Praise for Adam Cohen's *Nothing to Fear*

"In a lucid, intelligent narrative as fast-paced as the hectic Hundred Days, Cohen skillfully charts the course of events with just enough detail, building by accretion a portrait of the stop-and-start process by which sweeping change is made." —*Los Angeles Times*

"Cohen brings this brief but extraordinary period in American history to vivid life. An excellent writer and storyteller, he does so by concentrating not on its central figure, Roosevelt, but on a handful of his aides. . . . *Nothing to Fear* is a fascinating account of an extraordinary moment in the life of the United States, indeed a page-turner." —John Steele Gordon, *The New York Times*

"A deeply sympathetic and thoroughly convincing portrait of FDR and five of his senior advisers that unearths how the aides' interactions with Roosevelt helped to spawn the New Deal. . . . Cohen's smart study of Roosevelt's first hundred days vividly captures all of these achievements and reaffirms just how dramatic a break from the past the New Deal really was." —*The Washington Post*

"Timely and engaging . . . Cohen masterfully renders the backgrounds and personalities of Roosevelt's inner circle. . . . *Nothing to Fear* serves as an apt reminder of the possibilities of dramatic reform in the face of crisis and the role of human actors in bringing it about." —*Chicago Tribune*

"Cohen's well-told story belies the cliché about legislation and sausage-making: his narrative is absorbing and enjoyable to read." —David Greenberg, *The New York Times Book Review*

"Cohen's impressive ability to bring these five New Deal figures to life reminds us that administrations are made by more than the great man—someday it will be the great woman—elected by voters." —Lizabeth Cohen, *The American Prospect*

"Fascinating . . . Cohen . . . unfolds the clear, compelling story of how the circumstances of the nation—together with the character of its political leaders—reshaped American society in so brief a time. . . . Even those most knowledgeable about American politics will be surprised by some parts of the story." —*The Christian Science Monitor*

"In the veritable library of books about the New Deal, Adam Cohen's new entry deserves a prominent place on the top shelf. In my judgment, the story of the Hundred Days has never been told so well, nor the cast of characters rendered so compellingly."

—Joseph J. Ellis, author of *American Creation*

"An indispensable primer." —*Salon*

"Highly recommended . . . Cohen does an excellent job describing the backgrounds and personalities of key FDR policy makers."

—*The Huffington Post*

"This is thrilling history, bringing to life the full-dimensional, extraordinary band of people who shaped the modern United States in a hundred-day dash. Cohen's character sketches are sharp, his narrative moves along briskly, and the story itself is fresh—and full of drama. We are better off as a nation for having this chapter of our shared past told in page-turner fashion by Adam Cohen."

—Timothy Egan, author of *The Worst Hard Time*

"[Adam] Cohen delves into the New Deal archives to fashion an elucidating, pertinent and timely work on the makings of government. . . . Ambitious yet well focused—a marvelously readable study of an epic moment in American history." —*Kirkus Reviews* (starred review)

"FDR brought together brilliant people with divergent beliefs and was able both to manage and juggle them. In this fascinating book about his first hundred days, Adam Cohen looks at his innermost circle and provides wonderful insights about leadership, management, and creativity."
—Walter Isaacson, author of *Einstein*

"Cohen displays his strong prose style and research skills in this story of the precedent set by FDR against which later presidents are judged: the so-called honeymoon period after inauguration and before the media and the opposition inevitably begin to critique and attack. . . . [Cohen] presents a crucial human story which goes beyond that found in most FDR biographies. Superbly readable and informative."
—*Library Journal* (starred review)

"When Franklin D. Roosevelt became president in March 1933 he issued a spate of reform legislation which transformed America for the better. Now, Adam Cohen, one our finest historians, explains in vivid prose the backstory of how five members of his inner circle jump started those historic Hundred Days. *Nothing to Fear* is a riveting, indispensable book for our times."
—Douglas Brinkley, professor of history and Baker Institute Fellow, Rice University, and author of *The Great Deluge*

"Vividly written and profoundly researched, this reprise of FDR's circle is an exciting New Deal adventure for these troubled times. Adam Cohen's *Nothing to Fear* is filled with surprises, new stories and unique portraits of FDR's friends and enemies you have never met this way before."
—Blanche Wiesen Cook, University Distinguished Professor, John Jay College & Graduate Center, CUNY, and author of *Eleanor Roosevelt*

ABOUT THE AUTHOR

Adam Cohen is assistant editorial page editor of the *New York Times*, where he has been a member of the Editorial Board since 2002. He was previously a senior writer at *Time* and is the author of *The Perfect Store: Inside eBay* and coauthor of *American Pharoah*, a biography of Mayor Richard J. Daley. Before entering journalism, Cohen was an education-reform lawyer, and he has a law degree from Harvard.

NOTHING TO FEAR

FDR'S INNER CIRCLE AND THE HUNDRED DAYS
THAT CREATED MODERN AMERICA

ADAM COHEN

PENGUIN BOOKS

PENGUIN BOOKS

Published by the Penguin Group

Penguin Group (USA) Inc., 375 Hudson Street, New York, New York 10014, U.S.A.

Penguin Group (Canada), 90 Eglinton Avenue East, Suite 700, Toronto,
Ontario, Canada M4P 2Y3 (a division of Pearson Penguin Canada Inc.)

Penguin Books Ltd, 80 Strand, London WC2R 0RL, England

Penguin Ireland, 25 St Stephen's Green, Dublin 2, Ireland (a division of Penguin Books Ltd)

Penguin Group (Australia), 250 Camberwell Road, Camberwell,
Victoria 3124, Australia (a division of Pearson Australia Group Pty Ltd)

Penguin Books India Pvt Ltd, 11 Community Centre, Panchsheel Park, New Delhi – 110 017, India

Penguin Group (NZ), 67 Apollo Drive, Rosedale, North Shore 0632,
New Zealand (a division of Pearson New Zealand Ltd)

Penguin Books (South Africa) (Pty) Ltd, 24 Sturdee Avenue,
Rosebank, Johannesburg 2196, South Africa

Penguin Books Ltd, Registered Offices:
80 Strand, London WC2R 0RL, England

First published in the United States of America by The Penguin Press,
a member of Penguin Group (USA) Inc. 2009
Published in Penguin Books 2010

1 3 5 7 9 10 8 6 4 2

THE LIBRARY OF CONGRESS HAS CATALOGED THE HARDCOVER EDITION AS FOLLOWS:

Cohen, Adam (Adam Seth)

Nothing to fear: FDR's inner circle and the hundred days that created modern America / Adam Cohen.

p. cm.

Includes bibliographical references and index.

ISBN 978-1-59420-196-7 (hc.)

ISBN 978-0-14-311665-3 (pbk.)

1. United States—Politics and government—1933–1945. 2. Roosevelt, Franklin D.
(Franklin Delano), 1882–1945—Friends and associates. 3. Moley, Raymond, 1886–1975.
4. Perkins, Frances, 1880–1965. 5. Douglas, Lewis W. (Lewis Williams), 1894–1974. 6. Wallace,
Henry A. (Henry Agard), 1888–1965. 7. Hopkins, Harry L. (Harry Lloyd), 1890–1946.
8. United States—Economic policy—1933–1945. 9. United States—
Social conditions—1933–1945 10. New Deal, 1933–1939. I. Title.

E806.C5925   2009

973.917092—dc22   2008029791

Printed in the United States of America

DESIGNED BY MEIGHAN CAVANAUGH

To Beverly and Stuart Cohen

The beginning is the most important part of any work...for that is the time at which the character is being formed.

—PLATO, *The Republic*

CONTENTS

Introduction   *1*

CHAPTER ONE
"Action, and Action Now"   *13*

CHAPTER TWO
"Moley! Moley! Moley! Lord God Almighty!"   *46*

CHAPTER THREE
"The Hardest-Boiled Man in Washington"   *84*

CHAPTER FOUR
"Good Farming; Clear Thinking; Right Living"   *109*

CHAPTER FIVE
"Good Lord! This Is a Revolution!"   *133*

CHAPTER SIX

" 'Social Justice' . . . Has Been the Maxim of Her Life"   *157*

CHAPTER SEVEN

"Just So We Get a Public Works Program"   *195*

CHAPTER EIGHT

"He Must Be Part of This Historic Show"   *248*

CHAPTER NINE

"People Don't Eat in the Long
Run—They Eat Every Day"   *265*

EPILOGUE

"A Lot Happened Out of That Determination
of a Few People, Didn't It?"   *284*

Acknowledgments   *319*

Notes   *323*

Index   *363*

INTRODUCTION

E dmund Wilson, the well-known writer, toured Chicago in 1932 and found a "sea of misery." On one stop, he saw an old Polish immigrant "dying of a tumor, with no heat in the house, on a cold day." In the city's flophouses, Wilson encountered "a great deal of t.b." and "spinal meningitis" that "got out of hand for a while and broke nine backs on its rack." Worst of all were the garbage dumps, "diligently haunted by the hungry." In the summer heat, when "the flies were thick," a hundred people descended on one dump, "falling on the heap of refuse as soon as the truck had pulled out and digging in it with sticks and hands." Even spoiled meat was claimed, since the desperate foragers could "cut out the worst parts" or "scald it and sprinkle it with soda to neutralize the taste and smell." A widowed housekeeper who was unable to find work showed up with her fourteen-year-old son. "Before she picked up the meat," Wilson wrote, "she would always take off her glasses so that she would not be able to see the maggots."[1]

Wilson could have written a variation on this grim dispatch from any city in America. By 1932, the shock waves of the Crash of 1929 had brought devastation to every corner of the country. One-fourth of the nation's workforce was unemployed and *Fortune* estimated that 27 million Americans were without a regular income. People with jobs struggled to survive on wages that had plunged to near-starvation levels. An Arizona cotton picker could earn as little as thirty cents a week after food and housing were deducted. In the cities, there were long lines outside soup kitchens and plaintive "hunger marches" by the unemployed. In rural areas, the destitution was less obvious but just as real. The American Friends Service Committee visited the West Virginia and Kentucky hill country and found that up to 90 percent of the children in some schools were underweight, and many were drowsy from malnutrition. Americans were reaching the limit of what they could take. Radicalism was on the march, not only in cities, but in God-fearing parts of the Farm Belt. "The biggest and finest crop of little revolutions I ever saw is ripe all over this country right now," a National Farmers' Union leader warned.[2]

The nation was crying out for the government to respond, but President Herbert Hoover refused to acknowledge the seriousness of the crisis. "I am convinced," he said in the spring of 1930, "we have passed the worst." As the Great Depression held on for year after brutal year, Hoover began to concede that the crisis was real, but he still refused to provide the sort of relief that was needed. His free-market ideology taught him that private enterprise should be the source of all solutions, and his near-religious commitment to "rugged individualism" convinced him that giving aid to the Depression's victims would morally damage them. Hoover's callousness earned him the enmity of the nation's millions of unemployed, who got their revenge by turning his name into an epithet. They dubbed the bleak encampments they erected in parks and under bridges "Hoovervilles" and they called the old newspapers they covered themselves with at night "Hoover blankets." When Hoover ran for reelection, mobs of jobless men and women showed up at his campaign rallies and pelted his car with rotten eggs. His opponent, Franklin Delano Roosevelt, promised a new approach. Roosevelt's vision of what government should do was so different that Hoover declared the 1932 election to be a choice not between two men, but between two philosophies. Hoover's philosophy lost in a landslide in which he managed to carry just six states.[3]

When Roosevelt took office on March 4, 1933, he charted a new course. That course was determined during the first one hundred days of his presidency. The Hundred Days, as the press would later name the period, began with a remarkable inaugural address. After assuring a despairing nation that "the only thing we have to fear is fear itself," Roosevelt promised "action, and action now." More than his words and his confident manner, it was the flurry of activity he ushered in that raised the nation's spirits. During the Hundred Days, Roosevelt offered up what the historian Arthur M. Schlesinger, Jr., called "a presidential barrage of ideas and programs unlike anything known to American history." Roosevelt shepherded fifteen major laws through Congress, prodded along by two fireside chats and thirty press conferences. He created an alphabet soup of new agencies—the AAA, the CCC, the FERA, the NRA—to administer the laws and bring relief to farmers, industry, and the unemployed. In an editorial entitled "Laws for Everything," *The New York Times* declared Roosevelt's dizzying pace of accomplishments to be "little short of a marvel."[4]

The Hundred Days swept the old order away in quick and dramatic fashion. On inauguration day, the nation's banks were teetering on the brink of collapse. Thousands had already failed, and all forty-eight states had declared bank holidays, preventing more banks from failing by cutting depositors off from their money. Hoover had stood idly by, refusing to intervene. Roosevelt took a more active stance. Within days he had declared a national bank holiday and signed the Emergency Banking Act, which immediately put the banking system on a firmer footing. He then delivered a remarkable fireside chat that restored the public's faith in the banking system. When the banks reopened, the public rushed to put money in, not take it out, and the crisis was over. Before the Hundred Days had ended, he signed a second law, the Banking Act of 1933, which made deeper reforms.

When Roosevelt was sworn in, farmers were entering the second decade of their own, localized depression. At the end of World War I, commodity prices had plunged so low that for many farmers it no longer paid to plant. Farms were being lost to foreclosure at an alarming rate, and farm families were being thrown off the land. Hoover had made a few halting efforts to address the problem, but his ideology had prevented him from taking more effective steps. Within weeks, Roosevelt had signed a revolutionary new law, the Agricultural Adjustment Act, which increased farm prices by paying farmers not to grow crops. He combated farm foreclosures through the Farm Credit Administration, a new federal farm mortgage program.

Roosevelt also brought help to the urban unemployed. Hoover, who believed relief eroded character and encouraged idleness, thought the poor should be cared for by private charity or, as a last resort, by local government. Roosevelt created the nation's first federal relief program, the Federal Emergency Relief Administration, which supported the unemployed with federal money dispensed according to federal standards. He established two major public works programs. The Civilian Conservation Corps sent 250,000 jobless young people out into nature to plant trees and reclaim the land. The National Industrial Recovery Act allocated $3.3 billion for a wider range of projects. Roosevelt also created an agency, the National Recovery Administration, charged with helping industry get back on its feet. In exchange for that help, he got companies to agree to minimum wages and maximum hours, a legal right for unions to organize, and a ban on child labor.

There was more. Roosevelt passed a pathbreaking law, the Truth in Securities Act, which for the first time regulated issues of stock. He created the Tennessee Valley Authority, a new form of regional entity, to provide low-cost public power and improve conditions in one of the poorest regions in the country. Roosevelt took America off the gold standard, allowing him to battle deflation, which was causing hardship for anyone with a mortgage, especially farmers.

No presidential administration had ever done so much so fast. "The nation was bewildered, thrilled, happy with hope," the journalist Ernest K. Lindley wrote. "The new President had delivered with a vengeance the 'action' which he promised on March 4."[5]

It is hard to imagine the Hundred Days without Roosevelt in charge. He was so confident and charismatic, he spoke so eloquently and with such compassion, that the American people, whose hope had been all but defeated, trusted him unreservedly. "If he burned down the Capitol," Will Rogers declared, "we would cheer and say, 'Well we at least got a fire started anyhow.'" Ordinary Americans, who had seen Hoover as part of the problem, felt a personal connection to their new president. In Roosevelt's first week in office, 450,000 letters arrived at the White House. The following week, after he had revived the banking system and spoken to the nation in his first fireside chat, even the skeptics were won over. William Randolph Hearst, the newspaper baron, declared, "I guess at your next election we will make it unanimous."[6]

Roosevelt was such a compelling leader that history has generally laid credit for all of the accomplishments of the Hundred Days at his feet, and they are often thought of as his carefully planned response to the crisis. The truth is more complicated, and more chaotic. Roosevelt had vowed in a campaign speech at Atlanta's Oglethorpe University to respond to the depression with "bold, persistent experimentation." It was "common sense," he insisted, "to take a method and try it: If it fails, admit it frankly and try another. But above all, try something." When he became president, Roosevelt was true to his word. "The notion that the New Deal had a preconceived theoretical position is ridiculous," insisted Frances Perkins, his secretary of labor. "The pattern it was to assume was not clear or specific in Roosevelt's mind, in the mind of the Democratic party, or in the mind of anyone else." Raymond Moley, Roosevelt's top aide, agreed. "To look upon these policies as the result of a unified plan," he said, "was to believe that the accumulation of stuffed snakes, baseball pictures, school flags, old tennis shoes, carpenter's tools, geometry books, and chemistry sets in a boy's bedroom could have been put there by an interior decorator."[7]

Roosevelt arrived in Washington with no firm commitments, apart from his promise to "try something." At a time when Americans were drawn to ideologies of all sorts, he was not wedded to any overarching theory. Once, when a young reporter had asked Roosevelt his philosophy, he had replied, "I am a Christian and a Democrat—that's all." Roosevelt had just completed four years as a progressive governor of New York State, and his instincts were undeniably liberal, but on many of the most important issues facing the nation, his views were in conflict. The question he was most torn over was whether to undertake large-scale, and enormously expensive, programs to help the Depression's victims. Roosevelt cared about the people who were suffering, and as governor he had established the nation's first state relief program. In the 1932 campaign, he had vowed to help the unemployed, struggling farmers, and "the forgotten man at the bottom of the economic pyramid." He was also, however, a fiscal conservative who believed government budgets should be balanced. In the campaign, he had attacked Hoover for heading up "the greatest spending Administration in peace time in all our history," and promised to adopt "a stern and unremitting administration policy of living within our income." Roosevelt was committed both to spending more and to spending less, a conflict that created a built-in tension in the Hundred Days. There were other important issues on which he was torn. Roosevelt was highly skeptical of corporations and wanted to put in place greater regulations to force them to act in the public interest. At the same time, he believed strongly in market capitalism, which, Perkins said, he took "as much for granted as his family."[8]

Roosevelt did not have a deep understanding of many of the problems facing the nation. Moley, who played a major role in the banking crisis, said he doubted "either Roosevelt or I could have passed an examination such as is required of college students in elementary economics." Advisers like Perkins and Rexford Tugwell, the assistant secretary of agriculture, were struck at times by Roosevelt's inability or unwillingness to follow the details of the reforms they proposed. He was more focused on outcomes. Roosevelt's "mind may have been a *tabula rasa*, but the *tabula* had clearly labeled pages to be written on," Tugwell said. "He did not very much care *what kind* of farm relief, or *how* the principle of cheap and universally available power was arrived at. Banking regulations might be of any practicable sort, and the methods used for relieving the unemployed were open to argument. But he was committed to *some* action in all these matters."[9]

Roosevelt had an open mind, and he was willing to listen. He learned "not from books but from people," according to Adolf Berle, a Columbia University professor who counseled him on economics. At the start of the 1932 campaign, Roosevelt had asked Moley, a Columbia government professor, to establish a group of academics to advise him on policy. The

Brain Trust, as the group was quickly dubbed, developed proposals for farm policy, industrial recovery, and unemployment relief that worked their way into campaign speeches. After Roosevelt was elected, several members of the Brain Trust were given important positions in the new administration. "Instead of a kitchen, or a tennis cabinet, he preferred to lean on a cap and gown cabinet," one profile of the new president declared. Roosevelt's intention, the press reported, was to establish a new form of government—a "factocracy."[10]

A more ideological president would have surrounded himself with people who shared his single-minded vision. Roosevelt chose Cabinet members and top aides with a range of beliefs, reflecting his own conflicted views. In the Hundred Days, his advisers included social workers who advocated ambitious relief programs and businessmen who argued for cutting the budget. Factory workers, farmers, and bankers all had their champions. The pragmatic Roosevelt listened to all of them, looking for ideas that would work. Many of the initiatives adopted during the Hundred Days were thought up by Roosevelt's closest advisers, but others came from members of Congress, and even holdover members of the Hoover administration.

When the time came to make a final decision about how to proceed, Roosevelt called in Cabinet members, congressmen, and advisers to weigh the alternatives, and then he made his ruling. He was evaluating what he believed to be the best policy, but also what he thought would work politically. He took into account what the public wanted, what Congress would pass, and what was acceptable to his electoral coalition—from farm leaders, to union bosses, to Wall Street financiers. Sam Rayburn, the Texas Democrat who later became House speaker, said Roosevelt was "the best jury to listen and decide that I ever saw." From informal meetings like these, the policies of the Hundred Days fitfully emerged. The idea of Roosevelt imposing from on high a program to restore the nation to health could not be more wrong, according to those who were there. "Franklin Delano Roosevelt did not invent the New Deal; he does not own it," wrote John Franklin Carter, one of the era's leading journalists. "He is its master of ceremonies, not the manager of the theater; its chief croupier, not the owner of the casino."[11]

Roosevelt's distinctive leadership style meant that his inner circle had enormous influence—and a rare chance to shape history. Five of Roosevelt's advisers—Raymond Moley, Lewis Douglas, Henry Wallace, Frances Perkins, and Harry Hopkins—had the greatest impact on the Hundred Days. They did not have the biggest titles in the administration, although Perkins and Wallace were both Cabinet members. They were also not necessarily the closest to Roosevelt, although Moley and Douglas spent as much time with him as anyone. They were simply the people who, by virtue of their jobs, talents, rapport with the president, and force of personality, were able to leave the greatest mark.

Raymond Moley was at the center of Roosevelt's inner circle. His up-from-the-bootstraps rise had taken him from small-town Ohio to Columbia University. After heading the Brain Trust and serving as chief speechwriter in the campaign, Moley accepted an offer to join the administration as a top aide to Roosevelt. His work on the emergency banking law put him in the middle of the most serious crisis of the Hundred Days. Moley was Roosevelt's "closest, most intimate adviser," *Time* magazine said when Moley appeared on the cover. Moley wrote most of Roosevelt's speeches and congressional messages, helped recruit for the administration, and drafted key bills. He was also part of the two-man "bedside Cabinet" that met with Roosevelt each morning. Moley's early roots were in midwestern progressivism, but he had begun to move to the political center. He was, like Roosevelt, a pragmatist, less concerned with ideology than with identifying ideas that would work.[12]

Lewis Douglas, the director of the budget, was the other member of Roosevelt's "bedside Cabinet." Unlike Moley, he did have a strong ideology. Douglas was the scion of one of Arizona's wealthiest mining families, copper barons with a record of mistreating their workers. When he was elected to Arizona's at-large House seat, he became the strongest voice in Congress for slashing spending. His conservatism made him a surprising choice to play a prominent role in the New Deal, but Douglas appealed to Roosevelt's fiscally cautious side. Many progressives believed that his prescription was precisely the wrong one for the Depression, but Roosevelt made Douglas the star of the first months of his administration, and helped him push a major budget reduction measure, the Economy Act, through Congress. If Douglas had continued to enjoy the same level of support from Roosevelt that he did in these first months, the New Deal would have looked very different.[13]

At the opposite end of the political spectrum was Frances Perkins, the secretary of labor. Perkins, the first woman Cabinet member, was born into a conservative New England family, but she broke away after college and went to work with Jane Addams at Hull House, ministering to Chicago's immigrant poor. After moving to New York, she became an advocate for workers. Perkins was an eyewitness to the Triangle Shirtwaist Fire, which took 146 lives, and after it became one of the nation's leading crusaders for improved factory safety. She had served as Roosevelt's state industrial commissioner, and as a result had worked with him longer than almost anyone else in the administration. Before accepting her Cabinet position, Perkins had gotten Roosevelt to agree to support her ambitious progressive agenda: a major unemployment relief program; large-scale public works; and an array of workers' rights protections, including minimum wage and maximum hours laws and an end to child labor. In large part due to her efforts, much of this agenda was achieved in the Hundred Days.[14]

While Perkins championed urban workers, Henry Wallace did the same for the nation's farmers. Wallace, the secretary of agriculture, was a brilliant farmer, scientist, and journalist from Iowa, the third Wallace generation to edit *Wallaces' Farmer*, his family's farm journal. He came of age when agriculture was in a deep depression, and was determined to rescue the Farm Belt. Wallace became one of the nation's leading proponents of domestic allotment, the plan for propping up crop prices that was adopted during the Hundred Days. Working with Tugwell, his assistant secretary, Wallace got the first—and most sweeping— relief program of the Hundred Days signed into law. He then went to work setting up the elaborate administrative structure necessary to implement it.[15]

Harry Hopkins was the last to join the administration, arriving on day 79. After graduating from college in his native Iowa, Hopkins moved to New York's Lower East Side, where he worked in a settlement house. He became a prominent social worker, and after the Depression hit, headed the emergency relief agency that Roosevelt created in New York. With the help of Perkins and congressional progressives, Hopkins persuaded Roosevelt to create a $500 million federal relief program, which he went on to run. Within months, Hopkins established something America had never seen before: a relief program that distributed federal funds to the states and imposed national standards. Hopkins quickly moved beyond relief. Proclaiming the idea that people preferred to remain idle "100 percent wrong," he pushed to substitute jobs for relief, and eventually became the leading public works administrator of the New Deal.[16]

These five advisers did not work as a team. Far from it. There was a deep fault line, with Perkins, Wallace, and Hopkins on one side, Douglas on the other—and Moley in between. The Perkins group and Douglas represented two clashing traditions in American politics. Perkins, Wallace, and Hopkins were committed liberals—heirs to the Progressive Era—who argued that the government should take an active role in improving the lives of workers, poor farmers, and the unemployed. Douglas was a strict conservative who believed in the free market, low taxes, and small government. While the public story line of the Hundred Days was about how Roosevelt, through his eloquent public statements and legislative initiatives, rallied a desperate nation, behind the scenes his advisers were battling over what shape the New Deal would take. Perkins, Wallace, and Hopkins worked with members of Congress, farm leaders, union officials, and other progressives to promote their agenda. Douglas worked with business leaders and other conservatives to pull Roosevelt in the opposite direction. In the first month of the Hundred Days, through the passage of the Economy Act, Douglas's side prevailed. For the rest of the Hundred Days, Perkins's side did. While Douglas won the early battles, Perkins, Wallace, and Hopkins won the war.

The Hundred Days was more than the greatest burst of legislation in American history—it was a revolution. Roosevelt had promised as much in the fall of 1932, when he told a group of campaign workers in Indianapolis that the election would be not only a landslide but "a revolution—the right kind, the only kind of revolution this nation can stand for—a revolution at the ballot box." When the Hundred Days was over, administration insiders and journalists returned to that word again and again. Tugwell called his memoir of the time *Roosevelt's Revolution*. Lindley gave his book, which was written as the events were unfolding, the title *The Roosevelt Revolution: First Phase*. "No other word seems strong enough," he wrote, "to describe a change so swift and so fundamental."[17]

The Hundred Days was the third great revolution in American history. George Washington had guided the nation from breakaway British colony to constitutional republic. Abraham Lincoln had led the nation through a civil war that determined that it would be an indivisible union, with a single standard of citizenship. The Roosevelt revolution created modern America. When he took office, the national ideology was laissez-faire economics and rugged individualism, and the federal government was small in scope and ambition. "The sole function of government is to bring about a condition of affairs favorable to the beneficial development of private enterprise," Hoover had declared in 1931. Roosevelt and his advisers introduced a new philosophy, one that held that Americans had responsibilities to one another, and that the government had a duty to intervene when capitalism failed. He proselytized for this new philosophy in his speeches, fireside chats, and press conferences, and he made it a reality with the policies he put in place.[18]

The Hundred Days laid the groundwork for the rest of the New Deal. The relief and public works programs would be expanded into larger initiatives that put tens of millions of people to work, and established a safety net for the elderly, the unemployed, and poor children. The regulations imposed on banks and stock issuers would be the first building blocks of the elaborate regulatory state that emerged during Roosevelt's four terms, and after. The voluntary workers' rights protections introduced in the National Industrial Recovery Act would eventually be turned into mandatory national minimum wage and maximum hours standards, and a federal ban on child labor. Perhaps the most important transformation of the Hundred Days was Roosevelt's decision to engage in large-scale deficit spending to fund federal relief efforts. That decision to spend heavily, which he reached with considerable reluctance, would be one of the driving forces behind the New Deal.

The New Deal had its critics from the start. They were muted during the Hundred Days, when even conservatives were inclined to give Roosevelt a chance. As time passed, they became more outspoken. A small but entrenched minority called for a return to the Hoover approach to government. There was no question, however, that the great majority of Americans embraced the New Deal. In the 1934 midterm election, the Democrats added to their majorities in the House and Senate. In 1936, Roosevelt won in a bigger landslide than he had in 1932. In his second inaugural address, Roosevelt declared that the American people had changed their philosophy in the previous four years. They had come to appreciate, he said, that "we all go up, or else we all go down, as one people," and that the federal government had become "the instrument of our united purpose." There were still naysayers, as there would be throughout Roosevelt's presidency, but they were now relegated to the margins. Tugwell dismissed these stubborn anti–New Dealers as "willful beneficiaries of the Old Order, who—in the words of a gifted Englishman—sat 'waiting for the twentieth century to blow over.'" But the twentieth century did not blow over. A new America had been born.[19]

CHAPTER ONE

"Action, and Action Now"

On the morning of March 4, 1933, Frances Perkins, wearing a black dress and her trademark tricorn hat, strode through the ornate lobby of the Willard Hotel. The Willard held a venerable place in American history. Abraham Lincoln had slipped into its side door in early 1861, one step ahead of the pro-Confederate conspirators who were said to be plotting his assassination, and spent the night before his inauguration sleeping fitfully in one of its best suites. Later the same year, Julia Ward Howe returned to the hotel after reviewing Union troops near the Capitol and wrote "The Battle Hymn of the Republic." In March 1933, America faced a crisis every bit as dire as the one it confronted in 1861, and Perkins was on her way to an inauguration as momentous as Lincoln's. She was about to walk into history as the first woman Cabinet member, and as an officer in the New Deal army that Franklin Delano Roosevelt had assembled to fight the Great Depression. First, however, she had to locate a taxi, and there were none to be found.[1]

Perkins had spent a lifetime getting to this moment. As a young woman, she had fled a traditional New England upbringing in Worcester, Massachusetts, and her father's conventional plans for her, to join Jane Addams at Hull House, ministering to Chicago's immigrants. Perkins made a brief stop in Philadelphia to work for a fledgling organization that helped the poor, and rescued young women who were in danger of being lured into prostitution.

From there it was on to New York, where she studied at Columbia University for a master's degree and did social science research in the streets of Hell's Kitchen. She went on to become New York State's industrial commissioner, and an influential champion of working men and women.

Perkins was America's leading industrial reformer, and the scourge of unscrupulous factory owners. People who knew her only by reputation were invariably surprised when they met her. "Miss Perkins, though she was once a social worker, is not at all the settlement-house type; nor is she the type of fighting woman labor leader," Edmund Wilson observed. "She is an attractive lady from Boston, who dresses with considerable elegance." George Creel, a prominent journalist, considered Perkins "intense," but found her "intensities masked by suavity, splendid judgment, and a nice sense of humor." Even "in her crusading days she never called names," wrote Creel, "marching to her goals with a gay, disarming amiability that won over many an opponent." Still, people underestimated Perkins at their peril. One reporter who followed the career of this "small, determined woman" noted that those who had not observed her up close were unaware of "her skill at repartee, her scornful replies to vapid criticism, or her intellectual preparation for her job."[2]

Perkins had come down from New York by railroad the previous afternoon. When her train pulled into Union Station, Washington's soaring Roman-style terminal, the scene was "bedlam," she would later recall. The station was filled with out-of-towners who had flooded the capital for Roosevelt's inauguration. It was a long-awaited moment for Democrats, who had last seen one of their own sworn in as president sixteen years earlier, and for the entire nation, which was desperate for more forceful leadership.[3]

The bedlam at Union Station reflected a broader chaos. The nation was in the grip of a depression of unprecedented magnitude. Since the crash of October 1929, stock prices had plunged 85 percent. Manufacturing had all but ground to a halt. The automobile industry was operating at 20 percent of capacity, and the steel industry at just 12 percent. Between one-quarter and one-third of the workforce was jobless. People leapt at the mere possibility of a paycheck. An advertisement for 750 men to dig a canal in Birmingham, Alabama, for twenty cents an hour drew 12,000 applicants. New York City's streets were filled with unemployed people selling apples from makeshift stands. The city had almost no shoeshine boys before the crash, but now there were thousands. A reporter counted nineteen on a single Midtown block. Even many people who had jobs were scraping by on sharply reduced hours. In Pennsylvania, only 40 percent of workers were employed full-time. People were forced to work for sweatshop wages. A *New York World-Telegram* exposé told of girls in a Brooklyn pants factory earning six cents an hour, and of one worker who, after paying for carfare, lunch, and child care, took home just ten cents a week. "Hospitals were filling with women who had worked themselves into a state of collapse for a pittance," *Time* magazine reported.[4]

America had never before faced such despair. "Panic was in the air," Harold Ickes, the incoming secretary of the interior, recalled. "Millions of people were half-fed ... barely clothed, and living more like kennelless dogs than human beings." Grim jokes abounded, like the one about the hotel desk clerk who inquired when people asked for a room, "For sleeping or for jumping?" In the cities, families were forced to double and triple up in small apartments. "Only the other day a case came to my attention where a family of ten had just moved in with a family of 5 in a 3-room apartment," reported Dorothy Kahn, a Philadelphia relief worker. "It is almost an everyday occurrence in our midst." Worst off were the residents of "Hoovervilles," the grim encampments that were springing up in parks and under bridges, who had only wood planks, tar paper, and cardboard to protect them from the elements. People slept in rusted old hulks of cars and, in the case of one large family, an old piano crate.[5]

Soup kitchens ladled out meager portions to millions of hungry people, but they could not keep up with the demand. "You could hardly believe what they live on," *Atlantic Monthly* wrote of a Youngstown, Ohio, family of six whose breadwinner had lost his job. "The mother mixes a little flour and water, and cooks it in a frying pan. That is their regular meal." Fathers deserted families, wives moved back in with their parents, and children were left at orphanages. The Hoover administration insisted no one was starving, but that was willful ignorance. "There were great numbers of hospital cases of malnutrition reported, of babies dying, of men falling dead in parks, and frozen unemployed found in abandoned warehouses during the winter," recalled Matthew Josephson, an editor at *The New Republic*. More than 20 percent of New York City schoolchildren suffered from malnutrition, the city's Bureau of Health Education reported, which could "be attributed directly to unemployment."[6]

Conditions were no better in rural America. Farm income had plunged from $6.7 billion in 1929 to just $2.3 billion in 1932. Crop prices were so low that farmers could not cover their expenses. Many had stopped planting, and farm workers and sharecroppers were being thrown off the land. Large numbers of the dispossessed poured into the cities or headed west in search of work. Alabama congressman George Huddleston lamented that many of his constituents, especially the black tenant farmers, were "practically without food and without clothes, and without anything else, and how are they going to live?" In Iowa, one of the wealthiest farm states, fully one-seventh of the farms had already been lost to foreclosure. "The most discouraging, disheartening experiences of my legal life have occurred," a rural lawyer from Iowa declared, "when men of middle age, with families, go out of bankruptcy court with furniture, team of horses, a wagon and a little stock as all that is left from twenty-five years of work."[7]

Urban and rural Americans were united by a shared sense of desperation. Reinhold Niebuhr, who was then a Detroit pastor with a large number of autoworkers in his congregation, had just published an essay that declared, "Capitalism is dying...it ought to die." When the novelist John Dos Passos visited Detroit, he found the parks filled with Communists selling *The Daily Worker*. In the Farm Belt, radical farmers, enraged over the low price of milk, were putting nail-filled boards on the highways to stop delivery trucks. Mobs were showing up at farm foreclosures, stopping the proceedings by force and sending bank lawyers fleeing. In rural areas and small towns, talk of revolution was growing. "You would be astonished if you could attend these township and county meetings of farmers, crowded full of militant farmers—more militant all the time," Ella Reeve Bloor, the legendary Communist known as Mother Bloor, reported from Sioux City, Iowa. The president of the Wisconsin Farmers Union told a congressional committee that "there are more actual Reds among the farmers of Wisconsin than you could dream about."[8]

The most immediate crisis was the collapsing banking system. There had been more than five thousand bank failures, mostly caused by banks' reckless speculation with their depositors' assets. Since there was no deposit insurance, customers were losing their money, in many cases their life savings. The failures caused runs on the surviving banks by people desperate to withdraw their deposits while they still could. The runs, in turn, produced more failures. Across the country, states were declaring "bank holidays," which required banks to close their doors and stop allowing withdrawals. The holidays were necessary, since banks did not have enough cash to pay off all of their depositors, but they were creating new hardships.[9]

The banking system's problems were being felt at the inauguration. Some guests learned after they arrived that the banks back home had closed, and that the checks they had intended to use to pay their hotel bills would not be honored. Rexford Tugwell, who would soon become assistant secretary of agriculture, recalled that there was a "strange emptiness" in the air over inauguration weekend. The banking crisis detracted from what should have been a celebratory mood. Tugwell realized, though, that the problems of well-heeled inauguration guests paled beside those of poor people across the country who "faced worse possibilities than not being able to pay a hotel bill."[10]

Perkins understood better than almost anyone how the hard times were devastating ordinary Americans. As industrial commissioner, her job had required her to monitor the impact of the Depression on New York. Perkins had sought out some of the worst conditions in the state so she could speak about them later. She had made a point of visiting the Hooverville that had gone up in Central Park near Ninety-first Street, not far from her home. The men lived, she recalled later, in "little packing box carton shelters, with any kind of old rags hung around and little fires going, making their mulligatawny." Perkins had traveled the country and seen with her own eyes the "lost boys in the railroad yards in St. Louis and Kansas City," and the "people pulling the baseboards and woodwork out of the houses to chop up and burn" in Detroit. She drew on these experiences when she argued for relief for the unemployed, which she did often. Perkins made her case so crisply and with such command of the facts that *The Saturday Evening Post* declared that she "talks like an editorial in *The Survey*," the national social work magazine.[11]

There were great hopes riding on Perkins. *The Nation* magazine had spoken for liberal America when it pronounced her appointment "cause for profound jubilation." Perkins's value system, rooted in the Progressive Era and in her Episcopal faith, gave her a deep conviction that government had a duty to help those in need. Her New York friends, many of whom were active in the organized labor and settlement house movements, were imploring her to take quick action. Once Perkins arrived in Washington, however, she found that it was all she could do to locate a place to sleep. The Inaugural Committee, she learned to her dismay, had not reserved rooms for her or her sixteen-year-old daughter, Susanna, even though the city's hotels had been booked for months. The Department of Labor staff had proven equally indifferent to her arrival. Perkins had been forced to fend for herself, hurriedly contacting a New York friend who knew Mrs. Willard and pleading for a room at the Willard Hotel.[12]

Perkins was beginning to realize how little she understood Washington. The evening before the inauguration, she had taken a taxi through traffic-clogged streets to go to a reception hosted by the Pan-American Union, an organization promoting closer ties between North and South America. The invitation had been elaborate, and with no one to advise her, she had assumed it was the sort of event she should attend. But after crawling along for more than an hour, she could see when her taxi pulled up that the party was a mob scene. As she was trying to decide whether to go in, and risk not being able to find another taxi to take her home, Mrs. Woodrow Wilson, the widow of the former president, emerged and urged her to flee. The reception was "perfectly terrible," Wilson told Perkins, and it was so overcrowded it would be dangerous to enter. "If you'll take my advice," she said, "you'll go right away."[13]

Perkins returned to the Willard after midnight to find a message from Roosevelt's personal secretary, Stephen Early, marked "very important." When she called, Early expressed amazement at how she had spent the evening. "Oh goodness," he said, "didn't anybody tell you not to go?" The Pan-American Union reception was, he said, "just to entertain the riff-raff." Early had called to tell her that Roosevelt wanted his incoming Cabinet and any family members they cared to bring along to join him at ten o'clock the following morning at St. John's Episcopal Church.[14]

Now, Perkins was on her way, with Susanna in tow, for what would be her first official function as part of the Roosevelt administration. The service was beginning soon, but she had no idea where St. John's Episcopal Church was or how to get there. The doorman at the Willard was unequivocal: there was no hope of finding a taxi that would get her to the service on time. The church was close enough to walk, he told her. Perkins and Susanna hurried off on foot.[15]

St. John's was known as "the Church of the Presidents." The men who had endowed its building fund in the early 1800s had hoped it would be just that. When construction was complete on the late-Federal-style church, the second building to go up on Lafayette Square after the White House, they offered President James Madison a free pew. Madison joined, but insisted on paying his way. Many succeeding presidents had worshipped at St. John's, along with numerous Cabinet members and lesser officials, including Roosevelt, who had attended services when he was in the Wilson administration. St. John's unique history made it a logical place for Roosevelt to hold his inauguration day service, but there was another consideration. Though he took great pains to hide it, Roosevelt's mobility was severely restricted. He walked with the help of ungainly steel leg braces, leaning on his son James or an aide. He would have had trouble making his way through Washington Cathedral, the soaring gothic edifice that was the seat of the city's Episcopal diocese. St. John's was smaller and it had a side door leading directly from the street into the nave, which minimized the walking he would have to do.[16]

Roosevelt's disability was caused by polio, which he had contracted in the summer of 1921, a harsh moment of adversity in an otherwise privileged life.

He was born in Hyde Park, New York, in 1882, to James and Sara Delano Roosevelt, and had grown up in a sprawling estate on the Hudson River. "All that is in me," Roosevelt once wrote, "goes back to the Hudson." The Roosevelts were an entrenched part of New York's Dutch aristocracy. The Delanos were even more prominent, and wealthier. As the only child of doting parents, Roosevelt had a childhood that was in many ways idyllic, filled with ponies and European vacations. "His youth is summed up," the historian Richard Hofstadter observed, "in his mother's words: 'After all he had many advantages that other boys did not have.'" Roosevelt's childhood was also a solitary one, without siblings, close friends, or even peers his own age, an absence that may have contributed to the keen sense of loneliness he exhibited as an adult. After an early education by tutors, Roosevelt attended prep school at Groton, an Episcopalian academy in Massachusetts that educated the scions of America's upper class. He went on to Harvard College, leaving in 1904 with a history degree. Roosevelt was not an academic star, generally earning no better than "gentlemen's C's," but he was well liked by his classmates and distinguished himself by being elected president of the school newspaper, *The Harvard Crimson*. After college, Roosevelt moved to New York to attend Columbia Law School and married a distant cousin, Anna Eleanor Roosevelt. Eleanor, a shy orphan, was the favorite niece of President Theodore Roosevelt, who gave her away at the wedding. If Theodore Roosevelt was pleased by the union, Sara Roosevelt was not. She resented Eleanor's stealing away her only child at what she regarded as too young an age. After failing to break up the engagement, she would intrude endlessly on the marriage. Roosevelt spent three years at the law firm of Carter, Ledyard & Milburn, which represented large corporations and wealthy individuals, before deciding that he wanted to pursue another path.[17]

Tall and charismatic, with an easy speaking style and a famous last name, Roosevelt was a natural politician. Hudson Valley Democrats approached him in 1910 to run for the State Senate from a Republican district. He accepted, and he won the race in a strong Democratic year. Although he had been chosen by the local political bosses, Roosevelt had declared to the nominating convention that he was running "with absolute independence, I am pledged to no man." In the campaign, Roosevelt had spent little time in the Democratic stronghold of Poughkeepsie, the biggest city in the district, and instead focused on winning over Republican farmers. When he arrived in the legislature, Roosevelt made political reform his chief cause. He played a leading role in blocking the selection of William "Blue-eyed Billy" Sheehan, the Tammany Hall Democratic machine's choice for United States senator, an office that was still chosen by legislators, not popular vote.[18]

Mostly, though, Roosevelt was regarded as an upper-class dilettante—his colleagues, playing off of his initials, dubbed him "Feather Duster." In 1912, Roosevelt supported Woodrow Wilson, the Democratic presidential nominee, over his fifth cousin Theodore's Bull Moose candidacy. When Wilson was elected, he named Franklin Roosevelt assistant secretary of the navy, a position Theodore Roosevelt had once held. Roosevelt made an ill-advised run for the United States Senate in 1914, losing overwhelmingly to James W. Gerard, Wilson's wealthy and well-respected ambassador to Germany, who was backed by Tammany Hall. Roosevelt took away a lesson from the defeat: he made his peace with Tammany. In future years, it would be a mainstay of his political coalition.[19]

After his Senate loss, Roosevelt returned to the Department of the Navy, where he remained through the World War. During this period, Roosevelt began an intense relationship with Lucy Mercer, Eleanor's beautiful social secretary. Roosevelt and Eleanor came close to divorcing over the affair. In the end, under pressure from Sara, who was worried about the couple's five children, and Louis Howe, Roosevelt's political adviser, who was convinced divorce would ruin his prospects for elective office, Roosevelt broke off with Lucy. His political career soon resumed in dramatic fashion. In 1920, the Democratic presidential nominee, Ohio governor James M. Cox, asked the thirty-eight-year-old Roosevelt to be his running mate. "It was an obvious political move," Roosevelt's aide Raymond Moley would later say. "He was from the East, his name was Roosevelt and this was about all that figured in his nomination for the vice-presidency." The Cox-Roosevelt ticket lost to Warren G. Harding and Calvin Coolidge in an election that marked the beginning of twelve years of Republican rule.[20]

It was during the following summer that Roosevelt contracted polio, on a visit to his family's cottage on Campobello Island, New Brunswick. When the extent of his illness became clear, Sara urged her son, who was working as a bank vice president, to retreat to the life of a country gentleman, amusing himself with his books and stamps. Roosevelt, however, was not ready to retire. Eleanor, who thought retirement would have been a terrible waste, allied herself with Howe, and the two of them persuaded Roosevelt to hold on to his political ambitions. Their arguments, and Roosevelt's innate determination, won out. He bought a 1,200-acre rehabilitation center in rural Warm Springs, Georgia, where he worked to heal himself, and helped others with polio.[21]

Many people close to Roosevelt believed that his physical disability prompted a remarkable transformation in his character. Perkins, who knew him in his early years in New York society, and as a young legislator in Albany, had considered Roosevelt something of a prig. "His superficial feeling toward many people was that they were great bores, stupid and nonsensical," and he "didn't want to bother with them," she recalled. "After he was ill, flat, prostrated," he "had a total change of heart," she said. "Nobody was dull. Nobody was a great nuisance. Nobody made no sense. Nobody was good for nothing. Because they were human beings who could walk, and run, and exercise, they were all superior to him." Roosevelt hid his disability as much as he could, in what one historian called his "splendid deception," and few people knew just how difficult it was for him to move about. The public rarely saw him in his wheelchair, and almost never saw him being carried around like a small child. At the same time, the fact that Roosevelt was afflicted with polio was not a secret. When *Time* magazine named him its Man of the Year in 1932, it reminded its readers that he was a "helpless cripple," though it noted approvingly that his "attitude toward his affliction is one of gallant unconcern."[22]

A few years after contracting polio, Roosevelt took up politics again with renewed vigor. In 1924, he was chosen to nominate New York governor Alfred E. Smith for president at the Democratic National Convention at New York's Madison Square Garden. Roosevelt slowly worked his way up to the podium in his heavy braces. The delegates were transfixed, first by his halting but determined movement, and then by his extraordinary nominating address, in which he saluted Smith as a "Happy Warrior." With this single speech, Roosevelt catapulted himself to national prominence. *The New York Herald Tribune* declared that he had become "the one man whose name would stampede the convention were he put in nomination." Despite Roosevelt's eloquent words, Smith lost the Democratic nomination to John W. Davis, a prominent New York lawyer who went on to lose to Coolidge. Four years later, in 1928, Smith won the Democratic nomination. When he did, he personally appealed to Roosevelt to run for the governorship he was giving up. Smith lost to Herbert Hoover, who assured the voters, "We are nearer today to the ideal of the abolition of poverty and fear from the lives of men and women than ever before in any land." Roosevelt, however, bucked the Republican tide and won the New York governor's race by 25,000 votes. For the next two years, Roosevelt jokingly called himself the "one half of one percent governor," but in 1930 New Yorkers reelected him by a more than 700,000-vote margin. Roosevelt was widely regarded as his party's leading candidate for president in 1932. At the Democratic National Convention that year, he defeated Smith, getting the necessary two-thirds vote when Texan John Nance Garner, a third contender, threw Roosevelt his support. Roosevelt made Garner his running mate and rode the nation's deep dissatisfaction with Hoover's handling of the Depression to the presidency.[23]

Now, Roosevelt was about to gather his family and Cabinet for an inauguration day service of thanksgiving and prayer. It came as no surprise to people who knew him well that he would want to begin his presidency in church. During his childhood, Roosevelt and his family had been regular congregants at St. James's Episcopal, where his father had held the highest lay position. At Groton, he had come under the influence of Reverend Endicott Peabody, the formidable headmaster, who preached a steely, forward-looking brand of Protestantism. "O God, author of the world's joy, bearer of the world's pain, make us glad that we have inherited the world's burden," one of Peabody's favorite prayers beseeched, and "Let unconquerable gladness dwell." As an adult, Roosevelt still read the Bible and the Book of Common Prayer, and quoted liberally from both. Perkins, who was deeply religious herself, believed that Roosevelt's political views were rooted in his faith. "He saw the betterment of life and people as part of God's work," she would later say. James Farley, Roosevelt's campaign manager, who was about to join the Cabinet as postmaster general, had traveled down from New York on the "Roosevelt Special," a train that carried the president-elect, his family and friends, and a few reporters and photographers. Farley had been struck that Roosevelt had talked more on the way down about religion than affairs of state. He told Farley about his plans for an inauguration day church service. Roosevelt firmly believed, Farley later said, that "the fundamentally religious sense of the American people would be a great factor in seeing the nation through."[24]

Perkins finally found her way to St. John's Church, and she and Susanna made their way through the crowd that had gathered outside. Inside, about one hundred Roosevelt family members, friends, and Cabinet members and their families had packed into the pews. Perkins did not know most of her fellow Cabinet members, but she recognized some of them from their photographs in the newspaper. Moments before the service began, Roosevelt entered through a side door, accompanied by his son James, Sara, and Eleanor. Roosevelt moved slowly, struggling with his leg braces and grabbing on to James for support. He settled into his pew by the door just as the service was about to start.[25]

Roosevelt had asked Reverend Peabody to preside. Although he had voted for Hoover, whom he deemed the "more capable man," Peabody was happy to do his part for his old student. The service was a mixture of thanksgiving, homage to country, and supplication for the future. Peabody led the congregation in the hymn "Faith of Our Fathers" and recited a special prayer for the new president, which asked for the Lord's blessings on "Thy servant, Franklin, chosen to be President of the United States, and all others in authority." In twenty minutes, it was over. Roosevelt continued to kneel, his face cupped in his hands, even after the strains of the recessional had died out. The other worshippers looked on silently as Roosevelt pulled himself up and, as Perkins later recalled, "turned and smiled at all of us in a sort of friendly, fatherly way" before exiting through the same side door he had entered.[26]

St. John's emptied out quickly. The worshippers who knew their way around Washington had arranged to have cars waiting to take them to the inauguration. Perkins watched the incoming secretary of state, Cordell Hull, who had been in Congress since 1907, and the secretary of the navy, Claude Swanson, who had been in town even longer, escort their wives to waiting limousines. Harold Ickes, the interior secretary, and his wife and children headed off in another limousine. Other worshippers quickly hailed taxis and headed downtown. When the crowd dispersed, Perkins found herself standing on the sidewalk beside a man she recognized from his photograph as Henry Wallace, the incoming secretary of agriculture.[27]

The forty-four-year-old Wallace was in many ways Perkins's rural counterpart. He had spent his adult life advocating for the nation's beleaguered farmers, who had suffered at least as much from the ravages of the Depression as her urban workers had. Unlike Perkins, who had fled her family to find her life's mission, Wallace had been born into his. He represented the third generation of his family to edit *Wallaces' Farmer*, an influential Iowa journal, and now he was following in the footsteps of his father, who had served as secretary of agriculture in the 1920s. While Perkins had joined the administration to promote unemployment relief and public works, Wallace wanted to establish a program of government aid for agriculture. He was one of the leading proponents of "domestic allotment," a plan for propping up battered farm prices. Conservatives considered domestic allotment as dangerous as the unemployment relief programs Perkins was advocating. *Time* magazine's rightward-leaning editors had warned that "[a]round the Cabinet table" Wallace's "radicalism will probably need checking by cooler, more conservative heads."[28]

Wallace, despite his country-boy appearance, was no Farm Belt rube. He had traveled extensively throughout the United States and across Europe researching agricultural methods, and had visited his father in the Department of Agriculture. He was, however, a scientist at heart, more comfortable holding forth on the biology of hybrid seeds than navigating his way through a traffic-clogged city. Perkins, who was desperately looking for a way to get to the inauguration, did not realize that the Labor Department had two cars that were being used by outgoing officials. Wallace had the same problem. "We were very green, and knew nothing about the sort of arrangements that could be made," Wallace's wife, Ilo, said later, "not even that we could ask for a limousine from the Department of Agriculture."[29]

Perkins turned to Wallace and said, "I suppose we're all going to the same place."

"You're Miss Perkins, aren't you?" he responded.

"Yes," Perkins said. "You're the Wallaces, I'm sure." They shook hands, and Perkins introduced Susanna.

"We better make common cause, get the first cab we can, and go all together, don't you think?"[30]

Perkins agreed that they should. The incoming labor secretary and the incoming agriculture secretary ran in opposite directions and waved furiously until a taxi finally stopped. Then the four of them piled in and headed toward the fast-growing crowds that were descending on the Capitol.[31]

After the service at St. John's, Roosevelt returned to his suite on the seventh floor of the Mayflower Hotel. He made a few last-minute changes to his inaugural address and then headed to the White House. By tradition, the incoming and outgoing presidents traveled together to the swearing-in ceremony. This year, the journey would be awkward because of Hoover's undisguised dislike of his successor. The low regard that Hoover had for Roosevelt going into the 1932 election had turned into bitterness after his landslide defeat. Hoover was especially unhappy about the roles that history had assigned them. It was already clear that Hoover would be remembered for having failed the nation, while Roosevelt was looking like he might be its savior. Roosevelt could afford to be gracious to his predecessor. "No cosmic dramatist could possibly devise a better entrance for a new President—or a new Dictator, or a new Messiah—than that accorded to Franklin Delano Roosevelt," the playwright Robert E. Sherwood would later observe. "Herbert Hoover was, in the parlance of vaudeville, 'a good act to follow.'"[32]

It was not supposed to be this way. Hoover had been elected four years earlier as a progressive technocrat for an optimistic new era. An Iowa-born Quaker, he had been orphaned as a boy, and through his own ingenuity and drive had entered with the first class at Stanford University. After success in the mining industry, he acquired the nickname "the Great Engineer" and became a self-made millionaire. During World War I, Hoover turned his skills to humanitarian ends, serving as U.S. food administrator, which made him responsible for ensuring that there was enough food for the Allied armies and for Americans living in Europe. Hoover had considerable power over what crops farmers in the United States produced, how much those farm products sold for, and where they ended up. Rather than regulate or ration, Hoover led a food conservation program that relied on patriotic appeals, featuring posters with slogans like "Food Will Win the War." This approach, dubbed "Hooverizing," worked well. Domestic food consumption declined during the war by about 15 percent.[33]

When the World War ended, Hoover was put in charge of Europe's recovery. His success in distributing 30 million tons of food to the hungry and bringing medical care to the sick made him a hero at home and in Europe, where several cities named streets for him. When Hoover's European work was done, President Harding appointed him secretary of commerce. Hoover used his relatively minor Cabinet post to drive American business to modernize and become more efficient. He was reappointed by President Coolidge, and took on more wide-ranging responsibilities in the new administration. When the Great Mississippi River Flood hit in 1927, Coolidge sent Hoover to coordinate the massive relief effort. As he had during the war, Hoover relied on private entities and individuals to deliver the necessary aid. For Hoover, rugged individualism had become more than a personal philosophy. In his book *American Individualism*, he declared it to be nothing less than "the one source of human progress."[34]

When Coolidge decided not to seek reelection, Hoover was the leading Republican contender. He easily won the nomination, and his defeat of Al Smith continued Republican control of the White House. Hoover's individualistic ideology worked well enough at the start of his presidency, when the economy was strong. It left him unprepared, however, to deal with the Great Crash that occurred in the fall of his first year in office. Hoover's reverence for laissez-faire capitalism and his commitment to small government led him to see the Depression as a temporary economic aberration that would soon right itself. He blamed the economic crisis on international forces, a focus that blinded him to the measures that could be taken domestically. Even his approach to the international aspects of the Depression made things worse. Hoover signed the protectionist Smoot-Hawley Tariff Act of 1930, which Republicans had pushed through Congress, even though more than one thousand economists had signed a letter urging him not to. The law, which raised American tariffs to new highs—"a virtual declaration of economic war on the rest of the world," one historian called it—was precisely the wrong prescription, contributing to a global tariff war that made the hard times even worse.[35]

Many intellectuals were coming around to the view that the Depression was unprecedented and likely to persist for some time. "An Appeal to Progressives," which ran in *The New Republic*'s January 14, 1931, issue, asserted that it might be "one of the turning-points in our history, our first real crisis since the Civil War." Hoover did not take the blithe approach of Charles M. Schwab, the chairman of Bethlehem Steel. "Just grin, keep on working," Schwab declared. "We always have a way of living through the hard times." Hoover did, however, insist that the economy was improving. "I am convinced," he said, "we have passed the worst and with continued effort we shall rapidly recover." Reporters Drew Pearson and Robert Allen observed in their book *Washington Merry-Go-Round* that Hoover responded to the Depression with inaction. "Facts, statistics, plan, organization—there have been none, and when proposed by others have been rejected and stifled," they wrote. "One policy alone has dominated his course: not to do or say anything that would reveal the truth about the great catastrophe."[36]

Hoover's belief in rugged individualism led him to firmly oppose federal aid to the Depression's victims. He insisted that relief should come only from local governments and private charities. "The help being daily extended by neighbors, by local and national agencies, by municipalities, by industry and a great multitude of organizations throughout the country today is many times any appropriation yet proposed," Hoover declared. "The opening of the doors of the Federal Treasury is likely to stifle this giving." The federal relief proposals that were being put forward, he said, would be "disastrous." Hoover spoke against relief bills and vetoed them when they reached his desk, "usually accompanying his actions," one Washington journalist noted, "with homilies such as 'We cannot squander ourselves into prosperity.'" Hoover was echoing the views of big business. A special committee established by the United States Chamber of Commerce to look into the unemployment problem came out strongly against federal aid. Relief should be provided by "private contributions" and "state and local governments," it recommended. "There is every evidence that all requirements can in this manner be adequately met." In a debate over whether to provide the Red Cross with relief funds in early 1931, Senator David Walsh, a Massachusetts Democrat, declared that "not a single bill for adequate relief will pass this Congress" because of the Hoover administration's determination that "those who pay large income taxes and the corporation-income taxpayers of the country must not be burdened with relief obligations."[37]

The federal government that Hoover presided over was small and limited in scope. The government collected little revenue, and therefore it had little money to dispense. The federal income tax had been in effect a mere twenty years, and only about 5 percent of Americans paid it. The total federal budget was just $3.3 billion. Hoover did not believe the federal government should grow to any great extent to meet the challenges posed by the Depression. His first major response to the hard times was to establish, in the fall of 1930, the President's Emergency Committee for Employment, chaired by Colonel Arthur Woods. The Woods Committee did not actually provide relief. Its mission was to encourage states, localities, and the private sector to do more. The committee's efforts to encourage industry to hire more workers did not get far, since companies were more interested in cutting their payrolls to bring them in line with declining revenues. The committee's attempts to persuade local governments to undertake more building projects were no more successful, because so many cities and towns were bankrupt or close to it. Colonel Woods tried to persuade Hoover to reduce unemployment by increasing federal public works programs, and after Hoover refused, he resigned in frustration. In August 1931, Hoover created the President's Organization on Unemployment Relief. POUR, which was headed by American Telephone and Telegraph president Walter S. Gifford, had the same mission as the Woods Committee, and it was no more effective. It persuaded college football teams to play games for charity, and it distributed posters with the slogan "Of Course We Can Do It." POUR's impact on unemployment, however, was negligible. On his radio show in November 1931, Will Rogers imagined how the conversation must have gone when Hoover offered Gifford the position.

> "Gifford, I have a remarkable job for you; you are to feed the several million unemployed."
> "With what?" says Gifford.
> "That's what makes the job remarkable. If you had something to do it with, it wouldn't be remarkable."

Hoover's refusal to spend federal funds on relief reached a low point when a severe drought hit Arkansas. Hoover supported millions of dollars in loans to buy feed and animal seed, but he opposed relief for starving farmers. "Blessed be those who starve while the asses and mules are fed," Senator George Norris, a progressive Republican from Nebraska, fumed, "for they shall get buried at public expense."[38]

The calls for federal relief grew louder, but Hoover continued to resist. The "federal dole," he insisted, was foreign to the "philosophy and creed of our people." Hoover's prescription for the Depression was a pair of conservative standbys: keeping federal spending in check; and remaining on the gold standard, the policy that anyone holding dollars could turn them in for gold. Even some conservatives worried that by sticking so strictly to free-market capitalism, Hoover was actually undermining it. "They also serve who only stand and wait," two prominent economists wrote in a syndicated column, "but they serve the cause of Communism." Congressional progressives finally succeeded in getting Hoover to sign a bill drafted by Robert F. Wagner, Democrat of New York, that allocated $300 million to the Reconstruction Finance Corporation to distribute to the states for unemployment relief. The funds, however, would be given out in the form of loans, not grants. The problem was, the states that were in the worst shape would be the least likely to take the money, out of fear of making their financial situation even worse. As one critic pointed out, the federal government was asking "what can a state afford," not "what ought it to afford?"[39]

The incident that cemented Hoover's reputation for callousness came in the summer of 1932. The Bonus Army, which was made up of impoverished veterans of the World War, rolled into Washington. They were seeking early payment of a bonus that Congress had awarded to returning soldiers, which was scheduled to come due in 1945. Thousands of veterans camped out in Anacostia Flats, in southeast Washington, clamoring for relief. The Hoover administration did not merely turn down the Bonus marchers. It crushed them. Federal troops attacked, using tanks, bayonets, and tear gas, and they set fire to the shacks the veterans were living in with their families. The public was not entirely sympathetic with the veterans' demands for early payment of their bonuses, but they had even less sympathy with the Hoover administration's brutal response. Movie theaters across the country were soon showing newsreel footage of the clashes, which the narrator described as "a day of bloodshed and riot." The villain of the story was the current occupant of the White House.[40]

The reluctant steps that Hoover took to address the Depression, such as his approval of the RFC funds, have led some of his admirers to portray him as an activist president, a modest hero of the Depression, and even as the originator of New Deal values. In an influential 1963 essay, "The Ordeal of Herbert Hoover," the historian Carl Degler argued that Hoover should be credited with "breaking precedent to grapple directly with the Depression." These revisionist accounts have a kernel of truth, but they vastly overstate Hoover's role. As the historian Arthur Schlesinger, Jr., observed, a logical place to look to for an accurate assessment of Hoover is the accounts of the elected officials, journalists, and academics who were there in 1933. They were all but unanimous in seeing him as a conservative who resisted taking action against the Depression. It also makes sense, as Schlesinger argued, to take Hoover at his own word. Not only did Hoover not promote New Deal values—he fulminated against them as dangerous radicalism. "When the American people realize," he wrote in December 1933, "that they surrendered the freedom of mind and spirit for which their ancestors had fought and agonized for over 300 years, they will, I hope, recollect that I at least tried to save them."[41]

The 1932 presidential campaign was, Hoover declared, not "a contest between two men" but one "between two philosophies of government." Roosevelt and Hoover had some points of common ground. The two candidates sounded similar when they talked about government spending. Roosevelt campaigned on a pledge of "government economy," or slashing the federal budget, and he agreed with the Democratic Party platform, which called for reducing spending by 25 percent. On other issues, however, the differences between the two men were pronounced, especially on the one that dominated the campaign, the Depression.[42]

Hoover minimized the significance of the economic crisis and its impact on the American people. In an odd campaign tactic, he went to hard-hit parts of the country and tried to convince his audiences that things were not all that bad. In a speech in Iowa, which was reeling from low crop prices and soaring farm foreclosures, Hoover argued that "it could be so much worse that these days now, distressing as they are, would look like veritable prosperity." To a nation that was demanding government action, Hoover continued to preach his gospel of individualism. It is not the federal government's role, he insisted, to "relieve private institutions of their responsibility to the public, or of local governments to the States, or of state governments to the Federal Government."[43]

Roosevelt offered a clear alternative. He had been a progressive even before the Crash of 1929. He had been elected governor of New York on a promise of liberal social reform, in the tradition of his predecessor Al Smith, emphasizing the positive impact that government could make on the lives of ordinary people. As governor, he had been a strong advocate for public power, insisting that the state had a duty to harness water power and make it available to the people at the lowest possible rates. Roosevelt had supported workers' rights, fighting for safer workplaces and more generous worker compensation laws, and he had opposed the use of injunctions against striking workers. It was the Depression and his singular response to it, however, that had pushed Roosevelt into the top ranks of the nation's liberals. In a pathbreaking speech to the New York State Legislature in August 1931, he had declared that when citizens are unable to find work, the state must help them "not as a matter of charity, but as a matter of social duty." Roosevelt, who was governor of the nation's most populous and wealthiest state, then proceeded to establish a major relief program for the unemployed that became a model for other states.[44]

Early in the presidential campaign, in an April 7, 1932, radio address, Roosevelt promised to champion "the forgotten man at the bottom of the economic pyramid." It was one of the most talked-about, and most revolutionary, speeches of the campaign. Hoover and his Republican predecessors had governed in the interests of those at the top of the economic pyramid, insisting that their wealth would eventually trickle down to the rest of the country. Roosevelt was promising direct help to Americans who lacked money or social status. When the Democratic National Convention nominated him, Roosevelt broke with tradition and traveled to Chicago Stadium to address the delegates in person. In his acceptance speech on July 2, he made a historic promise. "I pledge you, I pledge myself, to a new deal for the American people," he said. The New Deal was not a platform. Voters had no way of knowing exactly what Roosevelt would do about the agricultural crisis or unemployment, but his pledge of a New Deal was a commitment to bring about change, rather than wait for conditions to improve. "It was a happy phrase," Frances Perkins would later say. "It made people feel better, and in that terrible period of depression they needed to feel better."[45]

Each candidate warned that victory by his opponent would spell disaster. Hoover's supporters argued that Roosevelt was a dilettante, unsuited to leading the nation even in the best of times. He was the sort of politician who told people what they wanted to hear, they charged—a "chameleon on plaid." Walter Lippmann, the most influential columnist of his day, dismissed

Roosevelt, in a much-quoted putdown, as "a pleasant man who, without any important qualifications for the office, would very much like to be President." Hoover was the most caustic of all in his criticism. The "inchoate new deal" Roosevelt was proposing would, he said, "crack the timbers of the Constitution" and "destroy the very foundation of our government." Hoover spoke of a Roosevelt victory in apocalyptic terms. "The grass will grow in the streets of a hundred cities, a thousand towns; the weeds will overrun the fields of millions of farms," he warned.[46]

Roosevelt, for his part, attacked Hoover for indifference to the plight of the Depression's victims, and for lacking an identifiable plan for turning the economy around. The Hoover administration, he insisted, "has been unable to do more than put temporary patches on a leaking roof without any attempt to put a new roof on our economic structure." In one of his last major speeches of the campaign, to a Baltimore audience, Roosevelt used an especially vivid image. He was waging war, he declared, "against the 'Four Horsemen' of the present Republican leadership: The Horsemen of Destruction, Delay, Deceit, Despair."[47]

Hoover began the campaign convinced he would prevail. Roosevelt was simply too insubstantial, he believed, to be elected. Even as it became increasingly clear that his opponent was headed for an overwhelming victory, Hoover would not be dissuaded. "He is living on an island that is getting smaller each day," a friend observed. Other than the candidate himself, few people were surprised when Hoover lost in a landslide, carrying only six states, or when Congress turned solidly Democratic. William "Big Bill" Thompson, the onetime Republican mayor of Chicago, noted dryly that "the history of American politics shows that the people don't vote for continued depression." When the election returns came in, Hoover was bitterly disappointed. To more objective observers, however, Roosevelt's victory was expected—and a sign of where the nation was headed. William Allen White, the influential Kansas newspaper editor, declared that the outcome reflected "a new attitude in American life...a firm desire on the part of the American people to use government as an agency for human welfare."[48]

After the election, relations between Hoover and Roosevelt were chilly. The Twentieth Amendment, which pushed presidential inaugurations forward from March to January, had been ratified but it had not yet taken effect. As a result, the transition from Hoover to Roosevelt was the last in which there would be four long months between election and inauguration. That was unfortunate since, as one journalist noted, "almost to a man...the country would have been delighted to see [Roosevelt] step into the Presidency at once." Hoover wanted to work with Roosevelt during the interregnum, as the press called the period, but it proved impossible. Hoover was only interested in doing things on his own terms. Roosevelt was reluctant to do anything that would associate him too closely with his repudiated predecessor. Although they met several times, and there was urgent business to be done, the two men were unable to agree on a course of action.[49]

Now it was eleven a.m. on inauguration day, and Hoover stood waiting at the White House's north door. A convertible pulled up and Roosevelt was inside looking, as a radio announcer observed, "magnificently confident." Hoover, by contrast, appeared, in Rexford Tugwell's words, "tired almost to death." The two men took off their silk hats and exchanged a perfunctory handshake before setting off for the Capitol. They drove down Pennsylvania Avenue, the grand boulevard linking the executive and legislative branches. Hundreds of thousands of onlookers lined the route, standing ten deep, or sitting on bleachers, soapboxes, or, as one news account put it, "anything that would bear their weight, and some things that wouldn't and didn't." The crowd roared when the convertible approached. Their excitement was about more than the chance to gawk at a pair of presidents. *New York Times* Washington bureau chief Arthur Krock detected "a note of jubilation that the day had come when [a] new philosophy was to replace the rejected theories of the old."[50]

Roosevelt smiled and waved at the crowd along the one-and-a-quarter-mile route. Hoover sat next to him "grim as death, looking stonily forward," James Roosevelt observed from the jump seat. Hoover did his best to ignore both the crowds and Roosevelt. When they passed a building under construction, Roosevelt exclaimed, "My, Mr. President, aren't those the nicest steel girders you ever saw!" Hoover did not respond, and Roosevelt stopped making an effort. When the car reached the Capitol the two men said good-bye and went their separate ways. Hoover retreated to the building's ornate President's Room and spent his final minutes in office signing bills and receiving well-wishers. Roosevelt settled into the Military Affairs Committee Room on the same hallway. At noon, he walked to the Senate chamber, leaning on James's arm, and looked on as his vice president, John Nance Garner, took the oath of office. Afterward, Roosevelt returned to the committee room and waited to be sworn in as the thirty-second president of the United States.[51]

Roosevelt was to take the oath of office on a platform that had been erected on the Capitol's East Portico, the setting of inaugurations going back to Andrew Jackson. The Inaugural Committee, which had carefully attended to the staging, could do nothing about the cold, windy day or the dark clouds hovering overhead. Close observers would notice another somber touch. The Capitol's flags were flying at half-mast in tribute to Montana senator Thomas Walsh, who was to have been Roosevelt's attorney general. The seventy-three-year-old Walsh, a liberal crusader who had investigated the Teapot Dome scandal, had died of a heart attack on a train headed to the inauguration, days after his marriage to Señora Mina Perez Chaumont de Truffin, a wealthy Cuban widow two decades his junior. His death was a major loss for the new administration, particularly for its progressive wing. Walsh's was not the only death haunting the inauguration. Weeks earlier, in Miami, Giuseppe Zangara, a crazed Italian immigrant, had fired on a car carrying Roosevelt. Zangara had missed his mark after a fast-thinking woman jostled his arm, but his shots had seriously wounded Chicago mayor Anton Cermak, who was now on the verge of succumbing to his injuries. This would be the most mournful inauguration since 1865, when Abraham Lincoln took the oath of office in the final throes of the Civil War, promising to strive "to bind up the nation's wounds."[52]

At precisely one p.m., a bugle sounded. Roosevelt, again leaning on his son, made his way through the Capitol's ten-ton bronze doors. As the Marine Band played "Hail to the Chief," he moved haltingly up a ramp leading to the inaugural platform. As he came into view, the crowd applauded and stomped their feet. At 1:06 p.m., Roosevelt faced Chief Justice Charles Evans Hughes and placed his hand on a Dutch Bible that his forebears had brought with them to the United States, the same one he had used both times he was sworn in as governor. It was open to a favorite passage of Roosevelt's, 1 Corinthians 13:13: "And now abideth faith, hope, charity, these three; but the greatest of these is charity." After taking the oath of office, Roosevelt launched into his inaugural address, which was broadcast over 178 radio stations, the first inaugural to be so widely aired.[53]

The American people were united behind Roosevelt. "In the present plight of the nation partisanship is forgotten," *The New York Herald Tribune* declared on inauguration day. "All feel that they are in the same boat and that the captain must be upheld." The nation expected Roosevelt to claim the powers of a dictator, or close to it. Senator William Borah, the legendary progressive Republican from Idaho, had announced that he was willing to put aside "partisanship and politics" and "agree to give our incoming President dictatorial powers within the Constitution for a certain period." Senator David Reed, a mainstream Republican from Pennsylvania, had declared, "I do not often envy other countries their governments, but I say that if this country ever needed a Mussolini, it needs one now." Even Walter Lippmann, usually a voice of studied moderation, was insisting that the use of "'dictatorial powers,' if that is the name for it—is essential." There were dissenters. The liberal *Nation* magazine asked on its cover, "Do We Need a Dictator?" and answered inside: "Emphatically not!" *The New Republic* decided that what the nation was looking for was not a dictator but a "Messiah." *Time* magazine put the nation's hunger for a bold leader in homier terms. Its inauguration week cover bore a portrait of Sara Roosevelt over a quote: "Franklin had a great habit of ordering his playmates around." Inside, *Time* completed the anecdote. "Once I said to him: 'My son, don't give the orders all of the time. Let the other boys give them sometimes.' 'Mummie,' he said, lifting a soil-streaked face, 'if I didn't give the orders nothing would happen!'"[54]

Roosevelt had been thinking for months about what he wanted to say. He had been working on his address since the previous fall with Raymond Moley, the Columbia University professor who was his chief speechwriter and closest aide. The two men had begun the outlining in September, on a trip to San Francisco. Roosevelt's western campaign swing was going so well that victory seemed assured. One night, he turned off the phone in his suite at the Palace Hotel, took the braces off his legs, and told Moley he wanted to begin drafting an inaugural address. They ended up talking until two in the morning. Roosevelt expected to be speaking in a time of crisis, to a despairing nation. He wanted to address the American people in a tone of utter seriousness, without any of the false optimism that they had been subjected to, but he also wanted to offer hope. Roosevelt was not prepared to declare a dictatorship, but he told Moley that he wanted to emphasize that he was determined to take the sort of action a leader would in wartime. It was important, he said, that Congress not be allowed to slow down his plans.[55]

Roosevelt and Moley had discussed the address again in early February, on a train ride from Warm Springs to Jacksonville, Florida. The depth of the Depression, and the grim conditions Americans were living under in early 1933, were having an effect on the writing. "The inaugural speech is going to the left," Moley noted in his diary in mid-February. At the end of the month, Moley arrived at Hyde Park with a final draft. He and Roosevelt retreated to the library for a night of whiskey and writing. Moley's draft was written out in longhand, but Roosevelt insisted on copying it over in his own handwriting because, he said, Louis Howe would "have a fit" if he thought Roosevelt had not written it. It would later strike Moley that Roosevelt had been trying to create physical evidence to support the claim that he had written the address himself. One major Roosevelt biography dutifully described the speech's creation just that way, recounting how the president-elect had written it himself at Hyde Park, while his ancestors' portraits looked down on him. In reality, the two men tinkered with Moley's draft, sentence by sentence, into the early morning. The speech was, in the end, a true collaboration.[56]

The address's best-known line was not in the version they completed that night. A story emerged that Roosevelt inserted the phrase "the only thing we have to fear is fear itself" after coming across the words in Henry David Thoreau's journals. It was actually Louis Howe who slipped it in, while he was tinkering with the speech. The source was almost certainly not Thoreau, or at least not directly. Howe read only "detective stories and newspapers," Moley said, and "may never have heard of Thoreau." Moley's best guess was that

Howe had seen the historic line in a newspaper advertisement. There were, in fact, many places Howe could have stumbled on the general idea, which was not an original one. Two years earlier, the chairman of the United States Chamber of Commerce had been quoted in *The New York Times* warning, "In a condition of this kind, the thing to be feared most is fear itself."[57]

When Roosevelt spoke on that blustery March day, he looked out on an audience as despairing as he had anticipated. Hoover had stood in the same spot four years earlier and addressed himself to a nation "filled with millions of happy homes; blessed with comfort and opportunity." His message had been one of boundless optimism. "In no nation are the fruits of accomplishment more secure," he had declared. The crowd of 100,000 that was now stretched out before Roosevelt—standing on the Capitol grounds, peering down from rooftops, hanging from trees—was worried it would never see good times again. "There was the most terror-stricken look on the faces of the people," Perkins recalled. Henrietta Nesbitt, who was about to start work as the Roosevelts' housekeeper, was struck by how care-worn the young people around her seemed. "We older folks expect to have qualms," she said, "but there is something terribly wrong when young people are afraid." The audience was, one reporter observed, "as silent as a group of mourners around a grave."[58]

Roosevelt launched into the address with his chin thrust out "as if at some invisible, insidious foe," as one press account put it. "This is a day of national consecration," he began, a characteristic bit of religious imagery that he had scribbled in at the last minute on his reading copy. Roosevelt pledged to speak to the American people "with a candor and a decision which the present situation of our Nation impels." He then declared that it was his "firm belief that the only thing we have to fear is fear itself," the inspired addition that would become among the most famous lines ever uttered by a president.[59]

The speech was not all soaring rhetoric. Roosevelt laid out the nation's problems straightforwardly. The government was short of income; industrial production had collapsed; "farmers find no markets for their produce"; and "the savings of many years in thousands of families are gone." He set out what his priorities would be. "Our greatest primary task," he insisted, "is to put people to work." Agricultural prices had to be raised, he said, so farmers could make a living. More had to be done to provide relief to the Depression's victims. Picking up on a theme from the campaign, he talked about the need to reduce federal spending. And he called for stricter supervision of banking, credit, and investments—"an end to speculation with other people's money." Striking the balance he had decided on in San Francisco, of being serious without leaving his audience despondent, Roosevelt shifted back and forth between gravity and reassurance. "Only a foolish optimist can deny the dark realities of the moment," he said at one point. At another, he reflected that the nation's difficulties "concern, thank God, only material things."[60]

The address's great theme was "action, and action now." Roosevelt underscored the sense of urgency through military imagery. He announced that he was assuming "unhesitatingly the leadership of this great army of our people" and set out "the lines of attack." The rhetorical high point was Roosevelt's full-throated assault on the banking industry. "Practices of the unscrupulous money changers stand indicted in the court of public opinion, rejected by the hearts and minds of men," he declared. Then, in another religious reference, Roosevelt invoked Jesus' temple cleansing from Matthew 21:12. "The money changers have fled from their high seats in the temple of our civilization," he said. "We may now restore that temple to the ancient truths." The crowd responded excitedly, though one observer noted that they were reluctant to applaud for long, fearing it would halt the momentum with which Roosevelt took on the nation's problems.[61]

Before the seventeen-minute speech was over, Roosevelt addressed on the talk of dictatorship directly. He would soon ask Congress, he said, to take on the nation's problems. He hoped to be able to tackle the crisis within the president's historic authority, but if he could not, he insisted, he was prepared to seek a "temporary departure." He would ask Congress to give him "broad Executive power to wage a war against the emergency, as great as the power that would be given to me if we were in fact invaded by a foreign foe." It was the most radical part of the whole speech, with its understated suggestion of autocracy, and it received an enthusiastic response from the crowd.[62]

When Perkins and Wallace got into the taxi in front of St. John's Episcopal Church, they were unsure of what route to take. The Inaugural Committee, which had not made reservations for Perkins, had also failed to tell her how to get to the inauguration. Perkins and Wallace told the driver to head to the Capitol, but when they got close, the taxi got caught in a traffic jam. A policeman told them they would have to travel the rest of the way on foot. They got out and, with the inauguration about to start, tried to make their way through the sea of humanity. "Henry, Ilo, Susanna, and I just ran," Perkins later recalled. "We elbowed our way."[63]

It suddenly seemed possible that the incoming labor and agriculture secretaries might not make it to the inauguration at all. Perkins and Wallace separated from Ilo and Susanna, whose tickets were for the distinguished visitors' section, and made a dash for the inaugural platform, which was far in the distance. "I hope you've got rubbers on," Wallace said. They climbed under ropes and cut across lawns that had been put off-limits. Perkins and Wallace arrived after the proceedings had already begun. They got there too late to claim their seats in a section set aside for the Cabinet. Instead, they settled unobtrusively into a section off to the side. They missed Roosevelt's swearing in and only heard his inaugural address when it was "about half through," Wallace recalled later. After she settled in, Perkins saw the speech's author, bending over, hands on his knees, sighing. Moley turned to Perkins, whom he knew from New York. "Well, he's taken the ship of state and he's turned it right around," he said. "We're going in the opposite direction."[64]

The crowd applauded one last time, and the ceremony ended at 1:34. Hoover had been a grim presence at the event. "I have seen people once or twice, standing at the brink of an open grave with that same look of despair," Eleanor "Cissy" Patterson wrote in *The Washington Herald*. Hoover did not enjoy Roosevelt's speech—"dark little knots of disagreement came and went" on his forehead, another news account observed. When it was over, he left for Union Station, where he caught a train for New York. He and Roosevelt would never see each other again. Hoover would soon embark on his next career of criticizing, and trying to derail, the New Deal. Other than Hoover, though, it would have been hard to find anyone in the vast crowd outside the Capitol that day who had not been moved and inspired. From the podium, Frances Perkins could see tears streaming "down the faces of strong men in the audience as they listened to it." The crowd's reaction was so emotional that Eleanor Roosevelt was worried. "You felt that they would do anything—if only someone would tell them what to do," she said. The inauguration had been, she concluded, "very, very solemn and a little terrifying."[65]

In tenements crowded with immigrants, parlors of elegant town houses, and isolated farmhouses, Americans had huddled around their radios to hear the address. Joseph Williams, who was listening in Detroit, was overcome by "a feeling almost impossible to describe." Roosevelt had inspired in him, he said, "a feeling of renewed hope, a feeling that this old world is again going to be a pretty good place after all, a feeling that soon this life will be worth living." The press gave the speech rave reviews. The *Chicago Tribune*, a Republican paper, praised its "dominant note of courageous confidence." *The New York Times* hailed it as "a Jacksonian speech, a fighting speech." Even Norman Thomas, the Socialist candidate for president in 1932, conceded that it had been "quite a fine talk as Democratic talks go." *The Daily News* in New York declared: "This newspaper now pledges itself to support the policies of President Franklin D. Roosevelt for a period of at least one year from today; longer, if circumstances warrant." Nearly half a million listeners were moved to send letters to Roosevelt over the next few days, and their praise was effusive. "I am quite sure it was not a mere bit of chance that brought you to the office you now hold," Mrs. William Showalter of Westmont, New Jersey, wrote. "I truly believe you have been sent directly by God to our nation, for such a time as this."[66]

Roosevelt walked down a ramp and into his car, and he and his family drove off, escorted by a team of cavalrymen. He entered the White House for the first time as president and sat down for a modest family buffet. The formal luncheon for five hundred that had been planned had been canceled out of respect for Senator Walsh. Roosevelt then went out onto Pennsylvania Avenue, where a six-mile-long inaugural parade was under way. He took his place in the official reviewing stand, a replica of Andrew Jackson's Tennessee homestead, the Hermitage, alongside his wife and mother, Cabinet members, armed forces leaders, and other dignitaries. The eighteen thousand marchers who filed by included governors of more than half the states, members of the Electoral College, and veterans, some from the Civil War. There were prancing horses pulling artillery caissons, a Sioux Indian bugle-and-drum corps, and Prohibition opponents from Boston shouting "We Want Beer!" More than one hundred military planes, and two dirigibles, flew overhead. Bands played "The Franklin Delano Roosevelt March," written by the incoming treasury secretary, William Woodin. Four black men pushed lawn mowers down the avenue, a retort to Hoover's warning that if Roosevelt became president grass would grow in the streets. Roosevelt, who had always enjoyed parades, declared this one "wonderful," and stayed for most of the three and a half hours it took to pass. By doing so, and exhibiting such high spirits, he was again reassuring the nation that everything would be all right.[67]

Eleanor left the reviewing stand to host a reception for 2,500 out-of-town visitors. The East Room, the White House's magnificent "great hall," in which James Madison held Cabinet meetings and Lincoln's body lay in state, was decorated with fine glass, silver, and red roses. The crowd of friends, family, and government officials filled the room and spilled out into the State Dining Room. Among them were thirteen people with polio who had traveled up from Warm Springs for the inauguration. At eight p.m., there would be a buffet supper for seventy-five members of Roosevelt's extended family, the largest gathering ever of Roosevelts and Delanos. After dinner, there would be a ball at the nearby Washington Auditorium. Eight thousand people had bought five-dollar tickets, and many more would be turned away.[68]

Roosevelt left the inaugural parade at dusk and made his way up to the Oval Room on the second floor. He had quietly arranged for the Senate to confirm his Cabinet that afternoon, and now he was about to do something that had never been done before: swearing in a full Cabinet at once. The incoming Cabinet members had been summoned to appear with any family members they wanted to bring, but they had not been told why. Perkins brought Susanna and her old friend Molly Dewson. When she arrived,

Roosevelt was seated at a large desk—looking, as Ickes later recalled, "courageous, competent, and confident." Perkins's fellow Cabinet members were arranging themselves in a circle around Justice Benjamin Cardozo, an old friend of Roosevelt's from his days on New York's highest court, who had just been appointed to Oliver Wendell Holmes's seat on the Supreme Court.[69]

The Cabinet had gotten a lukewarm reception when Roosevelt announced it. Arthur Krock of the *Times* declared that "its composite trait seems to me to be diligence; brilliance it lacks completely." The new Cabinet was criticized for lacking "big men," notably the candidates Roosevelt had defeated for the nomination, like the 1928 Democratic standard-bearer, Al Smith. One Republican congressman wisecracked that Roosevelt had kept his promise to look out for the "forgotten men," since his Cabinet contained "nine of them and one woman." Some of the people clamoring for "big men" lacked confidence in Roosevelt and wanted to be reassured that he had capable people around him. When the Eastern money interests talked about wanting big men, though, which they did loudly, they meant that they wanted conservative Cabinet members who would keep Roosevelt from doing anything rash, like nationalizing the banks or promoting inflation. "At its core," one journalist observed at the time, "the cry was the last effort of the financial powers which had been defeated at Chicago and on Election Day to retain control of the government."[70]

Roosevelt's Cabinet members may not have been well known, but they had been carefully chosen. There were Washington elder statesmen like Cordell Hull, the venerable Tennessee senator who was to become secretary of state, and people more in touch with what was happening in the states, like George Dern, a two-term Utah governor and a key Roosevelt supporter in the West, who would be secretary of war. The new agriculture secretary, Wallace, was revered in the Farm Belt, and the treasury secretary, William Woodin, was a businessman who was trusted by Wall Street. Roosevelt's instinct for political coalition building was on display. Three of the Cabinet members were progressive Republicans, a key constituency that had swung to the Democratic ticket in the last election, and that Roosevelt was eager to include in his administration. Overall, Roosevelt declared his Cabinet "slightly to the left of center," a characterization he also applied to himself. It was also the most diverse Cabinet in history. Roosevelt had appointed Southerners and Westerners. He had named two Catholics, including Senator Walsh, and the press noted that he had considered Jesse Isador Straus, the president of R. H. Macy & Co., and his old friend Henry Morgenthau, both of whom were Jewish. The appointment of Perkins was the most historic of all.[71]

Roosevelt announced to the Cabinet that Justice Cardozo would be swearing them in. "I hope you don't mind being sworn in on my old Dutch Bible," Roosevelt said. "You won't be able to read a word of it, but it's the Holy Scriptures, all right, isn't it?" He called off the names of the new Cabinet members in order of protocol, starting with Hull, whose department had the highest ranking. As each stepped forward, the silver-haired Justice Cardozo administered the oath of office, and Roosevelt extended a congratulatory handshake and a signed commission. Last to be called was Perkins, whose department, which turned twenty that day, was the most recently created.[72]

Roosevelt joked that he had sworn in the Cabinet right away so they could "receive an extra day's pay." The real reason was that he wanted them to begin work immediately, in a spirit of unity. Even without "big men," the Cabinet included men, and one woman, with a great deal of knowledge, experience, and commitment. The best of them had, as Walter Lippmann noted, something that would make them an important force during the next one hundred days: "convictions, which they have held to when it was neither profitable nor popular." *Time* magazine declared that the group "presaged good teamwork with a President who obviously would be its master," but the relationship would not be that simple. The Cabinet members gathered in the Oval Room, and many New Dealers not in the room, had very definite ideas about where they wanted to take the country, and on some of the most important issues of the day, they would be the ones taking the lead.[73]

CHAPTER TWO

"Moley! Moley! Moley! Lord God Almighty!"

With the start of the Roosevelt administration, Washington was suddenly seized with a new vitality and sense of purpose. Hoover administration officials, beaten down and dejected, had begun clearing out. In their place came waves of lawyers, economists, and aspiring bureaucrats, many of them recent graduates of the nation's best schools. They were eager to join the federal government, which was seen as the best hope for defeating the Depression. "We came to Washington because that's where the action was," recalled Thomas Eliot, who left a Buffalo law firm to be a lawyer in the Labor Department. There was another consideration. Many of them simply needed a job. These would-be New Dealers showed up with letters of introduction from governors, professors, and anyone they knew back home who had contacts in Washington. They passed around résumés short on work experience and interviewed feverishly. "A plague of young lawyers settled on Washington," George Peek, a businessman who would soon play a large role in Roosevelt's agriculture program, wrote grumpily in his memoirs. "They all claimed to be friends of somebody or other ... They floated airily into offices, took desks, asked for papers and found no end of things to be busy about."[1]

The new arrivals settled into once-dowdy neighborhoods like Georgetown and Foggy Bottom, and infused sleepy Washington with a level of energy it had never seen before. "They have transformed it," *Collier's* reported, "from a placid, leisurely Southern town, with frozen faces and customs, into a gay, breezy, sophisticated and metropolitan center." The New Dealers gathered for parties at which the fate of the nation was debated late into the night. "The most important things that happened in Washington in those days were over cocktails," a prominent New Deal lawyer recalled. Perkins's friend Molly Dewson, a leading Democratic Party activist, remembered that the capital was suddenly "as lively as an ants' nest that has been split open."[2]

This invigorating new spirit had also taken hold in the White House. The head of the Secret Service detail, Colonel Edmund W. Starling, noticed the difference as soon as he returned from dropping former president Hoover off at Union Station. The White House "had been transformed during my absence into a gay place, full of people who oozed confidence," he said. "The President was the most happy and confident of them all." Will Rogers was gratified that unlike Hoover, Roosevelt looked like he was enjoying himself. "A smile in the White House again," Rogers said, "seemed like a meal to us." Eleanor Roosevelt noted that the national crisis was having a "most exhilarating effect" on her husband. "Decisions were being made, new ideas were being tried, people were going to work and businessmen who ordinarily would have scorned government assistance were begging the government to find solutions for their problems," she wrote in her memoirs. The new sense of possibility worked its way through every level of the federal government. Milton Katz, a young lawyer who had joined the Reconstruction Finance Corporation, remembered it as a "virtually physical" difference. "The air suddenly changed, the wind blew through the corridors," recalled Katz, who would go on to become a distinguished Harvard Law School professor. "You suddenly felt, 'By God, the air is fresh, it's moving, life is resuming.'"[3]

Roosevelt's first priority had to be the banking system. The banks' troubles had begun, like the Depression itself, in the frothy economy of the 1920s. Americans had come to believe, along with President Coolidge, that the business of America was business. Over the course of the decade, the number of stockbrokers increased from fewer than thirty thousand to more than seventy thousand, and the public followed the market with a passion it had once reserved for baseball. Americans bought stocks at a frenzied pace, much of it on margin, putting up only a fraction of the price while banks often put up the rest. They also poured their savings into "investment trusts," speculative stock-buying syndicates that eventually plunged in value. Ninety percent of the stock purchased in the 1920s, by one estimate, was bought for speculation. It was not only Coolidge Republicans who were swept up. John J. Raskob, the chairman of the Democratic National Committee, told *Ladies' Home Journal* that by diligently investing a portion of their salaries "anyone not only can be rich, but ought to be rich." There were periodic calls for putting limits on margin buying, but they were quickly beaten back. "If buying and selling stocks is wrong the government should close the Stock Exchange," the influential newspaperman Arthur Brisbane declared. "If not, the Federal Reserve should mind its own business."[4]

Banks had been among the most eager participants in the speculative frenzy. Having piled up large cash reserves, they invested heavily in the stock market. After the crash, which sent stock prices down 85 percent from their highs, the banks found themselves with total assets that were worth less than they owed their depositors. The banks' loans added to their problems. In many cases, they had accepted as collateral for their margin loans speculative stock that had become all but worthless. When borrowers fell behind on their payments, the banks had nothing of value to collect. Banks in the Midwest and the South had the additional problem that the farm economy had been depressed for more than a decade. Low crop prices meant that many farmers could not meet their farm and home mortgage payments. The land that had been offered as collateral was, like the speculative stock, often worth less than the outstanding debts.[5]

Many banks could not survive. Between 1930 and 1932, 773 national banks and 3,604 state banks, with more than $2.7 billion in assets, had failed. As rumors of impending bank failures spread, depositors rushed to withdraw their money. These bank runs were often chaotic, and traumatic for the people whose life savings were at risk. "Long lines wound in and out of the lobbies of neighborhood banks," the writer Robert Bendiner recalled, "which proceeded to disgorge currency and gold at a rate to frighten and disgust those who had not yet taken theirs out." People who managed to retrieve their money hid it under mattresses, buried it in holes in their backyards, or sent it overseas for safekeeping. These panicked withdrawals exacerbated the problem, pushing many more troubled banks into insolvency.[6]

The bank failures started in Nashville in the fall of 1930, and spread through the South and the Midwest. In Hartford, three banks failed in unison, including the eighty-year-old City Bank & Trust Co. In South Carolina, the collapse of the forty-three-branch Peoples State Bank spread panic across the state. The most spectacular failure of all was the collapse of the New York–based Bank of United States in December 1930. Although it was a private bank, the name made many customers think it had the government's backing. When it went under, 450,000 depositors, many of them impoverished Jewish immigrants who worked in the garment industry, lost their savings. Four hundred thousand of the banks' customers had $400 or less on deposit. For many, it was all that they had. When word of the failure spread, 8,000 depositors lined up outside a single branch in the Bronx, watched over by a phalanx of police officers, in an unsuccessful attempt to retrieve their money. Similar stories played out across the country.[7]

Hoover was besieged by demands to take some kind of action. True to his ideology, and his experience as food administrator, he believed the private sector should solve the problem. Hoover initially proposed that the banks get together and pool their assets, so the stronger ones could rescue the weaker ones. The privately operated organization that the bankers set up at his instigation, the National Credit Corporation, quickly proved inadequate to the challenge of saving the nation's ailing banking system. Hoover learned how difficult voluntary action would be when he tried to set up a fund to save the failing Bank of Pittsburgh and his own treasury secretary, Andrew Mellon, himself a Pittsburgh banker, refused to contribute.[8]

With banks continuing to fail at an alarming rate, in 1932 Hoover yielded to congressional pressure and established the Reconstruction Finance Corporation. The RFC, which began with $3.5 billion in government funds and borrowing capacity, was authorized to lend money to troubled banks, mortgage companies, and other financial institutions that were able to provide adequate security. The RFC got off to a promising start, helping to shore up banks, particularly ones in small towns. Ultimately, though, it proved ineffective. One problem was that the RFC was required to publish the names of its borrowers. Many struggling banks did not apply for help because they feared being publicly identified. Hoover's bad luck continued with his choice of Chicago banker Charles Dawes, who had served as vice president under Coolidge, to be the RFC's president. When Hoover vetoed the bonus for war veterans, Dawes had called him a hero for resisting the "dole principle." It was, as a result, embarrassing when, weeks after Dawes resigned, it came out that a bank he headed had received a $90 million RFC loan. Critics joked that RFC stood for "Relief for Charlie," and argued that Dawes's double standard proved that the Hoover administration cared only about helping the wealthy.[9]

With the federal government flailing, states began to act on their own. In October 1932, Nevada's governor declared a bank holiday when the state's banks found themselves without enough funds to meet depositors' withdrawals. Louisiana followed in early February 1933. It was Michigan's banking crisis that same month, however, that started the nationwide panic. Like most things in Michigan, the banks were closely tied to the automobile industry. When the Depression struck, workers in the hard-hit automobile industry began depositing less and withdrawing more, straining the banks' liquidity. At the same time, more borrowers were failing to make their mortgage payments, and the banks found themselves with property as collateral that they could not sell. With every week that passed, it became harder for the banks to remain solvent.[10]

The Hoover administration asked Henry Ford to help a large, troubled Detroit bank by freezing his sizable deposits, but he refused. Ford had little sympathy for the banks, which he believed had brought on their own troubles. He had also long nursed a grudge against New York banks, which he believed were out to get him. Two top administration officials came to Dearborn to make a personal appeal, telling Ford that the state's banks were on the verge of failing, endangering one million deposits that supported three million state residents. If Michigan's banks failed, they warned, other states' banks would likely follow. "Let the crash come," Ford is said to have replied. "Everything will go down the chute. But I feel young. I can build again."[11]

When Ford did not come through, Governor William Comstock declared an eight-day bank holiday, closing 550 banks, on February 14. Michigan residents reacted calmly to "Comstock's Valentine," as the press dubbed it. Detroit paid city workers with the money it collected from railway fares, and other employers were equally resourceful. While Michigan adapted, bank customers in other states, who were still able to withdraw their deposits, panicked. "The news from Michigan jangled the American System from center to periphery," historians Charles and Mary Beard observed. On February 21, New Jersey restricted payments, and two days later, Indiana declared a bank holiday. On February 25, Maryland declared a bank holiday, followed in quick succession by Arkansas, Ohio, Alabama, Kentucky, Tennessee, and Nevada. The nation's anxiety level rose with each new declaration. "Urban populations cannot do without money," Thomas Lamont, a partner of J. P. Morgan, warned. "It would be like cutting off a city's water supply." In states where the banks remained open, currency and gold were being withdrawn at such a rapid rate that the system would not be able to survive for long. Demands for the federal government to act were growing more strident. "The credit structure of the U.S. is a disgraceful failure," William Gibbs McAdoo, Woodrow Wilson's secretary of the treasury, who had just been elected senator from California, declared. "Our entire banking system does credit to a collection of imbeciles."[12]

Hoover, who was bitter over his electoral defeat, was not up to handling the crisis. It seemed to Eugene Meyer, the chairman of the Federal Reserve Board, that the lame-duck president had gone "into a tailspin mentally—emotionally." The final weeks of his administration were, Meyer recalled, "a period of going along as best you could from day to day, knowing that you weren't getting anything but black looks in the White House." Hoover did not believe it was necessary to close the banks that remained open. He was also getting conflicting advice. His banking advisers were recommending that he declare a national bank holiday, invoking his authority under the Trading with the Enemy Act, a World War I–era law that authorized the president to regulate transfers of gold and currency. Hoover's attorney general, William D. Mitchell, doubted that the law gave him the authority to do so. Hoover decided that if he was going to do anything with lasting impact he needed to have Roosevelt's support. His efforts to enlist it, however, were ham-handed. He wrote a letter to Roosevelt during the Michigan bank holiday, in which he suggested that Roosevelt's election had produced a "steadily degenerating confidence in the future." After that insult, Hoover told the man who had defeated him that they should work together—on Hoover's terms. To restore the nation's confidence, he insisted, Roosevelt would have to promise to balance the budget, remain on the gold standard, and adopt an array of other conservative prescriptions. Hoover admitted he was trying to maneuver Roosevelt into accepting policies the voters had just rejected. "If these declarations be made by the President-elect," Hoover wrote in a letter to Senator David Reed of Pennsylvania, "he will have ratified the whole major program of the Republican Administration" and that would require "abandonment of ninety per cent of the so-called new deal."[13]

Roosevelt received Hoover's handwritten letter on the night of February 18, while he was attending the Inner Circle dinner, an annual gathering of reporters and politicians, at New York's Astor Hotel. Roosevelt did not pull himself away from the night of drinking and humorous skits to respond, and he would not answer for eleven full days. Roosevelt called Hoover's letter "cheeky," but it was not just its presumptuousness that put him off. Roosevelt was wary of squandering his political capital by joining forces with his unpopular predecessor. It made more sense, Roosevelt believed, to wait until after he had taken office, and a new, more Democratic, Congress was in place. During these panic-stricken days, when the future of the banking system was in serious jeopardy, Roosevelt remained calm, and confident that everything would work out. "It was Will Woodin and I who tore our hair over the reports of the mounting gold withdrawals and the growing number of bank suspensions and who sat up night after night pondering the possible remedies," Moley would later recall. "Roosevelt went serenely through those days on the assumptions that Hoover was perfectly capable of acting without his concurrence; that there was no remedy of which we knew that was not available to the Hoover Administration . . . and that, until noon of March 4th, the baby was Hoover's anyhow." Hoover tried again, in his final days as president. He was willing to overcome his reluctance and declare a national bank holiday starting on March 3, he said, if Roosevelt would agree to call Congress into special session on March 5 to ratify the decision. The state of the banks was undeniably worsening. In the previous week, another $732 million had drained out of the reserves, much of it ending up under mattresses or in overseas bank accounts. Roosevelt did not oppose the bank holiday, only the idea of joint action. He suggested that Hoover declare his own holiday until Saturday noon, the end of his own term in office.[14]

Hoover did not give up. He and Mrs. Hoover invited the Roosevelts to the White House the afternoon before the inauguration, as protocol dictated. When Roosevelt arrived with Eleanor and James for four o'clock tea, Hoover was waiting with his treasury secretary, Ogden Mills, and the chairman of the Federal Reserve Board, Eugene Meyer. Roosevelt felt he had been ambushed. "Father told me later that Mr. Hoover's ringing in of Ogden Mills at this meeting was one of the damnedest bits of presumption he ever had witnessed in politics," James later recalled. Roosevelt called in reinforcements, summoning Raymond Moley, who had been napping at the Mayflower Hotel. The discussion of the crisis, which lasted over an hour, ended in deadlock. For the last time, Roosevelt refused to be drawn in.[15]

Roosevelt invited Hoover to take his leave. There was a tradition that the outgoing president return the visit of the incoming president, but Roosevelt told Hoover that he should not feel obligated to do so. It was a considerate gesture, which was shot down sharply. "Mr. Roosevelt," Hoover said, "when you are in Washington as long as I have been, you will learn that the President of the United States calls on nobody." James later said he had wanted to punch Hoover in the nose. Roosevelt was offended by Hoover's manner that day, and over the previous few months. He "was not prepared to be treated like a schoolboy, or to have his own integrity thrown into question," Roosevelt's secretary, Grace Tully, said. With this final standoff, the matter appeared settled. Hoover would do nothing, and Roosevelt would inherit a failed banking system. "In all history there have been few such ironic coincidences," noted journalist Ernest K. Lindley, "as this collapse of an economic order in the last minutes of its zealous guardianship by the man who thought it fundamentally perfect."[16]

The man responsible for coming up with a solution to the banking crisis for Roosevelt was William Woodin, the incoming secretary of the treasury. Woodin had not been the first choice for the job. Roosevelt had offered it to Senator Carter Glass, the courtly Virginian who had helped create the Federal Reserve System in 1913, and who was the Democrats' leading expert on banking. But the seventy-five-year-old Glass, who had already briefly served as treasury secretary in the Wilson administration, was not eager to leave the Senate. He made clear that he would not join the Cabinet to promote an economic agenda he disagreed with. Glass told Moley, who was coordinating the search, that he would only accept if Roosevelt committed to remaining on the gold standard. Like many fiscal conservatives, Glass believed that going off gold would lead to dangerous rates of inflation and destroy business confidence. In his public statements, Roosevelt had supported the 1932 Democratic Party platform, which had called for "a sound currency to be preserved at all hazards." But in private, his views were less firm, and he was under intense pressure from his Farm Belt supporters to adopt an inflationary monetary policy, which farmers believed would get them out from under their crushing debt loads. Roosevelt had not decided whether or not to abandon the gold standard, but he knew he did not want a Treasury secretary who would lock him into one side of the issue. Glass also told Moley he would want to be able to name his own staff, including a J. P. Morgan & Company partner as his deputy. This demand, too, was unacceptable to Roosevelt. "We simply cannot go along with Twenty-three," Roosevelt told Moley, a reference to Morgan's address at 23 Wall Street. "If the old boy doesn't want to go along, I wouldn't press it."[17]

Moley had decided back in January that if Glass did not take the job, Roosevelt should offer it to Woodin, a lifelong Republican who would be almost as reassuring to Wall Street as Glass would have been. Woodin was the president of American Car & Foundry, the largest railroad equipment company in the world, and the successor to a company his grandfather had founded. A pillar of the Eastern Establishment, he served on twenty-one corporate boards and was a member of the Republican Union Club of Philadelphia and the Union Club of New York. Woodin was widely regarded as an economic traditionalist. "Woodin is big business," *BusinessWeek* declared, "holding all the orthodox views about sound money, guarantee of bank deposits, and a balanced budget." At the same time, he was firmly in the Roosevelt camp. He had broken with his party to support Al Smith in 1928, and in 1932 he had endorsed Roosevelt early and given $35,000 to his campaign. Woodin was not only a political supporter of Roosevelt, but a personal friend who served on the board of the Warm Springs Foundation. One of his biggest selling points was that unlike Glass and other leading contenders—and despite what *BusinessWeek* seemed to think—Woodin did not have strong views on banking or inflation, or at least none that he would hold to if Roosevelt felt otherwise.[18]

When Glass began making his demands, Moley approached Louis Howe and asked if he would help sell Roosevelt on Woodin. Howe liked the idea of appointing a Roosevelt loyalist who would also appeal to business leaders. Moley and Howe sent a coded radio message to Roosevelt, who was on a pre-inauguration sailing vacation on Vincent Astor's yacht: "PREFER A WOODEN ROOF TO A GLASS ROOF OVER SWIMMING POOL. LUHOWRAY." "Wooden" and "glass" referred to the two main contenders for treasury secretary, and "Luhowray" was a conglomeration of the message writers' names. At the same time, Glass's friends were urging him to reconsider, and it was not clear what he would do. "The Glass appointment was like King Charles' head," Moley complained. "It kept popping up." In the end, Glass made clear he was not interested, and Roosevelt chose Woodin.[19]

The appointment came as a shock, most of all to Woodin, who was not certain he was up to the job. The press shared his doubts. After being led to believe the position would go to the distinguished senator from Virginia, reporters seized on Woodin's diminutive size and spritelike appearance and quickly dubbed him "Wee Willie Woodin." The press's references to Woodin as "elfin" and "faunlike" were so frequent that Moley would later complain that it would seem, "to read the accounts of him, that he went dancing through directors' meetings wearing a conical hat…and playing on little pipes." The profiles also made sport of the fact that Woodin, an amateur composer, had written such classics as the "Raggedy Ann's Sunny Songs," to be performed by children on ukuleles. Many people who knew Woodin agreed with Roosevelt's budget director, Lewis Douglas, who considered him "a nice little man, not a particularly profound person, but very agreeable." The press and members of the administration were particularly skeptical that Woodin was the right person to confront the banking crisis. "His real business was manufacturing railroad locomotives," said Walter Wyatt, who would be influential in planning Roosevelt's rescue of the banks, "and he didn't know anything about how to handle the banking problems."[20]

Woodin was not sent to take on the bank crisis alone. Roosevelt asked Moley to work alongside him. It was an unusual arrangement, but an understandable one. Ever since he had come to Roosevelt's attention as head of the Brain Trust, the pragmatic Moley was the person Roosevelt turned to when he was faced with a difficult policy question. In addition to his formal role, Moley filled a special place in the new president's psyche. He was, for the moment, the occupant of a position as important as any Cabinet post: he was Roosevelt's professional confidant and alter ego. Despite his large family and extensive circle of friends and supporters, Roosevelt was essentially a lonely man. Throughout his adult life, he always had a male subordinate close at hand whose job was to be both chief adviser and friend on call. When he began his career it had been Howe, the former journalist who plotted his early political rise. At the start of the New Deal, when Roosevelt desperately needed to develop wise policies, it was the cerebral, strategic Moley who filled the role. "Through his ear," *Time* declared when it put Moley on its cover in May, "is the shortest and swiftest route to the heart of the White House."[21]

The public was largely unaware of Moley, who was most comfortable working behind the scenes. But people in Roosevelt's inner circle understood that he was, as one insider put it, "the second strongest man in Washington," after Roosevelt himself. As Moley's influence became better known, it became the subject of wry humor. Capital wits soon began replacing the word "Holy" in the name of the well-known hymn and proclaiming "Moley! Moley! Moley! Lord God Almighty!" An often-told joke had an old friend of

Roosevelt calling up and pleading, "Franklin, can you do me just one favor? Can you get me an appointment with Moley?" People eventually came to realize that the looks and demeanor of this stocky, balding, forty-six-year-old academic were deceptive. He was "about as different from the timid, absent-minded professor type of fiction as could be imagined," *Collier's* noted. "There is a jut to his jaw, a steel-trap effect around the mouth, and behind his glasses are a pair of clear eyes that have the bore of gimlets." This gimlet-eyed, behind-the-scenes operator was the person Roosevelt leaned on as he confronted one of the greatest challenges the nation had ever faced.[22]

Moley's route to the inner sanctum of the Roosevelt White House had been an improbable one. He had been born in Berea, Ohio, outside Cleveland, in 1886, the son of the owner of a struggling men's furnishings store. His lineage was Irish-French and yellow-dog Democrat, and his childhood hero was William Jennings Bryan, the great populist orator of the Plains. In three unsuccessful campaigns for president, Bryan told spellbound farm audiences that their troubles were due to manipulations of the money supply by Eastern financial interests. In 1896, in his famous "Cross of Gold" speech to the Democratic National Convention, Bryan decried the impact of the gold standard on the common man and woman. Young Moley could not follow the monetary arguments, but he was impressed by Bryan's oratory, and his concern for the disadvantaged. He put a picture of his hero up on his bedroom wall and, when Bryan lost, convinced his mother to let him miss three days of school so he would not have to endure his classmates' taunts.[23]

The Panic of 1893, and the serious depression it ushered in, forced the family to move to nearby Olmsted Falls, where Moley's grandparents owned land. Moley pursued an education as far as he could in the tiny local school system, leaving after tenth grade to attend college. He worked as a teacher in Olmsted Falls, and quickly became school superintendent, supervising three other teachers. At the same time, Moley embarked on a career in local politics. He was elected village clerk of Olmsted Falls in 1907, and mayor in 1911. The high point of Moley's brief mayoral career was a successful drive to bring electric lights to Olmsted Falls. Moley's youthful stint as a mayor hardly thrust him into the political big leagues, but it helped to prepare him for the greater challenges that lay ahead. When Roosevelt's campaign manager, James Farley, asked during the 1932 campaign, "What the hell do you, a college professor, know about politics?" Moley could say that he had been elected to office three years before Roosevelt entered the New York State Legislature.[24]

Moley's ambitions reached beyond small-town Ohio. He earned a master's degree at Oberlin College and began teaching high school history in Cleveland. In the early 1900s, Cleveland was a bastion of progressivism, and its municipal government was a leading innovator. Moley did his master's thesis on one of the city's leading institutions, the municipal court. While he was at Oberlin, Charles A. Beard, the noted Columbia historian, came through to lecture. Beard had just completed his Progressive Era classic, *An Economic Interpretation of the Constitution of the United States*, which argued that the Constitution reflected the Founding Fathers' personal financial interests. Moley struck up an acquaintance with Beard and, at his urging, continued his graduate studies in the fall of 1914 at Columbia, where Beard became his most powerful academic influence.[25]

Moley returned to Ohio in 1916 to take a position at Western Reserve University in Cleveland, and married Eva Dall, whom he knew from his school days in Olmsted Falls. He became active in progressive causes, including the drive to "Americanize" Cleveland's recent immigrants. Moley was considering entering elective politics when he accepted the position of director of the reform-minded Cleveland Foundation. A crime wave had hit the city, and one of Moley's biggest projects was an investigation of the criminal justice system. The Cleveland Crime Study, on which he collaborated with Dean Roscoe Pound and Professor Felix Frankfurter of Harvard Law School, led to major reforms. Moley went on to conduct similar studies in eight other states. On the strength of his criminal justice work, he was invited to return to Columbia in 1923 as an associate professor of government at Barnard College. Not long after their arrival in New York, Eva gave birth to twin boys. Moley became a full professor of public law in 1928, and he would soon publish two books, *Politics and Criminal Prosecution* and *Our Criminal Courts*.[26]

When Governor Al Smith appointed him research director of the Crime Commission of New York State, Moley came into contact with Louis Howe. Howe had gotten a position, with Roosevelt's help, on the National Crime Commission, and knowing little about crime, he sought Moley's guidance. When Roosevelt ran for governor in 1928, Howe invited Moley to help with the campaign. It was, for someone with Moley's interest in politics, an irresistible offer. Moley was impressed with Roosevelt from their first meeting at campaign headquarters. He was struck, he would later say, by Roosevelt's "handsome figure" and "the smile that was so soon to win the affection of many million Americans." Roosevelt asked Moley to prepare a memorandum on criminal justice reform that could be the basis for a campaign address. Moley wrote the memo, and Roosevelt turned it into a speech that he delivered in the Bronx, in which he called for the creation of a commission to explore ways to make the courts more efficient. When Roosevelt became governor, he appointed Moley to the State Commission on the Administration of Justice.[27]

After his reelection in 1930, Roosevelt began planning his presidential run. Roosevelt had experienced political advisers, including Howe and James Farley, the Irish-American state Democratic Party official who would manage the campaign. What Roosevelt did not have were policy experts who could advise him on the subjects a presidential candidate had to have positions on. Roosevelt's counsel, Samuel Rosenman, suggested that he invite a group of academic advisers to join the campaign, and Roosevelt readily agreed. Rosenman suggested Moley to head up the group. One of Moley's great strengths, as far as Roosevelt and Rosenman were concerned, was that, despite his youthful exposure to midwestern progressivism, he did not have particularly strong political views. Moley accepted at once. When the number of academic advisers began to grow, James M. Kieran, a reporter for *The New York Times*, wrote a brief story on the group, which he dubbed the "brains trust." The name, in slightly modified form, stuck. Rosenman and Moley would later battle over who deserved credit for creating Roosevelt's famed Brain Trust. Rosenman argued that the original concept had been his. Moley, who recruited the members and led the group, insisted the Brain Trust had been his doing. "Sometimes the lady who smacks the champagne bottle against the ship's prow," Moley said, "has the illusion that she is causing the ship to slide down the ways."[28]

Moley was the Brain Trust's chief recruiter. He began at Columbia because he thought it best to bring in people he knew, and he figured the proximity would make it easy to meet regularly. He did not have to look far for his first recruit, Rexford Tugwell, a young economist who lived one building down from him on Claremont Avenue, near the Columbia campus. Tugwell had been born in the town of Sinclairville in upstate New York, the son of a successful businessman who owned a vegetable and fruit cannery. He had studied economics at the University of Pennsylvania before joining the Columbia faculty, where he was an expert on agricultural economics. Although he was a New Yorker, Tugwell kept in close touch with farm issues across the country and abroad. He had traveled to the Soviet Union and Europe, and had written about farm conditions in both. His research had left him with the conviction that government planning was necessary to make farming more efficient. Tugwell had begun speaking of the importance of government, industry, and agriculture working together—an idea he would later brand a "concert of interests." Tugwell could see the toll the Depression was taking on farm communities and on his own neighborhood, where a Hooverville had formed and was rapidly expanding. He was angry that Hoover was doing so little. When Moley approached him, Tugwell quickly signed on. At his Brain Trust interview, the brilliant, charming, and strikingly good-looking Tugwell made a strong impression. "Rex was like a cocktail," Moley said. "His conversation picked you up and made your brain race along."[29]

Moley's next major recruit was Adolf A. Berle, Jr., a corporation law expert at Columbia Law School. Berle, a child prodigy, had graduated from Harvard Law School at twenty-one, the youngest graduate in the school's history. He had just finished writing a pathbreaking book with the economist Gardiner C. Means, which argued that modern corporations posed a greater threat to the public good than corporations of the past, and had to be more highly regulated. Berle had a reputation for being difficult—his critics said he continued to be a child long after he had stopped being a prodigy. Moley, however, was impressed with Berle's ideas about business. When Moley stopped by his office on a recruitment visit, Berle responded that he already had a candidate for president, Newton Baker, a former reform mayor of Cleveland who had been Wilson's secretary of war. Moley said that the campaign wanted his policy advice, not his political support, which was of little value. Berle laughed and accepted the invitation. He drew up a memorandum for Roosevelt that laid out what would become a New Deal article of faith—that the federal government had to start taking more responsibility for the nation's economic condition. "In 1932, this was a revolutionary and dangerous conception," Berle would later say. "The federal government was there to keep order, do certain reform work, assist from time to time, but the normal processes of laissez-faire economics were supposed to provide the results."[30]

Moley did not do the recruiting alone. He brought prospective Brain Trust members in to meet with Rosenman and Basil "Doc" O'Connor, Roosevelt's former law partner. If the lawyers approved, the recruits went upstate to meet Roosevelt. Tugwell vividly recalled his own meeting. "Roosevelt was sitting on the front porch of the big Governor's mansion, with his shirt open and his coat off although it wasn't a terribly warm day," Tugwell said. "He was smoking a cigarette as he always did in his long holder, with his chin up as it always was. He wasn't frightened by anything." Tugwell was invited to dine with Roosevelt, and they talked late into the night about agriculture and the plight of the farmers. Tugwell was deeply moved by his first encounter with Roosevelt. "Meeting him," Tugwell would later say, "was like coming into contact with destiny itself." Roosevelt had also been impressed. Tugwell made the cut, but not everyone Moley proposed for membership in the Brain Trust met with Roosevelt's approval. Another Columbia economics professor, Frederick C. Mills, was rejected because he had strongly held views on monetary policy. Roosevelt turned down other would-be Brain Trusters who showed up with fixed positions, inflexible "plans" for solving particular problems, or allegiance to one of the faddish movements, like "technocracy," that were sweeping the country. What Roosevelt was looking for, above all, was simply good advice about how to solve the nation's problems. "You tell me what you think and what you think I ought to do," Roosevelt told Berle. "Leave the politics to me. That's a dirty business."[31]

The Brain Trust was headquartered in the Roosevelt Hotel, separate from

Roosevelt's political advisers, who operated out of the Biltmore. While Farley and Edward J. Flynn, the Bronx Democratic boss, plotted strategy for winning the nomination, members of the Brain Trust researched policy issues and wrote memos that could be turned into campaign speeches. It was Moley who discussed the memos with Roosevelt and drafted the speeches. This arrangement was partly due to Moley's unusual skill at speechwriting, partly a matter of his desire to be in control, and partly a reflection of his conviction that, as he insisted, "a speech cannot be written by a committee." Moley led the group with a firm hand. He could be abrasive, and he was known for his occasionally sharp temper. Moley drafted the first of the Brain Trust speeches himself, a ten-minute radio address that aired on the *Lucky Strike Hour* on April 7, 1932. The speech, which argued for a stronger response to the Depression, introduced a phrase that Roosevelt would forever be associated with, "the forgotten man at the bottom of the economic pyramid." Other members of the Brain Trust got their own chances to shape Roosevelt's message. In a Jefferson Day address in St. Paul, Minnesota, Roosevelt gave voice to Tugwell's longstanding belief that the needs of farmers, workers, and businessmen had to be blended into a "a fair and just concert of interests." Berle's call for stronger regulation of corporations inspired a rousing September 1932 address to San Francisco's Commonwealth Club that came to be known as the "manifesto of the New Deal." In the speech, Roosevelt went further than ever before in laying out his vision of progressive government. "We are steering a steady course toward economic oligarchy," he warned. "The day of enlightened administration has come," Roosevelt declared, in which the federal government had no choice but to play a more active role in reining in corporate excesses and planning industrial policy.[32]

Early in the campaign, Moley, consulting with Tugwell and Berle, wrote a memorandum that distilled the Brain Trust's thinking, which had evolved over many conversations with Roosevelt. The overarching theme of the memo, which Moley completed on May 19, was that Roosevelt should present a clear alternative to Hoover, "not a choice between two names for the same reactionary doctrine." The key, Moley argued, was for Roosevelt to lead a party of "liberal thought" and "planned action," which would advocate an active role for the federal government in fighting the Depression and helping its victims. The memo called for centralized economic planning, a favorite idea of Tugwell's, which Roosevelt would incorporate into his first agricultural and industrial policies. It also advocated reform of the banking system and the securities industry, including separating investment and commercial banking. The memo urged relief for the unemployed and large-scale public works, but it also endorsed balancing the budget to restore confidence in the government. With those contradictory recommendations, the memo began to create a fundamental conflict—between spending more to fight the Depression and spending less to balance the budget—that would be a central tension of the Hundred Days. Moley's introduction to the memo used the words "new deal" for the first time. Six weeks later, Roosevelt included the phrase in his acceptance speech at the Democratic National Convention, and an era got its name.[33]

Over the next few months, Moley and Roosevelt formed a close bond. Roosevelt traveled extensively during the campaign—in the eleven months before his inauguration, he covered 27,000 miles and visited forty-one states. For Roosevelt, getting out and meeting the voters was, Moley said, "unadulterated joy." Moley often came along, carrying suitcases full of books, draft speeches, and policy memos, writing furiously as the campaign train traveled from town to town. It was an odd pairing, the easygoing, natural politician, born into privilege, and the somber, detail-oriented academic, who never forgot his modest Ohio upbringing. The two men were not friends—the gap in their roles and status was too great. Their relationship was, however, more than that of an ambitious candidate and an unusually talented and dedicated staff member. A real "intimacy developed," Moley recalled, that offered Roosevelt "the relief and satisfaction of thinking aloud when we were together."[34]

The Brain Trust kept working after the election, drawing up policy proposals for the new administration. The group worked on farm legislation, plans for regulating the securities market, and bankruptcy reform. Moley remained at the center of the action, "the one-man reception committee," as *Newsweek* put it, "through whom ideas had to go to reach Roosevelt." He also continued drafting the inaugural address. Moley's importance was under-scored during the interregnum when Hoover asked Roosevelt to come to the White House to discuss the handling of European war debts. England and other debtor nations had unilaterally announced their intention to defer payments on the debts they had incurred to the United States during the World War. Hoover was willing to negotiate, in exchange for those nations' making concessions on other matters. Roosevelt, whose focus was more domestic, knew little about the debts and did not want to be drawn too deeply into a discussion of them with Hoover. He asked Moley to look into the matter. Moley was not an expert on war debts, but working with Berle, he did extensive research and prepared index cards with relevant questions to bring along to the White House. To Moley's surprise, Roosevelt asked him to come to the November 22 meeting with Hoover. After a second meeting on the war debts in mid-January, Roosevelt instructed Hoover's advisers to speak directly with Moley about them.[35]

Moley was eager to find out what role he would play in the new administration. Despite his close relationship with Roosevelt, he was having trouble getting a firm commitment. In late January, Moley told Tugwell of his frustration. "I advised Moley not to go further in his present anomalous role," Tugwell wrote in his diary. "He has much work, many responsibilities, and no authority. F.D.R. is certainly not treating him—or me, for that matter—fairly in requiring so much of us without any acknowledgement of our position." In early February, at Warm Springs, Moley put the question directly to Roosevelt, who said he hoped Moley would come with him to Washington. "I don't have to tell you," he said, "that I've found it easier to work with you than anyone else." The obvious position for Moley was administrative assistant to the president, which would allow him to be Roosevelt's closest day-to-day adviser. What stood in the way of this logical solution was Louis Howe, Roosevelt's eccentric, longtime adviser, whom Tugwell described as "a little gnome of a man" who seemed likely to "blow away at any moment." Howe had guided Roosevelt's political career every step of the way, and as Samuel Rosenman noted, promoting Roosevelt "was his main, if not his sole, mission in life." Roosevelt, in turn, was tremendously loyal to Howe. In the new administration, Howe would be the presidential secretary, a position that would allow him to work out of a back office at the White House where he could be, as Roosevelt said, a "man of mystery." Howe would also move into the White House, where he would live until his death in 1936. There would be two assistant secretaries, Stephen Early, a forty-four-year-old former wire service reporter from Virginia, who would handle press relations, and Marvin McIntyre, an affable fifty-five-year-old Kentucky bachelor, who would be in charge of the president's calendar. The insecure Howe was pathologically jealous of anyone else getting close to his boss. "He guarded his man Roosevelt just like iron," Frances Perkins recalled. Howe was adamant that Moley not be given a job in the White House, and Roosevelt deferred to his old friend.[36]

That left the question of where to put Moley. Roosevelt said that he had been "digging through the Congressional Directory" and it struck him that assistant secretary of state would be the ideal job. It had no statutory duties, which would keep him free to work as Roosevelt's top aide, and it had the added advantage of being located in the State, War and Navy Building, across the street from the West Wing of the White House. That would be far enough away to satisfy Howe but close enough that Moley could easily shuttle back and forth to Roosevelt's office. Roosevelt conceded that assistant secretary of state was "nominally subordinate" to the secretary of state, but he insisted that if Moley took the job he would not have any significant State Department responsibilities. Moley told Roosevelt he thought he would be asking for trouble if he accepted that particular job. He was concerned about the vagueness of the job description, and it seemed to him that any Cabinet member would resent having an assistant who saw the president more often than he did. Moley joked that Roosevelt might as well post him in the Philippines, and Roosevelt replied, "No. You would be 8,000 miles away. I need you here."[37]

Moley, who was ambitious and status conscious, was not happy with the title and arrangement Roosevelt was offering him. He was being banished from the White House to a made-up job, and he would nominally report to a secretary of state he did not know and would have little to do with. Moley was thinking seriously of returning to teaching full-time. His influence on the world would be far less, but his ideas would be accepted, he reasoned, "on the basis of what I had to say, rather than because I was part of a governmental machine." Despite his reservations, Moley could not bring himself to walk away from the new administration he had helped to bring about, and he convinced himself that his country needed him. The lame-duck Congress was proving incapable of doing anything of consequence about unemployment, depressed agricultural prices, or the many other crises the nation faced. While Congress squabbled and equivocated, conditions in the country were only getting worse. It was looking increasingly likely that the nation would be lost to revolution or complete economic collapse if things did not improve quickly. There was no choice, Moley decided, but to accept the call. "If Roosevelt failed, in the weeks to come," he said, "no one's dreams of individual salvation would be worth a damn in any case."[38]

Moley accepted the job, but he did not make a long-term commitment. He kept his full teaching load, scheduling all of his classes on Thursdays to minimize the commuting back to New York, and asked Columbia to list his fall classes in the 1933–1934 course catalogue. While he was in Washington, Moley stayed at the Carlton Hotel, a short walk from his office, paying by the day and living out of a suitcase.[39]

Moley was an ideal person to help with the banking crisis. Roosevelt had come into office without a plan for reviving the banks, and Moley's greatest talents were identifying experts and developing policy proposals. Roosevelt also appreciated that Moley approached problems pragmatically. There were all sorts of ideas circulating in Washington for how to deal with the banks, including radical proposals to nationalize them, or to have U.S. post offices deliver basic banking services. Roosevelt was more interested in reforming the banking system than in taking it over, and he could count on Moley to promote cautious, nonideological solutions. People who knew Moley only by reputation, and from his work with the Brain Trust, were inclined to see him as Lewis Douglas, Roosevelt's conservative budget director, did: as "one of the passionate, collectivist New Dealers." But people closer to Moley, who listened to him discuss policy matters in what one observer called his "gleeful-depressed way," knew better than to lump him in casually with the administration's liberals. Moley's youthful progressivism had evolved into pragmatism, and now that pragmatism was evolving. As he had risen in status through his association with Roosevelt, and as he had begun spending more time with rich and powerful men, he had started to drift rightward. By the time of the inauguration, Moley was already one of industry's closest allies in the administration. Tugwell, who remained a strong progressive and a critic of big business, noticed the change in his old Brain Trust colleague. "Ray was somehow in process of being quite lost to me," Tugwell lamented.[40]

During the interregnum, Moley had helped Roosevelt make one particularly important decision. They decided that the people who knew the most about how to save the banking system were not in the Brain Trust, or even in the Democratic Party. They were, rather, the Hoover administration officials who had been working on banking issues for the past four years. "Great dif[ference] now is emergency," Moley wrote in his notebook on January 19, "turn over to people now on job—the things they are now doing." Moley and Roosevelt talked about working closely with Hoover's Treasury Department team to come up with a solution to the banking crisis. The idea ran counter to the spirit of the moment, which called for quickly pushing out tired, conservative Hoover holdovers and replacing them with dynamic New Dealers. After three terms of Republican presidents, however, there were not many Democrats who had direct experience in regulating the banking industry. The decision to work with the Hoover banking team turned out to be an inspired one.[41]

Hoover may have done little about the banking crisis, but it was not his staff's fault. He had a capable economic team, led by his secretary of the treasury, Ogden Livingston Mills, Jr. The aristocratic Mills, who had graduated from Harvard with Roosevelt in the class of 1904, was the grandson of Darius Ogden Mills, who had made his fortune in mining and banking in California during the gold rush. Ogden Mills had been a Republican congressman from New York and had run against Al Smith for governor in 1926. Although he had campaigned energetically for Hoover in 1932, Mills also believed that Hoover should have done more to confront the banking crisis, even if he could not persuade Roosevelt to go along. Mills's group—which also included Arthur Ballantine, the undersecretary of the treasury; F. G. Awalt, the comptroller of the currency; and Walter Wyatt, the general counsel of the Federal Reserve Board—had proposed an array of activist measures that Hoover could implement, including declaring a national bank holiday, which would have frozen conditions in place, stopping depositors from withdrawing currency and gold from individual banks, and from the United States. Hoover, however, resisted all of their suggestions. Mills and the others had worked around the clock in the administration's final days, hoping until the end that Hoover would relent. When Roosevelt took office, Hoover's banking team had assumed that their government service was done. They had no reason to expect that the new administration would ask them to stay on and work on a rescue plan for the banks. It came as a shock to them, Wyatt would later say, that Roosevelt and his advisers "apparently had no plans about the banking system, none whatever."[42]

The cooperation between the two administrations began the night before the inauguration. Within hours of his final fruitless meeting with Hoover at the White House, Roosevelt gathered his banking advisers at the Mayflower Hotel. He spoke with Moley, Woodin, Glass, and Jesse Jones, the chairman of the RFC, late into the night. The group made little progress toward a solution. Glass continued to push his conservative agenda on Roosevelt, trying to get him to commit to remaining on the gold standard, and insisting that the president did not have the legal authority to order a national bank holiday. Everyone was "indescribably tense," Moley recalled, "even Roosevelt." Hoover called twice during Roosevelt's meeting. At eleven-thirty p.m., he asked Roosevelt to approve an order from the president restricting withdrawals. Roosevelt turned him down. He was inclined to close all of the banks, not merely to limit withdrawals, and he believed it was better for him to act without Hoover. Hoover was still free, of course, to act on his own. At one a.m., Hoover called back to say that Mills and his other economic advisers were still at the Treasury Department, working on the crisis. Roosevelt thanked Hoover for the information, and the two men agreed they should turn in for the night.[43]

Moley was planning on going to bed when he bumped into Woodin in the Mayflower lobby. Woodin, who had left the meeting with Roosevelt earlier, had tried to go to sleep, but he was so worried he "couldn't even get to the stage of undressing." The two men decided to go over to the Treasury Department to see what the Hoover banking team was up to. When they arrived, they found Mills, Ballantine, and Awalt in the Federal Reserve Board's room looking bleary-eyed. Mills and his team were convinced the devastating bank runs and currency and gold withdrawals would continue on inauguration day if the banks remained open. They had hoped up until the end to persuade Hoover to declare a bank holiday, but it was now clear that he would not go along. Having failed at getting a national holiday, they were trying to achieve the same effect by persuading all forty-eight governors to declare state holidays.[44]

When Moley and Woodin arrived, there were only two holdouts, Illinois and New York. Governor Henry Horner of Illinois had not yet been reached, and Governor Herbert Lehman of New York, under pressure from his state's bankers, was holding out. Mills left the room repeatedly to call Lehman. Before the night was over both Lehman and Horner agreed to declare holidays. The crisis was not over, but it was finally on hold. Moley, who had been awake twenty hours straight, had napped through the moment of triumph. Woodin woke him in the middle of the night to say, "It's all right, Ray. Let's go now. Lehman's agreed." The two men walked past reporters and photographers and headed back to the Mayflower for a few hours of sleep before the inauguration. The evening had been an auspicious sign that the Hoover and Roosevelt teams would be able to work together better than their bosses had. It was not that the Hoover officials were lacking in partisanship. Mills, "like Hoover, viewed the Roosevelt ascension as a disaster for the nation," Tugwell said. But the men working at the Treasury Department that night had been able to keep their focus on the national interest and on the vital work at hand. "Mills, Woodin, Ballantine, Awalt, and I had forgotten to be Republicans or Democrats," Moley said. "We were just a bunch of men trying to save the banking system.[45]

The state bank holidays kept bank runs from breaking out on

inauguration day, but they were not a real solution to the banks' problems. In his inaugural address, Roosevelt would speak forcefully about money changers, and about restoring "that temple to the ancient truths," but it was still unclear how he intended to go about it. In a story headlined "Roosevelt's Plans Secret," *The New York Times* reported on inauguration day that "there was still no light on the details of any banking plan which would be submitted" to Congress. In fact, Roosevelt had decided on a course of action just that morning. Moley and Woodin had stopped by the Mayflower and told him that they had been at the Treasury Department most of the night. Mills and the rest of the Hoover team were advising, they said, that Roosevelt declare a national bank holiday. They also wanted him to call a special session of Congress to enact new banking legislation. Moley and Woodin were worried that Roosevelt would be unhappy that they had taken it upon themselves to start working with the Hoover officials. Roosevelt, however, was delighted to hear it and approved of the course of action they suggested.[46]

Moley and Woodin took a break from the banking work to attend the inauguration, where Moley was able to hear Roosevelt deliver the speech they had written together. Afterward, they returned to the Treasury Department and told Mills, Ballantine, and Awalt what Roosevelt had said. "They had been restrained—even frustrated—by Hoover's indecision so long," Moley said, that "Roosevelt's support gave them new energy and determination." Moley, Woodin, and the Hoover team worked late into the night. Mills and Ballantine drafted a presidential proclamation declaring a four-day bank holiday that would start on Monday, March 6. As authority, they relied on the Trading with the Enemy Act. The Hoover group had also begun drawing up a plan for reopening the banks after the holiday. The crux of it was dividing the banks into three groups: Class A, which could reopen immediately; Class B, which would need help reopening; and Class C, which might not reopen at all. There was still more work to be done, including drafting emergency banking legislation to authorize this sorting out of banks. Woodin went to the White House to tell Roosevelt about the idea for a national bank holiday and the plan for reopening the banks in phases. If Roosevelt called a special session for Thursday, March 9, Woodin said, they would have a bill ready to submit to Congress. Roosevelt agreed to the strategy. The White House issued a statement saying that he would declare a special session of Congress, though it did not specify when. It was still unclear how long it would take far-flung members of Congress to return to Washington.[47]

Woodin decided to invite some of the nation's leading bankers to Washington to get their thoughts and to give them an idea about what to expect. The following morning, Sunday, March 5, they began arriving. The bankers were greeted by Woodin—"a very worried little Mr. Woodin," in *Time* magazine's account—Moley, and Mills. It was the beginning, Moley would later recall, of "four interminable days and nights of conferences." The bankers were a traumatized group. One of them, Melvin Traylor, president of the First National Bank of Chicago, had been forced the previous summer to stand on a marble pedestal in his bank's lobby in the middle of a bank run, reassuring panicked customers that their deposits would be safe. The bankers agreed that Roosevelt should declare a national bank holiday, but they could not agree on much else. Although the bankers ended up having little impact on Roosevelt's emergency banking law, progressives were troubled by their mere presence. "The money changers whom Mr. Roosevelt drove out of the temples in his inaugural," complained journalist Ernest Gruening, were now "congregating in the White House and telling him what to do."[48]

That Sunday afternoon, at 2:30 p.m., Woodin and Moley went to the Cabinet Room, where the first formal meeting of the Cabinet was getting under way. Roosevelt presented Moley and Howe to the group, announcing that they were two of his top advisers. After the introductions, Roosevelt talked about the banking crisis and the legal problems it raised. He asked Homer Cummings, the Connecticut lawyer he had named attorney general at the last minute to replace Thomas Walsh, how long it would take him to prepare an opinion on whether the president had the legal power to declare a national bank holiday. "Mr. President," Cummings replied, "I am ready to give my opinion now." Cummings, who had spent much of inauguration day researching the question, agreed with Hoover's banking team that the Trading with the Enemy Act gave the president sufficient authority. Roosevelt said he would issue a proclamation closing the banks and call Congress into special session on Thursday. Woodin emerged from the meeting at three p.m. "I feel ten years younger than when I entered the conference and discussed the problem with the Cabinet," he told reporters on the way out.[49]

While work continued at the Treasury Department, congressional leaders met with Roosevelt at the White House to hear about the emergency banking legislation. Senator Glass of Virginia and Representative Henry Steagall of Alabama—the leading banking authorities in the two chambers—and Majority Leader Joseph T. Robinson promised to shepherd the bill through Congress. Late that night, the Treasury Department and White House meetings merged. Surrounded by members of his administration and Hoover's, Roosevelt was prepared to issue the banking proclamation. Walter Wyatt urged him to wait until after midnight so the proclamation would be issued early Monday, rather than late Sunday night. No harm would be done by the delay, since all of the banks were closed, and after starting off in his inaugural address on a well-received religious note, Wyatt argued, there was no reason to undo it by issuing such an important proclamation on the Sabbath. Roosevelt changed the date on the proclamation to March 6 and waited. He had by now made the Hoover holdovers' proclamation so much his own that the public would not be aware of the Hoover team's role, or the fact that the banking proclamation was itself a holdover whose first words had originally read: "Now, therefore, I, Herbert Hoover President of the United States of America."[50]

After midnight, early Monday morning, Roosevelt declared that "heavy and unwarranted withdrawals of gold and currency from our banking institutions" had created a "national emergency." Seated at a desk in his study, a cigarette poised in an ivory holder, he signed a proclamation invoking the Trading with the Enemy Act to declare a national bank holiday through March 9. In addition to stopping bank runs, the bank holiday prevented depositors from taking their money out in the form of gold, as they were otherwise legally entitled to do. A great deal of gold was being withdrawn, and much of it was being hoarded or exported. In the week before the inauguration alone, the Treasury gold reserves had decreased by $226 million, and Roosevelt was worried that the nation's gold reserves were being lost for good. The new rules appeared to take the nation off the gold standard, since depositors could no longer go to their banks and demand their money in gold, but Woodin denied it. "We are definitely on the gold standard," he insisted. "Gold merely cannot be obtained for several days." Two days later, at his first press conference, Roosevelt would be more equivocal, telling reporters at first that it was hard to say if the nation was still on the gold standard and, moments later, admitting that "what you are coming to now really is a managed currency." Roosevelt also signed a second proclamation, which called Congress back for a special session starting on Thursday, March 9. The bank holiday, which would necessarily impose a significant burden on the public, was the real start of the New Deal. It was, journalist Ernest K. Lindley observed, "the new regime's first application of the principle that the larger welfare stands above the individual right."[51]

The bank holiday was, in *The New York Times*'s estimation, the "most drastic" exercise of presidential power "ever taken in peacetime to safeguard the nation." By the time Roosevelt issued his edict, most of the country had already begun getting used to operating under state bank holidays, and finding ways to make do without access to cash. In many areas, scrip had began to circulate. An Akron newspaper paid its workers in its own hastily printed currency, which it persuaded merchants to accept and then took back in exchange for advertising. The Dow Chemical Company paid its employees with coins that it manufactured itself from a magnesium alloy that it dubbed Dowmetal. An Oklahoma City hotel announced it would accept payment in "anything we can use in our coffee shop," and a customer showed up with a pig. Canadian and Mexican money, stamps, streetcar tickets, and simple IOUs were used to settle debts. The humorist Robert Benchley wrote in *Harper's Bazaar*: "I see no reason why there should not be a new theatrical season, providing my proposed plan for using pressed figs and dates as money goes into effect fairly soon."[52]

Roosevelt's proclamation stopped the hoarding, but it could not bring back the gold that was already gone. Most of the hoarders were ordinary Americans worried about losing their life savings, who saw gold as a safe harbor. Given the last few years of economic turmoil and bank failures, the instinct was understandable. Roosevelt believed, however, that to shore up the banking system it was critical to get as much gold back as possible. Hoarders came under heavy pressure to turn in their holdings. People who held on to withdrawn gold were publicly vilified and blamed for the banks' weakened state. Reverend Christian Reisner, pastor of New York's Broadway Temple Methodist Episcopal Church, went so far as to denounce gold hoarders as traitors and called for them to lose their citizenship. Angry bankers, who saw the flight of gold as a risk to their institutions, demanded that hoarders' names be published, and that the offenders be taxed and fined. On Wednesday, March 8, the Federal Reserve Board ordered its member banks to report the names of everyone who had withdrawn gold since February 1, if they did not return it by the following Monday. Yielding to the bankers, the Federal Reserve threatened to publish the names of people holding on to hoarded gold.[53]

These new directives set off the "Gold Rush of 1933." Fearful of being taxed or fined, or simply vilified, bank customers who had withdrawn gold raced down to their banks on Thursday and Friday to return gold. They showed up with briefcases, paper-wrapped parcels, canvas bags, and children's wagons filled with gold bars and coins. Some even offered up their gold teeth, so worried were they about being prosecuted for hoarding. *The New York Times* declared it a "gold stampede in reverse," in which "men and women waited in long lines for the privilege of shoving coin and gold certificates through the tellers' windows." In St. Louis, a man showed up with gold coins he said he had saved for thirty years, some of which the teller had to pry apart with a chisel. At the Federal Reserve Bank of New York, tellers counted out gold pieces and crossed depositors' names off a list of gold hoarders that had been prepared to send to Washington. By the week's end, an estimated $200 million in gold and gold certificates had been turned in.[54]

Monday, March 6, after issuing the banking proclamation, Roosevelt began his first weekday as president with a scare. He ate breakfast in his strange new bedroom and read the morning newspapers. After he shaved and dressed, his valet, Irwin McDuffie, wheeled him into his office and left him to work. Roosevelt found himself alone in front of a bare desk. He knew the nation was waiting for him to implement the initiatives he had talked about in his inaugural address, but he could not even find a pad to scribble ideas on. Roosevelt looked with increasing agitation for a button to summon his aides, opening and closing desk drawers in vain. He ended up shouting for help. Missy LeHand, his personal secretary, ran in from a nearby office, and Marvin McIntyre, his appointments secretary, came from another.[55]

Roosevelt often told this story of his helpless first moments in his office. Rexford Tugwell, who heard it firsthand, was convinced that Roosevelt was invoking not just his physical incapacity, but something larger. "What seemed appalling to him," Tugwell would later write, "was the implication that the national paralysis had struck so nearly to the center and, for that short time, had reached the vital organ of direction." What would it have meant for the country, Roosevelt was asking, if his immobilization had been permanent?[56]

Roosevelt could not mull the question over for long. He had to attend a ten a.m. memorial service for Thomas Walsh, his late attorney general designee, in the Senate chambers. While he was there, he met briefly with congressional leaders and submitted several nominations for Senate confirmation, including Moley's. Afterward, he had to host a governors' conference. When he had invited the governors a month earlier, he had intended to talk with them about federal-state relations. When they showed up in the East Room, however, the subject quickly turned to the banking crisis. The governors wanted to know what his plan was for reopening the banks. Roosevelt was vague about the details, but he assured them that the bank holiday would end soon and that the banking system would survive. The governors' other main concern was unemployment relief. They were being inundated with requests for help, and state and local resources were quickly running out. Governors of states that were being flooded with impoverished migrants wanted to know what Roosevelt would do to help them handle the burden of the new arrivals. He offered no immediate solutions, but the governors were impressed by his commitment to take action. At the conference's end, the governors—"without regard to our political affiliations," as their resolution put it—expressed their unanimous "confidence and faith in our President."[57]

While Roosevelt met with the governors, Eleanor held the first press conference ever hosted by a first lady. The idea for the gathering, to which only female reporters were invited, had come from her good friend Lorena Hickok, a veteran reporter. Eleanor's motives were partly charitable. Women journalists had been hit especially hard by the Depression, and the press conference would provide them with stories they could sell to newspapers and magazines. Eleanor also hoped to help her husband's standing with women voters. Questions about politics were off-limits; the focus would be on homier subjects. Thirty-five reporters showed up in the Red Room, so many that some had to sit on the floor. Eleanor went into it with "fear and trembling," she would later recall, and tried to cover her nervousness by passing around a box of candied fruit. She spoke casually about her experiences so far in Washington. The White House was a "very delightful house," she said, and she was still "trying to unpack." The way to deal with the hard economic times, she said in response to a question, was with "courage and common sense on everybody's part." The press conference was the start of Eleanor's public role, which would far surpass anything any first lady had ever tried. Eleanor would begin writing a widely syndicated newspaper column, "My Day," and she would become her husband's roving ambassador, appearing in places that his crowded schedule and physical infirmity made it difficult for him to go. After a trip to a coal mining region or a farm county, she would report back to Roosevelt on the conditions she observed, and make recommendations for how they should be addressed. Her sympathies were always with the struggling people she met on her travels. "Some miner's child will receive glasses which he needs," a reporter observed, "but no one will ever know that they came from Mrs. Roosevelt."[58]

Proclaiming a national bank holiday was the easy part of dealing with the banking crisis—"the anesthetic before the major operation," Moley called it. The "operation" would require coming up with a plan to restore the nation's banks to financial health, and to restore the public's faith in the banks. The responsibility once again lay with Moley, Woodin, and the Hoover officials. On Monday morning, Moley had breakfast in his hotel room with his nominal boss, Secretary of State Cordell Hull. He then raced over to the White House, where he met with Roosevelt, who was still in bed, to update him on the progress that was being made on drafting an emergency banking bill. From the White House, Moley went to the Treasury Department. The visiting bankers were there and the "babble of tongues was so deafening," Moley complained, that he and Woodin found it impossible to get anything done. The two men retreated to Woodin's rooms at the Mayflower Hotel to work on the banking bill in peace.[59]

Moley and Woodin believed it was important to open as many banks as possible when the bank holiday was over, to build up public confidence. It was not clear how the banks would prepare themselves for the end of the holiday. Many bankers wanted the government to issue scrip, as it had done during the Panic of 1907, which they could use to pay off depositors who showed up when the holiday was lifted. Woodin decided instead to accept the prevailing view among the group at the Treasury Department that more dollars should be printed, which could be advanced to the banks against their assets. Currency would be more reassuring to depositors, Woodin believed. "It won't frighten people," he said. "It'll be money that looks like money." Moley and Woodin were convinced that the key to reviving the banking system was restoring the public's faith in banking. If depositors did not believe in the reliability of their own bank, they would continue withdrawing their money, and the banks would not be able to maintain the cash reserves they needed to operate. To reassure depositors, Moley and Woodin wanted Roosevelt to make a direct appeal to the public to put their faith in the banks. "There was magic, we knew, in that calm voice," Moley recalled.[60]

Tuesday morning, Moley and Woodin met with Roosevelt in his bedroom, where he was reading the morning's newspapers in bed. They updated him on the latest developments in the plan they were cobbling together. Roosevelt approved all of it, including the printing of currency. He wanted a bill ready for delivery to Congress at the start of the special session, which was then just two days away. Moley and Woodin returned to the Treasury Department, where the banking team was finishing up the drafting. The Emergency Banking Act formally authorized all of the actions Roosevelt had taken so far in the banking crisis, settling once and for all the question of whether the Trading with the Enemy Act gave him the power to close the banks. It also set up a system by which banks would be able to apply to the Treasury Department to reopen. The department would give licenses right away to banks that were financially sound. Banks in worse condition would be put under conservators, who would help restore them to financial health. Banks that could not be saved would be closed permanently. The bill authorized the issuance of currency not backed by gold, Federal Reserve bank notes, so banks would have enough money to pay off depositors who showed up to make withdrawals.[61]

On Wednesday morning, more than one hundred reporters packed into Roosevelt's office for his first press conference. Prodded by Stephen Early, a former Associated Press reporter, Roosevelt created a new set of ground rules for what he announced would be twice-weekly events. He would not require questions to be submitted in advance, as Hoover had. Roosevelt hoped that his press conferences would be, he said, "merely enlarged editions of the kind of very delightful family conferences I have been holding in Albany." When the press conference began, Roosevelt joked, "Now, as to news, I don't think there is any." The reporters immediately asked about the banks. Roosevelt would not go into detail about the emergency bill that was being drawn up, and he tried to lower expectations about it. "We cannot write a permanent banking act for the nation in three days," he said. Roosevelt promised that there would be more far-reaching banking legislation before long. He did not yet know what that broader bill would look like, but he made clear that he did not support federal deposit insurance. It would be a mistake, he said, for the government to "guarantee bad banks as well as good banks." Roosevelt warned the reporters that they should regard what he said about the banks as tentative. "Everything is subject to change these days," he said, "within twenty-four or even twelve hours." By the end, Roosevelt had thoroughly charmed the press corps. *The Baltimore Sun*'s correspondent declared the press conference "the most amazing performance of [its] kind that the White House has ever seen."[62]

Wednesday afternoon, Woodin and Moley sent the final version of the

Emergency Banking Act to the White House. That evening, they joined Roosevelt in briefing congressional leaders on it. Since there was not yet a draft available for distribution, Senate Majority Leader Joseph T. Robinson and House Speaker Henry T. Rainey, their Republican counterparts, and Senator Glass, Representative Steagall, and other influential members of Congress listened as Roosevelt read from his draft and explained what the new law would do. Three hours later, all of the attendees, Democrats and Republicans, pledged their support. When a reporter asked Woodin if the bill was finished, he responded wearily that it was. "Both bills are finished," Woodin said. "You know my name is Bill, and I'm finished, too."[63]

The banking bill arrived in Congress the morning of Thursday, March 9. "Our first task," Roosevelt declared in his congressional message, "is to re-open all sound banks." When the special session began at noon, the galleries were packed. It was, according to one newspaper account, "a grim Congress which met today, the most momentous gathering of the country's legislators since war was declared in 1917." Most members of Congress knew that they were being called in to vote on a banking act, but little more. Steagall, the chairman of the House Banking and Currency Committee, who had the only draft of the bill, one with pencil corrections scrawled on it, walked down the aisle of the House chamber, waving it overhead and shouting, "Here's the bill; let's pass it." The debate was over in forty minutes. Bertrand H. Snell, the House Republican leader, urged a "Yes" vote even though he had not been able to read the bill. Snell conceded that it was "entirely out of the ordinary" to vote on a bill that had not even been printed yet, but he said that "there is only one answer to this question, and that is to give the President what he demands and says is necessary to meet the situation." The bill passed without a recorded vote.[64]

By the time the Senate began considering the banking bill, copies had been distributed to the whole chamber. Glass walked his colleagues through the main provisions. Several progressive senators complained that the bill favored larger, wealthier banks, and suggested it was part of a plan to phase out small, state-chartered banks. Huey Long, the Louisiana populist who would be one of Roosevelt's great antagonists until his assassination in 1935, insisted the licensing provisions would make it difficult for smaller banks—the banks "at the forks of the creeks," he called them—to get approval to reopen. He accused the administration of planning to reopen only five thousand of the nation's nineteen thousand banks, while closing the rest. Long was fighting, he said, not for the banks themselves, but rather for "the men and women, the bootblacks, the farmers, and widows who have money in these little State banks." William Borah, the progressive Republican from Idaho, insisted that the bill would lay "the foundation for the creation of a financial dictatorship with headquarters in New York." Long introduced an amendment to help small banks, but Glass, who believed a healthy banking system should not prop up "the little corner grocerymen who run banks," fought against it. He had vowed to protect the bill from the "pin pricks" of amendments, and he succeeded. The Senate passed the bill as introduced, 73–7.[65]

Within nine hours of its introduction, Roosevelt signed the Emergency Banking Act into law. He then met with Moley, Woodin, and Ballantine to draft a proclamation extending the bank holiday, which was scheduled to expire that night. Earlier in the week, Roosevelt had said many banks would be able to open on Friday. It was now clear, however, that the Treasury Department would not be able to evaluate the banks that quickly. Roosevelt issued the new proclamation, extending the bank holiday and the gold embargo indefinitely. The following day, he announced that the first banks determined by the Treasury Department to be fit would open on Monday. That would be a pivotal moment. If depositors showed up and demanded all of their money, an already dire banking crisis would become even worse. Roosevelt decided that the night before the banks reopened he would speak directly to the American people to explain why they should now have faith in the banking system.[66]

On Sunday evening, March 12, Roosevelt addressed the nation. "The President wants to come into your home and sit beside your fireside for a little fireside chat," the announcer said, and an institution was born. Roosevelt described the banking crisis in calmly reassuring tones to an estimated 60 million people gathered around their radio consoles. "When you deposit money in a bank, the bank does not put the money into a safe deposit vault," he said.

"It invests your money." That did not mean, he emphasized, that the money would not be there when they wanted it. "I can assure you," he said, "that it is safer to keep your money in a reopened bank than under the mattress." Roosevelt set out the reasons he had declared a bank holiday and described what would happen next. The following day, Monday, March 13, banks that had been certified as financially sound would begin to reopen in the 12 cities with Federal Reserve banks. The day after, banks would open in 250 more cities, and more would follow. "Let me make it clear to you that if your bank does not open on the first day you are by no means justified in believing that it will not open," Roosevelt said. "A bank that opens on one of the subsequent days is in exactly the same status as the bank that opens tomorrow." He concluded with an appeal to his listeners that echoed his inaugural address. "You people must have faith; you must not be stampeded by rumors or guesses," he said. "Let us unite in banishing fear."[67]

This first fireside chat, a modest fifteen-minute radio talk, was a breakthrough in presidential communication. Roosevelt had spoken in a similar way to the people of New York when he was governor, as Al Smith had before him, but no president had ever talked to the American people on such friendly, informal terms. "I tried to picture a mason at work on a new building, a girl behind a counter, a farmer in his field," Roosevelt would later say. "There was no attempt at oratory," Samuel Rosenman observed. "It was as if the microphone had been removed and he was seated in the living rooms of America." Roosevelt's performance won accolades. *The New York Times* praised his use of radio as "a fresh demonstration of the wonderful power of appeal to the people which science has placed in his hands." His explanation of banking was so clear, Will Rogers declared, that he made everyone understand it, even the bankers.[68]

While Roosevelt spoke, Treasury Department officials were working around the clock, sleeping on couches and having sandwiches brought in, deciding which banks should be licensed to reopen Monday morning. Chartered airplanes were on standby to rush newly printed currency to the banks, so they would have enough on hand to meet depositors' demands. The power of Roosevelt's fireside chat became clear the following morning.

When the banks reopened, there was no need for the freshly printed money. There were long lines at the teller windows, but more customers had come to make deposits than withdrawals. Roosevelt's success in reopening the banks restored the nation's confidence and boosted the economy. When the stock market reopened on March 15, after having been shut since March 3, it soared 15 percent on heavy volume. By the end of March, the banks had taken in $1 billion in deposits. In April, another $1 billion flowed in. Walter Wyatt, the Federal Reserve Board general counsel, who had wanted Hoover to try to fix the banks before he left office, decided things had worked out for the best. "Roosevelt could inspire confidence in the measures proposed to rehabilitate the banking system," he later wrote. "Poor Hoover could not."[69]

With the banking crisis resolved, Moley seriously considered leaving Washington. He was tired of living out of a suitcase in the Carlton Hotel and commuting to New York to teach. He wanted to return to Columbia and perhaps write for a magazine. Roosevelt would not hear of it. No one else, he told Moley, could help him develop the New Deal he had promised. Moley knew the people drafting the key bills, Roosevelt said. He knew what had to be done to get the legislation through Congress. He knew what they were trying to achieve. It was an "intoxicating speech," Moley said, even if a good part of it was "blarney." Moley was still troubled by his title, assistant secretary of state, which bore little relation to what he actually did. Woodin offered to make him under secretary of the treasury, but Roosevelt vetoed it, saying he did not want to lose his chief aide to Woodin. In the end, Moley was caught up in Roosevelt's infectious enthusiasm and agreed to stay on, remaining as Roosevelt's de facto chief of staff. He continued in his role of adviser, spotter of talent, and assigner of critical tasks. In his memoirs, Moley would liken his situation to that of the chancellor of the duchy of Lancaster, who was said to have been the "maid-of-all-work" in the British Cabinet. Moley's behind-the-scenes influence remained substantial. "Policy is made not only in speeches and messages—those are merely the foam on the crest of the wave—but by myriads of day-by-day decisions," the New Deal–era journalist John Franklin Carter, who wrote under the pseudonym "The Unofficial Observer," said of Moley's role. At the end of a grumpy column, Westbrook

Pegler wrote that complaints "should be addressed to Prof. Raymond Moley, who has general charge of everything now."[70]

The Emergency Banking Act was the administration's first triumph, and it was a dramatic one. "Capitalism was saved in eight days," Moley exulted. Saving capitalism, or at least saving the banking system, did not sit well with all of Roosevelt's supporters. American banking was, *The New Republic* told its readers, "rotten to the center," and it had to be "made over." Some urban liberals and western progressives had been hoping for a public takeover of the banks, something Tugwell had also advocated. To some progressives, Roosevelt's first week in office seemed like an epic lost opportunity. "I think back to the events of March 4, 1933, with a sick heart," Senator Bronson Cutting, a pro-Roosevelt Republican from New Mexico, wrote in *Liberty* magazine the following year. "For then," he declared, "the nationalization of banks by President Roosevelt could have been accomplished without a word of protest." Roosevelt was not among those feeling regret. Although he promised he would do more to reform the system with a later banking act, there were limits to how far he was willing to go. "Nothing reveals so clearly Roosevelt's continued faith in the private enterprise system," Samuel Rosenman said, "as his refusal—even in banking—to change in the slightest degree our private property economy, or to curtail in any way the private enterprise system under which he had lived and America had grown."[71]

Though it was only a stopgap measure, the Emergency Banking Act set the tone for the entire New Deal. By restoring a cornerstone of the economic system to health, Roosevelt was faithful to the Thomas Babington Macaulay injunction that he quoted so often: "reform that you may preserve." At the same time, the banking act was quietly revolutionary. Roosevelt threw aside his predecessor's laissez-faire principles and made clear that he considered it the federal government's duty to ensure that the nation's economic institutions functioned properly. To meet that responsibility, Roosevelt injected the government more deeply into private enterprise than it had ever gone before, taking steps that his critics regarded as not only radical, but beyond his constitutional powers. He was saving American capitalism, but in the process he was transforming it into something entirely new.[72]

CHAPTER THREE

"The Hardest-Boiled Man in Washington"

While working on emergency legislation responding to the banking crisis, Roosevelt also began the first affirmative part of the New Deal. Progressives had been urging him to make his next initiative a well-funded relief program for the unemployed. Roosevelt's highest priority, however, was reducing the federal budget. When Roosevelt took office his views were, Moley later said, "as frostily thrifty" as those of Calvin Coolidge. In the 1932 campaign, he had embraced the Democratic Party platform, which called for cutting the federal budget by 25 percent. In a major address in Pittsburgh, he had railed against President Hoover's budget deficits, calling them "a veritable cancer in the body politic and economic." Now, he was about to introduce the Economy Act, a bill to slash federal spending. If there had not been a banking crisis when he took office, the Economy Act would have been Roosevelt's first legislative initiative.[1]

It is odd to think of the New Deal beginning with a large-scale reduction in spending. There were several reasons Roosevelt was so intent on government economy, as reducing government spending was known. In part, he was simply reflecting the state of economics at the time. John Maynard Keynes, the great British economist, had not yet published his classic treatise *The General Theory of Employment, Interest and Money*, which argued for deficit spending in times of depression. Most orthodox economists, including some of

Roosevelt's top advisers, insisted that the most important thing was to restore business confidence. The way to do that, they argued, was to root out waste and make clear that the government's resources would be carefully managed. There were dissenters, who believed that the best way to respond to a depression was to "prime the pump" with increased government expenditures. In early 1932, twenty-four prominent economists, including an influential group at the University of Chicago, had sent a telegram to Hoover urging him to increase spending. These views were, however, still in the minority.[2]

The economists' arguments for fiscal restraint were in line with Roosevelt's instinctive beliefs about economics, and about how budgets should work. Roosevelt liked to think of abstract policy issues in concrete human terms. He thought of the nation as being like a family, and the federal budget as being like a household budget. This was how Roosevelt explained the budget economy issue to his Pittsburgh audience. An overspending nation, he argued, like an overspending family, was one "on the road to bankruptcy." It was a vast oversimplification, but his progressive advisers had been unable to talk him out of this homespun argument for a balanced federal budget. "Nothing we had said," Tugwell would later write, "had shaken it."[3]

Roosevelt also had political reasons for wanting to cut federal spending. He had assiduously courted business leaders and wealthy individuals during the general election, and both groups were pressuring him to balance the budget. Bernard Baruch, the influential financier, who had contributed heavily to the Roosevelt campaign, was one of the loudest voices for government economy. "With the monotony and persistence of old Cato, we should make one single and invariable dictum the theme of every discourse," he declared. "Cut governmental spending—cut it as rations are cut in a siege." The views of Baruch, who, it was said, "owned 60 Congressmen," were not easily ignored. The National Economy League, which was funded by some of the nation's most affluent families, was also pushing for budget cuts and lower taxes. Its chief lobbyist, William Marshall Bullitt, a former solicitor general of the United States, urged Roosevelt and Congress not to pander to special interests, particularly veterans' groups that were trying to defend their current benefit levels.[4]

Not least, budget cutting simply appealed to Roosevelt's thrifty nature. Roosevelt disliked extravagance. In his private life, the journalist John Gunther noted, he was careful about the cost of long-distance telephone calls and flowers and "hated needless extravagence." Roosevelt proudly admitted to being careful with money, at times resorting to a stereotype that was not unusual for his social class at the time. "He claimed," Henry Wallace would later recall, "that the original Roosevelt in this country had married a Jewess when he came here in 1620 or thereabouts." Then, according to Wallace, Roosevelt would "rub his hands together."[5]

The Democratic Party platform called for "abolishing useless commissions and offices, consolidating departments and bureaus, and eliminating extravagance." Advocates for government economy argued that the biggest waste of all lay in the benefits given to veterans of World War I and the Spanish-American War. Fully one-quarter of the budget was going to veterans, and it seemed to many observers that their benefits had risen to excessive levels under pressure from the veterans' lobby. Roosevelt's economy bill called for slashing veterans' benefits. To get all of the savings he wanted, it also included layoffs of federal workers and reductions in government salaries. Roosevelt knew the opposition was likely to be formidable. Congress would be reluctant to approve layoffs in the depths of a depression. And the veterans were among the most feared lobbies in Washington. One of the American Legion's lobbyists was known for rounding up votes by bluntly telling members of Congress, "If you don't support this bill, your successor will."[6]

Roosevelt was convinced that if he wanted to make major cuts he would have to act quickly, while he was still in his honeymoon with Congress and the American people. At Roosevelt's request, the new budget director, Lewis Douglas, had been hard at work during the interregnum drawing up a draft economy bill. On March 5, at the height of the bank crisis, Roosevelt had devoted his first national radio address not to the banks, but to his plans to cut the budget. Speaking from a microphone in the White House library, he had insisted on an American Legion radio show that veterans had to be prepared to sacrifice for the sake of national recovery. Fifteen years earlier, during the World War, Roosevelt said, veterans had "offered for the welfare and preservation of our country the ultimate contribution that a human can give." Now, these same veterans had to enlist in a war on selfishness, inertia, laziness, and fear, "enemies with whom we never conclude an armistice." The draft Economy Act, which had not yet been made public, specified in detail the sacrifices veterans would now be asked to make.[7]

In making the Economy Act his highest priority, Roosevelt was lining up behind his hard-driving budget director. At first, Roosevelt had been drawn to Douglas because the thirty-eight-year-old Arizona congressman was the nation's leading advocate for government economy. But before long, Roosevelt developed a real affection for the lanky, sandy-haired Douglas, a man one profile described as "rugged faced," with "quizzical brown eyes," and "an air of engaging diffidence." Roosevelt and Douglas had much in common. Both men were scions of wealthy families who, after attending exclusive prep schools and colleges—Harvard for Roosevelt, Amherst for Douglas—had dedicated themselves to public service. Both were engaging, popular men whose sunny exteriors did not fully reflect their more complicated interiors. When Roosevelt appointed Douglas budget director, he elevated the office to Cabinet rank. It was not only an endorsement of the man, but a clear indication that, as *The Washington Star* observed, "Roosevelt means business in his promise to reduce government costs."[8]

At the start of Roosevelt's presidency, Douglas had an exalted status. In addition to his Cabinet rank, Douglas was, along with Moley, a member of the "bedside Cabinet" of two, which met with Roosevelt each morning in his bedroom to prepare him for the day. Douglas and Roosevelt formed an extraordinary bond. The affinity came quickly, but differences between the two men emerged gradually, as the problems with budget slashing at the height of a depression became clearer. Forced to choose between an abstraction like fiscal conservatism and actual people who were suffering, Roosevelt would eventually come down on the side of the people. Douglas, however, would insist on proceeding with the budget cuts, and he would not be talked out of it. "His soft brown eyes turned hard," Tugwell recalled. "Economy was the great need of the day, he said, not relief." Douglas's fixed ideas about what needed to be done would make him one of the most influential of the early

New Dealers, but also one of the most embattled. Douglas was more than up for the fight. "The mildness is delusive," *The Literary Digest* observed. "Ask any Congressman. He will tell you that young Lew Douglas is the hardest-boiled man in Washington."[9]

Lewis Douglas had a surprising background for a New Dealer. He was born on July 2, 1894, in the Arizona copper mining town of Bisbee, hard up against the Mexican border. At the time, the Arizona Territory, which was nearly two decades from statehood, was still viewed by people back East as exotic and more than a little dangerous. "The dawn of civilization has just broken in this part of the country," *The New York Times* reported from Tucson shortly before Douglas's birth. There were law-abiding residents in Arizona, the *Times* conceded, but they had the misfortune of living alongside "the roughest elements in the New World—some struggling for homes, others for wealth, and others still living by their wits upon the weakness of their fellows."[10]

If civilization had dawned in Arizona, its light had barely reached Douglas's hometown. Bisbee's town center was Brewery Gulch, a grim street that did double duty as the town's sewage system. It was "covered with slime several inches deep and about four feet wide," the *Tucson Citizen* reported, forcing women "while walking, to hold their skirts high." Brewery Gulch was lined with saloons and dance halls that were filled late into the night with drunken miners, Mexican migrants, and outlaws. Bisbee was not without its charms. Nestled atop mile-high Mule Pass Gulch canyon, it was surrounded by craggy hills, giving it a stark western beauty. But it had few of the amenities of life back east, and it had perils that big-city residents could scarcely imagine. The town's children attended school in an old miner's shack and scratched out their lessons on brown wrapping paper. When Apache raiders descended, a guidebook noted, "a whistle was blown four times—two shorts, one long, and one short—and the teacher led her pupils, trained by frequent Indian drills, to the nearest mine tunnel for protection."[11]

Mining towns like Bisbee were in many ways like outposts of imperial Britain, a historian of the region has observed. The miners worked underground in dark, dusty shafts while the administrators stayed above ground, leading lives of relative luxury. Adding to the colonial feel, most of the bosses had been deployed from the mining company headquarters back East. Bisbee was a rough, menacing environment in which to grow up. Douglas would later say that his views about society were shaped by his time "on the frontier which was occasionally sprinkled with threats of Indian depredations and raids."[12]

Douglas was born into the pinnacle of Bisbee society. His grandfather, James Douglas, was a Canadian-born mining engineer of Scottish descent who had discovered the region's copper reserves for the New York–based Phelps Dodge Company in the 1880s. The copper mines around Bisbee proved so successful that in 1909 Douglas became president of Phelps Dodge. Lewis's maternal great-grandfather, John Williams, was another town pioneer. Williams had run a brokerage in San Francisco with Judge Dewitt Bisbee that sold mining rights in the part of Arizona that would later bear the judge's name. James Douglas's son, James S. Douglas, and Williams's granddaughter, Josephine Leah Williams, married in 1891. Three years later, Lewis was born.[13]

James S. Douglas worked for his father's company. During much of Lewis's childhood, he supervised a mine in Nacozari, Mexico, ninety miles south of Bisbee. The Douglases were Nacozari's version of landed gentry. Lewis grew up in a mansion known as the "White House," while his friends lived in grim conditions on the other side of town. Lewis's father, a difficult man with a bad temper, acquired a reputation as a hard-driving businessman and the nickname "Rawhide Jimmy." James S. Douglas cofounded two small banks, including the Bank of Douglas, in a town his father helped establish. He began to make his own fortune when he started to buy up copper mines. By the time Lewis Douglas was a young adult, his father was one of Arizona's wealthiest men—and one of its thriftiest. When Douglas relocated to Washington, his father often wrote him letters on the backs of used envelopes.[14]

Lewis's grandfather, James Douglas, was a relatively benevolent copper baron. Conditions in his mines were hardly ideal, with temperatures often rising above 100 degrees and dangerous dust in the shafts. He made an effort, however, to pay his miners well, and not only to discourage them from joining unions. In the early 1900s, the Progressive Era came to Arizona. The territorial government enacted laws protecting workers' rights, and union organizers began to show up at the mines. Around the same time, James Douglas began to cede control over Phelps Dodge's operations to his son Walter, who shared his brother James S. Douglas's tough-minded approach to the mining business. Walter and James S., joined by other powerful copper bosses, used their influence in the Arizona legislature to fight workers' rights bills and invested in newspapers, skewing their coverage against unions.[15]

As America entered World War I, Arizona became a bitter labor battleground. The International Workers of the World, better known as the Wobblies, sent organizers into Arizona mining towns and fought to improve an industry that was marked by what one worker described as "one continued sickening mess of extortion, fraud, graft, and…shameless, unblushing robbery." When the copper bosses refused their demands for better wages, the Wobblies called the Bisbee miners out on strike. Walter Douglas, who was by now running Phelps Dodge, and his brother James S., Lewis's father, responded with the Bisbee Deportation, one of the most brutal antilabor acts in American history.[16]

The deportation began when, at Walter Douglas's request, the sheriff deputized a group that called itself the Bisbee Citizens' Protective League. The Bisbee sheriff declared that if the Wobblies insisted on remaining in Arizona, it would be "up to the individual communities to drive these agitators out." The Wobblies refused to leave, and on July 12, 1917, the citizens' league took up the sheriff's invitation to drive out the agitators. League members spread out across Bisbee, arresting more than one thousand strikers and sympathizers and holding them downtown at gunpoint. When a train owned by Phelps Dodge pulled up, the prisoners were forced into twenty-three boxcars and taken to the New Mexico desert, where they were abandoned without food or water. The strikers and strike sympathizers remained stranded until state and federal authorities rescued them.[17]

The Bisbee deportation caused a furor, particularly in the progressive press. *The Nation* called it unlawful and "practically foolish." The muckraking *New York World* declared that "we have nourished a nest of vipers." Samuel Gompers, the president of the American Federation of Labor, protested to President Woodrow Wilson that "a group of capitalistic anarchists" in Arizona had gone "far from any warrant of law." Harvard Law School professor Felix Frankfurter, who was a member of Wilson's Mediation Commission, went to Arizona to investigate. The commission declared the deportation to have been "wholly illegal," and based on its report a federal grand jury indicted twenty-one people, including Walter Douglas, for violating the deportees' constitutional rights. Prosecutors prepared an indictment for James S. Douglas, Lewis's father, but never served it because he had moved to France to work for the American Red Cross. The case ran up against a court system heavily tilted against workers. In the end, the U.S. Supreme Court ruled 8–1 that the Bisbee Deportation had not infringed on anyone's constitutional rights. Before the case was over, a miner reported that the copper bosses had already resumed "hunting out union men" and firing them.[18]

Lewis Douglas was not living in Arizona when his uncle and father were waging their war on organized labor. He had been sent back East for school at the urging of his grandfather. Douglas attended the Hackley School in Tarrytown, New York, close to where his grandfather was living at the time. Hackley, which had been founded in 1899 to teach the children of Unitarians and other religious liberals, was closer to Lewis's grandfather's worldview than to his father's. Rawhide Jimmy eventually transferred his son to the Montclair Academy, which was as strict as Hackley was permissive. Douglas did well in school, and despite spending his early years on the frontier, he was not intimidated by his prep school classmates. He left Montclair Academy with the medal for the upper-school student with "the highest attainment in character, scholarship, deportment, and manliness."[19]

In 1912, Douglas entered Amherst College, where he majored in economics. Even as a college student, he shared his father's and uncle's conservative, laissez-faire philosophy. Amherst's most prominent economics professors were progressives, who believed that government should rein in the excesses of capitalism, but they were not able to win over Douglas.[20]

When the United States entered World War I, Douglas volunteered for the American Expeditionary Force in France. He saw extensive battle, and was seriously gassed at Meuse-Argonne. At the war's end, he returned to Amherst to work as a teaching assistant and recover from his injuries. The following year, he went back to Hackley to teach chemistry and to be closer to a young woman he had met at an Amherst-Smith dance. Margaret "Peggy" Zinsser, who lived a few miles away in Hastings-on-Hudson, was the daughter of a wealthy German-American chemist who ran a factory that manufactured poison gas during the war. Douglas married Peggy in 1921 and brought his new bride back to Arizona.[21]

The Douglases moved to Jerome, the rough copper mining town in which Lewis Douglas's parents were now living, and Douglas went to work for his father's mining company. At his father's insistence, he entered the business at the bottom, starting out as a "mucker," or underground shoveler. Douglas found that he had little interest in mining, and although he had great respect for his father, he could not work for him. When Democratic leaders approached him to run for the state legislature, he agreed to let his name be put in nomination. Douglas's prominent family, war service, and wealth more than made up for the fact that he had only recently moved back to Arizona. He won the primary and went on to face the Republican incumbent. Douglas had the advantage of running during a recession, when the Republicans who were in control in both Washington and Phoenix were being blamed. He had to run on a ticket led by George W. P. Hunt, a progressive former governor whose pro-union stands and support for higher mining taxes had made him an enemy of the Douglas family. Douglas put aside his negative feelings for Hunt and campaigned for the full Democratic ticket. On November 7, 1922, Hunt was elected governor and Douglas won his race 686–396.[22]

In the state legislature, Douglas focused on government economy. He chaired a committee that identified waste in Arizona's highway department, an agency that was certainly in need of greater scrutiny. At the same time, Douglas began to exhibit the sort of callousness toward the disadvantaged that he would frequently be accused of later in his career. He campaigned against increases in veterans' benefits, and opposed a bill that would have given farmers, who had been hit hard by a postwar drop in commodities prices, relief from taxes and more time to pay off delinquent taxes. The bill was, he insisted, "vicious in principle." Douglas supported some progressive measures, and introduced an anti–Ku Klux Klan bill, but he carved out a generally conservative record that often put him at odds with his fellow Democrats. He opposed most workers' rights bills, including one to ban company stores, where miners were often coerced into spending their paychecks on poor-quality, overpriced goods.[23]

After two years in the legislature, Douglas briefly left politics to go into business with a friend. In 1926, he thought about challenging Governor Hunt, but instead ran for Arizona's at-large congressional seat. The thirty-two-year-old Douglas tirelessly traveled the state making speeches, often with Peggy at his side. The five other candidates in the Democratic primary tried to paint Douglas as beholden to the copper bosses—one opponent called him the "young man with the copper collar." But once again, Douglas's family name, war record, financial advantages, and campaigning skills were a winning combination. Douglas captured the Democratic nomination, and carried the state in November by nearly two to one.[24]

Douglas moved his family to Washington, where they settled into a house at 1805 Nineteenth Street, N.W., from which he often bicycled to the Capitol. In Congress, Douglas turned out to be as out of step with the Democratic Party as he had been in the Arizona legislature. After two years of being an unreliable vote, Douglas was chastised by John Nance Garner, the Democratic floor leader. Garner accused him of betraying his fellow Democrats, but Douglas was unapologetic. Every American has three loyalties, Douglas declared. "The first is to his country, the second to his state and the third is to his party," he said. "Whenever these three conflict, one with the other, his sense of responsibility compels him to resolve the conflict in favor of the higher loyalty." Despite his occasional run-ins with his own party, the affable Douglas was well liked by his congressional colleagues on both sides of the aisle, and he and Peggy quickly became fixtures on the Washington social circuit.[25]

Douglas was not greatly affected by the Crash of 1929. Compared to stocks, which had been devastated, the Douglas family's mining interests held up well. Many of Douglas's constituents back in Arizona were not so fortunate. As hard times swept the country, his fiscal conservatism stood out more. Democrats in Congress were calling for the government to help the victims of the Depression, but Douglas remained committed to the laissez-faire philosophy he had been raised on. He voted in favor of the Reconstruction Finance Corporation, Hoover's program for bailing out failing banks and troubled financial institutions, although he confided to his father that he regarded even the RFC's program of loans as "hazardous." Douglas strenuously opposed measures to help struggling farmers, as he had in Arizona, and public works programs for the unemployed.[26]

Douglas believed the way to combat the economic crisis was through a balanced budget, a stable dollar, and government policies that bolstered business confidence. He shared Wall Street's view that taxing the wealthy was counterproductive because it discouraged investment. Douglas argued instead for raising sales taxes, the burden of which fell mainly on the poor and working class. As the Depression wore on, progressives in Congress, led by Senators Robert F. Wagner of New York and Robert La Follette, Jr., of Wisconsin—the son of the legendary "Fighting Bob" La Follette—pushed for a large-scale public works program, beyond the modest ones Hoover had put in place. Douglas viewed this talk of an ambitious public works agenda with alarm. If the government increased public works spending without offsetting it with increased revenues, he insisted, the result would be the sort of runaway inflation that had struck Germany. Douglas lamented in a letter to a friend that if "we proceed on a theory which history has demonstrated to be unsound I do not know what the future is going to be."[27]

While progressives argued for increasing spending on the unemployed, Douglas became Congress's most outspoken advocate of budget slashing. As a member of the Appropriations Committee, he was in a good position to argue for reductions in spending, but he was continually frustrated. Most members of Congress resisted making the sort of wholesale cuts he was calling for during a depression. They "will make reductions, but not enough," Douglas complained in a letter to his father in early 1931. A year later, Douglas remained just as discouraged. "Nothing is being done and it appears that nothing will be done," he wrote his father. "Inflation is gathering more weight and momentum." James S. Douglas told his son the problem was "organized minorities" who had too much influence over government spending. The solution, he argued, was repealing the Seventeenth Amendment, so senators would once again be chosen by state legislatures, as they had been up until 1914. On the matter of spending, father and son agreed. "I do hope that the lame-duck session will balance the budget by a reduction of expenses and not by unwise new schemes for taxation," the elder Douglas wrote.[28]

In February 1932, Douglas took a new approach. He proposed establishing a bipartisan congressional economy committee, which would make recommendations for how federal spending could be cut. Douglas's resolution passed, and he was appointed to a seat on the new committee. Although John McDuffie, a probusiness representative from Alabama, was chairman, Douglas was by far the most energetic member. He pored over ledger books and interviewed federal bureau chiefs about their budgets. When the committee released its report, it recommended more than $200 million in spending cuts, with a particular focus on veterans' benefits and federal workers' salaries.[29]

Veterans' benefits quickly became the main point of contention. The $1 billion a year that veterans received was more than one-quarter of the federal budget, and the government economy bloc in Congress argued that their benefits had become excessive. Veterans' payments had grown substantially since the World War ended, and part of the reason was the government's increasingly expansive view of who was eligible. Payments to disabled veterans, which had once been limited to injuries incurred during wartime, had been extended to those that were merely presumed to have arisen from service. Veterans' groups insisted that some disabilities only manifested themselves in later years, and that the victims were still entitled to be compensated. The economy bloc maintained, however, that most of these payments were only being made to appease the veterans' lobby. In early May, Douglas rose on the House floor to deliver a rousing call for adopting the Economy Committee's recommendations. It pained him as a veteran to say it, he declared, but the nation could not afford the level of benefit it was paying to veterans. As long as he was in Congress, he said, he would "oppose every organized minority that attempts to impose on the United States a burden which cannot be justified." Douglas's colleagues gave him a standing ovation, but moments later they voted overwhelmingly against the proposed cuts. Arthur Krock argued in *The New*

York Times that by rising and cheering House members were "paying a tribute to honesty and courage," and by voting against the cuts they were recording their "belief that these attributes in a politician do not pay." There was, however, a good deal of compassion mixed in with the calculation. Many members of Congress agreed with Edith Nourse Rogers, a Massachusetts Republican, who called the proposed cuts "a most cruel way of economizing."[30]

The economy drive was, at least for the moment, dead. With the 1932 election approaching, Douglas did his best to inject government economy into the presidential campaign. When the *Times* asked seven "outstanding Democrats" to write short essays about what their party's platform should emphasize, his response stood out. While the others talked about public works or opening employment offices, Douglas said, "the most fundamental object to be sought is the establishment, maintenance and stability of the credit of the government." This required, he insisted, cutting spending, especially on veterans' benefits. "Grateful as a grateful people must be to those who carried arms in times of national emergency," he said, "we do not believe that gratitude should be carried to the extent of destruction."[31]

In July, Douglas attended the Democratic National Convention in Chicago. He hoped the nomination would go to a fellow conservative like Albert Ritchie, Maryland's patrician governor, who opposed unemployment insurance and believed the answer to the Depression was to let "natural forces take their course, as free and untrammeled as possible." When Roosevelt was chosen, Douglas told a friend glumly "we made a mistake." Douglas was heartened, however, that the delegates supported a platform plank calling for a 25 percent cut in federal spending, and he rallied to his party's nominee. Douglas, who was up for reelection, campaigned alongside Roosevelt in Arizona, introducing him to an enthusiastic crowd at a rodeo. Because of its temperate climate, Arizona had the highest concentration of veterans of any state. At Douglas's public appearances, hostile crowds of veterans showed up to pelt him with oranges and eggs. Douglas narrowly prevailed in the Democratic primary, and won more decisively in the general election, swept along by Roosevelt, who carried Arizona by a wide margin. "Sincere congratulations on your tremendous victory," Douglas wired Roosevelt. "[A]m starting east soon and will call upon you."[32]

Roosevelt was also eager for a meeting. During his Arizona campaign swing, on a stop at the ranch of Isabella Greenway, a Roosevelt family friend, Douglas and Roosevelt had spoken about government economy. The two men found that they agreed on a great deal. After the election, Roosevelt invited Douglas to Hyde Park to continue the conversation. Rexford Tugwell, who was meeting with Roosevelt at the same time, was wary of the young congressman. He wrote in his diary that he found Douglas "very intelligent: liked him a lot." Tugwell was troubled, however, by the way Douglas "lingered fondly over the possibilities of" budget cutting and "the almost vindictive way he spoke of bureaucrats." Tugwell tried to convince Roosevelt that Douglas cared more about government economy than about governing, but Roosevelt was clearly taken by his charming guest. Tugwell could see how easily Roosevelt took on Douglas's skepticism about the role of government, and it concerned him. "The federal government has no business to be doing research, for instance," Roosevelt told Tugwell, repeating something Douglas had said. "Enough of that is being done by the universities. I think we ought to cut it out altogether." Tugwell was starting to worry that Roosevelt was too impressionable, and that he would simply accept the advice of whoever happened to be around him at the moment—including Douglas, "whose counsel was certainly the worst of all."[33]

If Tugwell was afraid Roosevelt would be too aggressive about budget cutting, Douglas left Hyde Park with the opposite worry. Roosevelt was "flirting with the idea of funding a public works program," Douglas complained in a letter to his friend William Matthews, the editor of *The Arizona Daily Star*. There was "no difference between funding public works and funding a deficit," Douglas insisted. After the Hyde Park visit, Roosevelt invited Douglas to work with two other fiscal conservatives, J. Swagar Sherley, a former congressman from Kentucky, and Senator James F. Byrnes of South Carolina, on a plan to reduce spending. The assignment allayed some of Douglas's concerns about Roosevelt's budgetary intentions, and he accepted it enthusiastically. Douglas was soon reporting to his father that he had identified close to $900 million in cuts.[34]

Rumors were circulating that Douglas would have a prominent position in the new administration. *The Washington Daily News*'s "People and Politics" column gave him a rave review: "He is handsome, wealthy, personable and intelligent; it seems that all the good fairies were present at his birth." It also reported that Douglas's "ability is said to have made a great impression on Mr. Roosevelt and his professorial friends." There were rumors that Douglas was being considered for budget director, but the rumors had gotten ahead of the reality. Roosevelt was looking for a budget director who would help him carry out his campaign promise to reduce spending, but Douglas was not his first choice. Roosevelt initially offered the position to Sherley, who turned it down for health reasons. On Sherley's recommendation, he turned to Douglas.[35]

When Roosevelt called on February 22 to make the offer, Douglas was uncertain about whether to accept. He thought he might be able to do more by staying in Congress. Douglas was also wary of the attacks he would be subjected to if he did the kind of budget slashing he believed was necessary. It was one thing to promote economy legislation in Congress, and quite another to be the administrator wielding the budget axe. Roosevelt insisted to Douglas that no one else could do the job the way he could, and he offered Douglas Cabinet status, something no budget director had been given since the position was established in 1921. After extracting a promise that Roosevelt would back him up when he pushed for serious cuts in government spending, Douglas accepted. In the end, he decided the nation needed him. "In times like these, even more so than in times of war, individuals cease to be significant," he wrote to his boyhood friend Arthur Curlee. "Only the common welfare is important."[36]

When Roosevelt announced Douglas's appointment the next day, the reaction was largely positive. Conservatives were the most effusive. "I am well pleased with it," Representative Robert Simmons, a Nebraska Republican, declared, "and the sentiment on the Republican side of the House is universally that way." Business leaders were delighted, and a bit surprised, that someone who was committed to reduced spending and lower taxes would be presiding over the New Deal budget. "I would even have voted Democratic last fall," H. N. Conant of United Investment Counsel in Boston wrote to Douglas, "if I had thought that at least one part of the government would be placed in such capable hands!" Anyone who had followed Douglas's career knew what to expect of him. "Mr. Douglas has something of ruthlessness— but ruthlessness is necessary," the *New York Herald Tribune* would soon declare. "We seem to be out of the hands of the Family Physician and into the hands of the surgeon." Progressives like Tugwell were less jubilant, but they kept their reservations to themselves, out of deference to Roosevelt, and hoped for the best.[37]

Douglas began his new job warily. After all of his failed efforts to get Congress to back government economy, he would now be able to promote it from a powerful position in the executive branch, with a popular president backing him. But even under these favorable conditions, he knew it would be difficult during a depression to achieve the level of budget cutting he believed necessary. Douglas was also clear-eyed about the personal costs. As budget director, he would have a high profile, and he would be associated in the public's mind with firing government workers and slashing the benefits of men who had served their country on the battlefield. Douglas understood that with times as hard as they were, these moves would make him many enemies. He realized, he later said, that "by accepting the position of Director of the Budget, I was bringing my own political career to an end."[38]

Roosevelt's plan was to introduce a budget-cutting bill right after Congress passed the emergency banking bill. Douglas had worked steadily on it in the weeks leading up to the inauguration, and the drafting had been grueling. J. Swagar Sherley was a "man of great character but very sensitive and very slow and very talkative," Douglas wrote to his father. "The result," he said, "was that I never ended a day until midnight." On Wednesday, March 8, Douglas presented Roosevelt with a final draft. Moley liked the title Douglas had given it, "A Bill to Maintain the Credit of the United States." It put the emphasis where Moley thought it should be, on the importance of spending cuts for economic recovery. Roosevelt quickly approved the draft and asked Moley and Douglas to draw up a congressional message to go with it.[39]

The Economy Act, as the bill came to be known, included the sort of cost-cutting measures Douglas had long championed. It gave the president the authority to reduce federal salaries by up to 15 percent, and to rewrite the rules for veterans' pensions. Veterans who were injured moderately during their service could lose most of their benefits. "Presumptive cases," the veterans who came down with illnesses like tuberculosis after their service was over, could lose all of their benefits. There was little doubt that some of the presumptive cases were taking advantage of the system, and of the veterans' strong lobby, to get benefits for illnesses that were not related to their services. Douglas's bill, however, swung the pendulum to the opposite extreme, allowing the administration to cut off even presumptive cases who could make a strong case that their illnesses arose from injuries they suffered during the war. Douglas estimated that his bill would save at least $400 million in veterans' payments and $100 million in employee salaries. The $500 million that would be cut represented about 15 percent of the total federal budget. "The extremely onerous reductions," Douglas wrote in a confidential memo, "will break many eggs, but they *will* balance the budget. They *will* insure a sound currency. They *will* lay the foundation for recovery."[40]

While Congress finished up its work on the Emergency Banking Act, Moley and Douglas worked on their congressional message. They were aiming to persuade not only Congress, Moley said, but the general public, reminding them of Roosevelt's deep concern about "sound fiscal administration." Unlike the banking bill, which was broadly popular, the Economy Act was likely to face significant opposition in Congress. Moley and Douglas tried to ride the groundswell of support for the banking bill, arguing that the two pieces of legislation were similar. The federal budget was in as much of a crisis as the banking system, they argued in the congressional message, and required "equally courageous, frank and prompt action." The message's most famous line, one that the New Deal's critics would quote for years, was Douglas's. "Too often in recent history," it warned, "liberal governments have been wrecked on rocks of loose fiscal policy."[41]

Thursday evening, less than an hour after the banking act was signed into law, congressional leaders of both parties began arriving at the White House for a briefing on the new bill. Roosevelt explained why he regarded spending cuts as necessary for recovery. He tried to assuage the Congress members' fears about budget cutting by emphasizing that the bill would make him responsible for deciding where to reduce spending. The congressional leaders stayed until nearly midnight, but when they left they were still wary. Roosevelt had not yet offered up a single bill to create jobs, and now he was proposing to make even more people unemployed. Members of Congress had shown with their swift passage of the banking act that they wanted to give Roosevelt the tools he asked for. The Economy Act sorely tested Congress's willingness to defer to his leadership.[42]

The next morning, Douglas was back at the White House for a meeting of the bedside Cabinet. He asked Roosevelt if he wanted any last-minute changes in the Economy Act before it went to Congress later that day. It turned out that he did. Roosevelt wanted to add $300 million for a program to send unemployed young men out into nature to plant trees. It was a pet idea of his, and it would be a peace offering to progressives who were impatient for a program to help the unemployed. Douglas, who opposed the program on principle, couched his opposition in tactical advice. It would be a mistake, he told Roosevelt, to add public works to a budget-slashing bill. "Congress will either refuse to pass the Economy Act and appropriate the $300 million on the grounds that economy is not necessary, or it will pass the Economy Act and refuse the appropriation of $300 million on the grounds that economy is necessary," he argued. "You shouldn't, Mr. President, go in two directions at the same time. The Congress won't." Roosevelt agreed to keep his tree-planting program out of the bill.[43]

When the Economy Act was unveiled, the press generally greeted it with approval. The conservative *Wall Street Journal* praised Roosevelt for recognizing that "the national recovery depends upon maintenance of the national credit." The most outspoken opposition, not surprisingly, came from veterans' groups. Douglas had drafted the economy bill in secret so the veterans' lobby would have little time to organize against it. When it arrived in Congress, however, they were quick to mobilize. The American Legion, which only learned of the bill the day before it was introduced, sent an urgent bulletin to its 900,000 members nationwide, asking them to "wire your congressmen and Senators immediately." The veterans were not the only ones organizing against the Economy Act. Federal employees were upset with the sharp cuts in salaries and jobs. Women's groups objected to a provision that called for firing all federal employees married to federally employed men. Eleanor was one of the critics of the marriage rule, and of the entire Economy Act. She believed there should be more government services, not less, paid for by taxes on wealthy individuals and profitable companies. When she wrote a column in the *Women's Democratic News* opposing the bill, Roosevelt wrote his own column arguing for it.[44]

The Congress that received the Economy Act was one that was eager to give Roosevelt what he wanted. After the 1932 landslide, the Democrats controlled the Senate 60–35 and the House 311–116, and many of the Republicans were progressives, whose views were more in line with Roosevelt than with Hoover. Despite this strong pro-Roosevelt tilt, the economy bill was "a staggering dose for Congress to down," Moley noted. Henry T. Rainey of Illinois, the lumbering, white-haired new Speaker of the House, introduced the bill in a meeting of the Democratic caucus on Saturday morning. If it got a two-thirds vote, every Democrat would be bound to support it on the floor. The bill, however, met with fierce opposition. A trio of southern populists—John Rankin of Mississippi, Gordon Browning of Tennessee, and Wright Patman of Texas—argued that the current economic crisis was no time for government to slash spending. John McDuffie, the Democratic whip, who had chaired the Economy Committee Douglas had served on, worked hard to round up support, but a coalition that included southern populists and representatives from New York's Tammany Hall machine kept the vote under two-thirds. When the bill arrived on the floor, the Republican minority leader, Bertrand Snell of New York, assured McDuffie he could count on the overwhelming support of House Republicans. It was less clear how many Democrats would stand by their leadership and vote in favor. To keep the rebellions in check, McDuffie limited debate to two hours and barred amendments, restrictions that drew outraged protests from the bill's opponents.[45]

McDuffie, taking on the role that Douglas had once played in Congress, gave an impassioned speech on the floor in favor of government economy. He acknowledged that there were those who questioned the wisdom of cutting spending in a depression, but he insisted there was "no quicker way to shorten the bread lines" and "no quicker way to lessen unemployment in America than by putting this Nation on an even keel financially." McDuffie took direct aim at the veterans' lobby, arguing that it was "no time to talk about group legislation or hurting any one class of our people, when every citizen's welfare is involved." He concluded with a flourish that drew wild applause from the visitors' galleries. "Your President," he told his colleagues, "has called you to arms, and in the language of a great Federal naval hero of the glistening waters of Mobile Bay many years ago, the time has come to give the command, as Admiral Farragut did: 'Full speed ahead! Damn the torpedoes!'"[46]

The Economy Act's opponents were no less impassioned. John Rankin of Mississippi noted that the cuts would come right after the government's rescue of the banks. If there was money to "take care of the big financiers," he argued, there was money for "the disabled veterans of the World War and the Spanish-American war, and their widows and orphans." Patman, whose rural Texas district was so poor that fewer than 2,000 of his 255,452 constituents paid income taxes, attacked the bill as a sop to oligarchs. "I tell you now, my friends, Mr. Morgan, Mr. Mellon, Mr. Meyers, Mr. Mills, and Mr. Mitchell are the gentlemen who are profiting by such legislation as this," he declared. Gardner Withrow, a Wisconsin progressive, had a different objection, arguing that the bill could be an unconstitutional delegation of power to the president. "Mr. Speaker, if this measure is passed we should, in consistency, close the doors of Congress and go home," he said to cheers from the galleries. William P. Connery, Jr., of Massachusetts, who had carried the American flag as a color sergeant in France, spoke for his fellow veterans. "I think of what the big businessmen of the country told us when we went off to France," he said. "'Goodbye, boys, good luck, God bless you,' they cried. 'When you come back nothing will be too good for you.' And today they ask you to tear the hearts out of the disabled men by passing this bill."[47]

For many members of Congress, what mattered was not the substance of the Economy Act, but giving Roosevelt authority to address the Depression as he saw fit. Mary Teresa Norton, a New Jersey Democrat, argued that the bill should pass "not because of its merit," but because Roosevelt had asked for it. "The citizens of our country elected him with the largest majority ever given to a President, believing that he has the ability, desire, sound judgment, and humanity to lead a demoralized and heartbroken people," she said. "Can we as patriotic American citizens do less than support him?" John Young Brown, a newly elected Kentuckian, felt the same way. "I had as soon start a mutiny in the face of a foreign foe as start a mutiny today against the program of the President of the United States," he said. Even many Republicans were moved by a sense of loyalty to Roosevelt. "I am not going to throw a monkey wrench into the machine," their floor leader, Snell, declared. "The President says this is necessary to meet the emergency and I shall support him."[48]

Roosevelt, who would prove masterful at maneuvering bills through Congress, eased the Economy Act's path through the House with some well-timed arm-twisting and a not-so-veiled threat. Word reached wavering members that if they voted against the bill, Roosevelt would take to the radio to denounce them. The prospect of being attacked by the immensely popular Roosevelt kept the progressive rebellion in check. In the end, the bill passed the House by a vote of 266–138, and Roosevelt had won the first contested battle of his presidency handily. "The President," journalist Anne O'Hare McCormick declared, "holds all the cards in the new deal." It was a triumph, but not for party unity. Even with all of the White House pressure, 92 Democrats had defected. The Economy Act only passed because 69 Republicans voted for it.[49]

The bill still had to pass the Senate. When Douglas testified there on Saturday, March 11, he was met with opposition from progressive senators who, like their House counterparts, insisted that it made no sense to cut spending and jobs during a depression. Douglas wrote to his father that he got "a good grilling from McAdoo"—William Gibbs McAdoo, the newly elected Democratic senator from California—"and a few others," but he was convinced that "the Senate will stay with the President." Huey Long protested that the bill would benefit "Mr. Morgan" and "Mr. Rockefeller," while hurting the Depression's victims. "Let them balance the budget by scraping a little off the profiteers' profits from the war," he urged. It was not only the progressives who were troubled. Arthur Robinson, an Indiana Republican whom *Time* magazine described as a "G. O. Partisan," pointed to the "approximately 13,000,000 men" who were already "walking the streets tonight looking for work, with none to be found," and argued that the Economy Act would only add to their number.[50]

The bill also had its supporters. There were fiscally conservative senators who shared Roosevelt's concern about waste in the federal government. "I am not paying one dollar to any one who never heard a percussion cap or saw the Atlantic Ocean," Carter Glass declared. Henry Fountain Ashurst of Arizona, a friend of Douglas's, acknowledged the risk he was taking, since his state was home to so many veterans, but he said he had come to realize that while "the perpetuity of the Republic does not depend on my re-election to the Senate," it might "depend upon granting to the President the authority for economies called for in his message to Congress." As had been the case in the House, many of the bill's supporters were driven mainly by loyalty to Roosevelt. Robert F. Wagner of New York spoke for many progressives when he mentioned the "heaviness of heart" with which he supported the Economy Act.[51]

Roosevelt was worried that a minority of the Senate might try to block the Economy Act by filibuster. As an incentive for it to act quickly, he declared Sunday night at the White House, "I think this would be a good time for beer." Prohibition, which had been written into the Constitution in 1919, was on the way out. Congress had already passed the Twenty-first Amendment repealing Prohibition, which would soon be ratified by the states. In the meantime, Roosevelt was proposing a law to legalize beer of up to 3.2 percent alcohol content. Roosevelt's beer bill got an enthusiastic reception in Congress, particularly from representatives of urban districts. The opposition from rural members was muted, in part because beer sales were being promoted as an economic stimulant. Thomas H. Cullen, the Brooklyn congressman who sponsored the House bill, said it would create 300,000 jobs immediately and 1,000,000 over time. Congress would go on to pass the bill quickly, easily overcoming the resistance of the once-mighty "dries," including the Women's

Christian Temperance Union, which argued in vain that "no nation ever drank itself out of a depression." Most of the nation rejoiced, especially the big cities. In New York, the Waldorf-Astoria Hotel announced plans to open a beer tavern called the Roosevelt Room.[52]

Roosevelt's move to legalize beer had the effect he intended. It was, one journalist observed, "like a stick of dynamite into a log jam." Progressive senators put forward a series of amendments to lessen the Economy Act's impact. La Follette proposed limiting spending cuts to just 15 percent. Thomas Connally, a liberal Democrat from Texas, called for a limit of 25 percent. A third amendment, also from La Follette, proposed exempting federal salaries of less than $1,000. Roosevelt's allies defeated all three amendments, but for the last two it had to rely on Republican votes. On Wednesday, March 15, the economy bill finally passed, on a 62–13 vote. There was no White House signing ceremony for the Economy Act. Rooosevelt signed it while eating lunch at his desk, looking up from a bowl of soup, and gave the pen to Douglas. The new law was, like the Emergency Banking Act, an extraordinary new grant of presidential power. *The New York Times* declared nervously that it would give Roosevelt "more arbitrary authority than any American statesman has had since the Constitution was framed."[53]

Getting Congress to approve deep cuts in the federal budget in the middle of a depression was an impressive political victory for Roosevelt. It was also a triumph for Douglas. Roosevelt's admiration for his charismatic young budget director had reached new heights. In early April, Roosevelt told Colonel Edward M. House, a Democratic Party elder statesman, that Douglas was "in many ways the greatest 'find' of the administration." In a letter to his father, Douglas expressed amazement at his new life. "It is so queer to telephone at any hour to a President, to go into his bedroom at one in the morning, in fact to have entree at any time and to be writing a Presidential message," he wrote. "How strange," he marveled, "for an insignificant young man from Arizona to be in such a position."[54]

Douglas's future looked bright. Roosevelt told Moley that one day Douglas would make "an excellent candidate for President." It was the only time, Moley said, that he had ever heard Roosevelt mention a possible successor.

Douglas's triumph on the Economy Act did not alleviate his anxieties about fiscal matters. After the bill passed, he wrote to an officer of the National Economy League that "there are a great many other items in the national budget that need tending to." He was concerned not only about current spending, but about the new programs his progressive colleagues were working on to help the unemployed. The Economy Act, however, finally gave Douglas the power he had long sought to fight back against the tide of government spending. On March 31, he proposed new regulations governing veterans' benefits. The new law gave the president considerable discretion about how much to cut, and many people had urged Douglas to be restrained, given the hard economic times. Douglas, however, did not hold back. He ordered all of the "presumptive" cases off the rolls, even though many veterans with legitimate service injuries would be affected. He also substantially cut the benefits of veterans whose injuries had occurred during wartime. The regulations called for closing Veterans Administration regional offices, and suggested that veterans' hospitals would also be shut down.[55]

Members of Congress complained that they felt betrayed. "We who voted for the Economy Act were assured that it would be justly and liberally applied," Park Trammell, a Democratic senator from Florida, protested. Trammell told of receiving a letter from a veteran who said he had only two comrades who could confirm when his injury had occurred, "one of whom is dead and the location of the other of whom he did not know." There were, Trammel said, many similar letters in his files. Veterans also responded with outrage. Douglas's secretary dutifully filed away the hate mail that poured into his office. One veteran sent a brief news item about a Spanish-American War veteran from Toledo, Ohio, who hanged himself after his pension was cut off. At the bottom, the letter writer had scribbled, "Gloat, you murderer, gloat." Another clipping, of an Arkansas veteran who shot himself in the heart, came with the handwritten message: "This is the 10th suicide of a Spanish War veteran. What a glorious achievement." Douglas was not deterred. He expected to be "much more unpopular by the expiration of two or three months than any other man that you can think of," he told his friend John Gaus, a University of Wisconsin political science professor. "Incidentally, I do not exclude Herbert Hoover."[56]

With the passage of the Economy Act, the administration had gotten off to an unexpected start. The first two laws Roosevelt presented to Congress had pleased the nation's bankers and business leaders, but despite his campaign-trail promise to govern on behalf of "the forgotten man at the bottom of the economic pyramid," he had still done nothing for the millions of victims of the Depression. That, however, would soon change. While Douglas was slashing spending, impoverished farmers, the unemployed, and ordinary workers would not be ignored much longer. The Hundred Days was about to head in a very different direction.[57]

CHAPTER FOUR

"Good Farming; Clear Thinking; Right Living"

Henry Wallace had arrived at the Department of Agriculture on Monday, March 6, ready to get to work. The department was familiar terrain for Wallace, who had visited a decade earlier, when his father was secretary of agriculture. Wallace had renewed his acquaintance with the department more recently, the Friday before the inauguration, when he had stopped by and met with Arthur Hyde, the departing secretary, and introduced himself to the bureau chiefs. Wallace settled into the secretary's imposing office, which looked out over the Mall and the Washington Monument, and began to make the room his own. He filled the table behind his desk with notebooks containing commodity price calculations that he had been compiling since his midtwenties, and he had an oil portrait of his father taken from a hallway and hung on one of the walls.[1]

Despite his inherited connection to the position, Wallace was an unlikely person to head up a department of over forty thousand people. He had never run anything larger than *Wallaces' Farmer*, his family's farm newspaper back in Iowa. At forty-four, Wallace was the youngest member of the new Cabinet, and he looked it. His wiry build, boyish face, and unruly shock of reddish-brown hair gave him, in the words of one journalist, the look of a "perennial farm boy." Before the inauguration, Wallace had gone shopping for a new wardrobe at a Fifth Avenue store with Rexford Tugwell, an Ivy League professor with cosmopolitan tastes. The salesman, Tugwell later recalled, could hardly believe that his oddly clothed customer was about to join the president's Cabinet. With Tugwell's help, Wallace bought striped trousers and other fancy garb to wear in Washington, but the effect would be negligible. Wallace's clothing "never fit very well to begin with," *Elks* magazine observed in a profile, "and after a week or so, they look as if they had been slept in, and a hard restless night at that." Old Washington hands considered Wallace's appearance out of place for someone of his lofty status. "I could not but note that the shoes he wore were still the same as those worn by farmers in small towns in Iowa and that his hair was cut as the barbers in these towns cut hair," a State Department official recalled of their first meeting. *Life* magazine noted that Wallace's manner was "deceptively informal," and that he "sat during important meetings with his feet propped on the rim of his wastebasket."[2]

Wallace was taking over the Agriculture Department at a time when the state of the farm economy was grave. Commodity prices had fallen 50 percent from their prewar levels. Farm foreclosures were occurring at a record pace. Almost eight in one hundred farms were in foreclosure, compared to just five a year earlier. Farm communities were emptying out, as family farmers and sharecroppers abandoned the land and headed to places like California and Florida, in a desperate search for better conditions. Farmers who stayed on the land were responding to their bleak circumstances with extreme politics and lawlessness. In January, in Pilger, Nebraska, a crowd of hundreds of farmers had shown up to disrupt a foreclosure sale. At a foreclosure sale the same month in Le Mars, Iowa, a crowd had dragged a lawyer from New York Life Insurance Company down the courthouse steps. His life in danger, the lawyer had telegraphed his employer and asked for permission to bid the full amount the farmer was asking. Farmers were becoming more radicalized by the day. Edward O'Neal, president of the Farm Bureau Federation, warned Congress that "unless something is done for the American farmer we will have revolution in the country within less than twelve months."[3]

Wallace was eager to begin helping these desperate farmers, but he was not sure how to get started. "What sort of a job is this, anyway?" he asked in his first few days. "All I do except talk to people is sit here and sign my name." His first important decision was naming Tugwell assistant secretary. There was an element of gratitude in the choice of Tugwell, who had energetically promoted Wallace for the position of agriculture secretary, but it was also an obvious choice. The brilliant and charismatic Tugwell was a distinguished economics professor with a deep knowledge of agriculture, who had played a large role in the Brain Trust days of shaping Roosevelt's thinking on the subject. Tugwell's strengths neatly complemented his new boss's. Wallace was a farm leader, with decades-old friendships spread across the Farm Belt. Tugwell was a New York academic, with extensive contacts on the East Coast. Tugwell, a much-published economic theorist, had thought about agriculture in ways Wallace had not. In 1927, he had traveled to the Soviet Union with a trade union delegation and had seen collective planning up close. He had come back with ideas about how American agriculture could be improved through greater government intervention. Tugwell's views would make him a favorite target of Roosevelt's critics, who dubbed him the "Lenin of the New Deal," and "Rex the Red." The attacks, however, were misplaced. "Liberals would like to rebuild the station while the trains are running," Tugwell explained. "Radicals prefer to blow up the station and forgo service until the new structure is built." Tugwell was not a radical. He was a liberal who tirelessly preached reform. The journalist Ernest K. Lindley regarded Tugwell as "the philosopher, the sociologist, and the prophet of the Roosevelt Revolution, as well as one of its boldest practitioners."[4]

In the first few days of the administration, it was hard to get Roosevelt's attention for anything but banking and budget cutting. Once the Emergency Banking Act and the Economy Act were under way, however, Wallace saw an opening. He made an appointment to drop by the White House to see Roosevelt on the evening of March 8. Wallace brought along Tugwell, who knew the president better than he did. The scene in the White House was chaotic, with crowds of supplicants and reporters milling around. Wallace and Tugwell pushed their way through. In a brisk meeting, Wallace proposed quickly drafting a major agricultural bill, so they could start getting help out to the Farm Belt. Roosevelt agreed right away. Wallace's timing had turned out to be excellent. It was already clear that Congress was moving rapidly on Roosevelt's first two bills, and he wanted to introduce more.[5]

Roosevelt had many reasons for wanting act quickly on agriculture. He had a strong affinity for farmers, and based on his agricultural work at Hyde Park, considered himself one. Farmers had also always been an important but elusive part of his political base. That had been true in his first run for office, when he was elected to the legislature from a Republican district in large part by persuading farmers to vote for him. "You have no notion what early success means to a young politician," Moley said of his boss's affinity for farm issues. Republican-leaning farmers had come through for Roosevelt in the 1932 election, and he wanted to keep them in the Democratic column. And Roosevelt believed that reviving agriculture, which employed more than 20 percent of the workforce, was necessary to get the larger economy moving again. There were also agricultural reasons for acting quickly. The spring planting schedule was fast approaching. If Roosevelt delayed any longer, the impact of his agriculture program would be put off by a full year. Not least, there was the rising tide of radicalism. The talk of imminent revolution coming out of the Farm Belt was beginning to sound all too real.[6]

In the White House meeting, Wallace was hoping to get guidance about what kind of farm bill Roosevelt was looking for. Roosevelt's instructions were simple: he wanted a bill the farmers themselves would support. That came as no surprise to Tugwell, who had observed weeks earlier in his diary that Roosevelt did not have "much judgment of a positive sort" about what approach he wanted to take, but was inclined to follow "the lead of the farm leaders." Roosevelt told Wallace to summon farm leaders to Washington for a meeting at which he would be able to poll them about their preferences and lock in their support. Roosevelt turned out to be in an even greater hurry than Wallace. When Wallace suggested holding the farmers' meeting on March thirteenth, Roosevelt said it should be on Friday the tenth, just two days later. In the meantime, he warned Wallace and Tugwell to watch out for the lobbyists who would descend. "You can send them over here if they give you too much trouble," he said.[7]

Roosevelt wanted what the farmers wanted, but it was not clear what that was. Many farmers now supported "domestic allotment," the approach Wallace and Tugwell favored, which called for increasing agricultural prices by paying farmers to grow less. But there was significant opposition to domestic allotment across the spectrum of farm opinion. Conservative elements in the farm community, including equipment makers and mill owners, still favored McNary-Haugenism, a 1920s farm movement that called for the government to boost prices by dumping crops overseas. At the other extreme, farm radicals were demanding "cost of production," government price supports that would guarantee farmers a healthy profit no matter what price their crops sold for. To get a farm bill enacted into law, Wallace would have to forge a consensus among these and other fragmented farm constituencies, and then work with Roosevelt to maneuver the bill through Congress. That left the fate of a large swath of the nation in the hands of a remarkable scientist, journalist, and farmer the public knew little about.[8]

Henry A. Wallace, who had been born in a farmhouse in Adair County, Iowa, on October 7, 1888, was the third in a line of extraordinary Henry Wallaces. The first, known as "Uncle Henry," had been born in Pennsylvania, the son of a Scots-Irish immigrant. Intent from a young age on becoming a minister, he decided at age eighteen to hop a railroad and head west. Uncle Henry, who was described by an Iowa reporter as "tall, bearded, with strong even features, and the glint of a Messiah in his eyes," attended seminary in Illinois. Afterward, he became pastor of Presbyterian congregations on opposite sides of the Mississippi, one in Rock Island, Illinois, the other in Davenport, Iowa. When he came down with tubercular symptoms, Uncle Henry moved his wife and five children to the healthier environment of the Iowa countryside. He settled in Westminster, in Adair County, took up farming, and gradually recovered. Uncle Henry began writing for local newspapers. He proved to be a naturally gifted polemicist, railing against political machines and railroad monopolies. But after a series of run-ins with newspaper editors and owners who objected to his views, he lost his journalistic platforms.[9]

Uncle Henry's oldest son, Henry Caldwell Wallace, was responsible for establishing the family newspaper. Harry Wallace, as he was known, had been born in Rock Island and grew up on the Adair County farm. He attended Iowa State, and after two years married a fellow student, May Brodhead, an Easterner from an old New England family who had been sent to live with an aunt in Iowa. When one of his father's tenant farmers left, Harry took over the land. He farmed it for the next five years, while May gave birth to two children, Henry A. Wallace and Annabelle. Harry's farming years coincided with a deep agricultural recession. Prices were so low, *The Literary Digest* noted, that "all around him farmers were working themselves into premature graves." Harry sold his farm equipment and returned to Iowa State to get his degree. On the recommendation of "Tama" Jim Wilson, a prominent faculty member and friend of his father, Harry was hired as an assistant professor and put in charge of the Dairy Department. While teaching, Harry bought a small, semimonthly newspaper with a friend. He soon began working at the paper full-time. With help from his father and his brother John, Harry bought out his friend's stake and changed the paper's name to *Wallaces' Farmer*. He offered his father the job of editor and stayed on as assistant editor.[10]

The tone that *Wallaces' Farmer* strove for was expressed in its motto: "Good Farming; Clear Thinking; Right Living." The editorial content was a mix of opinion on issues like tariffs, practical advice for farmers, and old-time religion. *Wallaces' Farmer* managed the neat trick, the literary critic Dwight Macdonald once observed, of "being respected for the soundness of its views on infant damnation and on hog cholera." Early on, the newspaper promised that its orientation would be populist. Its voice "would not be that of a corporation without conscience or soul, but of a living man responsible at once to public opinion and that higher law by which men are judged." Uncle Henry, who still thought of himself as a Presbyterian minister, regarded *Wallaces' Farmer* as his pulpit. His column, "Uncle Henry's Sabbath School Lesson," quickly emerged as the paper's most popular feature.[11]

Uncle Henry became a powerful force in Farm Belt politics just as William Jennings Bryan was making his first run for president. Bryan was an agrarian populist who championed farmers and insisted that the gold standard was at the root of their troubles. "Burn down your cities and leave our farms, and your cities will spring up again as if by magic; but destroy our farms and the grass will grow in the streets of every city in the country," Bryan told the 1896 Democratic National Convention. He ended his address with one of the most famous declarations in American politics: "You shall not crucify mankind upon a cross of gold." Much of the Farm Belt was swept up in Bryan's fiery rhetoric. Farmers were convinced that abandoning the gold standard, which would pave the way for inflation, was their best hope of getting out from under their crushing debt loads, since it would allow them to pay off their mortgages with cheaper dollars. Unlike many of his neighbors, Uncle Henry considered inflation a threat to national prosperity, more damaging in the long run to the Farm Belt than the gold standard. Uncle Henry made his views, and his opposition to Bryan, known in the pages of the family newspaper. When William McKinley defeated Bryan, Uncle Henry was a leading contender for secretary of agriculture, but he did not want the job. He threw his support behind "Tama" Jim Wilson, who served as agriculture secretary under McKinley, Theodore Roosevelt, and William Howard Taft. Uncle Henry was seated in church in 1916 when he died suddenly and, as *Wallaces' Farmer* put it, "in a moment the Grim Reaper had gathered in the richest sheaf in the harvest."[12]

With Uncle Henry's death, the editorship of *Wallaces' Farmer* passed to Harry. Like his father, he was a loyal Republican. Henry A. Wallace's first political memory was hearing his father say after the 1892 presidential election that hard times were coming because a Democrat, Grover Cleveland, had won. As editor, Harry fiercely championed farmers' interests. He clashed over farm prices with Herbert Hoover, who was serving as the head of the U.S. Food Administration under President Wilson. In a series of editorials, Harry accused Hoover of trying to "bamboozle" farmers by promising them one price for hogs and giving them less when the hogs were actually brought to market. Henry Wallace was not involved in his father's feud, but it left a strong impression on him. He took away from it, an editor at the paper said, "a profound distrust of the Hoover type of mind."[13]

Harry was also active in politics. In 1920, he helped Warren Harding's campaign for the presidency. When Harding was elected, he appointed Harry secretary of agriculture, the job Uncle Henry had not been interested in. Harry arrived in Washington during a crisis. The Farm Belt was already in the grip of a depression, a decade before it hit the rest of the country. During the World War, American farmers had planted 40 million new acres to compensate for the reduced production in Europe. At the war's end, European farmers began producing large harvests again, creating a global surplus and driving down crop prices. While American farmers' incomes plunged, the amount they had to pay for mortgages, taxes, and consumer goods remained the same. Caught in the "scissors" of falling income and constant expenses, farmers were struggling. Harry lobbied Harding to do something about it, but Hoover, who was now secretary of commerce, insisted that the federal government should not get involved. Just as Harry thought he was on the verge of prevailing, Harding died unexpectedly. Calvin Coolidge, who served out the remainder of Harding's term, was a champion of Eastern interests, and more implacably opposed than Harding to farm relief.[14]

In the Farm Belt, a movement was forming. The rallying cry was "parity." Farmers saw the era before the World War as a golden age, when rural Americans had been on an equal footing with city dwellers. Throughout the 1920s, urban salaries had risen steadily while farm income dwindled, due to economic factors outside the farmers' control. Farmers wanted the government to restore crop prices to the level that would bring their income back to the same ratio to urban salaries as before the war. The leading proposal for achieving "parity" of this sort was the McNary-Haugen bill, named for Senator Charles McNary, Republican of Oregon, and Representative Gilbert Haugen, Republican of Iowa. It called for the federal government to dump surplus crops overseas, driving up prices at home. McNary-Haugen's supporters argued that since the government propped up the prices of industrial goods through high tariffs, it was only fair for there to be a similar government program dedicated to driving up the prices of farm products. For much of the 1920s, McNary-Haugenism was the great populist dream of the Farm Belt, and the Wallaces were true believers.[15]

That Farm Belt dream "beat its head in vain against the imperturbable

When Franklin D. Roosevelt delivered his inaugural address on March 4, 1933, one-quarter of the workforce was unemployed, thousands of banks had failed, and the farm economy was on the brink of collapse. In his speech, Roosevelt promised a terrified nation "action, and action now." *Franklin D. Roosevelt Presidential Library*

Herbert Hoover barely spoke to Roosevelt during their joint ride to the inauguration ceremony. Hoover was bitter about his landslide loss and insisted that Roosevelt was unqualified to assume the presidency. After the inauguration, Roosevelt and Hoover never saw each other again. *Franklin D. Roosevelt Presidential Library*

In the 1932 election, Roosevelt and his running mate, John Nance Garner, had campaigned on a platform of change. Roosevelt declared that he was fighting "the 'Four Horsemen' of the present Republican leadership: The Horsemen of Destruction, Delay, Deceit, Despair." *Associated Press*

Raymond Moley, a Columbia University government professor, presided over Roosevelt's famous "Brain Trust" during the campaign. As chief speechwriter, Moley wrote an historic phrase into Roosevelt's speech to the Democratic Convention: "I pledge you, I pledge myself, to a new deal for the American people." *Franklin D. Roosevelt Presidential Library*

During the Hundred Days, Moley was Roosevelt's "closest, most intimate advisor," as *Time* magazine declared in a cover story. Moley was a pragmatist who focused more on reviving the banking system and shepherding legislation through Congress than on promoting a particular agenda. *Associated Press*

Lewis Douglas was Roosevelt's first budget director. The son and grandson of Arizona copper barons, he was an outspoken fiscal conservative. During the Hundred Days, Congress passed the Economy Act, which he drafted, a law that slashed federal spending, even though the nation was reeling from the Depression. *The New York Times*

Douglas opposed liberal solutions to the nation's problems, including public works programs, warning that the Roosevelt's policies would be "the end of Western Civilization." When Douglas lost these battles, he became increasingly embittered. He eventually resigned, saying he did not want to "destroy myself inside." *The New York Times*

Henry Wallace, the son and grandson of Iowa farmer-journalists, was a leader of the nation's beleaguered Farm Belt. When he accepted the position of secretary of agriculture, he declared that he would "make good for the farmer, or I will go back home and grow corn." *Associated Press*

Wallace oversaw the drafting of the Agricultural Adjustment Act, which propped up farm prices by paying farmers to grow less. The A.A.A. was the first New Deal law that committed the government to helping the Depression's victims. *The New York Times*

Frances Perkins, who grew up in a conservative New England family, became an expert on factory safety early in her career. As New York State industrial commissioner under Governor Roosevelt, she was a leading advocate for working men and women. *International Film Service*

Perkins went to Washington with Roosevelt, becoming his secretary of labor, and the first woman Cabinet member. Perkins was a leader of the progressive forces in the Cabinet, and clashed frequently with Lewis Douglas, particularly over whether the government should embark on large-scale public works programs. *The New York Times*

Before Perkins—seen here sewing in a National Recovery Administration label— agreed to join the Cabinet, she made Roosevelt promise to support federal relief and public works, minimum-wage and maximum-hours laws, a ban on child labor, and other progressive initiatives. By the end of the New Deal, her entire agenda had become law. *The New York Times*

Harry Hopkins, an Iowan who made a name for himself as a social worker in New York City, became administrator of the Federal Emergency Relief Administration during the Hundred Days. He quickly began handing out money to the states—and creating the nation's first federal welfare program. *Harris & Ewing*

In his later years, Hopkins became one of Roosevelt's closest advisers and confidantes. But Perkins believed that his finest accomplishment was his early work establishing "a decent, reasonable, human relief system," which she called "perhaps the most creative thing that has been done in the whole New Deal." *The New York Times*

Mr. Coolidge," as one journalist noted. Coolidge, a believer in laissez-faire, opposed the McNary-Haugen bill as an unjustified intrusion on the free market, and made clear that if it passed Congress he would veto it. Coolidge's opposition did not stop Harry from testifying before Congress in favor of the bill. Back in Iowa, *Wallaces' Farmer* was urging its readers to start a "prairie fire" of enthusiasm for the McNary-Haugen bill. But the Farm Belt's excitement could not overcome the entrenched opposition of business interests. When the bill came to a vote in the House on June 3, 1924, it failed by a 224–154 vote. There was widespread speculation that Coolidge would fire his rebellious agriculture secretary after the November election, but he never had to. With his McNary-Haugen campaign defeated and his Cabinet position in peril, Harry's health declined. After an operation to remove his gallbladder, he died on October 25, at the age of fifty-eight. Beleaguered farmers lost a fierce advocate, and the Wallace family mantle passed to the next generation.[16]

Henry Agard Wallace was the eldest of Harry and May's six children. He had many of the Wallace family attributes, including love of farming, spirituality, and iconoclasm. He would later say, however, that his mother had a more profound influence on him than his father. An heir to her family's flinty New England traditions, May Wallace did not smoke or drink, and she liked things that were simple and traditional. Henry would later recall that she resisted salads as "some new-fangled notion that was being foisted on the American people by women's clubs." May was as much of an agriculturalist as her husband. It was May, an enthusiastic gardener, who taught Henry how to crossbreed pansies.[17]

Henry grew up doing farm chores, including caring for a cow, a horse, a sow, and piglets. He had the good fortune as a child to come under the influence of George Washington Carver, an Iowa State teaching assistant who would grow up to become a world-famous botanist. Carver, the son of slaves from Missouri, had moved north to escape racial discrimination, finding Iowa more tolerant than the other places he had lived. When he visited the Wallace home, he took six-year-old Henry on "botanizing expeditions," in which he pointed out flowers and parts of flowers. Henry would later say that his mother and Carver were "responsible for my acquiring a love of plants at a very early age," while his father was somewhere "in the background of it." One day, Henry found a seed catalogue and ordered six kinds of strawberries. It was the beginning of his passion for plant breeding. Henry was convinced he had found his life's calling. His interest in agriculture was not merely intellectual, or even professional. He would later write in *Wallaces' Farmer* that "the individuality of corn plants is almost as interesting to me as the personality of animals or human beings." For Henry, plants had an almost spiritual significance. Later in his life, after becoming secretary of agriculture, he would deliver a speech entitled "The Strength and Quietness of Grass."[18]

At the age of fifteen, Henry attended a corn show put on by Perry G. Holden, an Iowa State teacher and "corn evangelist" who traveled the Farm Belt. At his corn shows, Holden invited farm boys to help him pick out the most beautiful ears, which he insisted would produce the highest yields. Henry did not believe that the most attractive corn was the most productive, and when he challenged the relationship, Holden invited him to take home the highest- and lowest-rated ears, plant them, and compare the crops they produced. Henry planted them, and at harvest time he found that the most beautiful corn had not produced the largest crops. He wrote up his results in *Wallaces' Farmer* and began a crusade against what he called "pretty ear" shows. He succeeded in discrediting the idea that attractive corn was productive corn, and put an end to corn shows.[19]

In 1906, Wallace enrolled at Iowa State. He continued his plant studies, including more breeding experiments, and began to extend his love of experimentation to his own body. He put himself on unusual diets, including a regimen of corn, soybeans, and cottonseed and linseed meal. After reading a magazine article on fasting by Upton Sinclair, the muckraking journalist, Wallace went a week without eating at all. It was in college that Wallace's views on agricultural policy began to take shape. He studied with Benjamin Hibbard, a maverick economist who was skeptical of laissez-faire economics. Hibbard taught that market competition hurt farmers, pitting them against each other and driving down prices. He got Wallace thinking about ways to insulate farmers from the ravages of the free market.[20]

After graduation, Wallace went to work full-time at *Wallaces' Farmer*. He proved to be the family's most talented journalist. Wallace wrote on a wide range of agricultural issues, often breaking new ground, as he did with his exposé on corn shows. In 1913, Wallace met Ilo Wilson, the daughter of a prosperous local businessman, at a picnic in Des Moines. Wallace was taken with her immediately, and they married the following year.[21]

Wallace's agrarianism, like Thomas Jefferson's, had a strong political component. He believed that rural America was a repository of virtue, and that it played a crucial role in counterbalancing the corruption of the cities. Wallace worried that farm life was being overwhelmed by fast-spreading urban culture. By the end of the 1920s, about 25 percent of the nation's 123 million people would be living on farms, down from more than 40 percent at the turn of the century. Wallace saw the encroaching urbanism as a threat to the farmer's way of life. "We want to prevent our countryside being merely a field for the extension of town habits," he said.[22]

Wallace developed an interest in farm pricing, and soon became an expert. His first book, *Agricultural Prices*, argued that the free market interfered with farmers' ability to make a living. If they were ever going to get a fair price for their crops, he maintained, they would have to take control over the amount that they produced. The book laid the groundwork for the New Deal agricultural programs to come.[23]

While working at the newspaper, Wallace continued with his agricultural experiments. He was particularly interested in hybridization, crossing different seed types to produce new varieties. Hybrid vigor, the idea that a cross of plant breeds often produces heartier, higher-yielding plants, was still a radical idea at the time, and Wallace became one of the nation's foremost advocates for hybrid seeds. He regularly extolled the virtues of hybridization in *Wallaces' Farmer*, explaining hybrid vigor and reporting on his discussions with researchers from across the country. In 1926, he founded the Hi-Bred Corn Company with the backing of family and friends. Using the slogan "Developed—not discovered, made to fit—not found by chance," the company made hybrid corn widely available. Wallace's efforts paid off handsomely. Within fourteen years, 90 percent of the corn being sold in the farm belt was hybrid, and the Hi-Bred Corn Company was the source of much of it. In the late 1990s, the company, which had been renamed Pioneer Hi-Bred, would be sold for more than $9 billion, about one-quarter of which went to Wallace's descendants.[24]

Wallace's other great passion, along with agriculture, was spirituality. "Fundamentally I am neither a corn breeder nor an editor but a searcher for bringing the 'Inner Light' to outward manifestation," he once said. That search for the "inner light" took Wallace away from the Presbyterianism of his grandfather and father and set him on a lifelong religious quest. Wallace's far-ranging journey took him to meetings of the Theosophy Society, the free-thinking movement that embraced pantheism, and into a lifelong fascination with mysticism. Later in life he would fall under the influence of Nicholas Roerich, a Russian-born mystic, and Charles Roos, a Finnish-American who fancied himself a Native American medicine man. Wallace's experiments in spirituality—he once described himself as a "practical mystic"—would provide considerable grist for his critics later in his career.[25]

Wallace's years at *Wallaces' Farmer* coincided with the postwar farm depression that his father confronted as agriculture secretary. Wallace did not excuse farmers from all responsibility for their condition. He believed in the "gospel of success," and constantly preached the importance of hard work and good farming practices. "It would be interesting," he wrote, "to search out the fourteen unluckiest farmers in Iowa. We could make out a score card for them, giving points to ignorance, laziness, slack business methods, lack of conveniences and out-of-date machinery." At the same time, Wallace insisted that the farmers' biggest problems were due to factors beyond their control. The farm and nonfarm economies had diverged, he believed, and farmers had been left behind. "The population of a great democratic nation can not indefinitely remain 'half slave and half free,' as is the case today," he wrote, "with city labor getting twice the pre-war wages and the farmer getting little more than enough to pay his interest and taxes." Wallace wrote articles in *Wallaces' Farmer* supporting his father's efforts to get government help for struggling farmers. He was convinced that the Republican Party, with its devotion to laissez-faire economics, would not be the farmers' savior. In the

1924 presidential election, weeks after his father's death, Wallace broke with family tradition and voted for Wisconsin senator Robert La Follette, the Progressive Party nominee.[26]

After the election, which Coolidge won handily, Wallace continued his campaign for farm relief. He traveled across the Farm Belt, speaking directly to farm families, to augment the campaign he was waging in print. He went to grange meetings, churches, and state fairs, explaining farm issues and urging his audience to demand that the government take action. His message was a simple one: that "a greater percentage of the income of the nation" should "be turned back to the mass of the people." Wallace started out as a "terrible speaker," a *Wallaces' Farmer* colleague recalled, with a "bad platform presence." He "wriggled" and either "tucked his chin in his collar and talked to the floor," or "looked at the rafters and talked to them." Wallace improved with practice, though he never became a riveting orator, and he was prone to speak for as long as an hour and a half. What he excelled at was explaining complex issues like the tariff or monetary policy to ordinary people. Wallace would look out at a room full of farmers and their wives, lean forward, and say: "This is a little hard to understand. It's complicated. But we need to know about it to know what we have to do next."[27]

As Wallace saw it, the farmers' plight stemmed from a single problem: oversupply. Manufacturers could cut back on their production when prices were low, but farmers planted and harvested as much as they could, no matter how bad the market was. A decade before it became a popular view, Wallace argued that limits on production were the key to increasing crop prices and rescuing the farm economy. Writing in *Wallaces' Farmer* under the slogan "Less Corn, More Clover, More Money," he urged farmers to voluntarily reduce production. "There is such a thing as over-production," he argued in 1922, "and if the farmers of the corn belt don't believe it, they can soon convince themselves ... if they continue to produce 3,000,000,000-bushel corn crops year after year." Ultimately, though, Wallace understood that voluntary reduction was problematic, because the economic incentives worked against it. It was in the interest of farmers as a group to reduce their production to drive up prices, but it remained in the interest of any individual farmer to produce as much as he could. For crop reduction to be effective, Wallace concluded, the government would have to get involved.[28]

Although he believed crop reduction was the best solution to the farmers' problems, Wallace also supported McNary-Haugenism. Despite the bill's setbacks, farmers were still flocking to its promise of "equality for agriculture." McNary-Haugenism had another important constituency: the businesses that made money on agriculture, which wanted the farm economy to revive but did not want to see a reduction in the amount of crops harvested. Two of the leading advocates for McNary-Haugenism were George Peek, the president of Moline Plow Company, and his colleague Hugh S. Johnson. The two men, who were close associates of the financier Bernard Baruch, freely admitted that they were motivated largely by financial self-interest. "You can't sell a plow to a busted customer," Peek liked to say. In 1927, Congress yielded to the Farm Belt pressure and passed the McNary-Haugen bill. President Coolidge vetoed it, as he promised he would. The following year, Congress passed it a second time. *Wallaces' Farmer* printed the full text of the bill and made an urgent appeal to Coolidge to sign it, but he vetoed it again.[29]

Coolidge's resistance to McNary-Haugen pushed Wallace even further from the Republican Party. The veto, he wrote, "has made it impossible for any farmer with self respect to vote for Coolidge or for any candidate who, like Hoover, supports [the] Coolidge policy toward agriculture." When Coolidge decided not to run again in 1928 and the Republicans nominated Hoover, Wallace began giving serious consideration to supporting the Democratic nominee. Al Smith, the governor of New York, was good on farm issues, and he supported the McNary-Haugen bill. Many farmers, however, could not look past Smith's Irish-Catholic background and his origins in the slums of the Lower East Side. Wallace went to hear Smith speak in Iowa and came away impressed. He did not make up his mind to support Smith, he later said, until the next day, when he went to a restaurant and heard his fellow diners make bigoted comments. Wallace supported Smith in *Wallaces' Farmer* and campaigned for him. Despite his efforts, Hoover carried Iowa by a nearly two-to-one margin on his way to a landslide victory.[30]

Wallace returned from a trip to Europe in the fall of 1929 to watch the stock market crash and the farm economy go into free fall. Crop prices, which had been depressed for most of the decade, plunged further. There was no longer much hope for McNary-Haugenism, since Hoover had made clear that he would veto it, and the bill's supporters did not have the votes for an override. Hoover's response to the farm depression was to establish a Federal Farm Board, with a $500 million budget. It was authorized to help farmers store crops and market them, but it was not allowed to buy crops or pay farmers to produce less. The farm board went further than Hoover's Republican predecessors had been willing to go, but it did not address farming's fundamental flaws, and its impact was minimal. Any modest good that Hoover did for farmers was more than outweighed by his disastrous tariff policy. In June 1930, Congress passed the infamous Smoot-Hawley Tariff Act, which raised tariffs on manufactured goods to historic levels. When more than one thousand economists had signed a petition urging Hoover to veto the bill. Wallace joined them, calling Smoot-Hawley "iniquitous." The bill would hurt farmers as consumers, he argued, because high tariffs would drive up the price of the manufactured goods they bought. It would also hurt them as producers because it would invite other countries to impose their own tariffs, making it harder for American farmers to sell their crops overseas. Hoover signed Smoot-Hawley, and it set off the round of retaliatory tariffs that Wallace and others had feared, cutting into the export market for American farm products.[31]

In 1931, Wallace began to turn to "domestic allotment," a new plan for farm relief being developed by M. L. Wilson, a professor at Montana State College, and other agriculture experts. It took the approach that Wallace had long favored, inducing farmers to work together to reduce their production, and since its creators were readers of *Wallaces' Farmer*, his own writings may have helped to inspire it. The goal of domestic allotment, as with McNary-Haugenism, was to return agricultural prices to prewar "parity" levels. It proposed to do this by having the government pay farmers to take some of their land out of production. Farmers could choose to participate or not. The funds to pay farmers not to grow would come from a tax on agricultural "processors"—flour mills, canneries, packinghouses, and other businesses that acted as middlemen between farmers and consumers. The plan's creators saw the processor tax as the best way of ensuring that domestic allotment would be self-financing. The processors would protest, but the plan's drafters envisioned that they would have no trouble passing the cost on to consumers. Wallace became one of the leading proponents of domestic allotment, arguing for it in the pages of *Wallaces' Farmer* and in his speaking tours across the Farm Belt.[32]

At the same time, Wallace was campaigning for a new monetary policy. A generation earlier, Uncle Henry had opposed William Jennings Bryan's populist call for abandoning the gold standard. Wallace was now convinced that going off gold and promoting inflation were necessary if farmers were ever going to get out from under their debt. Writing in *Wallaces' Farmer*, he advocated for the "honest dollar," a term Bryan had used in the 1896 presidential campaign. To Wallace, an honest dollar was one that restored farmers' buying power, relative to urban residents, to where it had been before the war. Wallace testified in favor of inflation before the Senate Committee on Banking and Currency. He put the issue in scientific terms. Technology of all kinds was fast improving, he said, enabling manufacturers to improve efficiency and raise the nation's standard of living. What America needed now, he argued, was "up-to-date machinery for industrial and social justice equivalent to our industrial progress and development." A new monetary policy, Wallace insisted, was "part of the machinery."[33]

Wallace was increasingly being recognized as a national leader on farm issues. In August 1931, he attended the Conference on Economic Policy for American Agriculture, a gathering of prominent agricultural reformers, at the University of Chicago. While M. L. Wilson looked on, the conference formally endorsed domestic allotment. Wallace continued to talk up the plan and to speak out against Hoover's modest version of farm relief, which he dismissed in a March 1932 speech to the National League of Women Voters as "nonsense."[34]

The Farm Belt depression continued to deepen. Between 1929 and 1932 farm income had fallen by another two-thirds, and the foreclosure crisis was becoming ever more serious. Farmers were increasingly responding with radical politics and violence. In May 1932, two thousand farmers descended on the state fairgrounds in Des Moines to form the Farmers' Holiday Association. The group, headed by the fiery Milo Reno, a longtime Iowa farm activist, urged farmers to declare a "holiday" from farming. Operating under the slogan "Stay at Home—Buy Nothing—Sell Nothing," members vowed to withhold their corn, beef, pork, and milk until the government addressed their problems. As one piece of Farmers' Holiday Association doggerel put it:

> Let's call a Farmers' Holiday
> A Holiday let's hold
> We'll eat our wheat and ham and eggs
> And let them eat their gold.

More violent forms of protest also began to break out. In Sioux City, farmers put wooden planks with nails on the highways to block agricultural deliveries. The "red army" of Nebraska, one of many vigilante groups that were forming, showed up at a foreclosure sale and saw to it that every item that had been seized from a farmer's widow sold for five cents, leaving the bank with a total settlement of just $5.35. A wave of "penny auctions" of this sort swept the Farm Belt, forcing creditors to proceed with caution. The threat to the nation's well-being was clear. "When the American farmer comes out to the road with a club or a pitchfork," Kansas newspaper editor William Allen White observed in *The Saturday Evening Post*, "the warning flag is out."[35]

Wallace looked on the growing extremism with dismay. The Wallace family had always kept its distance from Farm Belt radicals. *Wallaces' Farmer* had been founded as a Republican journal for the "conservative type of farmer," which it defined as those with "no mortgages or low mortgages." Wallace supported the Farm Bureau, the old-line lobby that represented the "four-hundred-acre" farmers, rather than the upstart Iowa Farmers Union, which fought for the least well-off. The radicalism that was sweeping through the Farm Belt may have "served a purpose," Wallace would later say, "but it wasn't my way of doing things." Wallace believed in working through the system. He also had a more modest view than the farm radicals of what sort of reforms were needed. He believed that if crop prices could be increased, farmers would do fine in the capitalist system. He did not see a need for a war on Eastern bankers, or for any of the farm radicals' other revolutionary stands. Wallace was worried that if Hoover did not do more, the Farm Belt would be in complete rebellion. "I think the Republican administration was gravely culpable," he later said. "I'd blame them far more than I would Milo Reno."[36]

Wallace was still waiting for a Farm Belt savior. In June of 1932, the signs of one began to appear. Wallace attended another farm conference in Chicago, where he met Rexford Tugwell. The two men hit it off right away. Tugwell thought Wallace was a bit eccentric—he noticed that when they went out for a beer, Wallace would always order an ice cream soda. Tugwell was impressed, however, with Wallace's "keen mind," and with Wallace and M. L. Wilson's idea of domestic allotment. Tugwell acted quickly to inject it into the presidential campaign. He sent the proposal to Roosevelt, who was about to address the Democratic National Convention. "To show how close a margin we worked on," Tugwell said later, the domestic allotment plan that he had picked up in Chicago "went to Albany by wire; and it came back to Chicago by plane—incorporated in Mr. Roosevelt's acceptance speech." Roosevelt kept the reference to domestic allotment brief, to avoid alienating its critics, but the speech marked his first endorsement of the idea. Before long, Henry Morgenthau, Roosevelt's good friend, showed up in Iowa. He was on a mission to round up farm support for Roosevelt. Morgenthau, who owned a fourteen-hundred-acre fruit and dairy farm near Hyde Park and published *American Agriculturist* magazine, talked to Wallace about Roosevelt's concern for farmers. Wallace was beginning to believe that Roosevelt could be the farmers' champion that he had been waiting for, but he still was not sure. He was not even entirely certain, he would later say, whether he was still a Republican or on his way to becoming a Democrat.[37]

Roosevelt, who had received positive reports from Tugwell and Morgenthau, invited Wallace to Hyde Park in mid-August. Wallace went, but he was still wary. To save money, he accepted an invitation to lecture first

at Cornell University, which paid for the trip. "I was rather leery of politicians," he later recalled. "I didn't intend to go out of my way to see him, but
as long as I could get my expenses paid I was willing." Over lunch, Wallace
talked with Roosevelt and Morgenthau about conditions in the Farm Belt
and laid out the case for domestic allotment. Wallace was impressed by his
host's energy. "I had heard that his legs were paralyzed, and I feared that he
would be completely tired out," he wrote in *Wallaces' Farmer.* "Imagine my
great surprise, therefore, to find a man with a fresh, eager, open mind, ready
to pitch into the agricultural problem at once." On his return to Iowa, Wallace signed on with Roosevelt.[38]

In his campaign against Hoover, Roosevelt spoke out strongly for farm
relief. He reminded voters that he was a farmer himself. "I am not, as
you say, an 'urban leader,'" he wrote to a South Dakota newspaper, "for
I was born and brought up and have always made my home on a farm in
Dutchess County." Roosevelt also reminded voters that although New York
was known for its tall buildings and teeming immigrant neighborhoods, it
was also a farm state, first in the nation in income from dairy cows and hay,
second in production of apples and grapes, and sixth in overall farm income.
On his swings through the West and the South, Roosevelt echoed Wallace's
complaints about the plight of the farmer. Farmers had to bring two wagon-
loads of produce into town to buy the same clothing, farm implements, and
other manufactured goods they used to buy with one wagonload, he said.
Roosevelt emphasized that farm relief would help the whole country, not just
farmers. Nearly half of Americans made their livings directly or indirectly
from agriculture, and when they lost buying power, the whole economy was
dragged down. "No Nation can long endure half bankrupt," Roosevelt had
declared that spring in his "Forgotten Man" speech. "Main Street, Broadway,
the mills, the mines will close if half the buyers are broke."[39]

Roosevelt was scheduled to deliver a major agriculture address in Topeka,
Kansas, in mid-September, which M. L. Wilson would draft. He asked Wilson to work on it with Wallace since, as Moley observed, no one was more
familiar than Wallace "with the tastes and prejudices of the great farm
area whose traditional Republican allegiance Roosevelt had to destroy to be

elected." Wilson and Wallace's draft of the speech made a strong case for domestic allotment. Moley kept in the promise of domestic allotment, but he toned down the references to make the speech more acceptable to supporters of rival plans, including McNary-Haugenism, and to Easterners, who worried that farm relief would be expensive and that it would drive up the cost of food. Moley was pleased with the final draft, which he believed was pivotal in winning Roosevelt the votes of Midwestern farmers "without waking up the dogs of the East."[40]

Wallace barnstormed for Roosevelt across Iowa, driving to church suppers and county fairs in his Model A Ford. In the final days of the campaign, *Wallaces' Farmer* made its endorsement. "The only thing to vote for in this election is justice for agriculture," Wallace wrote. "With Roosevelt, the farmers have a chance—with Hoover, none." Iowa put aside its traditional Republican sympathies and gave Roosevelt nearly 60 percent of its votes. Farm regions across the West and the Midwest that had been Republican for generations joined the new Roosevelt coalition, which also included big cities and the solidly Democratic South. In the beleaguered Farm Belt, Roosevelt's victory brought a measure of hope. "I was going to tell the loan company to take my farm, but now I'm going to make a fight to hold it," a farmer told Wallace after the election. "It looks to me, for the first time in years, as if we farmers had a chance."[41]

The speculation began right away over who would be the next secretary of agriculture. George Peek, the farm equipment manufacturer who had long championed McNary-Haugen, was eager for the job. Morgenthau also desperately wanted to be agriculture secretary. Although he was an old friend of Roosevelt, the odds against him were heavy. *The Nation* bluntly explained that he was seen as "too Eastern and too Judaic" to oversee American farming. Tugwell, who scoffed at Morgenthau's ambitions for the job, was himself not a viable candidate, as a New York academic. Tugwell was pushing for Wallace, and had enlisted Moley to talk to Roosevelt on his behalf. Roosevelt did not require much convincing. He regarded agriculture secretary as a position that should go to a farm leader. Wallace was one of the nation's most prominent farm leaders, his views were compatible with Roosevelt's, and the two men had hit it off when they met in Hyde Park. Wallace had the further advantage of being a Republican, a group Roosevelt was especially eager to see represented in the Cabinet.[42]

Roosevelt invited Wallace to Warm Springs, and in the bungalow where Roosevelt was staying, they resumed the discussion they had begun at Hyde Park. Roosevelt asked Wallace to go to Washington to keep an eye on farm legislation pending in Congress, and to meet with Marvin Jones, the Texan who used his chairmanship of the House Committee on Agriculture to look out for the interests of Big Cotton. There did not appear to be much chance of a farm bill emerging from the lame-duck Congress, or of Hoover signing one if it did, but Roosevelt wanted to monitor what was going on. Over lunch, Roosevelt, Wallace, Moley, Morgenthau, and Senator John Bankhead of Alabama discussed farm policy while Roosevelt expertly carved a Georgia wild turkey. In the afternoon, Wallace, Moley, and Morgenthau discussed what they wanted to see in a farm bill.[43]

In Warm Springs, Wallace was exposed to Roosevelt at his most charming. He watched as the president-elect sent Morgenthau out to find liquor for cocktails, no easy feat in Prohibition-era Georgia. At dinner, Roosevelt held forth about a hunt for hidden treasure on an island off the coast of Nova Scotia. The exotic Georgia property, the bootleg liquor, and the devotion of much time at a moment of national crisis to a rambling pirate's tale left Wallace thinking he had wandered into "something out of this world." Wallace went away with a new appreciation for his host. "Roosevelt does not have the extreme pride of personal opinion that has characterized some of our more bull-headed presidents," he wrote in *Wallaces' Farmer*. "He knows that he doesn't know it all, and tries to find out all he can from people who are supposed to be authorities." Roosevelt returned the admiration. It was most likely on this visit that he decided to appoint Wallace secretary of agriculture.[44]

In early December, Wallace went to Washington, as Roosevelt had requested. He, Tugwell, and Morgenthau met with Congressman Jones to discuss farm legislation. There were divisions in the ranks of the Roosevelt contingent. Wallace and Tugwell argued for domestic allotment, while Morgenthau made the case against it. Jones did not have much to say either way. It did not take Wallace long to conclude that the lame-duck Congress was not going to take action on a farm bill. On December 12, also in Washington, Wallace attended a conference of farm leaders representing about half of the nation's organized farmers. To Wallace's great satisfaction, a consensus had begun to form in favor of domestic allotment. The conference made a formal recommendation that the government pay farmers to reduce production, and finance the payments through a tax on processors. When word of the conference's endorsement of domestic allotment spread, the processors who would be taxed to pay for it protested loudly. The chairman of General Mills declared that there was a growing sense "that Mr. Roosevelt has been alienating himself from his conservative friends and leaning toward the more radical elements in his party."[45]

Wallace returned home to Iowa, where he was still editing *Wallaces' Farmer.* In January, he wrote to Roosevelt to tell him about the "pathetic letters" he was receiving. Wallace enclosed a letter describing the dire situation of tenant farmers, which was, he said, "even more desperate than that of the unemployed in the cities." Roosevelt was close to making a decision about agriculture secretary. Moley, who was helping screen Cabinet selections, had asked a Washington lawyer to review Wallace's writings. After examining six years of *Wallaces' Farmer,* the lawyer reported back that Wallace was a "distinctly effective" stylist and that "much of his writing on Hoover is as devastating as anything I have read." Testimonials for Wallace poured in from across the Farm Belt, including a letter from 105 farmers from Bon Homme County, South Dakota. Whether out of modesty or conviction, Wallace was dismissive of his own prospects. In a February 2 letter to a friend, he said he thought that his outspoken advocacy on controversial subjects would work against him. "I have not failed during the past month to express myself with the utmost freedom on the money question," he noted.[46]

Within days, a letter arrived from Roosevelt inviting Wallace to join "my official family." Wallace was uncertain whether to accept the job that his grandfather had spurned and that had made his father so miserable. He did not respond for days, and Moley finally had to call him to press him for an answer. Wallace told his friends and family in Iowa that, in the end, his desire to help the nation's farmers overcame his reluctance to move to Washington and enter public life. Moley radioed Roosevelt, who was vacationing on Vincent Astor's yacht, "Corn Belt in the Bag," their code for Wallace accepting. The news of Wallace's appointment was greeted enthusiastically throughout the farm states, and especially in Wallace's home state. "IOWANS LAUD FARM CHOICE," *The Des Moines Register* announced in a front-page headline. In the same paper, a cartoon captioned "Turning the Case Over to the Family Physician" portrayed "Agriculture" as an old man in his sickbed and Wallace as a doctor holding a black bag.[47]

Wallace headed to New York to meet with Roosevelt. He stopped off to see his sister, who lived outside Detroit, and saw firsthand the distress that had hit industrial America. Michigan's banks were on the brink of insolvency, and the state's residents were panicked about whether they would see their savings again. At his brother-in-law's invitation, Wallace visited Father Charles Coughlin, the radio demagogue, in his suite in the opulent Book-Cadillac Hotel. Wallace knew that Father Coughlin had supported Roosevelt in the election, but little more. It came as a surprise that the first thing his host said when he arrived was, "We're going to take the gold away from the Jews." The visit underscored for Wallace how angry many Americans had become, and what sort of leaders were waiting in the wings if Roosevelt failed.[48]

When Wallace arrived at Roosevelt's East Sixty-fifth Street town house, he got his first real exposure to the new team he would be joining. He was introduced to William Woodin. The incoming secretary of the treasury seemed "very gentle" with "a lovely personality," Wallace said later, but he did not understand why Roosevelt had chosen him. He also met Louis Howe, who struck him as "a cynical, critical soul" who was "utterly loyal to Roosevelt," but also a "pure opportunist." Wallace and Roosevelt talked some more about agriculture, but this time Roosevelt introduced a new and, for Wallace, unwelcome subject. Roosevelt said he was intent on reducing government spending, and that Wallace should expect to cut his department's budget by one-third. Wallace was able to bargain the president-elect down to a reduction of one-fourth, but he was troubled to see how enthusiastic Roosevelt was about budget cutting.[49]

Wallace returned to Iowa to wrap up his affairs. Two weeks later, he headed to the inauguration on a special train with the Iowa delegation. Wallace was embarking on a mission, and a new kind of challenge. He had spent his entire career giving advice from the safe perch of a farm journal. Now, he would be setting national farm policy and carrying it out, and he would be responsible for the results. Wallace set off in a spirit of optimism. "When I come back to Iowa, I hope prices will be higher, mortgages and taxes lower," he wrote in *Wallaces' Farmer*'s March 4 issue. When he arrived in Washington, Wallace took a room at the Cosmos Club, while his family remained behind in Iowa until May. It was fitting that he moved into temporary quarters, because he made clear that his tenure as agriculture secretary might be brief. "This department will make good as far as the farmer is concerned," Wallace told reporters, "or I'll go back home and grow corn."[50]

CHAPTER FIVE

"Good Lord! This Is a Revolution!"

After Roosevelt gave Wallace and Tugwell the green light to draw up a farm bill, they hurried back to the Agriculture Department. Wallace immediately began calling farm leaders, inviting them to attend a conference two days later. He called representatives of the three main farm groups: the Farm Bureau, an establishment organization centered in the Midwest and South; the National Grange, which represented many farmers in the Northeast and New England; and the National Farmers' Union, whose membership was made up of the poorest and most radical farmers. Wallace announced an ambitious schedule. He wanted to have a bill passed by Congress and signed into law by March 15, so it could affect the spring planting.[1]

Wallace continued to support domestic allotment, but he had reservations. As a lover of plants, he did not like the idea of growing less. As a humanitarian, he was troubled by the idea of reducing production when people were hungry. On March 9, Russell Lord, a journalist and sometime Agriculture Department employee who would later write a book on the Wallace family, had lunch with Wallace and Tugwell. Wallace was "downright in his hatred of reduced production," Lord found, but also "glumly and completely determined" that "it must be done." The main reason he favored it was that the alternatives seemed worse. The McNary-Haugenites were still pushing to dump surplus crops overseas, but Wallace thought it was unrealistic to think that Europeans, who now had surpluses of their own, would want to buy American crops. The Farmers' Union was still promoting cost of production, which called for the federal government to fix prices based on what it cost farmers to produce their crops, including a salary for the farmer and a fixed rate of return on the land. Cost of production appealed to farmers, who liked the idea of a guaranteed income, but its champions never bothered to explain the details, and Wallace and Tugwell considered the whole concept "mythical." Wallace insisted that even if it could be achieved, "cost of production" would hurt farmers in the long run, by in effect turning farming into a regulated utility.[2]

Although it was his own preferred plan, Wallace did not want the farm leaders to back domestic allotment exclusively. He hoped instead that they would endorse the sort of broad delegation of authority to the president that the Emergency Banking Act and the Economy Act contained. That would help get the bill through Congress, because all of the farm groups would rally around it. Once it became law, a broad delegation would let Roosevelt and Wallace try a variety of approaches and adapt to changed circumstances. Wallace knew from the December farm leaders' conference that there would be strong support for domestic allotment, but he also knew there would be influential forces on hand trying to block it. George Peek would promote McNary-Haugenism, and there would be radicals pushing cost of production. In his calls inviting people to the conference, Wallace began making the case for a farm bill that gave the president broad authority and he got a good response. A group of farmer leaders held a late-night conference on the train to Washington and agreed among themselves to support a broad delegation of power. "Before the last of the farmers went to bed that night," Clifford Gregory of the *Prairie Farmer* said, "the plan of the new relief had taken definite shape."[3]

On March 10, Tugwell welcomed the farm leaders to the Department of Agriculture. Wallace largely stayed away. The farm leadership respected him and appreciated that he was not a "Pennsylvania Avenue farmer," a Washington farm politician with few ties to the land. But Wallace knew that there were "tremendous jealousies among the farm organizations," and since he had been active in some but not others, he thought it best to remain in the background. While the leaders were meeting, Wallace spoke to the American people. At the end of the first day, he delivered his first national radio address, in which he began to make the case for an agricultural relief bill. "Emergency action is imperative," Wallace declared, and the proper course of action was to "adjust downward our surplus supplies." He took direct aim at the business interests that were already lining up against domestic allotment, and emphasized the need to move quickly. "We can't legislate next June," he cautioned, "for a crop that was planted in April."[4]

On the second day, Saturday, March 11, the conference ended up where Wallace had hoped it would. The farm leaders endorsed domestic allotment while also calling for a broad delegation of power to the president. In an attempt to mollify Peek, their report left open the possibility of dumping excess crops overseas. Wallace arranged for a delegation to present the recommendations to Roosevelt. "We could be excused a certain euphoria when we marshaled the leaders first in our building, then in the White House lobby," Tugwell said later. When the delegation told Roosevelt what they had agreed on, he accepted their report enthusiastically, and asked Wallace to get to work drawing up a bill. While the supporters of domestic allotment celebrated, the agricultural processors who would be taxed to pay for it braced for a fight. The McNary-Haugenites were not placated by the conference's tepid acceptance of crop dumping. Peek would later complain that the delegates had "muffed their big chance" and had "left the field open to the professors." The Farmers' Union was the most outraged of all. "They wanted to be in a position to raise hell to the limit," Wallace said.[5]

For Wallace, the conference was a great success. He had "made the first significant dent in the walls of agricultural sectionalism," *The Saturday Evening Post* declared. "The spectacle of those fifty agricultural lambs and lions lying down together was proof of it." When the farm leaders left, work began on the bill. The drafting was done in Tugwell's office "at the cost of a good deal of sleep," Wallace would later say. The drafters were Tugwell; Peek; Mordecai Ezekiel, a respected Agriculture Department economist;

Jerome Frank, a University of Chicago Law School graduate who would soon be general counsel to the agricultural agency the bill established; and Frederic Lee, former head of the Senate drafting bureau. "Occasionally," Wallace recalled dryly, "I was suspected of having had something to do with it."[6]

The Agricultural Adjustment Act that the drafters came up with was designed to bring the prices of seven basic agricultural commodities—wheat, cotton, corn, hogs, rice, tobacco, and milk and its products—up to prewar levels. It did all of the things the farm leaders recommended. It authorized the agriculture secretary to take land out of production using money from processor taxes. It included a McNary-Haugen provision allowing processor taxes to be used to pay for losses on crop dumping. And it delegated broad powers to the president—"so broad," *Time* magazine said, "that few could see their limits." The bill said domestic allotment would be temporary, ending when the president declared the agricultural emergency over. When the drafting was done, Wallace delivered the bill in person. Roosevelt was delighted with it. He liked that it included both domestic allotment and discretion to try other approaches. He especially liked that it paid for itself, so there would be little burden on the Treasury.[7]

While the final touches were being put on it, opposition to the bill was growing on both the left and the right. On March 12, the day after the farm leaders' conference ended, the Farmers' Holiday Association held a raucous 3,000-delegate convention in Des Moines. Milo Reno, who presided, called Wallace an "ignoramus" and insisted that he had never known a member of the Wallace family who was not unbalanced. The delegates demanded a more ambitious farm bill than the Agricultural Adjustment Act, advising Congress "not to go to the expense of hearings on the non-sensical domestic allotment plan." If Congress did not provide farmers "legislative justice" by May 3, the delegates warned, there would be a nationwide farmers' strike. Wallace had little patience with the radicals, whom he dismissed as "left wing farmers...demanding $1.50 wheat and $10 hogs inside of six weeks."[8]

At the same time, business interests were lining up against the Agricultural Adjustment Act. Hugh Johnson, George Peek's colleague, delivered an "impassioned tirade" against domestic allotment to Moley on a train ride from New York to Washington, and pleaded for the administration to back McNary-Haugenism instead. When the processors realized they could not stop the bill, they tried to change the processor tax to a general sales tax, and argued for a one-year limit on the law. Roosevelt, siding with Wallace, rejected the processors on both counts. On March 14, representatives of the meatpackers, grain handlers, and millers met with Wallace to once again protest the processor tax. Wallace had no difficulty standing up to business interests. One of his colleagues recalled a high-powered lawyer coming in to lobby on behalf of a "great food-dealing concern" on a matter worth millions of dollars to the company. Wallace simply said "No." When the lawyer persisted, Wallace raised his hand to cut the man off and said wearily, "Unless we learn to treat each other fairly this country is going to smash." In a similar manner, the processors were turned away unsatisfied. Tugwell suspected they would simply take their complaints elsewhere. "The packers, millers, and spinners are quite adequately represented in Congress," he lamented in his diary. Having lost his battles to derail it, Johnson declared that Wallace's bill "breaks my heart." Lewis Douglas was no less despondent. Government payments to farmers offended his laissez-faire sensibilities, and he was concerned that administering the act would prove too costly. James Warburg, a young scion of the famous banking family, who was close to Douglas, reported that Wallace's bill had left Douglas "very depressed."[9]

On March 16, Roosevelt met with Wallace and Tugwell and signed off on a final draft of the bill. Roosevelt was excited enough about it that he wrote the congressional message himself, rather than asking Moley. He scrawled it on a yellow legal pad, while seated at his desk, as Moley, Wallace, and Tugwell looked on. Roosevelt explained that he had decided to extend the special session because the farm crisis was of "equal importance" to the bank crisis. The farm bill would, he said, be "a new and untrod path"—a phrase that soon had Washington wits questioning if a path was a path at all if it was "untrod." The goal of the bill was both to help farmers, Roosevelt said, and to give a boost to the larger economy by increasing farmers' purchasing power. He urged quick action "for the simple reason that the spring crops will soon be planted and if we wait for another month or six weeks the effect on the prices of this year's crops will be wholly lost."[10]

The Agricultural Adjustment Act was attacked as soon as it became public. For the "radicals...it is not enough," Tugwell wrote in his diary; "for conservatives it is too much." Congressional conservatives saw the bill as a radical interference with the free market and a power grab by Roosevelt and Wallace. "I can't permit the passage of such legislation," Republican senator David A. Reed declared. "If the people of Pennsylvania knew what its passage would mean, they'd riot in the streets." There were also widespread objections to the cost, even though much of it would be paid for by the processor tax. *The New York Times* objected that the bill would in effect impose a "sales tax, resting heavily on food." Wallace appeared on the *National Farm and Home Hour* radio show to try to build popular support for his bill. It was the farm leaders, he insisted, who had asked him and the president to take on "very broad powers." Consumers would be protected, he argued, because the slight extra expense imposed on them "will be more than compensated for by the revived power of farmers to buy the goods and services the city has to sell." The bill could have split the nation along rural and urban lines, but most big-city representatives had long accepted that higher farm prices would benefit the entire nation. "Suppose, you will say, the price of commodities increase; what will your workers in the city do?" said Representative Fiorello La Guardia, a liberal Republican from New York City. "We are prepared for that. We will demand increased wages. That is the other half of the answer."[11]

In the House, the leaders were intent on pushing the Agricultural Adjustment Act through quickly. Debate was limited to four hours, and no amendments were allowed. Opponents attacked the bill as a $1 billion tax on consumers and called domestic allotment socialism. The overwhelming sentiment, however, was that Roosevelt should be given authority to deal with the crisis as he saw fit. William Lemke, a Republican congressman from North Dakota, said that normally there were not enough Democrats in his state to fill the postmasterships, but his constituents wanted him to back the president. As the bill moved forward, violence continued in rural areas. On

March 21, Pennsylvania farmers attacked three sheriff's deputies conducting a sale, ripping the uniform off of one of them. The following day, the Agricultural Adjustment Act passed the House, 315–98.[12]

The bill's path through the Senate was rockier. Wallace testified before the Senate Agriculture Committee, which questioned him energetically but then voted for the bill. "The President told the Agricultural Committee that [the new law] would take 10 years off my life," Wallace joked in a letter to Dante Pierce, a newspaper friend back in Iowa. "Tugwell says that's the reason the committee voted it in." Conservative critics continued to attack the bill as socialist and dictatorial. One senator sneered that it was unduly complicated "due to its translation from the Russian." The strongest opposition came from the processors, who were still not resigned to paying the tax. A representative of the Farmers' National Grain Dealers Association told the Senate that the bill was "a futile attempt to legislate prosperity." The government should cut taxes and help farmers secure overseas contracts, he said, but other than that, the people he represented wanted "to be left alone for awhile."[13]

Farm radicals also came out in opposition. John Simpson, president of the National Farmers' Union, took direct aim at domestic allotment. Farmers "are not producing too much," he told the Senate Agriculture Committee. "What we have overproduction of is empty stomachs." Simpson painted a dark picture of where things were headed in the Farm Belt. The Farmers' Holiday Association had "the spirit of 1776," he warned. Its members had "thrown ropes around the necks of attorneys that brought the foreclosure proceedings," he said, "until they begged for mercy and made settlements according to the terms of the farmers." Simpson's impassioned account of militant farmers on the march led the committee chairman to ask, to laughter from the galleries, if there were any signs "that they are moving toward Washington."[14]

Wallace worked around the clock trying to get the bill passed. "We are skating over the thin ice so fast that it doesn't break through," he wrote Dante Pierce. The last major obstacle was the chairman of the Senate Agriculture Committee, Ellison "Cotton Ed" Smith of South Carolina, a man Tugwell described in his diary as "a dodo and filled with big business propaganda."

Smith was aligned with the processors, and he wanted to substitute his own version of the farm bill. When Wallace told Roosevelt that Smith was the holdup, Roosevelt wrote out a statement asking him to let the bill through. Because time was short, Wallace read the statement to Smith over the phone. It made the agriculture chairman "perfectly furious," Wallace later recalled.[15]

While the Senate was considering the farm bill, Roosevelt made an important addition. Wallace's draft had not addressed foreclosures, the issue roiling the Farm Belt. To placate Farm Belt radicals, and members of Congress from farm states, on March 27 Roosevelt issued an executive order creating the Farm Credit Administration. The new agency, which he appointed his old friend Henry Morgenthau to head, would use $1 billion in new bonds to lower the principal on farmers' loans; cap interest rates at 4.5 percent; and postpone mortgage payments for up to fifteen years. The new program would put an end, Roosevelt told Congress, "to the threatened loss of home and productive capacity now faced by hundreds of thousands of American farm families." The plan appealed not only to farmers, but to mortgage lenders, insurance companies, and other holders of farm debt, which were losing hope of ever seeing some of their loans repaid.[16]

Roosevelt also reached out to conservatives with a key personnel choice. On April 5, he asked George Peek to head the Agricultural Adjustment Administration, the agency that would be created by the new law. The appointment of Peek, with his plow-manufacturer background and ties to Bernard Baruch, would help to reassure the processors, and other business interests, that the new agriculture program would not go off in a radical direction. Peek resisted at first, insisting that Baruch would be a better choice, but he soon accepted. Wallace and Tugwell were concerned that Peek, who had never abandoned his support for McNary-Haugenism, would try to use the position to resist domestic allotment. "He may run away with the show since he is older and wealthier than H.A. or I, and since he is close to a crowd of powerful people," Tugwell wrote in his diary, "but we shall have to make out as best we can." Wallace understood Roosevelt's reasons for favoring Peek, and he was willing to hope for the best. "George is difficult in some ways as you know," he wrote to Dante Pierce, "but I believe I can learn how to handle him."[17]

Supporters of cost of production scored a surprising win on April 13, when the Senate yielded to pressure from Western progressives and added it to the bill, by a 47–41 vote. The amendment was Roosevelt's first major congressional loss, and it was a significant one. The administration had made clear that it would not accept a cost of production amendment, which left the Agricultural Adjustment Act in limbo. Wallace had originally hoped the bill would be signed into law within two weeks of its introduction so it could have an impact on the 1933–34 growing season, but that deadline had now come and gone. By the second week of April, South Carolina's farmers had already planted their cotton, Iowans were about to plant corn, and Kansas was sowing spring wheat. With the bill still in limbo, "John Farmer was starting his 1933 crops," *Time* magazine reported, "on the same haphazard plan of the past."[18]

While the Senate wrestled with the agriculture bill, Roosevelt turned to two related issues. He introduced the Home Owners' Loan Act of 1933, which would extend to home mortgages the sort of relief he had just provided for farm mortgages. Homeowners had gotten less attention than farmers, but they were also being squeezed by the gap between what they were able to earn in the Depression economy and what they owed on their mortgages. One thousand urban homes were being foreclosed on every day. The bill would create a Home Owners' Loan Corporation that would refinance home loans at 5 percent interest and lengthen repayment schedules. The government loans would be capped at $20,000, to ensure that benefits were reserved for poor and middle-class homeowners. When he signed the bill, Roosevelt urged lenders to institute a moratorium on foreclosures until the program could get up and running. The new law was a great success. The HOLC would soon hold one-fifth of all urban mortgages.[19]

The second issue, inflation, was forced on Roosevelt. The farm bloc in Congress had long been pushing for an inflationary monetary policy to reduce the burden of farm debt. Farmers were the most outspoken advocates of inflation, but they had powerful allies. Insurance companies, retailers, and other businesses with farm customers stood to gain from a looser money supply, which would leave their customers with more to spend. The Committee for the Nation to Rebuild Prices and Purchasing Power, which counted top executives from Sears, Roebuck among its membership, was an influential pro-inflation force. At the same time, members of the silver lobby, led by senators from silver-producing states, were pushing for inflation for their own reasons. They were calling for free coinage of silver, which would produce inflation and, not incidentally, increase the demand for silver. The pro-silver senators were adamant about their cause. "The nation must adopt bimetallism," Senator Burton K. Wheeler of Montana declared, "or face bolshevism." The farm bill provided a convenient vehicle for them. Wheeler introduced an amendment calling for gold and silver to be coined in unlimited amounts at the ratio William Jennings Bryan had once advocated, sixteen ounces of silver equaling one ounce of gold. Pro-inflation forces in the Senate rallied to the Wheeler Amendment, and it looked like it was on its way to passing.[20]

It was unclear how Roosevelt would respond. He had run in 1932 on the Democratic Party's "sound money" platform, and he had spoken out on the campaign trail against inflation. Now, he was being pulled in two directions. Powerful forces in Congress, and his own Farm Belt supporters, were pushing him to support an inflationary monetary policy. At the same time, fiscal conservatives were pressuring him to hold firm. Bernard Baruch insisted that even modest inflation was "sheer nonsense." It would only benefit one-fifth of the nation, he said: "unemployed, debtor classes—incompetent, unwise people." Lewis Douglas was the most outspoken of all. He argued that inflation would push America in the direction that Germany, where Adolf Hitler had just become chancellor, was headed: "social disorder." Despite Roosevelt's public pronouncements, there had long been signs that he was considering supporting inflation, including his refusal to promise Carter Glass, during Cabinet selection, that he would remain on the gold standard. With Congress increasingly clamoring for some kind of inflationary policy, Roosevelt seemed to have quietly made his mind up. In early April, he wrote to Democratic Party elder statesman Edward M. House, "It is simply inevitable that we must inflate...though my banker friends may be horrified."[21]

If Roosevelt had any doubts about whether to abandon the gold standard and embrace inflation, the Wheeler Amendment forced his hand. Farm Belt senators were threatening to vote against the farm bill if it lacked an inflation provision. Roosevelt's main objection to the Wheeler Amendment was that it was mandatory, which would put Congress, rather than him, in charge of monetary policy. He made clear to the Senate that if the Agricultural Adjustment Act came to him with the amendment, he would not sign it. The administration went to work lobbying individual senators. William Borah of Idaho, who had initially been inclined to support the amendment, committed himself to voting against it and brought others along. When it came to a vote, the Wheeler Amendment got thirty-three votes, up from just eighteen in January. Although the administration won that round, Walter Lippmann reported that at least eleven of the senators who voted no did so "not because they are by conviction opposed to inflation, but because they wish to give the Administration more time to formulate a policy." Senator James Byrnes of South Carolina, a close ally of the administration, warned Moley that the Wheeler Amendment could not be held back much longer. In the end, Moley was convinced, Roosevelt was shaken out of his ambivalence about inflation by a simple "counting of noses in the Senate."[22]

On April 18, Roosevelt gave his answer. At a meeting with Woodin, Douglas, other economic advisers, and congressional leaders, he announced that he was supporting an amendment introduced by Oklahoma senator Elmer Thomas. The Thomas Amendment would give the president broad authority to induce inflation by expanding the currency supply, lowering the gold content of the dollar, or coining silver. When Roosevelt issued his bank holiday proclamation on March 6, which barred the exchange of currency for gold, many people wondered if he had abandoned the gold standard. If it had been unclear then, his decision to back the Thomas Amendment removed all doubt. Roosevelt had also decided to stop issuing gold export licenses, a further step in taking the nation off gold.[23]

When Roosevelt announced that he was abandoning the gold standard,

Moley recalled, "hell broke loose in the room." Lewis Douglas and his fellow anti-inflationists spent two hours trying to get Roosevelt to change his mind. They painted a grim picture of the damage runaway inflation could do, but Roosevelt held firm. After the meeting ended, a morose Douglas declared that going off gold would be "the end of Western civilization." Douglas was on the verge of resigning over the president's "thoroughly vicious bill," as he described it to his father. Instead, he spent a night with Moley and other Roosevelt advisers in Moley's rooms at the Carlton Hotel making changes to the Thomas Amendment. With the revisions, which included a cap of $3 billion on the amount of currency the president could issue, Douglas decided the bill was no longer "thoroughly vicious," merely "pretty discouraging."[24]

Conservatives in the Senate reacted to the Thomas Amendment with outrage. Arthur Vandenberg, Republican of Michigan, declared it to be nothing less than "the most revolutionary proposal that has ever been presented in the history of the government." A tearful Carter Glass begged his colleagues not to take the "immoral" step of going off gold. The pro-inflation forces, however, were unstoppable. "There is no choice any longer between inflation and no inflation," Walter Lippmann wrote. The only choice, he insisted, was "between inflation by statute and inflation by monetary management." Roosevelt was simply taking the more flexible course. The Thomas Amendment passed the Senate and the House by wide margins. With its passage, Roosevelt kept control over monetary policy for himself, and cleared the way for the Agricultural Adjustment Act to move forward.[25]

While Congress deliberated, anger in the Farm Belt boiled over. On April 27, farmers in Le Mars, Iowa, a small town that was developing a reputation for lawlessness, pulled Judge Charles Bradley off the bench while he was hearing foreclosure cases. They carried him out of the courthouse and, when he refused to swear not to sign any more foreclosures, threw him into a farm truck and drove him to the outskirts of town. The mob pulled down his pants and put a noose around his neck. The farmers stopped short of a lynching, content merely to empty a hubcap full of grease on the judge's head and leave him dazed by the side of the road. The mob attack on Judge Bradley—and the fact that several Iowa counties were being placed under martial law—increased the sense of urgency in Washington.[26]

The administration's allies were still working to strip the cost-of-production amendment out of the bill. Senator Joseph T. Robinson, the majority leader, insisted that it was of no practical value, since Wallace had made clear that he would not use the authority, while it would embarrass Roosevelt. After the House voted 283–109 against cost of production, the Senate gave in and rescinded its amendment, and the bill was headed to Roosevelt for his signature. On May 12, at a White House ceremony attended by Wallace, Tugwell, M. L. Wilson, and a crowd of farm leaders, Roosevelt signed the Agricultural Adjustment Act and the Emergency Farm Mortgage Act. The AAA radically changed the economics of American farming, and it also marked an early milestone for the New Deal. It was the Roosevelt administration's first law that committed the government to caring for its destitute citizens. It was "the farmers," declared *The New Republic*, "with their solidarity, their faith in mass action, their courage in the face of violence and arrest, who have supplied us with one of the few hopeful signs in the depression."[27]

Roosevelt considered delivering a fireside chat on the new law. Instead, on May 13, Wallace spoke to a national radio audience about the AAA, which he called "A Declaration of Interdependence." Wallace explained domestic allotment, and how processor taxes would be used to adjust agricultural output downward. He emphasized that farmers, distributors, and processors should not expect to sit back while the government solved their problems. The Department of Agriculture would create the framework, Wallace said, but "these industries must work out their own salvation." The AAA was greeted enthusiastically in the Farm Belt, even by farm radicals, who had given up their insistence that it did not go far enough. As soon as Roosevelt signed it into law, Milo Reno called off a farm strike that had been scheduled for May 13. "We believe in giving the Federal administration an opportunity to redeem pre-election promises to farmers," he declared. Wallace was under no illusions that implementing domestic allotment would be easy. He understood that it ran counter to farmers' natural inclination to grow as much as they could, and he realized that the processors would continue to oppose the law. "I hope that we can start this thing in somewhat the same way in which you start an automobile," Wallace said. "I would like to do it by going into low gear and then intermediate, and then into high, without stalling the engine."[28]

Roosevelt had originally intended for the special session to be brief, with Congress handling only "four or five" emergency pieces of legislation and then adjourning. But the success of his first few efforts put him in a more expansive frame of mind. At a March 17 press conference, his fourth, he told reporters that he had spoken with congressmen over the past few days, and they wanted to stay in session. Roosevelt said he would have to "work twice as hard as I had planned to work" to prepare the legislation necessary to keep the special session going. Two of the bills Roosevelt sent to Congress were pathbreaking measures not directly related to the economic crisis. They represented the sort of progressive reform agenda Roosevelt might have pursued more single-mindedly if he had not taken office in the middle of a deep depression.[29]

The first concerned public power. Its chief champion, George Norris, a progressive Republican senator from Nebraska, had for years been fighting a lonely battle to build a power facility in Muscle Shoals, Alabama. Muscle Shoals was on the Tennessee River, whose fast-churning water made it ideal for generating hydroelectric power. The government had begun building a dam there during the World War to produce electricity for military use, but abandoned it when the war ended. Norris, who had arranged a state take-over of Nebraska's largest power company, had introduced a bill to get the federal government to finish the dam and produce electricity for the region. He argued that public power would be cheaper than the electricity the private power companies were selling and, no less important, it would put the people in charge of a vital public utility. Norris favored regional authorities, so control over public power would not reside in Washington. Hoover and conservative Republicans in Congress, who did not believe the government should be involved in making or distributing electric power, had repeatedly blocked Norris's Muscle Shoals bills.[30]

With Roosevelt's election, public power had a new life. Roosevelt had championed public power since his days in the New York legislature. It was an issue he felt deeply about. "When he talked about the benefits of cheap electricity he did not think in terms of kilowatts," his counsel, Samuel Rosenman, said. "He thought in terms of the hired hand milking by electricity, the farm wife's pump, stove, lights, and sewing machine." As governor, he had established a public power authority, fought to construct hydroelectric plants on the Saint Lawrence River, and battled to keep the rates of private power companies in check. The power companies had attacked his efforts as socialism, but Roosevelt firmly resisted the label. It was wrong to call public power supporters "Bolsheviks or dangerous radicals," he insisted. Roosevelt believed that public power worked on the same principle as the Post Office— that government should undertake activities that it could perform better than anyone else.[31]

In the 1932 election, Roosevelt had campaigned on public power, which helped him appeal to progressive Republicans. In a speech in Portland, he had argued that government-produced electricity could be a "birch rod in the cupboard." If private power companies acted badly or raised their rates excessively, he maintained, communities should be able to punish them by turning to public power instead. In addition to being a "birch rod," Roosevelt believed public power could serve as a "yardstick" to help government regulators learn how much it cost to produce public electricity and therefore how much private companies should be charging.[32]

The location of the Muscle Shoals project gave it a special appeal for Roosevelt. His years of going to Warm Springs for rehabilitation had exposed him to the poverty of the rural South, and had given him an affinity for poor Southerners. The Tennessee Valley region around Muscle Shoals, forty thousand square miles spread out over seven states, was among the poorest in the nation. Its nearly three million residents had an average income that was just 45 percent of the national average. Farming was made difficult by the fact that the region's topsoil was regularly washed away by heavy rainfall. A well-managed series of dams could generate inexpensive power for the people of the Tennessee Valley, and also help farmers by protecting the region's topsoil. Roosevelt also liked the fact that the project promoted interstate cooperation, a cause he had promoted as governor of New York.[33]

In late January 1933, Roosevelt visited Muscle Shoals with a delegation that included Norris. Afterward, he gave a speech from the portico of the state capitol in Montgomery supporting the project in which he said he hoped to move a bill on it through Congress quickly. When Roosevelt told Norris that it should be a happy day for him, Norris responded, with tears in his eyes, "I see my dreams come true." Later, in Warm Springs, Roosevelt expanded on his remarks. The project he was envisioning, he told reporters, would be "probably the widest experiment ever conducted by a government." It would include, he said, low-cost hydroelectricity, flood control, and reforestation, and it would eventually employ 200,000 people.[34]

Roosevelt's sweeping vision for Muscle Shoals, Moley observed, had "out-Norrised Norris." There were plenty of critics, including *The Washington Post*, which insisted it made no sense "in this period of hard times" to "waste still more of the taxpayers' money on this futile project." But Roosevelt was not deterred. In a March 13 letter, he asked Norris to take the lead in drawing up a new Tennessee Valley bill. The most controversial issue it would have to resolve was whether the project should include transmission lines, in addition to dams, which would give the government the ability to deliver electricity directly to consumers, putting it in head-to-head competition with power companies. The power companies were bitterly opposed to government-owned transmission lines, but Roosevelt decided that he wanted them for Muscle Shoals. He had become convinced that publicly owned transmission lines were key to keeping electricity rates reasonable.[35]

On April 10, Roosevelt sent Congress a bill to create the Tennessee Valley Authority. The TVA would, he said, be "a corporation clothed with the power of Government but possessed of the flexibility and initiative of a private enterprise." Roosevelt's goal was to follow the TVA with even bigger projects, which would, as Tugwell noted, "furnish yardstick power on a scale" that energy companies' "worst dreams had never pictured." In Congress, Democrats and progressive Republicans rallied to the bill. So many power executives showed up to oppose it that an extra day of hearings had to be scheduled. "The power companies are willing and want to work with the government toward the development of the valley," the vice president of

Tennessee Electric Power Company told Congress, "but we want to be protected." The biggest sticking point was the transmission lines, but the bill's supporters would not give in. "This is a national resource," Representative John Rankin of Mississippi declared, "and we should build lines to carry electricity to the ultimate consumer."[36]

On May 18, Roosevelt signed the TVA bill into law. The House had balked at including the transmission lines provision, but Roosevelt had held firm. At the signing, Roosevelt turned to Norris and asked, "George, are the transmission lines in here?" When told they were, Roosevelt jokingly asked where the representative of Alabama Power was. The signing was an emotional moment for the seventy-one-year-old Norris, who declared it the culmination of twelve years of struggling "on behalf of the common people against the combined forces of monopoly and human greed."[37]

Roosevelt's second reform initiative was the Securities Act of 1933. Its purpose, like the TVA's, was to use the government's power to rein in corporate excess. The villains this time were not greedy power companies, but dishonest issuers of stock. Stock market malfeasance was not as critical a problem as the farm crisis or mass unemployment, but the symbolism loomed large. The Crash of 1929 was widely regarded as the cause of the Depression, and the public blamed the crash in large part on lax government supervision of the stock market. Roosevelt, who regarded stock fraud as a moral issue as well as an economic one, had made the need for tighter regulation a theme in the 1932 campaign. He promised, in a speech in Columbus, Ohio, to promote "truth telling" in the sale of securities. "Government cannot prevent some individuals from making errors of judgment," he said. "But Government can prevent to a very great degree the fooling of sensible people through misstatements and through the withholding of information." When he took office, a law regulating stock sales was, Moley said, "a 'must' of the first order."[38]

At Roosevelt's direction, Moley had started working on the problem back in December. Busy as he was, Moley had enlisted Samuel Untermyer, a prominent New York securities lawyer, to come up with a bill. Untermyer, an old-line progressive, had been counsel to the House Committee on Banking and Currency, better known as the Pujo Committee, when it held hearings in 1912 into the "money trust," Wall Street financiers who exerted a pernicious influence on the nation's finances. The hearings had generated national headlines and had prompted states to adopt "blue sky" laws, so called because they imposed limits on stock issuers, who were known for trying to sell unsophisticated buyers "everything but the blue sky." During this "money trust" era, Untermyer and his fellow progressives had failed to pass a federal securities law, but now Roosevelt was giving them another chance. In January, Untermyer delivered a draft of his securities bill. Moley could see right away that there were problems with the bill, which made the dubious suggestion that the power to regulate securities should be given to the Post Office.[39]

While Untermyer was drafting his securities bill, Roosevelt asked Commerce Secretary Daniel Roper and Attorney General Homer Cummings to take on the same project. Duplicate assignments of this sort would be a common occurrence during the New Deal. On another occasion, Moley recalled, Roosevelt had asked five people to take on the same project "and was flabbergasted when they all turned up with elaborate reports." In the case of the securities bill, Moley believed the duplication was simply the result of Roosevelt's absentmindedness. But Roosevelt may also have figured that with two bills being drafted, he would get two approaches to the problem, allowing him to choose the one he liked best. When he realized that two securities bills were being produced, Roosevelt did what he generally did in such circumstances—he invited all of the drafters in to meet with him so they could agree on a single draft.[40]

When Roosevelt sat down with Untermyer, Roper, and Cummings it became clear their bills had gone off in different directions. The Untermyer bill took on stock sales in general, and held out for the Post Office as the regulatory body. Roper and Cummings had brought in Huston Thompson, a former chairman of the Federal Trade Commission, to help them with their draft. The Roper-Cummings-Thompson bill was limited to new stock issues, and put the regulatory power in the Federal Trade Commission. At the meeting with Roosevelt, both groups dug in. Roosevelt gave up hope of combining the two approaches, and settled on the Roper-Cummings-Thompson bill. The Roper-Cummings-Thompson bill addressed a far smaller part of the problem than Untermyer's bill. The portion it carved off was also of little immediate consequence, since the Depression had all but ended the issuing of new stocks. In going with the Roper-Cummings-Thompson bill, Roosevelt may have wanted to start out regulating a manageable part of the problem, or he may simply have been acting out of loyalty to his Cabinet members. He insisted, though, that there would be a future bill that covered trades of existing stocks.[41]

Roosevelt sent the Securities Act of 1933, also known as the Truth in Securities Act, to Congress on March 29. His congressional message, which was drafted by Moley, said that while government could not vet every new stock, it could insist that issuers provide full and accurate information to prospective buyers. "This proposal adds to the ancient rule of *caveat emptor*," Roosevelt said, "the further doctrine 'let the seller also beware.'" The bill was initially well received. "The measure is in the main so right in its basic provisions," *The Wall Street Journal* declared that "the country will insist upon its passage." When members of Congress looked closely, however, the bill struck them as riddled with problems. Some provisions seemed too draconian, including one giving buyers the right to return stocks for a full refund if a registration statement was untrue in any material respect. At the same time, *New Republic* columnist John T. Flynn insisted that the bill did too little. "There is hardly a stock abuse which ran wild during the last dozen years which would have been curbed if this bill had been on the statute books," he wrote. In the face of growing resistance in Congress, Sam Rayburn, the chairman of the House Commerce Committee, which had jurisdiction over the bill, urged Moley to come up with a new draft.[42]

Moley asked Felix Frankfurter to take on the project. An old friend of Roosevelt's from the Wilson administration, Frankfurter had turned down the position of solicitor general, but he remained a trusted adviser. "Three of us will arrive at the Carlton Friday morning," Frankfurter wired Moley. "Please reserve room for us." When he showed up, it was in a group of four: himself, James Landis, Benjamin Cohen, and Thomas Corcoran, who was already living in Washington. Landis, a young colleague of Frankfurter's at

Harvard Law School, was an expert on blue sky laws, and a former law clerk to Justice Louis Brandeis whose book *Other People's Money* laid the groundwork for regulating the securities industry. Cohen was a soft-spoken lawyer who had helped Frankfurter fight for minimum wage laws and other progressive causes. William O. Douglas, the New Deal lawyer turned Supreme Court justice, would later call Cohen "the best and most intelligent man in the New Deal." Corcoran—or "Tommy the Cork," as he would soon be known—was working at the Reconstruction Finance Corporation. A former student of Frankfurter's, Corcoran was the most outgoing of the three. The arrival of Frankfurter and his three young draftsmen was a milestone for the New Deal. Landis, Cohen, and Corcoran were among the first Frankfurter protégés to join the administration—a group that would soon acquire its own nickname, Frankfurter's "Little Hot Dogs." Corcoran and Cohen would go on to become a famous New Deal team, Cohen taking the lead in writing some of the era's most important laws and Corcoran in lobbying for them. Moley was impressed with Cohen and Corcoran when he first met them, but he was wary. After getting to know them better, it seemed to him that "they entertained a deep suspicion of bankers, of Wall Street lawyers, and of corporation lawyers in general."[43]

After Frankfurter returned to Harvard, Landis, Cohen, and Corcoran settled into the Carlton Hotel and worked around the clock. By April 8, they had a new draft securities bill. It borrowed from the Roper-Cummings-Thompson draft and from the British Companies Act, which required issuers of securities to file a prospectus in advance. In Britain, a government office merely checked that the prospectus was properly signed and dated. The Cohen-Landis-Corcoran bill was more demanding, requiring that a registration form be filed with the FTC thirty days before the stock was issued and authorizing the commission to block the stock issue if there were misrepresentations or important omissions. On April 10, the Frankfurter group attended a House Commerce Committee meeting. With Roosevelt's help, they convinced Sam Rayburn, the committee chairman, that their draft should be the basis for the new law. Cohen and Landis worked on revisions, clashing often in the process. "Teamwork," Cohen complained to Frankfurter, "is impossible." Landis wanted to give the FTC authority to specify what information stock issuers had to disclose. Cohen, who was more skeptical of Wall Street, wanted the bill to state in detail what was required. The dispute went all the way up to Roosevelt, who sided with Cohen.[44]

On April 21, a final draft was complete. At the insistence of Moley, who had become big business's go-to man in the administration, Rayburn met with a group of corporate lawyers led by John Foster Dulles. Dulles's group had a list of ways they wanted the bill watered down. Rayburn listened politely but did not yield. The committee reported out the Landis-Cohen bill to the full House. Rayburn arranged for debate to be capped at six hours, and for amendments to be limited. He made the first appeal for the bill, arguing that as much as half of the $50 billion in new stocks that had been issued in recent years had turned out to be worthless. The result, he said, had been "tragedy in the lives of thousands of men and women who invested their life savings." The House passed the Landis-Cohen bill on a voice vote on May 5. "Rayburn did not know," Landis later said, "whether the bill passed so readily because it was so damned good or so damned incomprehensible." On May 8, the Senate passed its own version of the bill. Rayburn presided over the conference committee that was charged with reconciling the two bills. He used his position to ensure that the House version won out.[45]

On May 27, Roosevelt signed the Securities Act of 1933. Selling securities "is really traffic in the economic and social welfare of our people," he declared, which "demands the utmost good faith and fair dealing." The new law was a victory for the administration's Brandeisians, who insisted that big business had to be closely regulated to ensure that it did not trample on the public. The act, which marked the federal government's first intervention into the stock market, alarmed Wall Street. *Time* magazine lamented that corporate lawyers had been outsmarted by Frankfurter, and worried that "the so-called Securities Act had made it practically impossible for any corporation to raise any new capital." While *Time* was sounding the alarm for capitalism, reformers were complaining that the bill did not go far enough. It did nothing to regulate the sale of existing stocks, nor did it require the government to evaluate the quality of new issues, as long as all of the required information was provided. In a *Fortune* article, Frankfurter declared the new law "a modest first installment of legislative controls," and insisted that more remained to be done.[46]

It had taken two months, not the two weeks Wallace had hoped, to get the Agricultural Adjustment Act through Congress. As a result, the planting season was well under way when Wallace embarked on what Mordecai Ezekiel called "the greatest single experiment in economic planning under capitalist conditions ever attempted by a democracy in times of peace." Suddenly, the Department of Agriculture was the white-hot center of the New Deal. "From early morn until midnight and often later," Wallace would later say, dairymen, cotton growers, wheat growers, and cling peach producers showed up looking for ways "to make the new machinery whir into action in their behalf." Presiding over the frenetic scene was Wallace himself, easily the most energetic person in the building. He woke at five a.m. and walked three miles to the department offices, where he invariably worked late into the night.[47]

When Peek arrived to head up the Agricultural Adjustment Administration, he was still a committed McNary-Haugenite. "He plowed just one furrow...and plowed it straight," Russell Lord observed. The day the Agricultural Adjustment Act passed, he had asked Wallace to give him the powers the new law gave to the secretary of agriculture. Wallace turned him down, after checking with Roosevelt, but realized that the request was not an auspicious start to their working relationship. Peek also told Wallace that he wanted to use his position to dump surplus crops overseas, and Wallace said no to that as well. Wallace tried to persuade Peek to give up on McNary-Haugenism. He asked M. L. Wilson, who had become chief of the Wheat Division, to sit down with Peek and make a pitch for domestic allotment. Wilson returned from an hours-long meeting admitting defeat. "Did you ever try to corner an ornery old sow in a fence-corner?" Wilson asked Wallace. "First you whack her on the left side of her head, and she turns; then you whack her on the right side; then zip! She's gone, right between your legs!" That, Wilson said, was how it had gone with Peek.[48]

Peek had a strong following within the department. "This is the man who ought to be Secretary," they would say as the hard-charging Peek arrived for a meeting, "and there," they would say, nodding toward the rumpled, soft-spoken Wallace, "is the man who is." The department broke into warring camps. On one side of the divide were Peek and his coadministrator, Charles J. Brand, who had played a large role in drafting the original McNary-Haugen bill. Heading up the other side was Jerome Frank, the University of Chicago Law School graduate Wallace had appointed to be counsel for the AAA. Frank was another protégé of Felix Frankfurter, who called him a "lawyer who watches the breadlines more closely than the price-quotations." Frank, in turn, brought in other so-called "urban liberals," including Adlai Stevenson, Abe Fortas, and Alger Hiss. Peek refused to rely on Frank for legal matters, and instead used his own salary to hire Frederic Lee, the drafter of the AAA, to be his private counsel. Peek insisted that Frank and his young, well-educated hires knew little about farming. They were socialists, Peek said, who wanted to change the AAA "from a device to aid the farmers into a device to introduce the collectivist system of agriculture into this country." Frank was just as critical of Peek, whom he regarded as right-wing, behind the times, and inflexible, and Brand, whom he dismissed as "a man of limited ability."[49]

Wallace's first order of business was getting the domestic allotment program started for wheat, which would be planted in the fall. In late May, he invited wheat farmers, processors, and consumers to a conference at the Department of Agriculture to discuss how to proceed. "We had no carefully prepared plan, but we knew that we had in that room all the elements necessary for one," Wallace said. The groups put their usual differences aside and agreed on how to proceed. By mid-June, half a million wheat producers had signed up. Wallace, with his spiritual connection to plant life, remained uneasy about taking farmland out of production and, even more so, about destroying crops. He was fortunate, however, in the case of wheat. With the

1933 crop already planted, it at first seemed inevitable that some of it would have to be plowed under before the summer harvest. As it turned out, the crop was hit by a severe drought, and there would not be any surpluses. "Our press section breathed a sign of relief," Wallace recalled, because "it would not be necessary to write about the logic of plowing under wheat while millions lacked bread."[50]

Wallace turned to cotton next. One-third of the nation's farm population relied on cotton for their survival. But the price had fallen to under five cents a pound and surpluses had reached 26 million bales. Farm leaders had come to Washington to tell Wallace that the South would not survive another season of five-cent cotton. The weather forecasts were good, suggesting that there might well be another bumper crop like the 17-million-bale harvest of 1931, and continued low prices. When the Agricultural Adjustment Act became law, half of the cotton crop had already been planted. The skeptics said American farmers, who were known for their stubborn individualism, would never be convinced to act collectively, but Wallace proved them wrong. He sent 22,000 workers out to 955 counties to sign up cotton farmers, and he agreed to pay over $100 million to plow under 10 million acres, or one-quarter of the 1933 cotton crop. When someone suggested that photographers should be discouraged from taking pictures of the plow-down, to avoid bad publicity, Wallace would not go along. "We must clear the wreckage before we can build," he insisted. "Rub their noses in the facts."[51]

After years of talking about paying farmers to grow less, Wallace was finally doing it, with an energy that left observers in awe. "The agricultural wing is performing its prodigious task with more thoroughness and intelligence than…any other department," journalist John Franklin Carter declared. That summer, Department of Agriculture employees worked around the clock in a room that took up half a city block, sending out as many as eighty thousand checks a day to participating farmers. A Russian visitor to the department exclaimed, Wallace recalled, "Good Lord! This is a revolution!"[52]

CHAPTER SIX

" 'Social Justice' ... Has Been the Maxim of Her Life"

Frances Perkins woke up at the Willard Hotel on Monday, March 6, ready to start work. The previous day, the Sunday after the inauguration, she had hosted a reception at the hotel for visiting New Yorkers. When she had not been greeting old friends, she had been wading through congratulatory letters and invitations and dictating responses to her longtime secretary, Frances Jurkowitz. Perkins had expected that someone would contact her to tell her what to do, or even how to get to the Department of Labor, but no one had. So she looked up the telephone number and called the department, where she reached the outgoing labor secretary, William Doak, in her office. "You know I've been sworn in, don't you?" she asked. Doak said he did, but that he had not been sure she intended to stay around Washington. Perkins told him that she was staying, and that she would be arriving shortly.[1]

Perkins found her way to the Department of Labor, which was located in a ramshackle former apartment building on G Street, wedged between a rooming house and a garage. From the outside, it seemed to her like "not a very suitable building." When she got inside, it looked worse. The offices were in suites of rooms laid out like apartments. The secretary's outer office was filled with hard, uncomfortable chairs, ashtrays overflowing with cigarette butts, and piles of crumpled papers that had been half-heartedly thrown in the direction of wastepaper baskets. The men hanging around matched the décor. They were, it appeared to Perkins, "typical politicians who were busy on the telephone all the time about nothing in particular."[2]

Perkins was ushered into the secretary's office, whose chief features were an unattractive portrait of Doak, a beaten-up desk, and a spittoon. Doak, a railroad yardman turned railroad union official, explained that the men in the outer office were "the boys from the labor unions" who hung out there all of the time. Perkins found Doak's knowledge of the department limited, and his views on labor issues disturbing. There was a lot of talk about public works, Doak told her, but it was a bad idea. "It'll cost a lot of money and wreck the treasury," he said. What interested him was immigration, especially illegal immigration. Pursuing illegal immigrants was, Perkins concluded, "the only thing anybody could think to do around the Department of Labor."[3]

Doak had not made any effort to pack up. He "just thought you wouldn't come for a while and things would go on as usual," his assistant secretary, Robe Carl White, explained. Perkins told Doak that she would have his assistant begin putting his things in boxes. His driver could take him to lunch, she said, but afterward he would report to her. When Perkins opened a drawer in her new desk, she discovered that the office was infested with larger cockroaches than she had ever encountered. The next time Miss Jurkowitz went to New York, Perkins asked her to buy J-O Paste, a potent insecticide. "They often talk about a new broom coming in and cleaning house when a new administration comes in," Perkins said. "We actually had to sweep, clean and get rid of cockroaches before we could do much of any important work."[4]

The Labor Department required a lot more cleaning up. It was a sinkhole of corruption and cronyism, perhaps the worst in the whole federal government—a "happy hunting-ground," as one contemporary account put it, "for superannuated labor union officials and the headquarters of some of the dirtiest deals in the history of the United States." The department's fetid reputation reached as far as New York. Before Perkins left for Washington, a New York City police lieutenant had warned her about the "awful strange mess" she would find on her arrival. In the first days of the administration, while Roosevelt was consumed with the banking crisis, Perkins had to focus on rooting out corruption.[5]

The center of the "awful strange mess" in the department was Section 24, the special immigration unit. It took its name from the section of the Immigration Act of 1917 that made it illegal for employers to bring in foreign workers to do contract labor. Section 24 was run by Murray and Henry Garsson. The Garsson brothers presided over a team of agents that they dispatched to locate and deport illegal immigrants, particularly alleged Communists. Section 24 agents regularly overstepped their legal authority. In one notorious case, they raided homes in Detroit and imprisoned more than six hundred immigrants on charges of being in the country illegally. Only two of the immigrants turned out to be legitimately subject to deportation. Section 24 agents were as corrupt as they were lawless. When they raided homes, workplaces, and social halls, they regularly shook down the immigrants they found for bribes, threatening them with deportation if they did not pay up.[6]

Section 24's misconduct was well known, but no one had been willing to take the unit on. Its agents had been allowed to operate by their own rules, traveling the country on expense accounts and handling their cases with almost no supervision. Doak had steered clear of Section 24, Assistant Secretary White explained to Perkins, because the Garsson brothers "have something on him." Rather than try to rein in Section 24, Doak had entrenched it further by recommending to Hoover that its agents get civil service protection. But Section 24 had a major vulnerability, White told Perkins. It had spent virtually all of the $200,000 that Congress had appropriated for it. If the unit did not get new funding, it could be eliminated. White warned Perkins, though, that if she intended to take the Garssons on she should act quickly "because they'll plant something on you."[7]

Perkins called Murray Garsson in and confronted him with what she had heard about the unit. When he was unable to defend his unit, she decided to put an end to it right away. She met with Roosevelt and told him she did not intend to renew the unit's funding. He told her she was "lucky" to have "thought of that way of doing it." Perkins mentioned that there could be agents in the unit with ties to powerful Democrats in Congress, but Roosevelt told her not to worry. "Anybody who works in that kind of an outfit ought not to be protected, no matter who he is," he said.[8]

On March 8—the day Douglas was presenting Roosevelt with a final draft of the Economy Act, and Wallace and Tugwell were meeting at the White house to propose a farm bill—Perkins asked Murray Garsson for his resignation. She terminated Section 24 and ordered that its work be returned to immigration officials at the state level. The next day, Perkins returned to the department after dinner. When she arrived, she heard voices. An elderly security guard told her that Garsson was on the fourth floor. Perkins found him and the other members of Section 24 rifling through files. She asked Garsson why he was still in the building, since he no longer worked there. He insisted he had come back to retrieve personal correspondence, but the files he was rummaging through looked like immigration files. Perkins could not tell if the Garssons were looking for files that were incriminating to them, or information that could be used to blackmail others, but she told them to leave at once and take nothing. She took Murray Garsson's key, locked the file room, and sent for an extra guard to watch over it. The next day, she had the locks changed.[9]

Perkins quickly fell into a grueling work schedule, arriving at the office at nine a.m., eating lunch at her desk, and returning after dinner to work until midnight. In her first days at the department, she was inundated with a steady stream of family, old acquaintances, and favor-seekers. While greeting this wave of visitors, Perkins accidentally snubbed a powerful senator, Pat Harrison of Mississippi, the incoming chairman of the Finance Committee, who stopped by without an appointment. Doak's secretary had not bothered asking who he was. After waiting briefly, Harrison stormed off. Perkins managed to catch him at the elevators to apologize, but word quickly spread on Capitol Hill that he had not been received properly. Perkins would later say that she learned two things from the encounter: that it was important to have competent staff and "that no Senator can even comprehend that there is anybody in the world who doesn't know him."[10]

If Perkins was still confused by Washington, the feeling was mutual. The capital, particularly its press corps, did not know what to make of a woman Cabinet member. Profiles invariably focused on Perkins's physical appearance, which made her uncomfortable. *Time* magazine was struck by her "dark and brilliant" eyes and "shapely white hands that flutter expressively as she talks," but seemed taken aback that she used "no powder, no rouge, no perfume" and dressed "mostly in severe blacks and dark browns." A popular newspaper column, "The Once Over," informed its readers that Perkins's appointment would "keep profanity down to a minimum at Cabinet meetings." Other press accounts simply ignored her gender. The *Chicago Tribune* used the headline "LEADERS LIST 8 MEN LIKELY TO GET POSTS" to report the imminent appointment of seven men and Perkins."[11]

To those who knew Perkins the attention to her sex was misplaced. It was her background and personal qualities, more than anything else, that made her selection significant. Roosevelt had taken a department that had been the preserve of corrupt labor insiders and handed it to one of the nation's leading advocates for working people. Perkins had spent a lifetime fighting for factory safety, workmen's compensation, minimum wages and maximum hours laws, and relief and public work. Her successes in New York, where she had been Roosevelt's industrial commissioner, had helped make the state a model for other states. Now, she had arrived in the president's Cabinet at an ideal moment to bring these fights to the national level.

After her first few days of cleaning up the Department of Labor, Perkins was ready to take on bigger issues. When she met with Roosevelt about closing down Section 24, she had also pressed him to put in place "some kind of quick relief program." Perkins had brought it up, she later said, because the unemployment situation was grave and "there was no one else to help him with it." Roosevelt was interested in establishing a system of relief, as he had done when he was governor, but he had no plans for getting it done. "Go ahead and get together everything you can," he told her. "Keep your eye on this and try and help develop something." From that first meeting, Perkins would be the driving force within the administration for relief. That would come as no surprise to people who had followed her career. It was inconceivable that she would "confine her activities to routine departmental affairs," *The New York Times* observed at the time of her appointment. " 'Social justice' is more than a shibboleth with her; it has been the maxim of her life."[12]

Fannie Coralie Perkins was born in Boston on April 10, 1880. She was descended through both parents from old New England families. Her most famous ancestor was the American patriot James Otis, the author of the 1764 tract *The Rights of the British Colonies Asserted and Proved.* The Perkins family had farmed in Maine since colonial times, and they had long manufactured brick in the coastal town of Newcastle. Maps still designated the site of the ancestral home and the family brickworks as "Perkins Point."[13]

Perkins's parents were Congregationalists, steeped in the Yankee virtues of simple living, hard work, and thrift. She would carry the family's ways into adulthood—the Maine accent, with a vague upper-class intonation, and the plain, dark clothing she had seen while growing up. Perkins's unmistakable New England manner would not stop political opponents, later in her life, from questioning her lineage. Clare Hoffman, a Republican congressman from Michigan, attacked her as "the wife of someone, though God alone knows what her true name may be, and no man yet has published the place of her birth." The DAR would launch an investigation, at the height of the New Deal, into whether Perkins was actually a Russian Jew. Perkins produced the prominent doctor who had delivered her, while insisting "I know that I am I." She further infuriated the DAR by declaring that had she been Jewish, she would have been proud of it.[14]

Perkins's father, Frederick, left Maine for Boston to study accounting, and ended up in Worcester, running a stationery store. In the summers, the family vacationed on the family farm in Maine, where Perkins came under the tutelage of her father's mother. Cynthia Otis Perkins was an unsentimental woman whose stolid life lessons included, "If you walk through a room and there are bodies on the floor, just keep walking." The advice that Perkins quoted most often was "if anybody opens a door, one should always go through. Opportunity comes that way."[15]

The Perkins family had enough money to employ an Irish maid and cook, and to move into successively nicer homes. In his spare time, Perkins's father studied law and read poetry and drama in the original Greek. Perkins grew up sharing her father's interest in the classics. She had less in common with her mother, a large and exuberant woman who sketched and hand-painted china. Susan Perkins guided the less intellectual aspects of her daughter's development. When Perkins was twelve, her mother took her to Lamson & Hubbard, Boston's leading milliner, and bought her a tricorn, which would become her trademark. "There, my dear, that is your hat," her mother declared. "Never let yourself get a hat that is narrower than your cheekbones, because it makes you look ridiculous."[16]

Perkins graduated from Worcester Classical High School, a private academy that sent many of its male students on to Harvard. In 1898, a time when few women attended college, she enrolled at Mount Holyoke, which had started out as a female seminary. Mary Lyon, the school's founder, tried to instill in her students a drive to improve the world, and many became missionaries or social workers. Perkins majored in chemistry and physics. Later in life, after years of touring factories and poring over technical reports, she would tell the *Alumnae Quarterly* that she had made the right choice. Science courses "temper the human spirit, harden and refine it, make it a tool with which one may tackle any kind of material," she said. The course that changed her life, though, was Elements of Political Economy. Professor Annah May Soule sent her students into the local mills and had them write a report on the lives of the workers. Perkins had been brought up to believe that people were poor because of some kind of moral failing. Soule's class made her realize that people could fall into poverty due to harsh circumstances and not simply, as her parents believed was generally the case, because they were lazy or drank too much.[17]

In Perkins's senior year, Florence Kelley, the head of the National Consumers' League, came to campus to speak. Kelley, the daughter of a Pennsylvania congressman, had worked in Illinois as a special investigator of child labor conditions. The Consumers' League fought against sweatshops and in favor of minimum wage and maximum hours laws. Perkins, who helped organize a school chapter of the National Consumers' League, would later say that meeting Kelley was what convinced her to dedicate her life to social reform.[18]

"Perky," who was elected president of the senior class, graduated in 1902. She was offered a job as a factory chemist but her father would not let her take it. The one field he would let her enter was teaching, and in 1904 she accepted a position at the exclusive Ferry Hall School in Lake Forest, Illinois. She taught physics and biology and began educating herself about poverty, reading books like Jacob Riis's *How the Other Half Lives*. Her new life took her far from her parents' world. If her father had read Riis's study of New York City tenement life, she was convinced, his reaction would simply have been, "Oh well, that's New York." Perkins found herself "deeply moved" by Riis's stark black-and-white photographs, and "sure something was wrong."[19]

In her time teaching at Ferry Hall, Perkins began reinventing herself. She replaced her girlish given names, Fannie Coralie, with the more sober Frances. She also joined the Episcopal Church, which was more upper-class, and had more elaborate rituals, than the austere Congregationalism of her parents. Perkins also threw herself into the lives of the poor. She spent her 1905 Christmas vacation at Chicago Commons, a settlement house in Chicago's impoverished seventeenth ward. "I never got so many ideas in my life as I did in those three weeks," she wrote to friends. She spent weekends and vacations there and at Hull House, Jane Addams's legendary settlement house, which served immigrants of many nationalities out of a run-down mansion on Chicago's Near West Side. Hull House looked like an ordinary charity mission. Addams's goal, though, was not merely to hand out relief, but to take on the root causes of urban poverty.[20]

Perkins was drawn into Hull House's vibrant intellectual community. It was, a history of the settlement house movement noted, "a place where one might meet a distinguished visitor, a statesman, writer or scholar from almost anywhere in the world," and one where university graduates could "meet other young men and women just getting started on careers in writing or business, or city planning." The thinkers who passed through helped open the nation's eyes to the immigrant poor. Robert Hunter, the social reformer who wrote the classic 1904 book *Poverty,* was inspired by several years of living at Hull House. Henry Demarest Lloyd, a prominent muckraking journalist who lectured at Hull House, called it "the best club in Chicago."[21]

In an era in which government provided little in the way of social services, Hull House delivered food and provided visiting nurses to needy families. It ran an employment bureau and housed the Jane Club, a cooperative residence for working women. Addams also believed in filling the educational and cultural voids of working-class life. Hull House ran a library and offered classes in music and lectures on Shakespeare. It established Chicago's first playground, and prodded the city to open municipal playgrounds. Addams and her colleagues lobbied for the poor in the state legislature. Since Hull House's neighborhood was full of sweatshops in which children worked up to sixteen hours a day, child labor was a particular priority. Advocates from Hull House played a major role in the passage of the Illinois Factory Act of 1893, which put restrictions on the use of child labor and mandated regular factory inspections.[22]

Perkins's assignments at Hull House brought her into contact with desperate poverty for the first time. She went out with nurses on visits to squalid homes full of sick children and drunken husbands. She also helped neighborhood residents extract their paychecks from sweatshops, which often refused to pay their workers. One day, after helping put on a show for the neighborhood, she wondered aloud how more systemic change could be brought about. "Is this going to go on forever," she asked a colleague, "these people being so poor that we have to give out free milk,…free nursing services, the babies die, [and] there's nothing to do on a Sunday afternoon but get drunk?" The young man replied that the only answer was organizing people into trade unions. Perkins had never given much thought to unions, which she had considered "an evil to be avoided," but she found herself wondering if they were the answer.[23]

Perkins would soon be exposed more directly to labor unions. Most of Chicago's unskilled workers, especially in the needle trades, were not organized. Nonunion workers were often made to work twelve-hour days and longer, and wages were low. Perkins was assigned to help Gertrude Barnum, a prominent organizer from the Women's Trade Union League who was focusing on "bundle women," sweatshop workers who carried home bundles of unfinished garments so they could continue to sew at night. Perkins helped round up women to hear Barnum's pitch, which gave her many opportunities to hear it herself. "I was quite unprepared for the things that she said and for the very emotional drive that she made," she would later say. Perkins was also struck by how hard it was to organize poor workers. The audience was "pretty well worn down," she said, and they "didn't have much energy left."[24]

By now, Perkins was ready to leave teaching behind. She found a job, through a college friend, with the Philadelphia Research and Protective Association. The fledgling group worked with Philadelphia's poor and, in keeping with the Progressive Era ethic, did social science research that could be used to promote reform. One of the association's projects was meeting women who arrived in the city by boat, especially black women from the rural South, before they could be lured into prostitution. The group rescued these women from the pimps who gathered by the docks, and it worked to close down the unscrupulous "employment offices" and rooming houses that were in on the racket. Perkins had found her calling. "Don't worry about me," she wrote to her mother, "because while I realize that I'm not so well off financially as I would have been in teaching, I'm much happier and am really on the track of work that will amount to something in the end."[25]

The job exposed Perkins to the extremes of Philadelphia society. She solicited contributions from the city's old-money elite, visiting town houses that had, as she said, "marble steps that a maid wiped off every morning." She also went into squalid slums, notebook in hand. "Ten cent lodging houses, employment agencies, the offices of the Philadelphia political 'gang' and the two police courts all became my haunts," she told her Mount Holyoke classmates. Late one night, Perkins was followed home by two owners of an employment office she was trying to close. She shouted the name of one of the men while defending herself with an umbrella. When people stuck their heads out of windows to see what the commotion was about, the men fled. The Research and Protective Association succeeded in closing down the employment office, and achieved larger reforms. The city shut down several other offices, and the police started meeting every boat that discharged new arrivals to ensure that the women were not taken advantage of.[26]

While she was living in Philadelphia, Perkins went back to school. She studied at the University of Pennsylvania with Simon Nelson Patten, a renowned economist. Patten disagreed with pessimists like Thomas Malthus, who argued that resources were scarce and man's future was bleak. Patten believed the modern economy produced enough wealth for everyone as long as it was properly managed and distributed. He was an early exponent of the idea that economies are driven by consumption, and that spending was what kept the economy strong. One article he wrote had the title "Extravagance as a Virtue." Patten advocated social welfare programs for those in need. He was also an early supporter of the emerging field of social work, which he regarded as "a new kind of charity...not to undermine energy and productive ability or to create a parasitic class, but to distribute the surplus in ways that will promote general welfare." He saw promise in Perkins and helped secure her a fellowship to pursue a master's degree at Columbia.[27]

When she arrived in New York, Perkins moved into Hartley House, a settlement house in Hell's Kitchen, a gritty neighborhood on Manhattan's West Side. While taking classes at Columbia, she worked as an investigator on a study of poor children in the neighborhood. The homes she visited were as bad as any she had seen in Chicago or Philadelphia. Before long, she moved to Greenwich House, a settlement house in Greenwich Village that had been founded by the reformer Mary Kingsbury Simkhovitch. In these prewar years, the Village was a center of bohemianism. Literary radicals were launching *The Masses*, a journal that promoted women's suffrage, free love, and workers' rights. Mabel Dodge was setting up her famous salon on lower Fifth Avenue. Greenwich House itself resembled a literary salon, with intellectuals like the philosopher John Dewey regularly stopping by to dine and lecture.[28]

After receiving her master's degree from Columbia in 1910, Perkins went to work for the New York City Consumers' League, the local affiliate of Florence Kelley's national organization. When Perkins joined, the league was coming off a major legal triumph. Kelley had persuaded Louis Brandeis, the Boston lawyer and future Supreme Court justice, to write his famous "Brandeis brief," which provided the sociological data the Supreme Court relied on in the 1908 case of *Muller v. Oregon*, which upheld a maximum hours law for women. In addition to litigating, the league lobbied and used the buying power of its well-off members to promote safer consumer products and better conditions for the workers who made them. The Consumers' League was an auspicious place for Perkins to land. "There were some," *The New York Times* would later observe, "who said that the entire New Deal relief program was nothing more than an expanded version of the Consumers' League platform."[29]

Perkins had arrived in New York at a tumultuous time for the labor movement. In the fall of 1909, more than twenty thousand workers who made shirtwaists, or women's blouses, had walked out of nearly five hundred factories. The Shirtwaist Strike of 1909 protested $6-a-week wages, workdays that stretched from seven a.m. to eight p.m., and tyrannical and unsafe factory conditions. The strikers, mainly young immigrant Jewish women, took to the streets with pro-union banners and yelled "scab" at anyone who walked by to take their place at the sewing machine. The police responded brutally. Perkins was shocked to see photos in the newspaper of young women whose faces had been bloodied by police nightsticks.[30]

Perkins had supported unions since her Hull House days, but she did not see them as the answer. "I'd much rather get a law than organize a union," she insisted. Like many middle- and upper-class reformers, Perkins believed the reach of unions was too limited. A union contract only regulated working conditions for the workers covered by it, while a workers' rights law protected everyone. Perkins also thought unions cared only for their own members, which was largely true at the time. Samuel Gompers, the American Federation of Labor's president, insisted that all improvements for workers had to come by union-negotiated contracts. If they were won by legislation, he believed, workers would not feel the need to join unions. Following his lead, unions opposed minimum wage, maximum hour, and workmen's compensation laws. Perkins saw this opposition firsthand when she tried to rally labor support for the Consumers' League's legislative agenda. When she and a colleague spoke to a labor meeting in upper Manhattan seeking support for a bill to reform workmen's compensation, the audience was "as near ugly to us as I ever met," she said. It was clear to her that the men did not care about injuries to workers who were not union members.[31]

Perkins spent much of her time lobbying the legislature. In January 1911, she headed to Albany with a legislative wish list that included child labor bills, a compulsory education bill, and a bill to require department stores to let women sales clerks sit down at work. The Consumers' League's highest priority was a fifty-four-hour bill, which would cap the workweek for women at fifty-four hours. A few years earlier, the Supreme Court had struck down maximum hours laws for men as an intrusion on freedom of contract, but in *Muller v. Oregon*, which invoked the special health needs of women, it had cleared the way for laws like the fifty-four-hour bill. The league had been trying for several years to get the bill passed, but Perkins brought a new energy to the cause. She spoke to legislators about the abuse women workers were subjected to and brought along pictures taken by the noted photographer Lewis Hine. The state legislature was not friendly territory for reformers, and Perkins and her fellow lobbyists had another disadvantage: many were women, and represented groups with heavily female memberships, at a time when women did not have the vote. "So the approach was 'please help,' not 'we demand,' " Perkins later said.[32]

Perkins recruited unexpected allies, notably Tammany Hall, the city's Democratic political machine. Upper-class Protestant reformers generally disdained immigrant-dominated political machines, but Perkins had gotten to know the local Tammany leader while living in Hell's Kitchen, and she had found that she could work with him. After the Democrats swept the 1910 elections, Tammany leader Charles F. Murphy installed Al Smith as Assembly majority leader and Robert F. Wagner as Senate majority leader. Smith and Wagner were Tammany members "in harness," as one civic leader put it, who could be counted on to back Murphy on patronage and other issues the machine cared about. But the two men, who grew up in New York City immigrant families, had great sympathy for the poor, and Tammany Hall had no objection to their acting on it. When Perkins approached Smith about the fifty-four-hour bill, he pledged his support. At the same time, he warned her that factory owners would fight hard to block it.[33]

On March 25, 1911, Perkins witnessed a catastrophe that would stay with her the rest of her life. She was having tea at a friend's town house on Washington Square when the butler announced that there was a fire. Perkins followed the sirens to the nearby Asch Building, whose top floors were being engulfed by flames. Workers from the Triangle Shirtwaist Company, most of them young immigrant women, were standing on the ledges, trying to escape. Firemen had arrived, but their ladders were too short. They scrambled to put up nets while shouting at the women not to jump. When they could not stand the heat, or when the flames reached them, many of the workers did jump. Others fell to the ground when they lost their balance or their grips gave out. "Never shall I forget," Perkins would later say, "that cold, sinking feeling at the pit of my stomach as I watched those girls clinging to life on the window ledges until, their clothing in flames, they leaped to their death." The fire was extinguished in less than half an hour, but in that time 146 people died.[34]

When word spread that the bosses had locked the factory doors—to keep the employees from stealing, it turned out—the city's sorrow turned to anger. On April 2, a mass memorial service was held at the Metropolitan Opera House, which was jammed to the rafters. The speakers included some of the city's most distinguished religious leaders, but Perkins, like much of the audience, was most moved by Rose Schneiderman, a short, red-haired union activist who had been trying to organize the workers. "I would be a traitor to those poor burned bodies if I came here to talk good fellowship," Schneiderman told the spellbound crowd. The only way working people could save themselves, she declared, was with "a strong working-class movement."[35]

The Triangle Shirtwaist Fire "was a torch that lighted up the whole industrial scene," Perkins would later say. Responding to the anguished cries for reform, the city's business and social elite established a Committee on Safety to look into factory working conditions and recommend appropriate health and safety standards. The governor and the state legislature created a second body, the Factory Investigating Commission, with Robert F. Wagner as chairman and Al Smith as vice chairman. Its mandate was to investigate unsafe factory conditions of all kinds across the state.[36]

Perkins suddenly found herself in great demand. In her year at the Consumers' League, she had become a leading expert on factory safety. She had investigated a wide array of workplace hazards, including textile machines that caught women workers' hair and scalped them and mangles that crushed laundresses' arms. She had also investigated two previous industrial fires. In keeping with the Consumers' League's mission, Perkins had also looked into conditions that endangered customers. In one investigation, she identified unsanitary conditions in one hundred bakeshops, declaring that she had seen "white pastry materials so black from the drippings of water from above that I mistook the mixture for chocolate." After the Triangle fire, elected officials and reporters called Perkins for advice on how to prevent another such tragedy. She made enemies in fire departments and city halls when she said that there were hundreds of factories across the state at risk of an equally deadly fire. She worked closely with both the Committee on Safety and the Factory Investigating Commission, sharing what she had learned in her work for the Consumers' League.[37]

The surge in sympathy for workers after the Triangle fire gave new life to the fifty-four-hour bill. In the legislative session that began in January 1912, it seemed to be on the brink of passing. The bill had the support of most Democrats, including the Tammany Hall bloc, and many Republicans, who now wanted to be seen standing up for working people. The biggest remaining obstacle was the powerful cannery industry. The canners were insisting on an exemption, arguing that their work was seasonal and had to be done around the clock to avoid spoilage. They were threatening to block the bill if it covered them. Perkins was convinced the Consumers' League leadership would oppose a bill that excluded canneries. Perkins, however, was more pragmatic than most of the idealistic reformers she worked with—one friend called her "a half-loaf girl: take what you can get now and try for more later." She decided to back the compromise. "This is my responsibility," she told a colleague. "I'll do it and hang for it if necessary." The fifty-four-hour bill with the cannery exemption passed. Perkins feared she would be fired when she got back to the city. After taking a midnight train and staying up all night, she reported to the Consumers' League, where Kelley embraced her warmly and congratulated her for getting 400,000 women workers covered. A year later, the cannery exemption was removed.[38]

One legislator who did not come through for Perkins was Franklin Delano Roosevelt, who had just been elected to the State Senate. They had met before, at a dance in Manhattan's Gramercy Park neighborhood, and their paths had crossed at other parties. Perkins was struck by his "unfortunate habit—so natural that he was unaware of it—of throwing his head up." That gesture, "combined with his pince-nez and great height, gave him the appearance of looking down his nose at most people," she later recalled. Roosevelt was making a name for himself as a reformer. He had led a campaign that succeeded in blocking Tammany Hall's choice for United States senator, a position that, before the Seventeenth Amendment, was still filled by the state legislature. But when Perkins asked Roosevelt to support the fifty-four-hour bill, he refused. His priorities, he made clear, were reform and the environment. Although he ended up voting for the fifty-four-hour bill, he did not endorse it publicly or try to win over his colleagues, even though it desperately needed help. Perkins never forgot Roosevelt's disappointing stance. "I took it hard that a young man who had so much spirit," she wrote in her memoir *The Roosevelt I Knew*, did not support a bill that "was a measure of the progressive convictions of the politicians" of that era.[39]

In May, Perkins left the Consumers' League to become executive secretary of the Committee on Safety, which gave her a more prominent platform for promoting safe working conditions. She campaigned against hazards like flammable dust and inadequate fire stairways and promoted "measured occupancy." There should be no more workers on a factory floor, she insisted, than could be evacuated in three minutes. Perkins did not limit herself to factories. She led an investigation of unsafe living conditions that identified forty-one loft buildings in one neighborhood, housing more than twenty thousand people, that had the same sort of unsafe conditions as the Asch Building.[40]

While working for the Committee on Safety, Perkins also lent her expertise to the Factory Investigating Commission. She organized factory tours for the commissioners, so they could see firsthand how workers in the state were being put in danger. When a Republican commissioner claimed that no children were employed in New York factories, Perkins took Wagner, Smith, and the rest of the commission on a surprise visit to a cannery, where they could see workers as young as five years old snipping beans and shelling peas. On another factory visit, Perkins had Wagner climb down an ice-covered iron ladder that ended twelve feet above the ground, which the workers were supposed to use as a fire escape.[41]

The Factory Investigating Commission issued a multivolume report enumerating hazardous conditions and making suggestions for reform. The legislature adopted many of its recommendations, including requiring automatic sprinklers for buildings of seven or more stories and fire drills for factories with more than twenty-five employees. The legislature would adopt no fewer than thirty-six factory safety codes over the next few years, remedying nearly all of the problems that had been present in the Asch Building at the time of the fire.[42]

The Progressive Party, which was running Theodore Roosevelt for president in 1912, invited Perkins to be a delegate to its national convention. The Bull Moose party, as it was widely known, was promoting many of the causes she was fighting for. Perkins was a socialist at the time, like many people in her circle, but the party recruiters assured her it would not be an obstacle. Perkins was flattered to be asked. "Think of it!" she wrote to a friend. "F.P. actually in the game and mighty few women with that chance." In the end, she decided she could not trade in socialism for Bull Moose progressivism. "They were shocked and pained," she told her friend, "when I said I guessed I'd stick by the proletariat and that I believed more in the class struggle than I did in politics."[43]

Perkins's life was not all work. The lively, dark-haired industrial reformer, who was by now in her early thirties, socialized with the journalists, intellectuals, and avant-garde artists who flocked to Greenwich Village before the World War. She went dancing with Will Irwin, a muckraking journalist who would soon cover the war for *The Saturday Evening Post*, and she met Winston Churchill through mutual friends. Perkins read early drafts of novels for Sinclair Lewis, whose books *Main Street* and *Babbitt*, and Nobel Prize in literature were still ahead of him. One summer evening, Lewis proposed marriage to her at the top of his lungs through the open windows of her apartment.[44]

In the fall of 1913, Perkins got married, but not to Lewis. Paul Wilson, a wealthy Chicagoan who had attended Dartmouth and the University of Chicago, was a progressive economist working in the reform New York mayoral campaign of John Purroy Mitchel. Perkins, who had come to believe that she "liked life better in a single harness," surprised even herself when she accepted Wilson's proposal. When the news was announced, Pauline Goldmark of the Consumers' League lamented the end of a promising career. "Oh dear," she told Perkins, "you were such a promising person." Perkins said she knew Wilson well, enjoyed his company and his friends, and had concluded she "might as well marry and get it off my mind." Despite her unsentimental account, the letters she and Wilson exchanged revealed a deeply affectionate bond.[45]

The marriage was unconventional. The thirty-three-year-old Perkins and the thirty-seven-year-old Wilson were late to wed by the standards of the day. The ceremony, which was held on September 26, 1913, at Grace Church on lower Broadway, had only strangers as witnesses. Once she was married, Perkins broke with convention and kept her own name. In a letter to Mount Holyoke's alumnae secretary, she complained that "letters from women who do not know me by sight and who cannot possibly know or care about my marriage come addressed to me under my husband's name." Perkins said she wanted to avoid the appearance of a conflict of interest if Wilson joined a Mitchel administration and she ended up lobbying it. It seems clear, however, that Perkins was also reluctant to give up a name that, through years of hard work, was beginning to gain some prominence. Later in life, she would say that by keeping her name she had been making a statement about women's "personal independence."[46]

Against the odds, the thirty-four-year-old Mitchel defeated the Tammany Hall candidate, becoming the youngest mayor in New York City history. When he took office, he ushered in a new era in City Hall. Wilson became budget secretary for the "boy mayor," and while he threw himself into municipal reform, Perkins added women's suffrage to her list of causes. She had always been more interested in workers' rights than women's rights, but when suffragists put a referendum on the 1915 New York ballot to allow women to vote in state elections, she gave it her support. She attended teas and club events, spoke at public meetings, and joined tens of thousands of women and men in a parade up Fifth Avenue. The all-male electorate defeated the referendum by nearly 200,000 votes.[47]

In December 1916, Perkins gave birth to a daughter, Susanna. Now that she was a mother, Perkins became more interested in maternal health. She helped form the Maternity Center Association, which ran clinics in poor neighborhoods that offered prenatal care and child-care education. She became executive secretary of the group, a job that allowed her time to care for her own child.[48]

The 1917 election brought mixed news. The state passed a women's suffrage amendment, but Mitchel was defeated. He had undertaken significant reforms, notably in taxation and transportation, but he had also alienated key constituencies and was seen as too high society. His problem, Theodore Roosevelt said after the returns came in, was "too much Fifth Avenue; too little First Avenue." Wilson had to find a new job.[49]

Unemployment was, however, the least of Wilson's troubles. He was starting to show the first signs of what Perkins called "an up and down illness." He ricocheted between excitement and depression, the start of a lifelong struggle with mental illness. From this point on, Perkins said of her husband, "there were never anything but very short periods of reasonably comfortable accommodations to life." Wilson would hold down a series of jobs over the next decade, though Perkins was never sure how much real work he was doing. He cycled in and out of institutions. When he was home, he often had an attendant. Wilson's disorder made him reckless, including with money. He had considerable family money, but during his manic spells he had squandered it. Wilson's condition caused great anguish for Perkins, who was intensely private. She kept it a secret from everyone except Henry Bruere, a close family friend, who had worked with Wilson in the Mitchel administration.[50]

Perkins suddenly had to take responsibility for supporting the family. Her career got a boost in the next election, when Al Smith ran for governor. It was the first New York election in which women could vote, and Perkins did outreach to this new voting bloc for the campaign. When Smith was elected, he offered his old factory tour guide a seat on the state's five-member Industrial Commission. Smith admired Perkins a great deal, but he also saw the political advantages of appointing a woman. Critics argued that it was inviting trouble to name a woman to a position that required giving orders to working men, but the women activists Perkins had worked with for years were delighted. When she told Florence Kelley the news tears ran down her mentor's cheeks. "Glory be to God," Kelley said. "I never thought I would live to see the day."[51]

It was not only the gender breakthrough that made Perkins a daring choice. Her advocacy for safer factory conditions had made her enemies among manufacturers and their allies in the legislature. The State Senate confirmed Perkins, but half of the Republicans voted against her, including one senator who charged that she did not represent employers, workers, or even women, only "agitation." On the Industrial Commission, Perkins found herself setting policy for the first time, instead of merely lobbying those who did. The job required her to hear workmen's compensation appeals, which gave her new insight into the exploitation workers faced. One old carpenter whose arm had been crushed had gotten his medical bills paid, but had not received the $6,000 he was due for loss of an arm. When Perkins asked why not, the carpenter said that his employer told him it was all he was entitled to. "It never occurred to him," Perkins said, "that a man who had had the advantages of good education and an opportunity to know what was going on in the world would fool a poor old man like him."[52]

Perkins was not as radical as her critics feared. Industry was pleasantly surprised, but workers were disappointed to learn that they could only count on her support when they had the law on their side. "The conflict of opinion among the workers—those who bless Miss Perkins for her tenderness, and those pretenders and malingerers who get short shrift—creates a tornado around her," one profile observed. "She is their beautiful lady or their grim force, according to their fortunes." Perkins helped persuade her fellow commissioners to adopt an array of reforms. They cracked down on lawyers who overcharged workmen's compensation claimants and required hearing officers to notify workers that they did not need a lawyer. The job put Perkins in close contact with irate factory owners and disgruntled workers. At one hearing, a worker jumped up, cursed the insurance company representative, and pulled a gun. Perkins calmly got the man to give up the weapon.[53]

At the time of the appointment, Smith asked Perkins to become a Democrat. He succeeded where the Bull Moose party had not. In June 1920, Perkins traveled to San Francisco for the Democratic National Convention. She did not have credentials, but her Tammany Hall friends got her inside. Ohio governor James Cox won the nomination, but Perkins's greatest memory was of his running mate. Franklin Roosevelt appeared to have matured a great deal from his days as a haughty young legislator. He had served as Woodrow Wilson's assistant secretary of the navy, and his stint in Washington seemed to have made him more adept at interacting with people. Perkins saw him on the convention floor chatting easily and slapping backs. He had also grown into his looks, she noticed. "Nobody who saw it will ever forget how handsome Franklin Roosevelt was," she said later.[54]

That fall, a Republican tidal wave swept Warren Harding and Calvin Coolidge to victory over Cox and Roosevelt. It also dislodged Al Smith as governor. Perkins suddenly found herself looking for work. The Merchants' Association, a league of progressive businessmen, asked her to head up a new group it was forming to help immigrants. The offer came from the group's president, William Woodin, who would later serve with her in Roosevelt's Cabinet. Perkins accepted. As executive secretary of the Council on Immigrant Education, she promoted night school classes for adults and other programs designed to help immigrants assimilate.[55]

Smith was elected governor again in 1922. His Republican successor had replaced the Industrial Commission with a single industrial commissioner, who was in charge of the Labor Department, and a three-member Industrial Board, which took on the old commission's quasi-judicial duties. Smith named Perkins to be one of the three commissioners. She used her position to enlarge the scope of workmen's compensation. In one case, she ruled that a worker was entitled to benefits when he broke his leg on the steps of the building in which he worked, even though he had not yet reached the machine he operated.[56]

In 1924, Smith sought the presidential nomination, and Perkins went to the convention to support him. This time, as chair of the Women's Democratic Union platform committee, she had credentials and a seat on the floor. The highlight of the convention was Roosevelt's speech nominating Smith. Roosevelt had contracted polio since the 1920 campaign, and his appearance had changed dramatically. "To those of us who remembered the strong, radiant, successful Roosevelt of the San Francisco convention of 1920," Perkins recalled, "the man who appeared at Madison Square Garden in 1924 was deeply moving." Roosevelt made his way to the podium while leaning on his son James. Despite the difficulty of the walk, he threw his head back and flashed the broad smile that would become his trademark. He then delivered his famous speech hailing Smith as a "Happy Warrior." Smith battled his main rival for the nomination, William Gibbs McAdoo, Wilson's treasury secretary, through seventeen days and 103 ballots. In the end, after Will Rogers admonished the delegates that "New York invited you people here as guests, not to live," the convention broke its deadlock by nominating Wall Street lawyer John W. Davis. Davis lost to Coolidge in a landslide, but fortunately for Perkins, Smith held on to the governorship.[57]

The 1920s were shaping up as a deeply conservative decade. The World War had left disillusionment in its wake, as writers like Ernest Hemingway and Gertrude Stein were reporting from Europe. In America, the postwar generation turned inward. Jane Addams noted that young people, who had been the lifeblood of the settlement house movement, had "gone back to liberty for the individual" and lacked "reforming energy." With Republicans in control of the White House and Congress, progressives had little hope of scoring victories in Washington. Even if they could eke out a win, the aggressively pro-free-market Supreme Court was likely to take it away. In 1922, the court struck down a tax on factories that employed workers under age fourteen, ruling that it would "completely wipe out the sovereignty of the states."[58]

Progressives' only hope of advancing their agenda was working at the state level, and Smith was a leader in this effort. He built low-cost housing and improved public schools and hospitals. To win over the Republican-dominated legislature, Smith took his case directly to the voters, speaking to them over the radio. After the broadcasts, he could look out his office window and see piles of letters and telegrams arriving for legislators. His plainspoken radio talks were a forerunner to the fireside chats that Roosevelt would deliver as president. In 1926, Smith promoted Perkins to chairman of the Industrial Board. She continued to speak out for more humane working conditions. When a social work journal held a debate on the question "Do Women in Industry Need Special Protection?" Perkins took the affirmative position. The work world was set up for men, she said. Women's "only hope of a reasonably satisfactory life in industry," she argued, "is on the basis of the prevention of fatigue by short hours, good wages and healthful conditions."[59]

In 1928, Smith won the Democratic nomination for president. He persuaded Roosevelt to run for governor, convinced that he could do the most to help the Democratic ticket carry New York. Roosevelt, who was working on his rehabilitation at Warm Springs, was reluctant. It seemed to him that 1928 would be a Republican year, and he thought he would be better off concentrating on his health and waiting to run in 1932. Roosevelt eventually warmed up to the idea and, on the strength of Smith's support, his own record, and his family name—he once joked to Perkins that she should do nothing to dissuade upstate voters that he was not his distant cousin Theodore—he won the nomination by acclamation.[60]

Campaigning across the country, Smith met with hostility from voters who were skeptical of his New York accent, his Tammany Hall ties, and, most of all, his Catholic faith. When his train pulled into Oklahoma City, the Ku Klux Klan had placed fiery crosses along the tracks. Perkins campaigned for Smith, and tried to reassure her fellow Protestants. She brought one Ohio audience to tears with her assurances that Smith was a true Christian, but the obstacles were enormous. Perkins found herself having to refute false rumors that Smith's wife was a drunk and that Smith had purchased an estate near the White House for the pope's use. In Independence, Missouri, Perkins was greeted by protesters throwing tomatoes, one of which landed on her dress.[61]

Perkins also campaigned in New York for Roosevelt. He had grown, she could see, from his Albany days, and now proudly claimed Smith's progressive mantle. It also seemed to her that he had been transformed by his illness. Roosevelt came across as warmer and more empathetic, and she noticed that he now listened to ordinary people when they spoke to him, even when they rambled on. Perkins was moved by the courage and dignity he displayed on the campaign trail. At an appearance in Manhattan's Yorkville neighborhood, the only way he could get into the hall where he was to speak was to be carried up the fire escape. Perkins was overcome with emotion on seeing his helplessness, but she noticed that he smiled the whole time.[62]

Smith lost to Herbert Hoover in a landslide, failing to carry even New York. Roosevelt, who ran ahead of Smith upstate, won the governorship by 25,000 votes. After the election, he invited Perkins to Hyde Park and, while she was there, he offered her the job of industrial commissioner. The appointment would be a breakthrough. As industrial commissioner, in the new configuration, she would run the Labor Department, supervising the state's workers' compensation judges and factory inspectors. In their drive around Hyde Park, Roosevelt noted the pioneering nature of the appointment, but Perkins refused to congratulate him on his open-mindedness. "It was more of a victory for Al to bring himself to appoint a woman, never appointed before," she told Roosevelt, "than it is for you when I have a record as a responsible public officer for almost ten years."[63]

Perkins was not sure she wanted the promotion. As Industrial Board chairman, she was in charge of the Labor Department's judicial and legislative work, which allowed her to put legally binding safety codes in place and to set standards for how workmen's compensation cases were decided. As industrial commissioner, she would have more power in the bureaucracy but not necessarily more ability to affect policy. In the end, she followed her grandmother's advice that "if anybody opens a door, one should always go through." Before accepting, Perkins got Roosevelt to promise to back her up when she clashed with insurance companies and Republican legislators. Perkins told Roosevelt that she would not talk about the job offer until inauguration day in case he wanted to change his mind. If he did, she said, he should appoint someone else "and don't give me a moment's thought." Roosevelt laughed and insisted the job was hers, but he told people that he had been impressed with how Perkins had put his political concerns ahead of her own ambitions.[64]

In early 1929, Perkins took charge of the nation's largest state labor department, with 1,800 employees. Not long after taking office, she was honored at a luncheon at the Hotel Astor, attended by nearly 1,000 people. The event was not to celebrate her as a person, she told the gathering, but "Frances Perkins as the symbol of an idea." That idea, she said, was "that social justice is possible in a great industrial community." Perkins laid out a vision for her tenure as industrial commissioner that was the complete opposite of the business-oriented, laissez-faire policies coming out of the Hoover administration. In addition to safer working conditions, minimum wage and maximum hour laws, and the abolition of child labor, she said she would fight to affirm the dignity of work. It was critical, she said, that workers not be turned into "robots," a word that had been introduced earlier in the decade by the Czech playwright Karel Čapek. "We are committed to the belief that the human race is not destined for that kind of efficiency," she said.[65]

In his first message to the state legislature, on January 1, 1929, Roosevelt endorsed much of the Smith-Perkins agenda. He called for a maximum hours law that would limit the workweek of women and children to forty-eight hours, and for creating an advisory board for minimum wages, both issues that Smith had promoted but failed to get through the Republican legislature. Perkins was pleased that Roosevelt was promoting what she regarded as the right platform, but she could see that he was not like other progressives she had worked with. Perkins was used to people who thought about social problems at a theoretical level, contemplating the interaction of labor and capital, or the goals of the regulatory state. Roosevelt's focus was narrower. He preferred to take on specific problems and try to solve them. "He was not a scientific mind and he never had a scientific approach," she later said, and she was struck by how "illiterate" he was "in the field of economics." Perkins also discovered that she could not always count on Roosevelt to sympathize with workers. When she told him of her effort to get a bill through the legislature to guarantee women the right to sit on the job in seats with backs, he "roared with laughter." Perkins lectured him on how much it hurt women to operate machinery with no support for the small of the back. He looked back at her, she recalled later, with "bewilderment."[66]

Perkins scheduled an hour-long meeting with Roosevelt at least every ten days to keep him apprised of her work and to lobby him on issues. Even if he did not begin with all of the sympathies of an old-time progressive, she found that he was open to persuasion. Roosevelt did not "respond to hammering," she said, but he could be "manipulated." The best way to convince him, she discovered, was repetition. She first brought him a brief written proposal. After explaining the case for it, she laid out the disadvantages. When he agreed to the proposal, she repeated it and asked him to repeat it. With this "trick," she said, her idea became fixed in his memory, and he could make the point himself later. She found that Roosevelt was most receptive to stories of real people. To enlist his support for factory safety laws, she told him about men who contracted silicosis from polishing glass milk tanks and women who came down with radium poisoning from using their lips to point fine hair brushes while painting luminous dials on clock faces.[67]

Everything changed in October, when the stock market crashed and people of every economic class suddenly found themselves in dire straits. New Yorkers were losing their jobs and struggling to pay rent and buy food. Americans looked to Washington for help, but the Hoover administration insisted that the economy was recovering on its own. Perkins was riding to work on January 22, 1930, when she saw a front-page headline in *The New York Times*: "EMPLOYMENT TURNS UPWARD, HOOVER REPORTS; CHANGES FOR FIRST TIME SINCE STOCK SLUMP." Hoover had declared, based on information from his Department of Labor, that for the first time since the crash, "the tide of unemployment has changed in the right direction" and the Depression was in retreat. The secretary of labor, James J. Davis, insisted that the nation would soon be "well on the way to complete recovery." Perkins did not believe Hoover's employment numbers or Davis's upbeat prediction. The data she was seeing from New York State indicated that joblessness was as bad as ever. She was affronted by what she saw as Hoover's dishonesty, and worried that the inaccurate report would mislead people about how bad conditions were.[68]

When she got to the office, Perkins asked her chief statistician to look at New York's employment numbers. He reported back that the numbers for employees on hand, days worked, orders on hand, and other key indicators were all headed straight down. Perkins had him check with the head of the federal Bureau of Labor Statistics. It turned out that Hoover's top labor statistician agreed that the situation was grim, but he was unwilling to publicly contradict the president. Perkins called a press conference to announce what she had found out. New York's labor data, she told reporters, showed that employment was lower than any December since 1914, the first year records were kept. She was speaking out, she said, so people would understand the gravity of the situation, and not be deluded into thinking that nothing had to be done. It occurred to her that she had not told Roosevelt her plans. She called him and gave a full report. Her response to Hoover was already "in the city rooms," she said. "Are you going to kill me, or fire me?" Roosevelt said he thought her press conference was "bully," though he was glad she had not asked him first, because he might have told her not to do it. The next day, the *Times* reported that Perkins had challenged Hoover's numbers as "not statistical, and probably based on inadequate, improperly analyzed material." It would soon become clear that Perkins was right. The dispute was a coup for Roosevelt, whose administration appeared to have a better handle on the Depression than the White House. "Frances, this is the best politics you can do," Roosevelt told her. "Don't say anything about politics. Just be an outraged scientist and social worker."[69]

Perkins's clash with Hoover also helped in her ongoing campaign to persuade Roosevelt to take strong steps to help the victims of the Depression. Roosevelt had great sympathy for people who had lost their jobs, but he also had a limited view of the government's role. He was reluctant to take on responsibility for providing relief. At Perkins's urging, Roosevelt established a committee to investigate the unemployment problem and recommend a course of action. He called it the Committee for the Stabilization of Industry because, Perkins noted, "he did not like to appoint a committee against anything." In announcing the formation of the committee, the first of its kind in the nation, Roosevelt emphasized the role that New York's businesses could play in lessening the impact of the economic crisis. He urged them to display "the same good-will" they had demonstrated in confronting "industrial accidents, industrial diseases, child labor," and other "adverse conditions." Roosevelt still believed the private sector, not government, would be the key to helping the unemployed.[70]

Perkins was the driving force behind the Committee for the Stabilization of Industry. She chose the governor's appointees, including the chairman, Henry Bruere, her and Paul Wilson's old friend, who had done a major study of unemployment during the Mitchel administration and was now a vice president of the Bowery Savings Bank. The committee met at the Labor Department, and Perkins's staff provided investigative and clerical support. To determine how severe the unemployment crisis was, the committee held meetings around the state. It also sent out surveys to employers, asking what they were doing to prevent joblessness. Many companies responded that they were cutting workers' hours to spread the work among as many employees as possible. In late April, just weeks after it was created, the Committee for the Stabilization of Industry issued its first recommendations. Calling for "steady work the year around," the committee urged companies to adjust production schedules to keep as many people working as possible. It also called on government to do more. The committee encouraged local governments to plan purchases and construction projects so more of them were done in economic downturns. These government-funded jobs, the committee said, could put the unemployed to work right away. Perkins convened a conference of mayors in Rochester to encourage local governments to establish public works programs.[71]

In November, the committee issued a final report with more sweeping recommendations. If industry could not solve the problem, the committee said, "it seems inevitable that the state will." It called on the state government to establish a planning board to help develop public works programs at the state and local levels. "The public conscience is not comfortable," the report declared, "when good men anxious to work are unable to find employment to support themselves and their families." It also recommended that the state consider a compulsory unemployment insurance system to help workers caught between a layoff and their next job. Perkins struck similar themes two days later in a speech to the National Consumers' League convention in Philadelphia. The "new challenge" for industry, she said, was making workers secure in their jobs. Perkins emphasized the importance of making jobs available to anyone who needed one, and expressed regret that the stock market crash had caught the government off guard. "If we had any brains in this country we would have had a long-range plan of public works," she told a luncheon audience, "making it possible for the government in December of 1929 to have released at once orders for construction without having to pass emergency legislation."[72]

Armed with the committee report, Perkins tried to persuade Roosevelt that the state should take affirmative steps to help the unemployed. She was convinced that one reason he hesitated to act was that he knew little about how business worked. To fill in the gaps, she encouraged committee members to meet with him and educate him. As a result of these conversations, she said, Roosevelt came to "realize that unemployment was not just a closed book, and that something could be done about it." Still, he continued to resist specific proposals. When Perkins raised unemployment insurance, Roosevelt was skeptical. "I'm against the dole, Frances," he protested. "Don't you get any dole in here!" Perkins found Roosevelt's frequent references to the "dole" frustrating. He was afraid of a European-style welfare system in which it was so easy to get benefits that people would not work even when jobs were available. Perkins tried to explain that unemployment insurance was not a "dole." It was an insurance system in which the benefits that were paid out were financed by contributions from the same people who were eligible to receive them. Roosevelt "never could get it through his head," Perkins complained.

She kept hammering away, trying to persuade him that she was proposing a form of insurance. "I finally decided that we had to have a completely different set of words," she said.[73]

As times got worse, Roosevelt's thinking evolved. In a speech to the Governors' Conference in Salt Lake City in June 1930, he became the nation's first major political leader to endorse unemployment insurance. He cut the "three or four pages" that Perkins had written for the speech, and toned down the substance. Rather than support a particular plan, Roosevelt said the subject required "proper study," and he emphasized that any program should be self-supporting so it did not become a "mere dole" or a "handout." When Perkins heard the speech, she was initially disappointed in Roosevelt's changes, but she later decided that, as a political matter, his cautious approach had been exactly right. On issues other than unemployment insurance, Roosevelt's speech to the governors reflected his still-conservative approach to many aspects of the economic crisis. He criticized the Hoover administration for abandoning laissez-faire, and expressed skepticism about the modest efforts the administration was making to stimulate state and local public works programs. New York State had spent $20 million more on public works projects than it had a year earlier, he said, and local governments had also increased their spending. The cost was too great, he said, to continue spending at that level.[74]

Roosevelt ran for reelection in 1930. Although he had not come up with a solution to the problem of mass unemployment, he had nevertheless compiled an impressive record. He had made strides toward developing low-cost public power, increased hospital construction, and improved conditions in state prisons. He had also, with Perkins's encouragement, fought for workers in a wide array of areas, including expanding the scope of workmen's compensation. In the campaign, Roosevelt made clear he wanted to do more about the hard times, in part because Hoover was doing so little. The president's failure "either to estimate the situation correctly or to tell the truth about it," he said, "has thrown an enormous burden on the Governors of all the States." Perkins hit the campaign trail, appearing before business and labor audiences. She also spoke to women's groups, though she said they were "not my dish of tea, really." On election night, Roosevelt won a resounding 725,000-vote victory, including a 167,000-vote edge in Republican upstate New York. Will Rogers declared the next day, "The Democrats nominated their President yesterday, Franklin D. Roosevelt."[75]

In his second term, Roosevelt's response to the economic crisis became bolder. In January 1931, in his annual message to the legislature, he indicated that he was becoming more supportive of the sort of public works programs Perkins and the Committee for the Stabilization of Industry had been recommending. "Public works are being speeded to the utmost," he told the lawmakers, "all available funds are being used to provide employment; wherever the State can find a place for a man to work it has provided a job." He also promoted labor reforms that Republican legislators had been balking at, including setting up an advisory minimum wage board. The same month, Roosevelt hosted a conference of governors of eastern states to work together on the unemployment problem. The conference, another recommendation of the Committee for the Stabilization of Industry, had been Perkins's idea. Delegations from Ohio, Massachusetts, Pennsylvania, New Jersey, Connecticut, and Rhode Island descended on Albany. Perkins invited Professor Paul Douglas of the University of Chicago, the future senator from Illinois, and other progressive thinkers. The conference helped spread ideas that were percolating in New York, including public works and unemployment insurance, to states that had not given them much thought. It also strengthened Roosevelt's reputation as a national leader in responding to the Depression.[76]

In the late summer, with economic conditions continuing to worsen, Roosevelt called the legislature into special session. On August 28, he delivered a historic address to the legislature in which he set out a new philosophy of government. "What is the State?" he asked. It was, he declared, an "organized society of human beings, created by them for their mutual protection and well-being." One of the state's primary duties, he said, was "caring for those of its citizens who find themselves the victims of such adverse circumstances as makes them unable to obtain even the necessities for mere existence without the aid of others." To fulfill the obligations that he had just described, Roosevelt asked the legislature to allocate $20 million for relief for the unemployed, to be administered by the newly created Temporary Emergency Relief Administration. In the interest of avoiding "the dole," Roosevelt wanted as much of the money as possible to be used for public works, so the recipients would have to work for their benefits. If it had to be dispensed as relief, he wanted it to be given, as much as possible, in the form of food, clothing, fuel, and shelter. The legislature was reluctant to sign off on the plan, but Roosevelt won them over. Samuel Rosenman, his counsel, would later say that the special session "had more to do with making Roosevelt the national figure that he became than anything else."[77]

With the TERA, New York became the first state to establish a relief agency to help victims of the Depression. Roosevelt appointed a three-member board to run the new agency, chaired by Jesse Isador Straus, the president of R. H. Macy & Co. Harry Hopkins, a transplanted Iowan who headed the New York Tuberculosis and Health Association, was chosen to administer the new program. Hopkins energetically took on the job of setting up the new agency and dispensing the $20 million to the unemployed. The Temporary Emergency Relief Administration would be a model for other states— New Jersey established a similar body a month later, and Rhode Island and Illinois followed—and for New Deal agencies to come. In the next six years, the TERA would provide aid to about five million people, 40 percent of all New Yorkers.[78]

Roosevelt's focus in 1932 was his much-anticipated campaign for president. Perkins was not part of the campaign's inner circle. "I was regarded as an administrator, as a reformer, as a do-gooder," she said, "while they were doing their plotting." She was, however, seen as a political asset. She was dispatched to speak to audiences that were looking for a more activist government. Perkins, who was invariably introduced as the woman who had challenged Hoover's employment numbers, attested to Roosevelt's progressive values and recounted his good works as governor, much as she had told the nation about Al Smith's character. New York boasted "the most advanced labor laws in the country," she said in a radio address in St. Louis. "If Franklin Roosevelt is elected President, the same policies of putting social justice first will prevail in the Federal Government." Perkins also expanded on her own ideas about government. At an appearance at the Tremont Temple in Boston she declared that people were looking for "security of opportunity to earn a living; security to plan their lives." It was the first time she had used the word, three years before she helped usher the Social Security Act into law, and it got, she recalled later, "wild, thrilled applause."[79]

The progressive influence of Perkins, and of the Brain Trust, could be seen in the kind of campaign Roosevelt ran. He made frequent reference in his speeches to government's responsibility to care for its citizens. In an October 13, 1932, radio address from Albany, Roosevelt mentioned the $20 million he was spending on local relief programs, which had been supplemented with another $5 million, and quoted from his "What is the State?" message. "That principle which I laid down in 1931, I reaffirm," he declared. "I not only reaffirm it, I go a step further and say that where the State itself is unable successfully to fulfill this obligation which lies upon it, it then becomes the positive duty of the Federal Government to step in to help."[80]

On election night, November 8, Perkins went to the campaign headquarters to watch the votes come in. She was out of her element among the political foot soldiers and revelers. "The most ungodly looking women were kissing each other, kissing me, and others," she recalled. "I remember saying, 'You have to stand a lot for your country.'" When Roosevelt won his landslide victory, the speculation about what role Perkins would play in the new administration began right away. Even before any votes were cast, *The Washington Post* had declared that it "seems to be a foregone conclusion" that if Roosevelt won she would be his secretary of labor.[81]

Perkins was an obvious choice, and not only because of her close working relationship with the president-elect. In the twenty-three years since she had arrived in New York, she had acquired a national reputation. Ida Tarbell, the muckraking journalist, had included her on a list of the fifty foremost women in the United States, alongside Amelia Earhart and Helen Keller. William Allen White, the Kansas newspaper editor, said choosing Perkins would be a "master stroke," and praised her as "not the professional political woman, not the chronic female person but the broad-minded, competent person who happens to be a woman as an incident of life on the planet." All the same, women were not indifferent to the fact that Perkins could be the first female Cabinet member. "Many, many women of influence in both Republican and Democratic ranks" were "concentrating on Miss Perkins," The *Chicago Tribune* reported. Molly Dewson, a leader in the Roosevelt campaign's outreach to women, told Roosevelt, "half jokingly, and at proper intervals," that Perkins's selection was the price of the work she had done. One person who was not actively promoting Perkins was Eleanor Roosevelt. The women were cordial, but not close. Perkins, the unflappable rationalist, regarded her boss's wife as too emotional. "Eleanor was always saying, 'I feel this and I feel that,'" she complained, "and I wanted to say: 'Eleanor, if you only feel it, don't say it.'" Perkins also suspected that Eleanor, who had not yet found her footing as a public figure, envied her career. In her memoir, Eleanor denied that she had lobbied her husband for Perkins, though she said she was "delighted when he named her."[82]

Perkins told anyone who asked that Roosevelt would not choose her. It was, she insisted, just as well. In the fourteen years Paul Wilson had been ill, there had never been "anything but very short periods of reasonably comfortable accommodations to life," she would later say. It would be difficult to manage his care if she moved to Washington. The main thing holding Perkins back was her desire for privacy. Joining the Cabinet, particularly as the first woman to do so, would make her a national figure, something she did not want to be. Perkins, who had been shy her whole life, once said that having her picture in the newspaper "nearly kills me." In later years, she would be outraged when a census form asked how many toilets her home had. "She was just furious," her grandson, Tomlin Coggeshall, recalled. "I remember her saying, 'We're not going to answer that.'" Perkins's reticence was partly due to her background. Her friend Agnes Leach thought of her as "a very reserved, very sensitive New Englander." The biggest consideration, though, was her fear that her husband's condition would become public, something Wilson was also afraid of. Perkins later confided to a friend that one reason she hesitated was her fear that Wilson would escape his caretakers, and it would be a national news story.[83]

There were also good reasons to accept. The women Perkins had worked with for years were pressuring her to make history. Dewson told her that if she said no it could be another hundred years before a woman was offered a Cabinet position. Perkins felt an obligation to accept "for the sake of other women," but a bigger factor was the responsibility she felt for workers and the unemployed. She had recently finished an article for *Survey Graphic*, a national social work magazine, entitled "The Cost of a Five-Dollar Dress." In it, she declared that the real "price of the bargain dress is not paid by" the women who wear it, but "by the workers in the sweatshops that are springing up in hard-pressed communities." Most employers wanted to maintain reasonable workplace standards, she said, but they had to compete with "the shortsighted manufacturer who tries to evade the labor law, cuts wages, and resorts to contract labor and homework." Perkins would be in an ideal position to fight against conditions like these if she joined the Cabinet.[84]

On February 1, Perkins wrote to Roosevelt, urging him not to choose her. It made more sense, she argued, to adhere to tradition and appoint a union official, sending a clear message that "labor is in the President's councils." She assured Roosevelt that "whatever I might furnish in the way of ideas" would be available to him "without the necessity of appointing me to anything." Perkins did not directly mention her husband's situation, but she said that "grave personal difficulties" might "seriously impair my usefulness." There were all sorts of rumors about what Roosevelt would do, including a report in *The Washington Post* a few days later that William Green, the president of the American Federation of Labor, had been offered the position of labor secretary and had accepted. It was Perkins, however, who was invited to the Roosevelt town house on Sixty-fifth Street, and there was little doubt what the president-elect wanted to talk about. Dewson told Perkins that if she turned the job down "I'll murder you."[85]

Perkins had been compiling a list of causes she would want to fight for, writing them on slips of paper and dropping them in a drawer. At her meeting with Roosevelt, she said she would only accept if he promised to back her agenda. At the top of her list were aid to state and local governments for unemployment relief and a large-scale public works program. She also wanted a federal minimum wage and maximum hours laws, a ban on child labor, and unemployment and old age insurance.

"You know, Frances, I don't believe in the dole and I never will," Roosevelt said.

Perkins explained again that she meant these to be actual insurance plans, not a dole. Perkins wanted Roosevelt to hold a governors' conference early in his administration, like the one he had held in Albany, at which they could encourage the states, where most labor laws were enacted, to promote the kind of protections she had fought for in New York. It was a remarkably ambitious agenda, and Perkins was not sure how Roosevelt would respond.[86]

"I suppose you are going to nag me about this forever," Roosevelt said. Perkins assumed that he meant this as an invitation to nag him about it. "He wanted his conscience kept for him by somebody," she would later say.[87]

Perkins agreed to serve as secretary of labor, but she asked Roosevelt not to make a public announcement until she could talk it over with her husband. She visited Wilson in the institution where he was living and found him in a "good, controlled mood." He had been reading the newspapers and was aware she might be asked to be labor secretary. Wilson encouraged her to take the job, though he was worried about the publicity. "He dreaded the fact that somebody would inquire about him," Perkins said. "That was terribly hard for him to bear." Wilson did not want to move to Washington. She promised that they would keep the New York apartment, and she said she would come up to see him every weekend. After the meeting, Perkins went home and collapsed in tears. It was the only time, Susanna would later say, that she recalled seeing her mother cry. "To this day I don't know why I was crying, except that it just seemed as though I didn't want to go," Perkins said later. "I didn't want to venture out onto this great sea of the unknown."[88]

Organized labor felt betrayed by the appointment. The unions had been promoting Daniel J. Tobin, the president of the International Brotherhood of Teamsters, and they were unhappy that the job had gone to someone entirely outside of their movement. "The Secretary of Labor should be a representative of labor, one who understands labor, labor's problems, labor's psychology," William Green insisted. "Labor," Green declared, "can never become reconciled" to the choice. John L. Lewis of the United Mine Workers was particularly harsh about the selection of Perkins, dismissing her as a "mere social worker." Perkins, who had always found labor leaders to be too focused on their own members, was not surprised by Green's strong statement. She also believed another consideration was at work. "He wouldn't have been so excited," she said later, "if it had been a man not from the ranks of labor."[89]

Outside of organized labor, the choice of Perkins was widely acclaimed. *The New Republic* declared it the best of Roosevelt's Cabinet appointments, because it was "the most courageous and sensible." Perkins "is a better man than any Labor Secretary we have yet had," the magazine said, "so far superior to the last two that there is no real comparison." Felix Frankfurter wrote that the appointment "exhilarates me in the way in which the anticipation of a Kreisler concert exhilarates me." Even some conservatives found reason to celebrate. The *Los Angeles Times* focused on the fact that "Miss Perkins does not carry a union card and may, therefore, be able to consider the interests of the 93 per cent of working people who do not carry union cards either."[90]

Perkins tried to prepare for the spotlight that was about to fall on her. She went shopping with her friend Margaret Poole for a fancier wardrobe. They bought a simple black dress for everyday and a velvet dress with sequins for formal events. Perkins did not need to buy a new tricorn hat, since she already had an adequate supply. Her efforts to dress up for Washington would not be appreciated. The press corps would still comment uncharitably on her attire and joke that it was so drab she must have had it designed by the Bureau of Standards. Perkins packed up Susanna and said good-bye to her husband, who was reported by the press to be "ill with influenza."[91]

Perkins was already thinking about the work she would soon be undertaking in Washington. In an interview with The *Chicago Tribune*, she began to lay the groundwork for a large-scale public works program. "The depression is feeding on itself," she warned, drawing on the lessons Simon Nelson Patten had taught her. "We must have mass consumption or we will never get a market for mass production." Before leaving New York, Perkins traveled to Albany to deliver a valedictory speech to the legislature on March 1. She made a final appeal for minimum wage and maximum hours laws and for unemployment insurance, the causes for which she had been fighting for much of her adult life. She basked in applause from the packed legislative chamber before getting on a train and joining the southward migration of New Yorkers heading to Roosevelt's inauguration.

CHAPTER SEVEN

"Just So We Get a Public Works Program"

The Department of Labor that Frances Perkins inherited was a backwater. It was the newest Cabinet department, and one that had been created only grudgingly. Labor unions had campaigned since the dawn of the industrial age for a Cabinet office dedicated to workers. Industrial states had established their own labor departments, like the one Perkins headed in New York, as early as the 1880s, but business leaders and their allies in Congress had succeeded in blocking a federal department. In 1884, in a modest concession to organized labor, Congress established a Bureau of Labor, charged with collecting labor statistics and other data, and placed it in the Interior Department. Eventually, Congress created an independent Bureau of Labor, but the bureau did not have Cabinet status and it had little to do. After Democrats took control of the House of Representatives in 1910, Congress finally passed a bill creating a Cabinet-level department to "promote and develop the welfare of the wage earners of the United States, to improve their working conditions, and to advance their opportunities for profitable employment." William Howard Taft grudgingly signed the bill into law on March 4, 1913, the final day of his presidency.[1]

Twenty years after its creation, the Labor Department was little more than a ragtag assortment of bureaus. The two largest divisions were the Bureau of Immigration and the Bureau of Naturalization. There was a Bureau of

Labor Statistics, the one Perkins had sparred with over employment data, and a small Children's Bureau, but since the adoption of the exclusionary immigration acts of 1921 and 1924, 90 percent of the department's work had been pursuing illegal immigration. Under Republican leadership, the Labor Department had done little for working men and women. Although he had once been a union official himself, William Doak supported these priorities. He did not like strikes, and he did not consider it any of his business how much workers were paid. "It was never intended that the central government should be used as a charitable institution," he said. After the stock market crash, Doak stuck with his hands-off approach. When a reporter confronted him after a Cabinet meeting to ask what the administration was doing about the decline in wages, Doak replied with irritation, "What can be done about it?"[2]

There was little doubt when Perkins showed up that the department would change, something that became even clearer after she made quick work of Section 24 and the Garsson brothers. "Feathers are beginning to fly," Clara Beyer of the Children's Bureau wrote to a friend. "I wish you could see the men who threatened to resign if a woman was appointed; they are crawling on hands and knees." It was not only the men who were worried. There were reports that women were coming to work in smocks rather than the inexpensive dresses they usually wore because they were afraid of being harshly judged by the author of "The Cost of a Five-Dollar Dress."[3]

Perkins started to push out the cronies and the hangers-on, replacing them with employees chosen on merit. As department counsel she hired Charles E. Wyzanski, Jr., a 1930 Harvard Law School graduate and yet another Frank-furter protégé. Under Perkins, the Cabinet department that had been known for having the least capable staff began to acquire a reputation for competence, industry, and forward thinking. Among her hires in her years at the department would be Henry Hart, an influential Harvard Law School professor; Thomas Eliot, a future chancellor of Washington University in St. Louis; and Archibald Cox, the Harvard Law School professor who would decades later become Watergate special prosecutor. Wyzanski, not an entirely neutral observer, insisted that Perkins's staff stood "as a challenge for comparison with any department of government at any time in our history." Her allegiance to meritocracy came at a cost. Members of Congress and powerful Democrats at the state level believed they were entitled to their share of patronage jobs, an area James Farley, the postmaster general, coordinated, and they resented that Perkins had put her department off-limits. Perkins's opposition to patronage made her powerful enemies in Congress, who retaliated over the years by cutting the Labor Department budget and insisting that new agencies created during the New Deal not be placed under her supervision.[4]

One part of the department that Perkins was especially intent on reforming was the Bureau of Labor Statistics. When she had her showdown with Hoover on employment numbers, the head of the bureau, Ethelbert Stewart, had broken with the president and conceded that her figures were more accurate. Perkins had been impressed by his honesty, but she had been disappointed that he had not spoken out publicly when his words could have made a difference. When she got to the department, she saw that his office was badly run and that it was full of unproductive people who were out of touch with the latest ideas in labor statistics. It was not clear to her whether the seventy-five-year-old Stewart wanted to be reappointed, but she would not consider it. Perkins asked the American Statistical Association for a list of suitable appointees, and from it she chose Isador Lubin, a young Brookings Institution economist. Lubin had strong academic credentials, and he had helped Senators Robert F. Wagner and Robert M. La Follette, Jr., draft unemployment insurance bills. She settled on Lubin, she told him, because she was convinced that he would be interested in the people behind the figures.[5]

Another high priority for Perkins was reaching out to organized labor. When William Green said he would never become reconciled to her appointment, Perkins had responded that she was sorry to hear it, but that she would be "reconciled to him right away." To show that she harbored no ill will, she called his office to say she wanted to pay a visit. When his secretary said that she thought Green would want to come see her, Perkins replied, "I hope he will later, but I want to come, if I may, this afternoon." She did, and she and

Green had a friendly talk about what the administration could do for workers. From that day on, Perkins and Green got along well.[6]

Other union leaders were still reserving judgment. Dr. Leo Wolman, the Amalgamated Clothing Workers' head of research, called Perkins to say that Sidney Hillman, the union's hard-driving president, was "very restive" because nothing was being done for labor. The union had gotten its members, who usually voted socialist, to support Roosevelt, Wolman said, and they needed something to show for it. Perkins pointed out that the administration was still in its first week, but Wolman urged her to do "something quick—anything," so long as it was "something that can be put in the paper." He also said that Hillman wanted to see her. Perkins, who was going to be in New York that weekend, arranged to meet Wolman and Hillman in Pennsylvania Station Sunday night before she boarded the midnight train for Washington. The labor secretary and the union president spoke for an hour on a bench in the waiting room. Hillman said that the administration could show its concern for organized labor by convening a conference of labor leaders. Perkins was skeptical that any good would come of it, but instead of sleeping on the train back to Washington, she started planning a conference.[7]

Perkins wanted to reach out to the whole labor movement, which would not be easy, because it was so divided. She decided to ignore the internecine divisions and to be expansive with the guest list. She invited top officials of the American Federation of Labor, and the traditionally Republican building trades unions, which had backed Hoover. She included Hillman and the AFL leaders with whom he was at war. She also invited John L. Lewis, the combative head of the United Mine Workers, who had been so dismissive of her when she was appointed, and who could be counted on to stir up trouble. Perkins made a point of inviting women leaders, including Rose Schneiderman, the head of the Women's Trade Union League, whose speech after the Triangle Shirtwaist Fire had made such a strong impression on her years earlier. As an inducement to accept, Perkins held out the possibility that Roosevelt might meet with some or all of the leaders who attended.[8]

As the first woman Cabinet member, Perkins had to deal with novel issues. One of them was the question of what she should be called, a matter she found difficult to put to rest. After the first Cabinet meeting, a male reporter approached her and asked how she wanted to be addressed. Perkins said "Miss Perkins" would be fine, but the reporter insisted that since the men in the Cabinet were called "Mr. Secretary" there should be an analogous term for her. Perkins deferred to Henry T. Rainey, the Speaker of the House, who was leaving with her. He declared that she should be called "Madam Secretary," insisting it was all laid out in *Robert's Rules of Order.* Perkins said "Madam Secretary" was fine with her, but she found that reporters had trouble getting it straight. She was referred to as "The Madam Secretary," or "Madam Perkins," or even "The Madam," which struck her as having "a distinctly nasty connotation." There was also the question of where Perkins fit into Washington's elaborate pecking order. It should have been straightforward. Cabinet secretaries were ranked by the age of their departments, which made Perkins tenth out of ten. Washington protocol dictated that the wives of Cabinet members were ranked among themselves according to the rank of their husbands. To avoid offending the Cabinet wives, Perkins decided that when attending events with them, she would ask to be seated where the labor secretary's wife would be put. When Perkins was seated next to the king of Greece at a state dinner and Mrs. Cordell Hull, the wife of the secretary of state, was given a lesser seat, Perkins called her the next day to explain that she had not asked for her prominent placement. "Oh, I know you didn't, my dear," Mrs. Hull replied. "I know what your ruling has been."[9]

Perkins did not look for sexism. She had not been disadvantaged by her sex, she liked to say, "except in climbing trees." Throughout her career, she told a reporter, she had mainly worked with men, and they had generally treated her well. Although she rarely mentioned it, Perkins did at times encounter unequal treatment, even within the administration. One of her fellow Cabinet members, Daniel Roper, the secretary of commerce, did not hide his concern about "the premature recognition" of women. Even Rexford Tugwell referred to Perkins in his book about the Brain Trust as "old-maidish." One indication of a possible double standard was the attention Perkins's colleagues paid to how much she talked. Vice President Garner made a point of telling Perkins after the first Cabinet meeting that she had not been as talkative as he feared. "You're all right; you've got something on your mind," he told her. "You said it and then you stopped." Others found Perkins too effusive. Interior secretary Harold Ickes, who was known for his caustic nature, complained about Perkins in his diary, which he later published: "She talks in a perfect torrent, almost without pausing to take breath, as if she feared that any little pause would be seized upon by someone to break in on her." James Farley, the postmaster general, complained to Dewson that Perkins "lectured the Cabinet at length on things they did not want to be informed about." Perkins may in fact have talked too much, or it may have been, as Molly Dewson, Perkins's good friend, thought, that the men around her were threatened by her intelligence. Dewson also believed, however, that Perkins's manner might have contributed to the problem. "Perhaps she realized her intellectual superiority, and her impatience with less brilliant minds and less gifted speakers, had given her some unattractive habits," Dewson said.[10]

One area where Perkins was at a distinct disadvantage compared to her male colleagues was in finding a place to live. With her heavy workload, and her travels to New York every weekend, she was having trouble locating a house, and unlike her fellow Cabinet members, she had no one to help her. "Having no wife is a great handicap to a public official," she lamented. Perkins believed on principle that she should avoid extravagance in her social life and her living arrangements. "How terrible it would be to read in the paper that the Secretary of Labor attended a dinner at the White House," she said, "or a dinner at the British Embassy, which was set with the gold plate, the sweetheart roses, the gladiola ferns, and all the elaborate nonsense that the newspapers would write." After the inauguration, Perkins moved out of the Willard Hotel and into the Women's University Club, while she searched for a permanent home. The club was "not a plush hotel," Perkins reasoned. "Nobody can write up about how you are living in the magnificent gold-plated bathroom fixtured rooms of the Willard Hotel."[11]

Perkins seriously considered moving into a convent. There would be no telephones to disturb her, she reasoned, and the doors would close at night, so she would not have to worry about accepting social invitations. The only convent she knew in the area, the Visitation Convent in Georgetown, did not have any rooms available, and in any case, Perkins had decided that if she moved into a convent, the press corps would never stop writing about it. Instead, she decided to share a house in Georgetown with her old friend Mary Rumsey, the eldest daughter of railroad tycoon E. H. Harriman. Rumsey's husband, Charles Cary Rumsey, a sculptor and polo player, had died in an automobile accident. Rumsey was extraordinarily wealthy, but she was not extravagant. She was "altogether a remarkable person to be the daughter of one of our biggest railroad builders," one profile noted. "Democratic and informal, she is a terrific worker, and will call people up at two o'clock in the morning if she has an idea she must discuss with them." Perkins and Rumsey had met years earlier, when Rumsey served on the board of the Maternity Center Association. Rumsey had founded the Junior League, to encourage young society women to help the poor, and now she was a committed New Dealer who would soon chair the National Recovery Administration's Consumer Advisory Board. The house that the two women shared in Georgetown was simple, and Perkins insisted on paying her share. The arrangement worked out well for Perkins, providing her with companionship and the financial resources to entertain, which she and Rumsey did frequently.[12]

Perkins also found a spiritual home in Washington, St. James, an Episcopal church. Perkins remained as religious as ever, and during her time in Washington, St. James was one of her great sources of solace. Attending morning services was the best way she knew, she would later say, "to adjust myself to the painful realities of life, and to assure myself of the help and support of God." Perkins told Henry Wallace, who was always in search of spiritual sustenance, about the church, and he and his family also attended regularly. Perkins also paid regular visits to an Episcopal convent in Maryland, often staying overnight. She spent much of her time praying, and observed the convent rule about keeping silent for all but two hours of the day. The nuns knew who Perkins was, but she registered as Mrs. Wilson to avoid attracting attention.[13]

While she was putting her department in order, Perkins began moving forward on relief. There were about 15 million unemployed people, and the limited resources available to help them were running out fast. Community chests, which had been carrying much of the burden, were not able to keep up with demand. While the number of people who needed their help continued to climb, many private charities were missing their fund-raising goals because the incomes of their donors were declining. State and local governments, whose tax revenues were plummeting, were also short of funds. Hoover had long resisted any kind of federal relief program. When he did agree to support one, the Emergency Relief and Construction Act of 1932, the conditions he imposed rendered it ineffective. The small amount of money it sent out to the states, in the form of loans, did little to meet the enormous need for relief.[14]

Roosevelt was prepared to do more, though it was unclear how far he would go. He told progressive senators Robert La Follette, Jr., of Wisconsin and Bronson Cutting of New Mexico that he intended to have some kind of relief program, but he did not offer details. There was reason to believe that he would establish a national program along the lines of the Temporary Emergency Relief Administration that he had set up in New York, but there was also reason to believe that he might not. He was reluctant to make relief a federal responsibility, both because of his views on the role of the federal government, and because of his commitment to government economy. On March 6, Roosevelt had told the Governors' Conference that when it came to unemployment relief "the primary duty is that of the locality, the city, county, town." If the localities could not manage the burden, he said, "the next responsibility is on the States and they have to do all they can." Only if localities and states could not meet the needs of their unemployed, he insisted, was it "the duty of the Federal Government to step in."[15]

Perkins had always assumed when she joined the Cabinet that she would need to be the driving force pushing for a federal relief program. After her meeting with Roosevelt about Section 24 and the Garsson brothers, at which he had told her to "keep your eye" on relief and "try and help develop something," she felt that this role was official. Perkins went into Cabinet meetings carefully monitoring where her colleagues stood, and she was on the lookout for a good relief plan to bring to Roosevelt. At the first Cabinet meeting, the only subject was the banking crisis, but at the second one, Perkins recalled, "the question of relief was discussed with considerable intensity." She was pleased to see that when Roosevelt polled the Cabinet, all of them said "that relief and quick relief must be given." Even the more conservative members, like Claude Swanson, the secretary of the navy, and Cordell Hull, supported relief. Vice President Garner, whose views Perkins had been unsure of, pounded the table and shouted a little too loudly that they had to "do something for the poorer kind of people. By George! We've got to do it! And we've got to do it quick!" The discussion stalled, however, because there was no agreement about how to proceed or how much money should be allocated.[16]

Lewis Douglas did not oppose relief, or at least he did not speak out against it. He was intent, however, on keeping it modest in scope and inexpensive. Douglas argued that aid should be handed out as "relief-in-kind"—food, clothing, and other items that the unemployed might need. It was a position Roosevelt had expressed some sympathy for. Perkins led the opposition, arguing for cash payments. In-kind relief "was inefficient, awkward and so slow that people would die of hunger before we got it done," she said. The goods that were offered might not be what the recipients needed. If they had good shoes, left over from better times, they would still take new shoes if the government were giving them away, Perkins said, even though they would be better off if they were given the four dollars the shoes cost so they could spend it on "medicine for little Johnny." In addition to being inefficient, in-kind relief was demeaning to the people who received it, she argued. Perkins's side won the debate, and it was agreed that relief should be provided in the form of cash payments.[17]

Although she supported cash relief, Perkins's real goal was to establish a large-scale public works program. Public works was different from "work relief." Relief programs sometimes made people work off their benefits, but in these work relief programs, a social worker determined how much money a family needed and the recipient had to work off the value of the benefits. What Perkins and her fellow progressives wanted was public works, in which the government paid people real salaries at prevailing wage rates to take on real jobs, constructing government buildings, repairing infrastructure, and taking on other projects that promoted the public good. Perkins had been publicly advocating large-scale public works since the spring of 1930, when she encouraged the Committee for the Stabilization of Industry to recommend them. She believed that with jobs as scarce as they were, the government had a duty to provide work to the unemployed, so they could support themselves and their families and have the dignity of working for their livelihood. She had also argued, before John Maynard Keynes made it a matter of economic orthodoxy, that large-scale public works would "prime the pump," creating economic activity that would restore the economy to life.[18]

While Perkins was promoting public works inside the administration, progressives in Congress were fighting for it there. New York senator Robert F. Wagner, Perkins's old ally from the Factory Investigating Commission, had introduced a bill authorizing $2 billion in spending on public works, a cause he had long been fighting for. The "anciently stated first law of nature," Wagner declared, was "the right to work." Wagner also believed that public works would "prime the economic pump" and help move the nation toward recovery. Senators La Follette of Wisconsin and Edward Costigan of Colorado had introduced a bill to spend $5 billion on public works at both the federal and state levels. Neither bill had moved forward. Hoover had initiated some public works programs, but they were relatively small in scope, and they were limited by a requirement that most of the projects be "self-liquidating," or able to pay for themselves over time. With Roosevelt's election, progressives had begun to believe that the time for large-scale public works had finally arrived. "The best hope for the immediate future," *The New Republic* declared, "is the launching of the largest program of federal public works that can be financed, bringing immediate jobs to many thousands of persons all over the country, and pouring rivers of new money through the dried-up channels of trade."[19]

It was not clear, however, that Roosevelt agreed. Large-scale public works programs were in conflict with the government economy campaign that he was waging. Funding major construction projects, which meant paying for materials as well as labor, was far more costly than simply providing the poor with enough money to get by. Nor was it clear where the Roosevelt Cabinet stood. At the early Cabinet meetings, Perkins paid close attention to what her colleagues said about public works. A core group, including Wallace, Ickes, James Farley, and George Dern, the secretary of war from Utah, seemed to support it. Commerce secretary Daniel Roper, Navy secretary Claude Swanson, Attorney General Cummings, and Vice President Garner appeared to be more skeptical. The biggest skeptic of all was Douglas.[20]

Douglas was intent on blocking public works, but he was worried about where Roosevelt stood. Douglas objected to the expense of a public works program. In a letter to William Matthews, his newspaper friend back home in Arizona, he had argued that when Arizona tried public works, "the state and counties" had been "broken by the sheer weight of interest and amortization charges." Douglas's resistance, however, was more than just budgetary. His concerns about expensive government programs came from a deeper place, Tugwell found, one that "was not touchable by argument." Douglas lived in constant dread that society was unraveling, that socialism was on the march, and that capitalism was in mortal danger. Proposals for large-scale public works were the embodiment of all of his darkest fears. Douglas, who was prone to seeing things in apocalyptic terms, was alarmed by what he called "these forces that are being released" and "the philosophical base upon which they rest." He had, he said, "great apprehension for the future of my country."[21]

There was surprisingly little ill will between the liberal labor secretary and the conservative budget director. Douglas found Perkins, who sat next to him at Cabinet meetings, to be "gay" and "engaging," and he thought she "spoke beautifully." He would later say that "one couldn't help but being fond of her." Perkins had similarly positive feelings about Douglas and respected his abilities as a budget director. On the matter of public works, however, the battle lines between them were clearly drawn. Douglas had not "shown his hand" in the first Cabinet discussion of public works, Perkins later said, but she knew where he stood. She decided that she would "have to watch out for him," because "he had great influence with the President." It was not clear who would prevail. Roosevelt understood why Perkins and the other progressives wanted a large-scale public works program, but as Tugwell observed, "he was still open to the arguments of Douglas and the business leaders who insisted that economizing would restore confidence."[22]

Whatever happened with public works, it was not a short-term solution for the problems of the unemployed. Even if Roosevelt could be persuaded to back a large-scale public works program, it would take time to draw up plans for post offices, bridges, and other projects, and to work out the logistics. There was still an immediate need for a program of relief. Perkins had begun looking for a relief plan, as she promised Roosevelt she would, but she had not found anything yet. There was no shortage of ideas. Two thousand proposals had landed in her office and more were bouncing around the federal bureaucracy. "Some were pretty wild," Perkins said. They had strange notions about how to help the victims of the Depression, and bizarre names, like the "Schenectady Guaranteed Income Plan." It was not surprising that so many of these plans found their way to Perkins, given her advocacy for the disadvantaged and her openness to new ideas. This openness was not always an advantage. "Miss Perkins was a very natural point of approach for a large number of crazy people," her young counsel, Charles Wyzanski, recalled.[23]

About a week after the inauguration, an answer fell into Perkins's lap. Two social workers from her past showed up unannounced with a plan for creating a national system of relief for the unemployed. Harry Hopkins had set up the Temporary Emergency Relief Administration for Roosevelt, and he was still running it for Governor Herbert Lehman. William Hodson was the head of the New York City Welfare Council. No one had invited them to Washington, Perkins later recalled, "they just came," and they said it was "absolutely essential" that she see them. The capital was teeming with free-lance depression fighters, who were finding it impossible to get a hearing in the White House, and Hopkins and Hodson were two of them. Despite his work at the TERA, Hopkins did not know Roosevelt well enough to get past his gatekeepers. Perkins had a dinner conference scheduled the day Hopkins and Hodson contacted her, but she agreed to meet with them before it.[24]

Perkins invited the two New York social workers to the Women's University Club, where she was then living. She was surprised that when they met all of the tables were already full with, as she put it, "the kind of people who ate dinner at six o'clock." They found a bench and dragged it under a stairway. While the three of them sat on the bench, "cramped up" and "bent over," as Perkins recalled, Hopkins and Hodson presented their plan. They proposed creating a joint federal-state program. The funds would come from the federal Treasury and be distributed by the states according to federal rules. Roosevelt needed to act right away to get the money from Congress, they said, and an agency had to be created to hand it out as quickly as possible. The plan struck Perkins as "well thought out" and "practical." She had not mastered the fine points in the conversation under the stairs, but she believed there was no time to agonize over the details. Perkins agreed to present the proposal to Roosevelt and said she would get him to commit to it. "It's got to be done quickly or the country won't hold," the two social workers insisted.[25]

Perkins made an appointment to meet with Roosevelt and brought along Hopkins and Hodson. Roosevelt readily agreed that the administration should adopt their plan as its official program for unemployment relief. He asked Wagner, La Follette, and Costigan, the Senate's biggest supporters of relief, to draw up a bill modeled on the Hopkins-Hodson plan, which would become the Federal Emergency Relief Act. When Perkins asked Hopkins and Hodson who should be brought on to run the new relief agency that would be created, they said they thought it should be one of them, since no one else had as much experience with programs like it. As for which of them it should be, they told Perkins that Roosevelt should choose.[26]

While Perkins was working on the emergency relief plan, she continued to fight for large-scale public works. The signs Roosevelt had sent so far on the subject were not encouraging. Early in 1932, he had criticized Al Smith, who was challenging him for the Democratic presidential nomination, for taking a strong stand in favor of public works. In the general election, progressives had urged Roosevelt to come out for a $5 billion public works program, but he had resisted. He did not think there were enough projects worth undertaking to justify a major public works program, and he did not subscribe to the "pump priming" theory that many supporters of public works were using to justify the sizable expenditures. In early March, Moley had dinner at the Capitol with Senators La Follette and Costigan, and they had asked him whether he thought Roosevelt could be persuaded to back a large-scale public works program. Moley was not optimistic. He believed Roosevelt was "frankly leery of the arguments for public works." Moley told La Follette and Costigan that it might be worth trying to bring the subject up casually, but he advised them not to press Roosevelt too hard.[27]

When Moley asked Roosevelt about relief on the morning of March 14, he got a response he had not expected. Roosevelt launched into an enthusiastic description of a specialized public works program that he had been planning for some time. Roosevelt wanted to send unemployed young men out into the nation's forests to do conservation work. He was calling the program, which he had initially proposed to include in the Economy Act, the Civilian Reclamation Corps. The idea was Roosevelt's own, but it had historical antecedents. It was similar to what the Harvard philosopher William James had suggested in an influential essay, "The Moral Equivalent of War." James had argued for drafting young men into an "army enlisted against Nature," rather than a military army. Moley suggested to Roosevelt that he might have been influenced by vague student memories of Professor James. When Tugwell heard the idea, he startled Roosevelt by saying that Mussolini already had such a corps in place in Fascist Italy. The similarity "was never mentioned publicly," Tugwell later wrote, "for obvious political reasons."[28]

The inspiration for the Civilian Conservation Corps, as the program would soon be renamed, was Roosevelt's own life. He had acquired a love of the land growing up in the rustic world of Hyde Park. "The Boss was an ardent tree lover," his secretary, Grace Tully, recalled. "When reports of bad storms in the vicinity of Dutchess County reached him, his first thought was 'I wonder what it did to the trees.'" When the Depression first hit, during Roosevelt's governorship, he and his state conservation commissioner, Henry Morgenthau, had put ten thousand New Yorkers to work on reforestation projects. When he accepted the Democratic nomination for president, Roosevelt already had something much larger in mind. In his July 2 address to the convention, he had spoken of a plan to convert millions of acres of marginal and unused land into timberland by reforestation. This plan could, he declared, provide jobs for one million men.[29]

The Civilian Conservation Corps had many things to recommend it. The CCC would provide jobs for many young people who had few other prospects of finding work. Roosevelt envisioned that the workers would send much of their earnings home, helping their parents and siblings survive the hard times. Along with these financial benefits, the CCC would instill a sense of purpose in young Americans, many of whom had been adrift since the start of the Depression. Roosevelt would later say that one of its primary purposes was to "build up character in the coming generation." At the same time as it brought relief to the participants, the CCC would help rescue the nation's forests and national parks. Unrestricted timber harvesting had reduced the virgin forest from 800,000 acres to just 100,000, and the plight of forests and parks was being made worse by severe soil erosion. Water and wind were removing six billion tons of soil a year. With money tight, the government had not been able to do much to reverse the damage. The genius of the CCC was, as one study of the program observed, that it "brought together two wasted resources, the young men and the land, in an attempt to save both."[30]

For Roosevelt, the CCC had another distinct advantage—it was public works on the cheap. Young, unmarried men, the group the program was intended to help, would be willing to work for low wages, especially when their room and board were being provided. Roosevelt proposed salaries of just one dollar a day. The corps's other expenses would be equally modest. It cost far less to clear paths and preserve topsoil than it would to build the bridges, dams, and school buildings that Perkins, Wagner, and other progressives were calling for. Roosevelt, who was still actively promoting government economy, declared that because of its limited focus the CCC could be run for some time with the relief funds that had already been allocated by the Hoover administration, with "no additional burden on the Treasury."[31]

When Roosevelt introduced the CCC to his Cabinet and top aides, the response was largely enthusiastic. The main holdout was the ever-practical Perkins, who considered it a "pipe dream." It was not clear to her how Roosevelt intended to get people off breadlines and out to forests, or what he expected them to do when they got there. She envisioned unemployed people from New York City marching up to the Adirondacks and getting lost. Roosevelt's quick sketch of the plan did not get into any of this. "It was characteristic of him," Perkins would later say, "that he conceived the project, boldly rushed it through, and happily left it to others to worry about the details." Even if the logistics were worked out, Perkins was troubled by the dollar-a-day wage, and she knew labor unions would also be. It was fine "so far as reforestation is concerned," she told Moley, since that would be a program of limited scope, involving work that was not currently being done by anyone. If the dollar-a-day wage were applied to public works more broadly, she warned, it would pull down private-sector salaries, which would have a disastrous impact on working men and women. Most of all, Perkins wanted to make sure that Roosevelt's pet project did not interfere with her own goal of creating a large-scale public works program that would provide jobs with real salaries to millions of unemployed people.[32]

Roosevelt wanted to move quickly. He asked Moley to circulate a memo to the Cabinet members who would be most involved in launching the CCC—Perkins, Dern, Wallace, and Ickes. The memo, which went out on Tuesday, March 14, asked the four of them to consider themselves "an informal committee of the Cabinet to coordinate the plans." With that invitation, Perkins, Dern, Wallace, and Ickes decided to push for something more ambitious. The next day, they drew up their own memo urging Roosevelt to establish three programs. The first was the CCC as Roosevelt had described it, though they urged that it be expressly limited to forestry and soil erosion work. The second was a general relief program, along the lines of the Hopkins-Hodson plan, which would provide money to the states to dispense to the unemployed. "The details of such a Bill," the memo said, "are practically agreed upon between Senators Wagner, Costigan, La Follette and Secretary Perkins." Finally, the four Cabinet members urged Roosevelt to back the sort of public works program Perkins and others had been lobbying for. It should be, the memo said, "a large practical, labor producing program of public works under the control of a Board which can allocate them in such a manner as to drain the largest pools of unemployment in the country."[33]

Roosevelt agreed with the first two recommendations, the CCC and a relief program, but he was still not persuaded about large-scale public works. Wall Street was telling him that if the government spent billions on public works, it would cause the bottom to fall out of the bond market and destroy the government's ability to borrow. Douglas was making the same arguments from within the administration, and Moley was largely staying out of the dispute. On March 15, the same day the four Cabinet members were in Ickes's office drawing up their memo on relief, Roosevelt held his third press conference. He talked enthusiastically about the CCC. There would be at least 200,000 people in the national forests alone, Roosevelt said, working on reforestation and creating "fire breaks," swaths of empty land that would confine any forest fires that broke out to a limited area. When he was asked if he also planned to support "a vast public works program," Roosevelt was evasive. There were "quite a lot" of people who favored an "all-inclusive" public works bill, he said, but he was not sure if he would support one, or restrict public works to "putting people immediately to work on natural resources."[34]

With that question up in the air, Roosevelt asked Moley to call in Perkins, La Follette, Costigan, and Wagner to meet with him the following day. On March 16, the group once again made the case to Roosevelt for large-scale public works, separate from the CCC. Moley could not attend the meeting because it fell on a Thursday, the day he returned to New York to teach. He was sorry not to have been able to attend and "see these people operate," he later said. The meeting turned out to be a turning point in the administration's response to the Depression. "They must have been persuasive," Moley said later, "because when the meeting broke up F.D.R., who distrusted public works profoundly, had agreed to mention them in his message on relief." The following day, at the fourth press conference of his presidency, Roosevelt told reporters that he expected to introduce a "larger relief program," and that it would "probably include public works."[35]

On March 21, Perkins held her first press conference. Her office asked newspapers to send news reporters, not feature writers. Although she was the first woman Cabinet member, Perkins did not want to be treated "as a feminine feature," The *Chicago Tribune* noted. "She hopes her history will say it with facts, not flowers." At the appointed hour, reporters, many of them women, crowded into her office. Perkins talked about closing down Section 24 and answered questions about employment statistics and other substantive labor matters. She ended the conference by saying she had to go to the White House. "I always make it a rule to be on time at a Cabinet meeting," she said, "for I am not going to let the men members point to the woman as the late one." Perkins's debut performance before the capital press corps got good reviews. *The Washington Post* reported that "this little woman, still smaller back of the wide mahogany desk," demonstrated a "firm grip."[36]

It was not easy for Perkins to banter with reporters. Unlike Roosevelt, who genuinely enjoyed spending time with the press, Perkins could not help thinking of them as the enemy. "One of the worst things that Roosevelt did, was to introduce the press into the affairs of government," she insisted. Perkins was offended by reporters' unending questions. "What business of theirs is it where you're going for Thanksgiving?" she complained. She especially resented intrusions into her family life. She was irate that during her first few days as secretary of labor *The New York Times* had run an article about Susanna's Irish terrier, Balto, running away that included the family's home address, 1239 Madison Avenue. Perkins's biggest fear remained that the press would turn Paul Wilson and his condition into a national news story. As it happened, they never asked about him. Perkins suspected Eleanor Roosevelt had taken the women reporters aside to explain the situation and asked them to spread the word. The press kept the secret so well that most Americans were under the impression that "Miss Perkins" had never married.[37]

Perkins also disliked how the press covered her professional life. She found Washington reporters more cynical and sensationalistic than the ones she had dealt with in New York. They were constantly asking her what her "angle" was, she complained. Perkins issued press releases that focused on important matters—"not what I think of John L. Lewis's last outburst," she said. "That's not the news. The news is the government's inquiry into the wages and hours of the coal mining industry." Many of the press questions struck her as no-win. "They would say, 'Have you consulted Secretary Ickes about this?'" she said. "If you say 'No,' then Ickes is offended because they say, 'Perkins refuses to consult with other Cabinet officers.' If you say 'Yes,' then they've got to know just what you said, what he said, why he said that, and then they've got to go ask him what he said, what he meant." Many of the younger reporters struck Perkins as having a "Marxian outlook" that skewed their questions. When they asked about her support for unemployment insurance, she complained, they would say, "'I suppose, Madam Secretary, that that will be a way of preventing revolution, won't it?' Well, now, what if you say, 'Yes.' That means 'PERKINS EXPECTS REVOLUTION' will be the headline."[38]

Perkins continued holding press conferences, but they were not like Roosevelt's amiable gatherings. One major difference was that she did not provide the reporters with chairs. "I've learned that the best thing to do is to keep them standing," she said. "They don't stay so long." She made no effort to win reporters over by gossiping with them off the record. Perkins's stern approach did not win her any friends. "With newspaper reporters," a magazine profile observed, "she tries to be cordial, but only succeeds in being cold and distant." The chilly relations that Perkins had with the press corps at the start of her tenure in Washington would last her entire career. Years later, on a trip to St. Louis, a photographer took her picture despite her pleas not to. Perkins asked if she could look at his camera. When he handed it to her, she dropped it on the ground, stomped on it, and said, "that takes care of the picture." Perkins's prickly treatment of reporters caused her to receive some of the worst press of any member of the administration. "Of all the game in the Roosevelt preserve," one magazine declared, "Secretary of Labor Perkins has been the most frequently chased and the most savagely harried." She refused to let it bother her—or to let down her guard. "I'll let history judge my record," she said, "not the newspaper boys."[39]

On March 21, the same day as Perkins's press conference, Roosevelt sent his Civilian Conservation Corps bill to Congress. In his congressional message, Roosevelt was far more open to large-scale public works than he had been before his meeting with Perkins, La Follette, Costigan, and Wagner. He adopted the formulation that the memo from Perkins, Dern, Wallace, and Ickes had urged on him. He declared relief programs to be "essential to our recovery program." To carry out a "direct attack" on the problem, he said, would require three kinds of legislation. The first would enroll workers in "such public employment as can be quickly started." The second would be "grants to the States for relief work." Finally, he told Congress, there should be "a broad public works labor-creating program."[40]

The work program that could be "quickly started" was the CCC. In the version of the CCC bill that he sent to Congress, he included the proviso that Perkins and other Cabinet members had called for in their memo—that the forest jobs the program created should not interfere with "normal employment." Roosevelt told Congress that the program—which would be supervised by the departments of Labor, Agriculture, War, and Interior—could put as many as 250,000 unemployed men to work as early as the summer. The CCC would be doing much-needed work, including "forestry, the prevention of soil erosion, flood control and similar projects." The benefits, he argued, would be more than just financial. The CCC would, he said, help eliminate "the threat that enforced idleness brings to spiritual and moral stability."[41]

The second program in Roosevelt's triad of relief, "grants to the States for relief work," would provide the unemployed with money for food, clothing, and other material needs. The Hopkins-Hodson plan that Perkins had brought to Roosevelt would be the blueprint for the legislation to accomplish this.[42]

The third relief program, large-scale public works, was the most noteworthy. Roosevelt was now officially a convert to the cause. There were several bills floating around on Capitol Hill, including the ones introduced by Wagner, La Follette, and Costigan, but Roosevelt wanted to come up with his own plan. In the message, he was spare with details, saying only that he would "make recommendations to the Congress presently." For Perkins and her fellow progressives, what mattered was that Roosevelt had gone on the record with his support of the basic idea.[43]

For now, Roosevelt was only asking Congress to approve the CCC. The CCC bill was generally well received by Congress. Most members were pleased finally to have the chance to vote for a law that would create jobs for the unemployed. But as Perkins predicted, organized labor was firmly opposed. The president of the Brotherhood of Railroad Trainmen, A. F. Whitney, argued that the bill's dollar-a-day salary "would place government's endorsement upon poverty at a bare subsistence level." William Green of the American Federation of Labor objected not only to the salary, but to the army's role in supervising CCC workers. "We cannot believe that the time has come," Green said, "when the United States should supply relief through the creation of a form of compulsory military service."[44]

The administration mobilized to defend its bill. The day after it was introduced, Roosevelt invited leading members of the Senate and House to the White House for an evening briefing. With Perkins, Wallace, Dern, and Ickes on hand, Roosevelt made his case for the CCC and answered questions about the bill. By the time the meeting adjourned, most of the congressional guests had been won over. William P. Connery, Jr., of Massachusetts, the chairman of the House Labor Committee, was a notable holdout. The staunchly proworker Connery, whose district included the factory towns of Lynn and Lawrence, insisted that he could not support a program that created jobs that paid so little.[45]

The following day, March 23, Perkins, wearing a black dress and a tricorn hat, testified before Congress. She firmly turned back organized labor's objections. The CCC, she told a joint session of the House and Senate Labor Committees, was not an employment program, but a relief measure "to provide honest occupation to self-respecting Americans who have been forced to panhandling and similar practices." Perkins rejected Connery's claim that the CCC wage was comparable to "sweatshop work," arguing that since the men would be given food, shelter, and clothing, it was substantially more generous than sweatshops offered. When a California congressman objected that it was unfair to force men to leave their families for a year to earn a dollar a day, Perkins joked, "It might be the best thing that could happen" for some families, to applause and laughter from the galleries. Speaking more seriously, she said there was nothing "more destructive of the family than prolonged unemployment, where a man has to sit around the house and brood, and his only occupation is to go twice a week and get his basket or dole." [46]

In her first appearance before Congress as a Cabinet member, Perkins "made such a favorable impression," *Time* magazine reported, "that many a hostile vote was won over to the White House plan." Although she had shown herself to be articulate and well versed in the facts, Perkins was still regarded by many in Congress as a curiosity. A female reporter, Ruby Black, told her that after her testimony several congressmen sat in the cloakroom talking about it while they smoked cigars. "She did awful well," one congressman said. "But I'd hate to be married to her." Perkins and Black laughed over it. "You know, Ruby, it never occurred to me when I went up there that perhaps I could get a husband," Perkins said. "How unfortunate I didn't think of it!" Her reaction showed how unruffled she was by her encounters with sexism—and how secretive she was about the fact that she was already married. [47]

The CCC's critics also testified, urging Congress to reject or modify the bill. Green continued to argue that the pay scale would hurt private-sector workers. This Congress "will go down in history," he declared, as one "that has established a dollar a day wage for the payment of labor on the public domain." Green also insisted that putting so many civilians under the army's control "smacked of fascism, of Hitlerism, of a form of Sovietism." Herbert

Benjamin of the National Unemployment Council warned that the CCC's model of sending men out to the forests for extended periods would result in "the violation and destruction of the families of American workers." The administration dispatched witnesses to rebut these concerns. Douglas MacArthur, who was then the army chief of staff, promised that while the armed forces would select, train, and transport workers enrolled in the CCC, it was a "purely non-military function" and would have "no connection with the army's job" of "national defense."[48]

Roosevelt's reference to larger-scale public works in his congressional message had alarmed conservatives. While the CCC worked its way through Congress, powerful financial interests mobilized to try to block a broader program. On March 24, the same day MacArthur testified, James Warburg, the prominent young banker, met with Moley to convey Wall Street's strong opposition to large-scale public works. Spending billions of dollars on such programs would only put a small percentage of the unemployed back to work, Warburg said, but it would do irreparable damage to the government's credit. Moley listened sympathetically to the argument, which he had already heard from Douglas. He knew, however, that Roosevelt was moving in the direction of adopting the sort of program Warburg and Douglas feared.[49]

In the meantime, Roosevelt was holding his sixth press conference. It was not clear how he intended to establish major relief and public works programs while also implementing the Economy Act. He suggested to reporters that he might do it by creating two budgets, one for regular and one for emergency expenditures. Roosevelt still intended to cut spending on regular expenses, but he had not decided whether it was fair to include "expenditures that relate to keeping human beings from starving in this emergency" in the regular budget. "I should say probably not," he told the press corps. The idea of dual federal budgets was not new—Moley had floated it in his May 1932 Brain Trust memo. Still, conservatives were shocked when Roosevelt went public with the idea. *The New York Times* was troubled that some of the president's advisers seemed to think he could increase spending while balancing the budget through "a sort of painless arithmetic." Douglas was the most disturbed of all. Roosevelt had not consulted with Douglas in advance, no doubt because he knew how bitterly he would have objected. The talk of a dual budget was Douglas's first indication that Roosevelt's commitment to government economy was weakening. Douglas was deeply pained by Roosevelt's change of heart. By the end of the year, he would write an angry memo pointing to Roosevelt's decision to treat emergency expenditures as a separate category as perhaps the worst of any during the Hundred Days. "Why should we steel ourselves to the heart-breaking task of saving a billion dollars of ordinary expenditures, when with a prodigal hand, we scatter over seven billions upon extraordinary expenditures?" he asked. To Douglas, as long as expenditures were greater than receipts, the government's credit would be in peril. Separating some expenses off into a separate budget, he insisted, "fools no one."[50]

On March 28, the Senate passed the CCC bill on a voice vote, undeterred by the warning of L. J. Dickinson, Republican of Iowa, that "we will rue the day when we put so much power into one man's hands." The opposition was stronger in the House, led by organized labor's allies. Connery tried to amend the bill to raise the CCC wage scale to $50 a month for single enrollees and $80 for married ones. The Connery amendment failed. The House did, however, approve another amendment sponsored by Oscar DePriest of Illinois, the House's only black member, prohibiting the CCC from discriminating on the basis of race. The House passed its bill, and after it and the Senate's bill were reconciled, with DePriest's amendment remaining, Roosevelt signed the CCC into law on March 31.[51]

Before the bill passed, planning for the CCC was already under way. Perkins offered the job of running the Labor Department's part of the program, the selection of enrollees, to W. Frank Persons, the former superintendent of the Charity Organization Society in New York. Persons had run the Red Cross home service during the war, and Perkins had been impressed, she said, with his "knowledge of how to sort out the sheep from the goats." The army drew up regulations dividing the country into nine regions, and it began calculating how much it would cost to train, shelter, feed, and clothe 250,000 formerly unemployed men in camps in the forest. Roosevelt convened a meeting at the White House on April 3 to work out how the departments of Labor, War, Agriculture, and Interior would coordinate their efforts. On the same day, the call went out for the first 25,000 enrollees.[52]

Two days later, Roosevelt named Robert Fechner director of the CCC. Just as he had chosen Peek to run the AAA to placate the leading critics of the program, agricultural processors, the selection of Fechner, an executive in the International Association of Machinists and vice president of the AFL, was Roosevelt's attempt to assuage the unions, which remained uneasy about the CCC. Fechner, who had been born into poverty in Chattanooga, had dropped out of school at sixteen to peddle newspapers on trains in Georgia. He became a machinist and worked his way up the ranks of the union, but he never lost his rough edges. Fechner once said that among the New Dealers, many of whom arrived in Washington with lofty educational pedigrees, he felt like "a potato bug amongst dragonflies." Most of his clerks, he freely admitted, were better educated than he was. Roosevelt asked Fechner how long it would take him to set up the first CCC camp. When he replied "a month," Roosevelt said it was too long. "Two weeks?" Fechner asked. "Good," Roosevelt said. The CCC met its deadline. The first camp was established in George Washington National Forest outside Luray, Virginia, and it was called Camp Roosevelt.[53]

On March 31, the same day Roosevelt signed the CCC bill into law, Perkins presided over the labor conference Sidney Hillman had asked for. Several unions offered their buildings so the conference would not have to be held in the Department of Labor's ramshackle offices. Perkins thought the symbolism of hosting the conference at the department was important. She wanted to make clear that the administration was reaching out to labor. The largest space in the poorly laid-out building was Perkins's office, so she had all of the furniture removed and the sliding doors to an adjacent office opened up. When the seventy-five union leaders arrived, it was not only crowded but hot, because, as Perkins recalled later, "spring came very early that year."[54]

In her opening statement, Perkins emphasized Roosevelt's commitment to doing something about unemployment. The administration intended to fight it, she said, with both relief and programs to create jobs. She also talked about unemployment insurance, old-age assistance, child labor laws, and maximum hours laws. All of these were valuable, she said, not only as workers' rights measures, but as ways to take people out of the job market, leaving more work for those who needed it. There were tensions among the labor leaders. John L. Lewis was "less than happily welcomed," Perkins noticed, and the AFL leaders cast "a big pickle eye on Hillman." When they focused on substance, there was more agreement. George Berry, the Tennessean who headed up the International Printing Pressmen and Assistants' Union, spoke for the whole conference when he talked about how badly off his members were and urged the adoption of a federal relief program as quickly as possible. Other leaders offered more specific suggestions, including that the unemployed be allowed to sleep in public buildings. The suggestion struck Perkins as "inane coming from a group of labor leaders," and more what one would expect coming from a "warm-hearted, not very scientific charity organization." In the late morning, Daniel J. Tobin, the Teamsters union president, complained loudly about the accommodations, and insisted that the conference should move to larger, cooler meeting rooms at the AFL headquarters. Perkins thought that the facilities were "horrid," but vetoed the move. What seemed to be rankling Tobin was not the accommodations, but being passed over for labor secretary.[55]

After a nighttime meeting without Perkins, the labor leaders returned the next day and hammered out a ten-point program of action. It called for at least $1 billion in appropriations for relief and $3 billion for public works, the adoption of a ban on child labor, and labor representation on CCC advisory boards. The labor leaders were particularly intent on getting large-scale public works, which they saw as the best chance of getting their members jobs until the economy improved. A $3 billion public works program would directly employ one million workers, they said, and it would employ nearly one million more in manufacturing and transporting the materials needed for the projects. When the conference ended, Perkins took a contingent of labor leaders to the White House to report to Roosevelt. With William Green's consent, she let Tobin lead the group. Their recommendations were not unexpected, but the meeting served a dual purpose for Perkins. It allowed her to show union leaders that the president cared about what they thought, and it helped her to show Roosevelt how strongly organized labor felt about public works and the other programs she was urging on him.[56]

By mid-March, Roosevelt had already sent Congress the ambitious Agricultural Adjustment Act, but the administration did not have a comparable plan for reviving industry. The lack of industrial relief legislation left a vacuum that Congress was prepared to fill itself. The previous December, Senator Hugo Black of Alabama had introduced a "30 hour" bill, his attempt to boost nonfarm employment. The Black Bill called for banning from interstate commerce products made by workers who were employed more than five days a week or six hours a day. The idea was that if workweeks were capped at thirty hours, employers would have to spread the available work out among more employees. It was wrong, Black insisted in a radio address, for some workers to work as much as seventy hours a week "while others are driven into poverty and misery from unemployment." If his bill passed, Black argued, it would force employers to hire 25 percent more workers to make up for the lost hours, generating six million new jobs. The Black Bill had strong support from organized labor and it benefited from the absence of any other serious proposals for reenergizing the labor market. On April 6, the Senate passed the bill by a vote of 53–30.[57]

Perkins had first heard of Black's "30 hour" bill back in New York, and it had struck her as nonsensical. She talked to Roosevelt and found that he agreed. As they saw it, the bill had two basic problems. It was too inflexible, applying a single cap on hours to every job in the nation. Roosevelt believed it would put a particular burden on businesses, like canneries, that were located in rural areas, where labor was in relatively short supply. The thirty-hour limit might mean that these employers would not be able to keep up production at peak times of the season. The rigidity was particularly unsuited for specialized industries, like dairy farming, which could not simply send a new shift of workers onto the factory floor. "There have to be hours adapted to the rhythm of the cow," Roosevelt said. The bill's other major flaw was that if employees' workweeks were reduced to thirty hours, they would earn less money at a time when low wages were already making it difficult for working people to support their families. Roosevelt dispatched Perkins to try to stop Congress from passing the bill.[58]

Perkins met with Black and found him difficult to dissuade. "Ah think the President's in favor of this," he told her. Perkins was not impressed when she listened to Black explain his bill. He took out a pencil and paper and did complex calculations involving the number of people employed before the Depression, the number currently unemployed, and the total value of the nation's manufactured goods. He concluded, in a way Perkins found thoroughly unpersuasive, that the available work came to thirty hours per worker, employed and unemployed. After this presentation, Perkins never "felt quite easy" about Black. The mechanics of fighting unemployment were, she decided, "a matter he knew nothing about." She asked him what would happen to workers who were currently working forty-eight or fifty-four hours a week, who would see their income plunge if they were cut back to just thirty hours. Black said their wages would naturally adjust, which she considered "absurd." Perkins argued that the bill had to contain a minimum wage provision, to ensure that workers were not driven into poverty by the hour limits. Black, however, insisted that such a provision was unnecessary.[59]

If Black's bill was going to be stopped now, it would have to be in the House. That would not be easy, since the bill had momentum coming out of the Senate, and it had the support of progressives who were unhappy that the administration, which had been slashing salaries and benefits under the Economy Act, had still done nothing for workers. The AFL strongly backed the "30 hour" bill. Faced with unprecedented unemployment rates, it had abandoned its historic opposition to helping workers by passing laws. William Green hailed the Black Bill as "the first real practical step on the part of the government to constructively deal with the problem of unemployment." He predicted a universal strike if it did not become law. Green would not go along with Perkins's suggestion of a minimum wage provision. "Pass your bill," Green said, "and let us handle the question of wages." The AFL insisted that it was worried that a minimum wage would effectively become a maximum wage as well. It looked to Perkins, however, like another example of what she had seen in her Albany days: labor leaders opposing rights for workers that were provided by law, rather than through a union contract.[60]

On April 12, Perkins returned to Congress to testify before the House Committee on Labor. The administration would be willing to support the Black Bill, she said, if it was properly modified. Roosevelt wanted an "elasticity" clause that would allow industries, with the permission of a joint government-employer-employee commission, to put workers to work for forty hours a week for a limited number of weeks. Perkins also insisted that, despite labor's opposition, the bill had to have a minimum wage provision, to ensure that workers whose hours were reduced were not driven into poverty.[61]

While she tried to modify or derail the "30 hour" bill, Perkins kept fighting for public works. Along with her behind-the-scenes lobbying, she used her bully pulpit to build popular support. At an appearance before the Pennsylvania State Federation of Labor the evening of April 12, she called for a federal public works program and a federal minimum wage. Perkins continued to argue that public works would not only help the unemployed, but restore the whole economy by priming the pump. "Industry cannot go forward unless it has in back of it the tremendous purchasing power of the wage earners," she said. Two days later, Perkins told the Associated Press that she supported $2 to $3 billion in public works projects over the next four or five months—not "monumental" projects, but practical ones, such as roads, sewage systems, and low-cost housing that could be started right away.[62]

On April 18, Perkins sent the House Labor Committee a revised version of the Black Bill that met the administration's concerns. The bill provided for industry-by-industry boards that would have the power to allow businesses to extend their workweeks up to forty hours. It authorized the labor secretary to establish a board to set a minimum wage for an industry if she found that the workers were not getting subsistence wages. It also expressly exempted milk and cream from the limits, a concession to Roosevelt's concerns about the "rhythm of the cow." There was strong opposition to the modified Black Bill. Organized labor attacked the minimum wage provision. Manufacturers opposed the maximum hours in Perkins's bill, and in Black's original one. Critics branded the bill "Sovietism" and accused Perkins of trying to become a "Czar of Industry."[63]

Perkins was not prepared for the ferocity of the opposition to what she called her "modest plan to make the Black bill workable." On April 25, she returned to the House Labor Committee. The hearing attracted an unusual amount of attention because Eleanor Roosevelt brought British prime minister Ramsay MacDonald's daughter, Ishbel, who was visiting the White House. In a hearing room packed with spectators, cameras, and klieg lights, Perkins calmly made the case for her bill. When a committee member objected that it would require thousands of new Labor Department staff, Perkins replied, "I should resign at once if it did." The following day, labor and business testified against the modified bill. William Green attacked the minimum wage provision as a "dangerous experiment" that would "peg wages." Gerard Swope, the president of General Electric, endorsed the goal of spreading work among more people, but he argued that the bill was "too rigid for practical application." On May 10, the committee reported out a version of the Black Bill, but it no longer mattered. Roosevelt did not want to back a bill that faced such entrenched opposition. The administration was by now at work on its own industrial recovery bill, one that it expected both business and labor to support.[64]

In early April, nineteen-year-old Fiore Rizzo walked into an army building in downtown Manhattan and declared that he wanted to work in the woods. Rizzo was the first person to sign up for the Civilian Conservation Corps, one of an initial group of 25,000 enrollees. Henry Wallace talked up the CCC in a national radio address. "This is primarily a relief program," he declared, but "the men who enroll are not seeking charity; they want an opportunity to make their way." The CCC was an instant success. Young men loaded onto buses and trucks and took up work assignments in forests and parks across the country. By mid-July, 275,000 workers would be employed at more than 1,300 camps, a deployment larger than the number of Americans who enlisted in the Spanish-American War. Roosevelt took a personal interest in the details of the CCC, and reviewed the camp locations himself. There were some early glitches. Too many work sites were approved in the West and not enough in the East, where most of the unemployed were. There was a mini-scandal when Louis Howe approved the purchase of 200,000 toilet kits without competitive bidding, and congressional hearings revealed that they could have been purchased for far less. But for the most part the CCC worked just as Roosevelt had hoped. Young men enthusiastically built roads, trails, camps, and picnic grounds. They worked on erosion and flood control projects and planted trees. Most of the participants earned $30 a month, and sent $25 a month home, supporting an estimated one million family members.[65]

The money and work experience changed millions of lives. The CCC allowed Robert Shaver, a young man with a sixth-grade education assigned to a camp in Tennessee's Cherokee National Forest, to send $25 a month to his struggling parents back in Cedar Rapids. Louis I. Schneider's father was unemployed and unable to support his twelve children. Schneider worked at a CCC camp in Cascade, Iowa, so his siblings would be able to eat and stay in school. At a time when there were few ways for young people to learn basic job skills, the CCC was an invaluable training ground. Charles Krall, who took conservation courses while he worked at a camp in Montana, went on to a thirty-year career in the Soil Conservation Service. Joseph Aebisher, a New Yorker assigned to a Vermont camp, helped build a ski jump in Stowe and a picnic area near Rutland. When his service was over, he became a construction engineer in the army. The CCC, he later said, "gave me the job experience that I've built on during the rest of my life."[66]

At first, the CCC was limited to unmarried men. Eleanor Roosevelt suggested to Perkins that women should be allowed to sign up. On June 1, the two women jointly announced the opening of an experimental camp for three hundred young women in upstate New York, on the banks of the Hudson River. Rather than plant trees or build roads, the women would receive vocational training in dressmaking, weaving, and embroidering. Later, at a camp in Texas, women would undertake the more rugged work of building vacation cottages, but overall, the opportunities for women were limited. The CCC was not much more receptive to blacks, despite Oscar DePriest's antidiscrimination amendment. In both the South and North, blacks were not allowed to sign up in proportion to their numbers, and they were generally placed in segregated camps. In camps for black workers, the supervisory positions went to whites. Fechner, who was a Southerner, defended the discriminatory policies, insisting that whites in the surrounding communities would feel more secure having whites in charge of the camps. Native Americans had a surprisingly good experience. In April, Roosevelt opened the CCC to 14,400 tribal members, who were suffering from the effects of both the Depression and a serious drought. There were CCC operations on reservations in fifteen southwestern and western states. Many of the projects, which were chosen with input from the tribal councils, focused on combating soil erosion and insect infestations, both of which were having a devastating impact on Native American farming.[67]

Veterans ended up receiving special status in the CCC, thanks to the Bonus Army. A year had passed since the Bonus Army's bloody encounter with Hoover's troops. The army's leaders had decided to return to Washington to keep lobbying for immediate payment of their bonuses and to protest the deep cuts that Lewis Douglas was making to their benefits. Roosevelt took a different approach from Hoover's. He was as resolute as his predecessor had been about not paying out the bonus, which would have interfered with his government economy plans. But he did not want to be drawn into the sort of clashes that had done Hoover's reputation so much harm. Roosevelt invited the veterans to camp at Fort Hunt, an old army installation on the Potomac River. The government would provide them with meals, medical care, and entertainment by the navy band.[68]

About three thousand Bonus Army members showed up, far fewer than the twenty thousand who had come a year earlier. As they settled in, Louis Howe had an idea. One afternoon, he asked Eleanor to take a drive with him. When they approached Fort Hunt, he asked her to go out and meet with the veterans. "Get their gripes, if any, make a tour of the camp and tell them that Franklin sent you to see about them," Howe instructed. "Don't forget that—be sure to tell them that Franklin sent you out to see about them." Eleanor threw herself into the camp, drinking coffee with the men, recounting her visits to the European battlefronts during the World War, and leading the veterans in old army songs. She did not know what would happen to their bonus, she told them, but she declared, "I would like to see fair consideration for everyone, and I shall always be grateful to those who served their country." The veterans were moved that a first lady had come to see them, and had treated them with respect and humanity. "Hoover sent the Army," one veteran said. "Roosevelt sent his wife."[69]

Even after the visit, Roosevelt held firm on the bonus, which disappointed veterans and their supporters. The veterans had "fought for democracy and you got influenza, prohibition, and Hoover," Francis Shoemaker, a Farmer-Labor member of Congress from Minnesota, told the Bonus Army. "Now you have a new deal, a raw deal I call it." What Roosevelt did offer the men was a special path to signing up for the CCC. He issued an executive order setting aside 25,000 places for veterans of the World War and the Spanish-American War, and all Bonus Army members encamped at Fort Hunt would be guaranteed spots. Some members of the Bonus Army refused to give up their goal of getting the bonus paid, and their responses were in some cases indignant. A loud cheer went up at Fort Hunt when one army member cried out, "To hell with reforestation!" Maurice Miller, one of the leaders, told a reporter that "none of the men are going to do any work like that for $1 a day." Many of the rank and file, however, felt differently. Within days of Roosevelt's offer, the Bonus Army disbanded. More than 2,500 of its members joined the CCC, and those who chose not to were given free transportation home. Fort Hunt was transformed into a CCC camp.[70]

As soon as the Black Bill began moving in Congress, the administration began scrambling to develop its own plan for industrial recovery. The main idea that was emerging was that the federal government and businesses should work together to coordinate industrial activity. Moley and Tugwell had favored some form of business-government partnership since the Brain Trust days. Their bible was *Concentration and Control*, a 1912 book by University of Wisconsin president Charles Van Hise, which argued that the United States had entered a post-competitive age, in which companies were growing larger and industries were becoming more "concentrated." Van Hise insisted that there was nothing wrong with industrial concentration as long as there was corresponding "control" by government regulators. This approach was a sharp break from the previous generation of progressives, who had rallied to Louis Brandeis's warnings about the "curse of bigness" and his call for breaking up large corporations through vigorous antitrust laws. The Brain Trust believed, in Moley's words, "that economic bigness was here to stay" and that "it was the duty of government to devise, with business, the means of social and individual adjustment to the facts of the industrial age."[71]

Moley and Tugwell supported industrial planning for different reasons. Tugwell, one of the administration's most liberal members, had been greatly influenced by the two months he had spent in the Soviet Union in the summer of 1927, when it was about to embark on its first Five Year Plan. New Deal critics would later charge that he had become a Marxist on the trip. Tugwell scoffed at the charge—"as though," he would later say, "communism could be caught by contagion like mumps or measles." He was not a Communist, but the Soviet influence on his thinking was noticeable. He believed that the United States could benefit from greater centralized economic planning. He also argued that "profits must be limited and their uses controlled."[72]

Moley, who had grown increasingly close with business leaders, came to the issue from the opposite direction. He was interested not in limiting corporate profits, but in expanding them, and promoting "business confidence." Economic conditions were so desperate that big business was eager for government planning. The same industrial leaders who extolled laissez-faire in the 1920s were now pleading with the government to step in. They argued that unfair competition had driven prices so low that they could not operate. Business leaders supported a law that would authorize the government to convene meetings of each industry at which mandatory minimum prices would be set. If companies sold their goods below these prices, they would be fined or shut down. Meetings of this kind would require suspending the antitrust laws, something business had been seeking since they were adopted. When 1,400 corporate leaders gathered in Washington for the United States Chamber of Commerce's annual meeting in the first week in May, most of the speakers called for greater government control over industry. "We have failed to take the necessary steps voluntarily, so the element of force, government compulsion, becomes necessary," Paul W. Litchfield, president of Goodyear Tire & Rubber Co., told the group.[73]

Perkins did not support centralized industrial planning, and she was wary of proposals to relax the antitrust laws. The New Dealers fell into two camps, the "collectivists" like Tugwell and Moley, who wanted to create a big centralized structure to run industry, and the old-line "progressives" like Perkins, who believed in competition and trust-busting. Tugwell lamented that Perkins was "inclined to regard with Brandeis-like disapproval bigness of any sort and especially in government." Perkins would not actively oppose a program of industrial planning, but neither would she fight for one. What she cared about was using whatever industrial relief bill emerged to enact workers' rights protections. The probusiness Supreme Court had repeatedly held workers' rights laws unconstitutional, in cases like *Lochner v. New York*, which struck down a state maximum hours law for bakers, and *Hammer v. Dagenhart*, which invalidated a federal ban on products made with child labor. Given the court's hostility, Perkins thought the best way of establishing minimum wages, maximum hours, and a ban on child labor was to get businesses to agree to them voluntarily, which they might do in exchange for greater freedom to meet to agree on pricing. Most of all, Perkins was intent on seeing that the bill included public works. "I don't care about what they do about anything else," she said. "Let them do anything else they want to try—just so we get a public works program."[74]

Roosevelt's views on industrial policy were something of a riddle, as so many of his views were, but they appeared to be closer to Moley's and Tugwell's than to Perkins's. Roosevelt had never been a Brandeisian-style trust-buster. As early as 1912, in a speech in Troy, New York, he had argued that collective industrial action could promote the public interest more than competition. "Competition has been shown to be useful up to a certain point," he said, "but co-operation, which is the thing that we must strive for today, begins where competition leaves off." Roosevelt had also served, before he was governor, as head of the American Construction Council, a trade association. The industrial planners wanted to give organizations like the construction council greater authority to coordinate action among their members to boost profits and promote recovery. In the 1932 campaign, Roosevelt signaled that he would back some form of government-industry coordination. In his speech to the Commonwealth Club of San Francisco on progressive government, he had declared that "business men everywhere are asking for a form of organization which will bring the scheme of things into balance"—an apparent reference to industrial planning."[75]

On April 14, Arthur Krock reported in *The New York Times* that a plan that would combine industrial relief and public works was "being developed by the President's closest advisors." In fact, more than one industrial relief plan was being developed. Roosevelt had asked Moley to begin work on a bill. Moley had asked James Warburg, the young banker who had been advising the administration, to look through a stack of industrial recovery plans that had been piling up in his office and make a recommendation for how to proceed. After reviewing the plans and speaking with economic experts, Warburg came up with an elaborate scheme in which the federal government would guarantee industry's losses for a period of time, and share in any gains. Although Warburg was conservative, his plan for the "regimentation" of industry was complicated, intrusive, and likely to cost a great deal. Moley talked it over with Roosevelt, and they agreed not to pursue it.[76]

Moley got a second draft bill started when he bumped into Hugh Johnson, Bernard Baruch and George Peek's associate, in the lobby of the Carlton Hotel. "I fell into his arms and told him the whole sad story of my failure to deliver" with Warburg's draft, Moley later recalled. During the World War, Johnson had worked for the War Industries Board, which Baruch had headed. The board had stimulated wartime production by relaxing antitrust rules, which freed businesses to set their own production levels and prices. Moley thought that the War Industries Board was a good model for the industrial program he and Roosevelt had in mind. When Johnson agreed to try to draft a bill, Moley took him back to his own office, "routed someone out of a desk," and put him to work.[77]

Johnson, who had spent years in the orbit of the business-minded Baruch, saw the industrial crisis the way the leaders of industry did. He believed the main problem was irresponsible companies engaging in "cut-throat" competition, driving down prices and making it impossible for legitimate businesses to make a profit. The plan that Johnson drew up gave business leaders what they wanted—less competition. It suspended the antitrust laws, and it allowed companies in a trade association to work together—critics would say collude—to draw up codes of "fair competition." The codes, which would be legally binding if the president approved them, set limits on the hours factories operated and how much they produced. They also set minimum prices, to eliminate cutthroat competition. Companies that failed to comply with the codes could be shut down. Johnson consulted with Tugwell on the bill, and Donald Richberg, a union lawyer who worked on the landmark Railway Labor Act of 1926, helped with the drafting.[78]

Two other groups were drafting industrial recovery bills at the same time, a reflection of the administration's disorganized habits during the Hundred Days. Assistant Commerce Secretary John Dickinson, a onetime University of Pennsylvania law professor, was coordinating an administration team that included Perkins, Tugwell, and Ickes. Tugwell was promoting a tax on industries much like the tax on processors in the Agricultural Adjustment Act, which would be distributed as an incentive to companies that adhered to the codes. The third group, led by Senator Wagner, started meeting on April 25. The Wagner team was working from a plan for recovery promoted by Brookings Institution economist Harold Moulton, former congressman Meyer Jacobstein, and banker Fred Kent, which called for suspending the antitrust laws and allowing trade associations to work cooperatively to reduce competition and raise prices and wages. The Dickinson and Wagner groups, which had similar approaches, quickly joined forces.[79]

Throughout the drafting, Perkins focused on her issues. The Johnson plan included only a brief mention of public works, which would not be enough to get the sort of program started that she favored. Perkins recalled that when she joined the discussion Wagner's draft also did not contain any kind of public works provision. Although he was one of the biggest supporters of public works in Congress, Wagner apparently intended to keep public works in a separate bill. Perkins urged both groups to add large-scale public works provisions. She was intent, she later said, on seeing that "public works was not lost in the enthusiasm for what I still regarded as a somewhat exotic and thoroughly experimental scheme."[80]

Perkins's other preoccupation was ensuring that the bill contained strong workers' rights protections. It was, she realized, a rare opportunity. In the two decades she had been fighting for minimum wage and maximum hours laws, she had always come up against strong opposition from employers. Now, companies were in such a weakened state, and they were so desperate to be able to collude to prop up prices, industry leaders might be willing to make substantial concessions to workers in exchange. Wagner, who was one of organized labor's most reliable allies in Congress, did not require much convincing to include workers' rights in his draft. He had been working on his own with labor economists to see what the unions wanted in the bill. Perkins invited Johnson, who was less attuned to labor issues, to dine with her and Mary Rumsey in their Georgetown home. Over the course of several dinners, Perkins made her pitch. At this point, the drafting was still going on in secret. Perkins told William Green about the bill, and asked him what the AFL would want to see in it. Green said that organized labor's highest priority was establishing a right to organize workers who were not yet in a union. Perkins would later say that she had not seen the importance of the right to organize because it was so well established in New York. In the rest of the country, though, unions were met with hostile, and often violent, responses when they launched an organizing drive. Perkins agreed to support adding the right to organize to the bill.[81]

In order to include a large-scale public works provision in the bill, the progressives would have to overcome Lewis Douglas's opposition. When Perkins brought public works up at Cabinet meetings, Douglas used what she regarded as an underhanded tactic. He would say that it sounded like a valuable idea, worthy of further investigation, and that he would be happy to look into it. Instead of telling Roosevelt "'I will oppose it to the last breath of my body,' which would have been the truth," Perkins complained, "he would always say, 'I will look that up, Mr. President. I would like to have that considered by two or three of my men. I will give you a report on that.'" Perkins "knew the trick," she said, his strategy of blocking a program he opposed with "fine words and plausible and apparently cooperative statements." Having preempted the discussion at the Cabinet meeting, Douglas could then give his report to Roosevelt one-on-one, where he could raise his concerns without fear of contradiction. "Part of his reason for backing away from cabinet discussion," Perkins realized, "was that he could do better in private."[82]

The drafting work that Johnson, Wagner, Tugwell, Perkins, and the others were doing on the industrial recovery bill provided Douglas with a new argument against public works. He could now argue that the new law would go a long way toward reviving the economy and putting people back to work. That being the case, he insisted, there was no need for a large-scale public works program to do the same thing. Perkins was convinced that Douglas's uncharacteristic optimism about the industrial bill was insincere, and that it was merely a tactic to bring Roosevelt to his position on public works. Perkins was always open about her support for large-scale public works, and for the workers' rights agenda she was promoting. It disturbed her, she would later say, that Douglas was "so polite and so plausible, and yet deceitful."[83]

When Douglas was not fighting public works, he was using his powers under the Economy Act to slash spending. He came to the March 28 Cabinet meeting with detailed calculations of how much each department would have to reduce its budget. Cabinet members were not happy to be told that they had to cut back on programs when there was so much work to be done, or to fire workers who would have difficulty finding new jobs. Ickes, in his diary, called it "the saddest Cabinet meeting yet." When Cabinet members appealed these budgetary edicts, they invariably found that Roosevelt supported Douglas. He "took a great deal of pleasure in telling folks that they had to cut their appropriations way down," Wallace recalled, and he enjoyed saying, " 'here's the man who's going to do the job on you.' "[84]

Wallace did his best to resist. He was particularly incensed that Douglas wanted to eliminate practically all of the scientific research in the Agriculture Department, work for which Wallace felt a particular affinity. He considered Douglas "a very decent fellow," but he was convinced the budget director had a special antipathy for his department. Wallace found that it was impossible to argue about the cuts with Douglas, who was, in Tugwell's words, "stubbornly uninterested." Wallace focused on saving the state agricultural experiment stations, and he was not above making a political case for them. Most of the people he knew who would lose their jobs, he told Roosevelt, were Midwestern Republicans who had voted Democratic in the last election. "It is my opinion," Wallace warned, "that if the Douglas program is carried through there will be such a large number of well-informed and disillusioned, highly trained, intelligent and influential people thrown into the ranks of the malcontents that the Democratic Party will probably never be able to carry the Middle West again." Douglas eliminated more than five hundred jobs in agricultural research projects and slashed the salaries of many workers who remained, but Wallace was able to keep the projects alive. Douglas became "incensed" and "vindictive," Tugwell recalled, when anyone talked Roosevelt out of his proposed cuts, and as a result, Wallace and Douglas "were pretty much at war."[85]

Douglas had similar battles with other departments, and with members of Congress. When senators and representatives objected to his cuts, Douglas told them that if they wanted to restore funding for their favorite programs they had to come up with alternative cuts. "I've placed the top limit," he said. "I'm not primarily concerned with the distribution of the limit." Douglas won most of his battles, but the fighting took a toll on him. The first few weeks of April were "even worse" than the fights over the Economy Act in March, he wrote to his father.[86]

The department that put up the biggest fight of all was the army. Douglas proposed substantial cuts, and MacArthur, the army chief of staff, demanded a hearing to challenge them. MacArthur, who appeared at the Budget Bureau in full uniform, spoke for forty minutes about the damage the cuts would do to the national defense. His appeal was, Douglas conceded, "one of the most dramatic and one of the most brilliant displays of oratory fireworks that I have ever heard." When MacArthur was done, Douglas did what he would later say was "one of the meanest things I have ever done in my life." He asked MacArthur if he was anticipating violent dysentery breaking out in the following year. "No," the general replied. "Why, may I ask, do you ask?" Douglas said the army had put in for 378,000 sheets of toilet paper for each enlisted man and officer. "You could see the rage rising within him," Douglas later recalled. MacArthur stormed out of the hearing.[87]

Douglas was so successful in implementing his budget cuts that Raymond Clapper, United Press's Washington bureau chief, dubbed him "The Great High Executioner of Department Spending." Douglas extracted $80 million from the army, $75 million from the Post Office, and tens of millions more from other departments. Farley, the postmaster general, had a bitter view of Douglas's cuts, and his motives. As Farley saw it, Douglas reflexively represented big business and the wealthy, and his interest in government did not extend beyond balancing the budget and keeping taxes low. "He never, as far as I could discover, had anything definite to offer on how to feed the millions of people who were suffering from loss of jobs, loss of income, and loss of savings," Farley said.[88]

On April 29, Roosevelt made another attempt to resolve the issue of public works. He invited Perkins, Wallace, Ickes, Dern, and Douglas to the White House to discuss what a large-scale public works program would look like.

Perkins came armed with a draft bill that called for $5 billion in grants. Roosevelt was by now prepared to go along with a major public works program, but he was balking at the $5 billion that Perkins and other progressives were asking for. At a recent press conference, he had called the figure "wild." Roosevelt put a damper on the enthusiasm in the room by asking Douglas to talk about the impact large-scale public works would have on the budget. Douglas provided the grim prognosis everyone expected from him. Roosevelt then asked Perkins what projects there were to justify the large expenditures she was asking for. Perkins presented a list of projects that had been suggested by the construction industry. Roosevelt focused on the New York projects, which he was in the best position to evaluate, and, as Ickes recalled, he "proceeded to rip that list to pieces." Ickes wanted to come to Perkins's rescue, but he found that "she was perfectly able to handle it herself." Perkins did not convince Roosevelt to support $5 billion in public works, but he was becoming more comfortable with the idea of spending a substantial amount of money.[89]

In the end, Wagner's draft industrial relief bill included $3.3 billion in public works spending. There were various explanations for how the figure was arrived at. After Roosevelt's resistance to approving $5 billion, $3.3 billion may have been the most the progressives thought he would accept. Another explanation was that $3.3 billion was the cost of all of the worthwhile public works projects the drafters could identify. According to Ickes, the dollar amount was arrived at by accident. While Wagner was reviewing the draft bill he is said to have shouted to his secretary, Simon Rifkind, "Does the three billion for public works include the three hundred million for New York?" Rifkind replied, "I put it in," but Wagner only heard the last three words. Wagner crossed out the $3 billion in the draft, Ickes said, and wrote in $3,300,000,000. When Roosevelt called him in to discuss the bill, Wagner said his group had decided $3.3 billion was the amount that was needed to provide relief to the unemployed and to prime the pump. Roosevelt accepted the figure.[90]

On May 7, Roosevelt delivered his second fireside chat, which Moley had drafted. While the first had been focused on reassuring a frightened nation about the banks, this fireside chat laid out the administration's broader vision for recovery. Mere words and optimism would not be enough, Roosevelt said—"we cannot ballyhoo ourselves back to prosperity." He went through the bills that had already been enacted, or soon would be—the laws creating the CCC and the Tennessee Valley Authority; farmers and homeowners' mortgage relief and the federal emergency relief bill, both of which would soon become law. They were all, he insisted, part of a "well-grounded plan." What remained to be added, Roosevelt said, was an industrial recovery bill. One was being developed, he said, that would create a partnership between government and industry—"not partnership in profits, for the profits still go to the citizens, but rather a partnership in planning, and a partnership to see that the plans are carried out."[91]

Roosevelt explained what he intended to do using cotton as an example. Probably 90 percent of cotton manufacturers would be willing to stop overproduction—and to stop overlong hours, starvation wages, and child labor. That did not matter, he said, as long as the other 10 percent refused to go along. Government should have the power to intervene to end the unfair practices. The antitrust laws would have to be readjusted. They were still needed to prevent monopolies, Roosevelt said, but they were never meant to "encourage the kind of unfair competition that results in long hours, starvation wages and overproduction." Roosevelt also explained his decision to abandon the gold standard. It was inevitable, he argued, since the nation only had enough gold to redeem about 4 percent of the currency and securities that were nominally backed by gold. Going off gold allowed the government to manage the dollar, inflating it so debtors could pay off loans with dollars of the same value they had borrowed. He promised to get the balance right and not allow so much inflation that lenders were cheated. "We seek to correct a wrong," he said, "and not to create another wrong in the opposite direction."[92]

On the same day as the fireside chat, *The New York Times* ran an article on Perkins. She had put aside her aversion to reporters long enough to talk about the need to increase work, wages, and buying power. Drawing on the ideas of her old economics professor Simon Nelson Patten, she argued that greater consumption was needed to revive the economy. When families had no money, she said, neighborhood stores were empty. That meant the stores' suppliers also suffered, as did everyone those suppliers did business with. "Like the ripples eddying out from the pebble dropped into a pool, the circle grows until it has reached every part of the social structure," she said. "A general paralysis ensues—the lawyer, the physician, the artist, the music teacher are as much affected as is the wage earner. The spring of economic life dries up at its source." Perkins believed public works could play a major role in increasing consumption and reviving the economy, but she also, perhaps out of loyalty to the administration, expressed mild support for the government-industry partnership Roosevelt was moving toward. "There isn't a day when some big employer doesn't walk in to me and figuratively try to throw his industry on the bosom of the government," Perkins said. Industry had become so competitive that it was leading to quick and deep wage cuts, which were drying up the nation's purchasing power. It might be, she said, that only "a disinterested agency" could help industry to right itself.[93]

It was time, Roosevelt decided, to come up with a final version of the industrial relief bill. He asked Perkins and Wallace to bring the Johnson and Wagner groups together to try to broker a compromise. The Johnson and Wagner bills were similar in their overall approach to industrial relief, but there were differences. Johnson's draft contained tough licensing requirements, which would help the government to enforce the codes of fair competition. The Wagner draft had less draconian enforcement rules. The two groups also differed on which industries should be covered. Johnson wanted codes to be written for all industries engaged in interstate commerce. Wagner, afraid that a sweeping approach could create practical and constitutional problems, wanted codes only for major industries like automobiles and steel. The two groups were unable to bridge their differences. Johnson was "extremely sensitive," Tugwell complained in his diary, and did not "cooperate too well in working out ideas."[94]

On May 10, Roosevelt invited the two camps to the White House. He "lectured them a little bit about what a grand idea" industrial relief was, Perkins recalled, and told them to lock themselves in a room and work out their differences. He wanted them to finalize a draft bill that included both industrial policy and public works, and he wanted it ready to submit to Congress by the week's end. Roosevelt told Wagner, Johnson, and Richberg to take charge, and he asked Perkins to keep him informed about the group's progress. Those four, along with Tugwell, Dickinson, and Douglas, met in Douglas's office. Tugwell dropped his idea of a processing tax on industries, which attracted little support. The negotiations were often heated, but in the end, the group agreed on a draft. Johnson prevailed on the question of the scope of the law, which would cover all industries engaged in interstate commerce, and on having tough penalties. The final bill included a strong system of licenses for businesses, which the government could withdraw from companies that violated the codes. Douglas's attempts to remove public works from the bill were again unsuccessful.[95]

While Roosevelt and his advisers struggled to develop solutions, the nation remained in a state of crisis. Americans wanted to believe they would be able to turn the nation around, but they continued to fear the worst. Charles Wyzanski, the young lawyer Perkins hired as her counsel, would later say that Washington was more chaotic than at any other time he lived there, including when a world war broke out. "The country was on the verge of a panic," he recalled.[96]

The panic even extended to members of the administration. Perkins bumped into Adolf Berle, the former Brain Truster who had been informally advising the White House on economic policy, and was shocked to see how anxious he was. "The people can't stand this, you know," Berle said gloomily. "Don't you understand, Miss Perkins, that human beings will not endure suffering beyond a certain point, and the suffering has got so intense that it cannot be relieved and cannot be endured?" "Oh, nonsense, Mr. Berle," Perkins responded. "You've no idea how much more human beings can endure, particularly if they see a ray of hope." She reached for a sturdy New England image. "Didn't you ever swim against the tide when it seemed as though it was out of the question? Some stronger swimmer says, 'Come on, we'll make the point.' Then you go on."[97]

Berle remained uneasy. "Miss Perkins, the date of the trouble is June 15. It won't go beyond June 15. Something will happen." He added somberly: "I am getting my family out of the city and out into the deep country. I advise you to do the same well before the 15th of June. The cities will not be safe."[98]

Berle's apocalyptic vision did not faze Perkins, who had spent her youth tramping through tough urban neighborhoods and was not inclined to panic. She would not be able to get her family out of New York City by June 15, and in any case, they were already scheduled to leave for Maine later that month. Still, the encounter with Berle stayed with Perkins. "He spoke as though he thought a violent physical revolution was about to take place in which the *sans culottes* would murder all of the rest of us and our children in their beds," she said later. "The sense of impending disaster was considerable."[99]

Roosevelt planned to introduce the industrial relief bill in Congress on May 17, but there were some last-minute conflicts to be resolved. Under pressure from Perkins, Wagner, and several other negotiators, the right of unions to organize had been included in Section 7(a) of the bill, which required that every code of competition approved under the law guarantee workers the right to organize "through representatives of their own choosing." Business leaders strongly opposed the provision and tried to get it removed. Perkins and Wagner, however, held firm. "No 7(a)," Wagner said, "no bill." The dispute went all the way to Roosevelt. Perkins brought Green to the White House to emphasize how important the provision was to organized labor. Roosevelt ruled in favor of Section 7(a), which would later come to be known as the Magna Carta of the labor movement. With his endorsement "the die was cast," Perkins would later say. "It was as casual as that."[100]

There was one final fight over public works. Perkins found out on Friday,

May 12, that the $3.3 billion program that had been agreed to was no longer in the bill. It had been dropped so quietly that even Wagner, who would be introducing the bill in a matter of days, was not aware of it. The omission was not entirely surprising. Even after he gave his approval, Roosevelt had remained ambivalent about the public works provision. Perkins suspected that Douglas had lobbied behind the scenes for its removal and Roosevelt had acquiesced. When she investigated, she quickly learned that her suspicions were correct. Douglas had met privately with Roosevelt and persuaded him to put public works in a separate bill, intending to kill it later. Perkins was indignant that Douglas had not acted "on the level." When she called him up, he admitted that he had spoken to Roosevelt, but he insisted that it had been Roosevelt who wanted public works separated out. "I know as much about what the President thinks as you do," Perkins thought to herself. "I know you're putting things into his mind, if not words into his mouth." She called Roosevelt and said she needed to talk to him right away. He invited her to meet him in his study the next day, Saturday, at two p.m. She checked with his secretaries—"I wasn't above that," she would later recall—and learned that Douglas had asked to speak with Roosevelt about a matter of importance earlier the same morning.[101]

Perkins stayed up all night to prepare for the meeting. She brought along Wyzanski, the Labor Department's top lawyer, to help make the case. At the meeting, she repeated her familiar arguments for public works, insisting that it would benefit not just the unemployed, but the entire country. She reminded Roosevelt of the conference he had held for governors of eastern states in early 1931, and of how it had recommended public works as a practical, substantial thing that could be done to stimulate employment. "You've got to decide it right now, Mr. President," Perkins said. "Here on this beautiful sunshiny afternoon we have to decide if we shall put it in or leave it out." If it was left out, Perkins insisted, public works would not pass that year, when it was desperately needed. Roosevelt was persuaded and told Perkins that she should direct Wagner to put the $3.3 billion public works provision back into the bill.[102]

Perkins was not taking any chances. She had checked with Wagner in advance to find out where he would be, and she asked Roosevelt if they could call him. Perkins got through to Wagner and told him that Roosevelt had agreed that he should include the public works provision in the bill. Roosevelt himself got on the line and said, "Frances says that she thinks it's best, and I think it's the right thing, don't you, Bob?" Perkins knew that by having Roosevelt tell Wagner directly, the matter would finally be settled. Perkins had no regrets about her maneuvers, which she regarded as defensive. It was clear to her that Douglas would always try to go through the "back door" to get his way. "I never would have done it to Lewis Douglas," she would later say, "if he hadn't done worse to me."[103]

On May 17, Roosevelt sent the National Industrial Recovery Act to Congress. The bill's purpose was to address a national emergency of "widespread unemployment" and "disorganization of industry." Title I gave business leaders what they wanted: the right to work through trade or industrial associations to develop "codes of fair competition." Industries would be able to set standards for what constituted "destructive...price cutting." If the president determined that a company violated its industry's code, he was authorized to revoke its license to do business. For workers, the bill provided that the codes of fair competition could include minimum wages, maximum hours, and child labor protections. It also included the union organizing protections of Section 7(a). Title II authorized $3.3 billion in public works. The bill enumerated a wide array of projects that the money would be used for, including construction and improvement of highways and public buildings; conservation of public lands; water power and electricity development; slum clearance; and construction of public housing.[104]

Roosevelt's congressional message, which Moley drafted, declared that the NIRA would create "the machinery necessary for a great cooperative movement throughout all industry" that would "prevent unfair competition and disastrous overproduction." The premise of the act, Roosevelt said, was that industry should be able to rein in excessive competition. The bill contained a "rigorous licensing power" to deal with the "rare cases of non-cooperation and abuse." To make clear that business would not be the only beneficiary, Roosevelt emphasized that the machinery being created would also be used to expand the rights of workers. He also included a strong statement about the importance of public works. "A careful survey convinces me," he said, "that approximately $3,300,000,000 can be invested in useful and necessary public construction, and at the same time put the largest possible number of people to work."[105]

Business rallied to the NIRA. Henry Harriman, the president of the U.S. Chamber of Commerce, declared that he considered it "one of the most important measures ever presented at any time to any Congress." The National Electrical Manufacturers Association, representing companies that had employed 250,000 people in 1929, called the NIRA "wholly and utterly revolutionary" and gave the bill its enthusiastic endorsement. Organized labor also urged Congress to pass the NIRA. William Green declared it "the most outstanding, advanced and forward-looking legislation designed to promote economic recovery" that had ever been proposed, and predicted it would create six million new jobs.[106]

In the House, critics leveled the now-familiar charge that the NIRA would give Roosevelt dictatorial powers. When one of the NIRA's defenders argued that Roosevelt would be a benign dictator, James Beck, an anti–New Deal Republican from Pennsylvania, fumed that "you might as well talk of a peaceful murderer." Arthur Krock, writing in *The New York Times*, gave support to the critics, having written a few weeks earlier that the laws already enacted and proposed by Roosevelt would give him "more absolute power than the sum of the arbitrary authority exercised at various times in history by Generals Washington, Lee, Grant, and Sherman, Presidents Jackson, Lincoln and Wilson, and all the Emperors of the Ming dynasty." The alliance of business, organized labor, and the administration, however, proved unbeatable. The industrial relief bill passed 323–76.[107]

There was more opposition in the Senate. Wagner, who introduced the bill, spoke eloquently for it. Organizing industry was "the necessary consequence," the New York liberal told his colleagues, "of the growing complexity of our economic machinery, and of the increasing interdependence between one State and all States; between one industry and all industries; and between unemployment anywhere and employment everywhere." Once again, there were charges that Roosevelt was seeking to become an autocrat. Weren't the powers the bill gave him "too much to vest in a Mussolini or a Stalin or anyone?" the Oklahoma populist Thomas Gore asked. Senate critics were particularly troubled by the power the bill gave the president to withhold licenses from companies that failed to adhere to the industry codes. In a surprising revolt, the critics won a 12–7 vote in the Senate Finance Committee to strip out the licensing provisions. It was only after Roosevelt sent a letter to the committee that Chairman Pat Harrison, Democrat of Mississippi, was able to round up the votes to restore the licensing system, which the bill's supporters were calling the "very teeth" of the law.[108]

Business interests, led by the U.S. Chamber of Commerce, made a final effort to remove Section 7(a) from the bill. The president of the National Association of Manufacturers, Robert L. Lund, warned that the right to organize could "force employers to deal with communistic or racketeering organizations." At a meeting of the group in Washington, the members made a personal appeal to Hugh Johnson to have Section 7(a) taken out. The unions fired back that the manufacturers were happy to have a law that pushed up their own profits, but they were unwilling to let working men and women benefit. Bennett Clark of Missouri introduced an amendment declaring that nothing in the law "shall be construed to compel a change in existing satisfactory relationships between the employees and employers of any particular plant, firm, or corporation." Clark's amendment would have undone the bill's labor protections, but progressives, led by Senator George Norris, had the votes to defeat it.[109]

Senate progressives had their own objections. They were convinced that if the antitrust laws were relaxed, corporations would use their new freedom to collude against the consumer. The populists insisted that big businesses would use the law to drive small ones out of business. The losers, Huey Long declared, would be the "molasses maker and country sausage packer down in my country." Hugo Black protested that the NIRA would be "a very advanced step toward the ultimate concentration of wealth." William Borah took on price fixing directly, introducing an amendment to make it illegal. Industry strongly opposed the Borah Amendment, and the bill's sponsors worried that if it passed business leaders would block the bill. Wagner led the opposition to the amendment, insisting that the bill already contained sufficient protections against price fixing, including the president's power to reject codes that he found unsatisfactory. "What the Senator fears," Wagner insisted, "can result only from a faithless and disloyal administration of the act." There were other forces working against the bill, including a growing sense that the economy was already rebounding, and a major industrial program was no longer needed. In the end, the bill passed the Senate 46–39 on June 13, without Borah's anti-price-fixing language. It was "a tacit admission," *Time* magazine noted, "that price-fixing is to form a part of most trade agreements."[110]

The discussion about who would administer the NIRA had begun before the bill was introduced. The head of the National Recovery Administration would be one of the most powerful officials in government. He would have a major role in regulating production, setting prices, and establishing work standards, and he would be able to discipline, and even shut down, businesses that broke the rules. He would also be in charge of dispensing $3.3 billion in public works funding. Roosevelt was inclined to choose Hugh Johnson, who was intimately familiar with the new law, and who had experience regulating business from his time with the War Industries Board. The choice of Johnson, a businessman with close ties to Bernard Baruch, would also be reassuring to industry. Like the appointment of Peek—another Baruch associate—to head the AAA, installing Johnson at the NRA would be a way of signaling that a pathbreaking New Deal agency would not go off in a radical direction. The main argument against choosing Johnson was Johnson himself. He struck many people as too militaristic, too quick to anger, and too prone to use profane language. "There were dead cats, stinking rats, and all kinds of things" when Johnson spoke, Douglas recalled. The little Perkins had seen of Johnson left her wary. Even Baruch did not think his longtime associate was a good choice. While the NIRA was pending in Congress, Baruch had visited Perkins and Rumsey in their Georgetown home. "He's dangerous and unstable," Baruch told Perkins. "He gets nervous and sometimes goes away for days without notice." He would be a good number two or three, Baruch said, but not a number one.[111]

Perkins relayed Baruch's concerns to Roosevelt. When he asked Perkins what she thought, she conceded that Johnson might be a little unstable, but he also struck her as capable and hardworking. "It's going to take a queer temperament to do this job," she said of the industrial recovery part of the position, and a "good, flat-footed administrator would never walk into" it. Perkins was concerned, however, that Johnson was not as detail-oriented as an administrator of a $3.3 billion public works budget should be. She recommended that Roosevelt divide the job in two, something Secretary of the Interior Harold Ickes was also urging. Roosevelt named Johnson administrator of the NRA, and put the public works program under Ickes. Johnson was greatly disappointed. He saw public works as an integral part of industrial recovery, and intended to use the funds not merely to put the jobless to work, but to stimulate specific industries that needed help. Perkins, who had fought so hard for public works, was pleased to see that it was being put under the control of Ickes, who she thought could be counted on to administer the program with "the utmost of careful controls, of integrity, and of cautious, businesslike legal procedures."[112]

With the passage of the NIRA, the last important piece of Hundred Days legislation had fallen into place. Tugwell saw it as a counterpart to the Agricultural Adjustment Act. The AAA "authorized the shaping of agricultural policy by the voluntary cooperation of the nation's farmers," he said. "The recovery act would similarly authorize the shaping of industrial policy through the cooperation of its operating units." Roosevelt was well aware that the NIRA envisioned fundamental changes in the nation's economic system. When he was working on the second fireside chat, Moley pointed to a section that called for a "partnership" between government and industry. "You realize, then, that you're taking an enormous step away from the philosophy of equalitarianism and laissez-faire?" Moley said. Roosevelt was silent, Moley recalled, and looked as grave as he had at any time since the inauguration. "If that philosophy hadn't proved to be bankrupt, Herbert Hoover would be sitting here right now," he responded. "I never felt surer of anything in my life than I do of the soundness of this passage."[113]

CHAPTER EIGHT

"He Must Be Part
of This Historic Show"

O f all the changes the New Deal was ushering in, none was more radical than the administration's approach to relief. The Hopkins-Hodson
plan that Roosevelt had endorsed in mid-March was a sharp break with the
nation's traditions. American welfare policy had descended directly from the
harshly punitive "poor laws" of Dickensian England. The English poor laws
assumed that the poor were to blame for their condition, and that they had to
be forced to overcome their laziness and go to work. When aid was absolutely
necessary, English law held that it was a local responsibility, to be carried out
at the parish level. American poor laws proceeded from the same ungener-
ous assumptions. They left care for the poor to local governments or private
charities. To ensure that aid would go only to the truly needy, many jurisdic-
tions gave it out in the form of "indoor relief," which meant that the poor had
to live in almshouses to receive it. Even when aid was given out as "outdoor"
or "home" relief—aid that poor people could receive while living in their
own homes—the eligibility rules were exacting, the benefit levels were low,
and the money budgeted for relief was woefully inadequate.[1]

The Depression challenged the nation's beliefs about the poor. After the
economic crisis threw millions of Americans out of work, it was clear that
poverty could be caused by brutal economic circumstances, not just weak

character. It was difficult to blame a once-successful lawyer who had lost all of his clients due to the Depression or a steelworker whose entire industry had ground to a standstill for being unable to earn a living. The economic crisis had also broken down the traditional methods of caring for the poor. Even wealthy cities like Philadelphia had run out of money to help their unemployed citizens. In less well-off parts of the country the situation was far worse. John L. Lewis, the United Mine Workers president, pointed out that many of his members lived in remote mining towns that barely had local governments, much less relief programs for destitute families. Private charities were unable to take up the slack. When the Depression began, charities were providing one-quarter of the relief given nationwide, but they could not keep up with the fast-growing demand. Between 1929 and 1932, about one-third of the private agencies that cared for the poor closed down for lack of money. Many of the remaining ones teetered on the brink of insolvency.[2]

Progressives in Congress and advocates for the poor had tried to persuade Hoover to take a new approach to relief. Hoover, however, held firmly to his traditional views. His belief in rugged individualism had convinced him that government aid would harm the recipients. "Must Americans perish miserably," *The Nation* magazine demanded of Hoover, "because of your fear that their characters may be sullied?" Hoover also believed strongly in local responsibility. If government had to get involved in distributing relief, his administration insisted, it should be the "local political division where such conditions exist." Most of all, Hoover believed voluntary efforts by businesses and charities were the answer. He set up two committees to help the unemployed—the President's Emergency Committee for Employment, and later the President's Organization on Unemployment Relief—but only provided them with money for administrative expenses. The committees' job, as Hoover saw it, was to lobby private industry to create more jobs. Congressional progressives introduced several strong relief and public works bills, but Hoover resisted all of them. John Nance Garner, who would soon be vice president, tried to rally support for a program to put the unemployed to work building post offices, but Hoover insisted that the plan was "not

unemployment relief," but rather "an unexampled raid on the public treasury." Walter S. Gifford, the chairman of the President's Organization on
Unemployment Relief, testified before the Senate and said he had faith that
states and localities could handle the crisis. When Senator Edward Costigan
of Colorado snapped, "You are always hopeful," Gifford responded, "I find it
pleasant, Senator, to be hopeful."[3]

When Hoover finally yielded and supported a federal relief program, it
was an inadequate one. Because he did not believe that relief was a federal
responsibility, Hoover would only agree to a program that distributed aid to
the states in the form of loans. Other constituencies were quick to impose
their own conditions. Southerners, led by Senator Hugo Black of Alabama,
insisted that states be given full control over how their funds were spent, to
ensure that federal administrators could not require that blacks and whites
be treated equally. Conservatives demanded that no new federal bureaucracy
be created to manage the program. Wagner drafted a bill that took account
of all of these concerns. It authorized the federal government to make $300
million in loans to the states. To avoid creating a bureaucracy, it called for
the funds to be distributed by the Reconstruction Finance Corporation, an
agency that already existed to help ailing businesses. States would be allowed
to run their programs without federal intervention. The Emergency Relief
and Construction Act proved woefully inadequate. The biggest problem was
that allocating aid in the form of loans did not work. The states in the worst
financial shape, which needed relief funds the most, were the least willing
to take on more debt. Although the law made $300 million available, by the
end of 1932, the states had borrowed only $80 million, which barely began to
address the needs of the nation's millions of unemployed.[4]

The Hopkins-Hodson plan would take relief policy in a new direction.
The bill that Wagner, La Follette, and Costigan drew up at Roosevelt's
request, the Federal Emergency Relief Act of 1933, allocated $500 million to
the states in the form of grants, rather than loans. Half of the funds would
be distributed based on a formula of $1 for every $3 that states and localities contributed. The other half would go to states and localities with no
requirement of a match, allowing the federal relief administrator to direct

the funds to poor states that had little or no money of their own to spend. In defiance of congressional conservatives, the bill called for creating a new government agency, the Federal Emergency Relief Administration, to distribute the money. Over the objections of the Southerners, the bill authorized the FERA to set the rules for state relief programs.[5]

The law rejected Hoover's approach to relief, but it also marked a new direction for Roosevelt. As governor of New York, Roosevelt, who had a strong states' rights streak, had resisted the idea of federal responsibility for relief, even though he could have used the aid. He emphasized that caring for the poor was a local responsibility. When he introduced the Temporary Emergency Relief Act in the New York state legislature, he had underscored "that the distribution of relief of the poor is essentially a local function." Roosevelt had stuck to this principle during the 1932 campaign. In a speech in Detroit, he continued to insist that localities bore "the first responsibility for the alleviation of poverty and distress and for the care of the victims of the depression." On the campaign trail, Roosevelt had criticized Hoover for many things, but—according to a book written in 1937 by two of Hoover's Cabinet members—Roosevelt had never faulted Hoover for failing to establish a federal relief program. Now, Roosevelt was supporting not only a program to dispense $500 million in federal funds, but a federal agency to oversee it.[6]

The Wagner bill immediately drew Republican attacks. "It is socialism," Representative Robert Luce of Massachusetts protested. "Whether it is communism or not I do not know." Senator Simeon D. Fess of Ohio, whose unswerving loyalty to the Republican Party earned him the nickname "Faithful Fess," complained that "Uncle Sam is looked upon as a Santa Claus to give alms." The critics, however, were heavily outnumbered. The Senate and House passed the bill by lopsided margins, and Roosevelt signed it into law on May 12, the same day he signed the Agricultural Adjustment Act. The relief law, the fifth of the fifteen major laws that would be passed during the Hundred Days, marked the first time the federal government gave funds to the states to fund relief programs. The $500 million appropriation was a substantial infusion of money, but Roosevelt recognized that it was just a small fraction of what was needed. When he signed the bill, he made clear that he expected the states and localities to put in significant amounts of their own money as well.[7]

There was still the question of who should run the new relief program. When Perkins told Roosevelt that Hopkins and Hodson hoped he would choose one of them, Roosevelt asked for her recommendation. Perkins considered both men "extraordinary," but she thought they had different strengths. Hodson, a Harvard Law School graduate who was New York City commissioner of public welfare, was the "smoother operator," she told Roosevelt. Hopkins, who had engaged in social work projects from the streets of the Lower East Side to flood-ravaged New Orleans, was the "more dynamic person." Even though Hopkins had run his New York emergency relief program, Roosevelt did not know him well. A major factor in his decision was that the mayor of New York did not want to give Hodson up. Roosevelt sent a telegram to Governor Herbert Lehman saying he wanted to bring Hopkins, who was still running the state relief program, to Washington. Roosevelt said it was "imperative that I get a man on the job immediately," but he suggested that the appointment would only be temporary. On May 19, a week after the Federal Emergency Relief Act became law, Hopkins was preparing to move to Washington. "It was as simple as that," Perkins recalled, "the beginning of the Hopkins rise."[8]

Harry Lloyd Hopkins was born August 17, 1890, in Sioux City, Iowa. Hopkins's paternal grandfather had left Maine as a young man to fight in the Civil War. At the war's end, he settled in Iowa with his wife and a young son, who grew up to be Hopkins's father. David Aldona Hopkins, who went by "Al," was an adventurous spirit. As a young man, he had joined an expedition into the Black Hills, which was Sioux territory, in search of gold. When the expedition failed, Al settled into the life of a small-town businessman. Hopkins's mother, Anna, was the daughter of Canadian homesteaders. She had worked briefly as a schoolteacher, but after marrying she quit her job and gave birth to six children in quick succession: Adah, Lewis, Rome, Etta (who died in infancy), Harry, and John.[9]

Hopkins's parents were opposites. Al was unfocused, particularly about work. He drifted from making harnesses to selling them, and then to running a sundries shop, struggling all the way. Al spent much of his time on fraternal organizations and bowling, which he liked to gamble on. Anna Hopkins was as quiet as her husband was gregarious, and as driven as he was easily distracted. She took her children to church as often as six days a week, and taught them hymns around the family pump organ. While Al bowled, Anna gave her time to the Methodist Home Missionary Society of Iowa, of which she would eventually become president, and impressed on her children the importance of good works. For Anna Hopkins, "service to others was the most important way to manifest one's religious feelings," her great-granddaughter, June Hopkins, has written. As a child, Hopkins navigated between these two strong personalities. One night, his father showed him $500 that he had just won bowling. "I wasn't supposed to tell my mother there was that amount of money in the house," Hopkins recalled, because "she would have made Dad give it away to church missions."[10]

The family moved often—across Iowa, Nebraska, and Illinois—as Al searched for business success. When Harry was eleven, Anna steered the family to Grinnell, Iowa, to expose her children to two things she valued highly—education and religion. Grinnell was home to Grinnell College, a progressive institution built on land donated by the abolitionist minister Josiah Bushnell Grinnell. Grinnell attracted, as the college bulletin noted, "cultivated and intelligent people," making it a sophisticated outpost on the Iowa prairie. At the same time, Grinnell had been founded as a temperance community, and the religious influence of the New England Congregationalists who founded the town remained strong.[11]

These were the disparate influences that shaped young Harry Hopkins. He would be, a family friend observed, a great case study for anyone interested in genetics. From his mother he got his industriousness, his moral compass, and his drive to reform the world. His father gave him his gregariousness, his love of adventure, and his charitable attitude toward people in difficult circumstances. Joseph E. Davies, who served with him in the Roosevelt administration, declared that the adult Hopkins had "the purity of St. Francis of Assisi combined with the sharp shrewdness of a race track tout."[12]

Hopkins enrolled at Grinnell College in 1908. More than a decade before he arrived, the Social Gospel movement—with its emphasis on establishing the kingdom of God on earth by pursuing justice and social reform—had taken hold at Grinnell. The passion for the Social Gospel had died down, but it could still be felt throughout the college. The curriculum included a political science course in which students were sent into town to study local government, and a course on the settlement house movement. In attending Grinnell, Hopkins was following in the footsteps of his sister Adah, who had been a leading member of her own class. Adah had taken several courses with Edward Steiner, the Applied Christianity teacher who lectured about settlement houses, and in her junior year she had delivered a fiery speech against child labor. After being named outstanding senior at commencement, Adah went to work with the poor in Philadelphia and then New York, where she would once again pave the way for her younger brother.[13]

Hopkins was a prominent figure on campus. He played on several sports teams, was elected senior class president, and formed a Democratic club. Hopkins absorbed Grinnell's social justice ethic, taking courses like Professor Steiner's "The Development of Social Consciousness in the Old Testament." In the spring of his senior year, he discussed his future with Louis Hartson, a professor with whom he had studied social reform. Hopkins was considering writing for a newspaper in Bozeman, Montana, but Hartson had heard from a friend back East that Christodora House, a settlement house on New York's Lower East Side, was looking for a counselor for its summer camp. New York City appealed to the adventurous spirit Hopkins had inherited from his father, and the city's vast immigrant neighborhoods were an ideal setting for the good works his mother expected him to engage in. When Hartson offered to give Christodora House his name, Hopkins accepted enthusiastically.[14]

After graduation, Hopkins traveled to New York with Hartson. They stopped in Chicago and Hopkins attended the Republican National Convention, talking his way onto the floor by claiming to be New York senator Elihu

Root's secretary. He watched as Theodore Roosevelt made his historic break with the Republican Party, on his way to becoming the Progressive Party candidate for president. Hopkins and Hartson also made a detour to Baltimore, where Woodrow Wilson won the Democratic nomination. When his travels were over, Hopkins reported to Christodora House's summer camp in New Jersey. The experience was eye opening. Most of the boys at Northover Camp lived in tenements near Tompkins Square Park, the neighborhood around Christodora House. Hopkins had never encountered children like these, who had been brought up in rough urban poverty. He had also never seen a Jewish boy before. Northover was Hopkins's introduction to the settlement house ethos. "It is not a 'fresh air' or 'health' camp," the staff was told. "It strives to give each camper a proper experience through a well-balanced program, in living as an individual in a democratic community."[15]

When the summer ended, Hopkins moved into Christodora House to help run the boys' clubs. The settlement house was founded in 1897 by Christina MacColl and Sara Libby Carson, who met while working for the Young Women's Christian Association. They established Christodora House, whose name is Greek for "gift of Christ," to answer what MacColl called a "sob of the spirit." The two women had been looking for the neighborhood most in need of a settlement house, but the one they chose was difficult terrain. The Lower East Side had the densest population of any neighborhood in the United States, and among the highest percentages of foreign-born residents. Adding to the challenge, the vast majority were Jews, who would resist MacColl and Carson's Christian message. The women's goal was to run a "social center" that was "educationally effective," "tolerant," and "non-sectarian." They did, however, try to win people over to Christianity, something not all settlement house workers did, and they were pleased when they could claim a convert.[16]

Christodora House preached optimism, and emphasized poor people's ability to rise above their grim surroundings. Its official song implored participants:

Look forward! move onward! the new work to do
Will strengthen our sinews, create life anew!

The splendor that beckons is life—it is youth
The sweetness of hope and the freshness of truth.

Newly arrived Eastern European immigrants eagerly signed up for English classes and courses to prepare for civil service examinations. There were lectures on current events and debates on subjects like "Resolved, that reading of history is more instructive than reading of novels." Christodora's clientele "entered college as soon as they entered the door of the House," a history of the settlement house reported, "and when they left it they carried the college home." There were clubs for all ages and both sexes, as well as "entertainments, musicals and social gatherings."[17]

Hopkins had landed as far from Grinnell as any place in America. The gangly Iowan, a country boy with a cowlick, now lived in a neighborhood crowded with immigrant hordes, where the storefront signs were in Yiddish. The newsstands sold *The Jewish Daily Forward*, the Yiddish-language democratic socialist daily. The streets were jammed with peddlers selling fruits, vegetables, eggs, and kitchen utensils from pushcarts. The cafés rang with heated political conversations. It was a colorful world, but an oppressive one. The tenements were grossly overcrowded—less than one-quarter of families slept two to a room; half had three or four people in each room; almost one-quarter had five or more. The air, which barely circulated, was full of tuberculosis. One Lower East Side history noted "the assault of the smells: the odors of human waste only intermittently carried away from back-yard privies by a careless sanitation department, the stench of fish and meat starting to rot on pushcarts, the foulness of neglected sewers and gutters." Hopkins decided to stay.[18]

The twenty-two-year-old Hopkins found himself at the center of life in Christodora House. He presided over the Club Council, which planned social events and attended to the physical plant. He was also editor-in-chief of the in-house journal, which printed such locally important news reports as "Loyalty Dance a Great Success." In his free time, Hopkins wandered the gritty streets of the neighborhood and witnessed firsthand its foreign cultures, crushing poverty, and criminality. He watched bottle fights and kicked gangsters out of settlement house dances. He also got his first introduction to radical politics, something the Lower East Side had in great supply. "I climbed tenement stairs, listened to the talk of Morris Hillquit and William English Walling"—two renowned socialist politicians—"and really got exposed to the whole business of how the working class lived," he recalled.[19]

Hopkins's guide for much of this journey was Ethel Gross, a young secretary who worked alongside him. Gross had been born to a Jewish family outside Budapest, where her father's family owned a glass factory. When he died of tuberculosis, her mother sailed for America with her five children. Gross grew up in a tenement and left school after eighth grade. While many of the young women around her led lives centered on family and synagogue, Gross was what Hutchins Hapgood, a Yankee journalist who published a study of the Lower East Side in 1902, called "The Modern Type"—emancipated and career-oriented. She grew up blocks from Christodora House, where she began working at age twelve, helping to run children's programs. After taking lessons in secretarial skills, Gross became secretary to a wealthy woman who had founded the Equal Franchise Association to campaign among the upper classes for women's suffrage. When she returned to Christodora House, Gross was far more knowledgeable about the world.[20]

Hopkins was immediately attracted to the pretty, dark-haired Gross. "I'm so happy Ethel," Hopkins wrote her shortly after they met, "for I always felt there must be some girl like you on this earth somewhere but I must confess that I didn't expect to find her working in a Settlement." Gross admired Hopkins's idealism, and she was taken by his Iowa farm-boy manner, which made him a living piece of the America she yearned to assimilate into. She was also charmed by his happy-go-lucky ways, a rare thing in the ghetto. "He was gay," she said, "and he used to go every place singing and whistling." When Hopkins proposed marriage, Gross was taken by surprise. "At the settlement at that time there were all these young college people who had all of these advantages, who had come from beautiful homes and were giving their time," she said. "I had him all paired off, first with one and then another and they all liked him, at least so it seemed to me."[21]

The couple married on October 21, 1913, at the Ethical Culture Society. Hopkins had left his mother's intense Methodism behind. He had come to believe, Gross said, that "service to other was the most important way to manifest religion." It was in many ways a shocking marriage, and one that upset Hopkins's parents greatly. Ethel was foreign-born, working-class, poorly educated, and perhaps most disturbing of all to them, she was Jewish. As unhappy as his mother was, Hopkins assured Gross that his father was no less disappointed. "Ye Gods—it is lucky that he hasn't any money for he certainly would leave me out," he wrote to her. Hopkins was proud, however, of the new and very modern life he was making for himself.[22]

To bring in more money, Hopkins began working nights for the Association for Improving the Condition of the Poor, a seventy-year-old charity that was one of the nation's largest. Like the settlement house movement, AICP aimed not only to offer aid to the poor, but to transform their lives. Its declared purpose was "to relieve none...whom we cannot elevate." AICP's director, Dr. John A. Kingsbury, hired Hopkins to do work along the waterfront, an even rougher area than the Lower East Side. The extra $60 a month that Hopkins earned came in handy after Ethel gave birth, in October 1914, to their first son, David, named for Hopkins's father. The job took Hopkins beyond the narrow world of Christodora House, and brought him under the guidance of one of the most important men in the social welfare field. Hopkins grew extremely close to Kingsbury and his wife. He moved his family to the same suburb the Kingsburys lived in, and got a summer home near their Woodstock, New York, retreat. He took on his mentor's pastimes, including joining him on weekend mushroom collecting outings.[23]

Kingsbury soon gave Hopkins a full-time job running AICP's employment bureau. In these years just before the World War, New York State's unemployment rate was above 16 percent, and the jobless were becoming more desperate by the day. Mobs had begun marching for relief, and showing up at churches demanding aid. In late 1913, Hopkins undertook a major study of the unemployment problem. His report—which was impressive for a twenty-three-year-old newly arrived in the city and inexperienced in social science research—challenged the widespread belief that, as he put it, "the men who can't find work are drunkards and vagrants or else downright lazy." Hopkins found that the vast majority of the unemployed were victims of a rapid influx of unskilled workers into the city. He recommended that the government create employment offices to help the jobless find work. Later, working with the head of AICP's family welfare division, Hopkins put together one of the city's first work relief programs. Using private funds, AICP paid one hundred men two dollars a day to work three days a week on a construction project at the Bronx Zoo. With the limited resources at his disposal, it was the best Hopkins could do, but the AICP initiative was a forerunner of the more elaborate programs he would create during the New Deal.

In the fall of 1915, John Purroy Mitchel, the reform mayor who hired Frances Perkins's husband as his budget director, created a Board of Child Welfare to help poor mothers and children. With the backing of Kingsbury, who had become Mitchel's commissioner of public charities, Hopkins was named executive secretary. At age twenty-five, Hopkins controlled a sizable budget and had the power of the government behind him. Hopkins got money out to eligible mothers quickly and, in keeping with the social work precepts of the day, his staff helped them decide where to live, what schools to send their children to, and how to spend their money. Hopkins ran weekly meetings at which he helped his caseworkers analyze their cases, and lobbied for legislation to help the groups he served. His performance was widely praised. *The New York Herald* reported that "the mere mention of his name appears to exert a magic influence on the widowed mothers." Despite his success, Hopkins's tenure was brief. He clashed with his bosses and grew frustrated by how limited his resources were compared to the number of mothers and children who needed help. When Mayor Mitchel lost in 1917, Hopkins moved on.[25]

With the United States entering the World War, Hopkins applied to work for the Red Cross's Division of Civilian Relief, which gave aid to the families left behind by the men serving overseas. He ended up being put in charge of disaster relief for the gulf division, based in New Orleans. The division, which covered Louisiana, Mississippi, and Alabama, helped victims of crises in the area, including a major flooding of Lake Charles. "Thousands homeless," Hopkins informed Ethel by telegram. "Am in charge of all relief work." The Hopkins family moved to New Orleans, though Ethel and David spent the summer in Far Rockaway, New York, with her family to escape the southern heat. While they lived apart, Ethel began to have doubts about her husband's faithfulness. She would later say that unlike the "social workers in the North who were trained and were very serious minded," the women Hopkins worked with in the South were often "just beautiful southern girls" eager to help in the war effort, and she understood that several were in love with her husband. During this time, she gave birth to a daughter, who died in infancy of whooping cough, and the following year, 1921, to a second son, Robert.[26]

When the war ended, Hopkins was put in charge of the Red Cross's Atlanta-based southern division, running operations in nine states. Without the sense of mission that the war provided, however, he enjoyed the work less, and in 1922 he returned to New York. After taking on a few other social work jobs, in 1924, with the help of his old mentor Kingsbury, Hopkins was named executive director of the New York Tuberculosis Association. The "white plague" was the scourge of the city's immigrant neighborhoods. The situation had improved since the turn of the century, when one in four deaths of New Yorkers between fifteen and sixty-five were from tuberculosis, but the disease still claimed the lives of thousands of New Yorkers every year. Hopkins fought for better medical care and healthier living conditions. "He never failed to point out," Frances Perkins recalled, "that poor people could not get the milk, eggs, fresh air [and] sunshine" they needed. Hopkins, whose work for the disadvantaged had always been combined with personal ambition, pushed the Tuberculosis Association to take on new diseases. Under his leadership, it absorbed the New York Heart Committee and renamed itself the New York Tuberculosis and Health Association. The association also entered an alliance with the Children's Welfare Federation, extending its reach still further. Hopkins, who was now in his thirties, exhibited the personality traits that he would carry with him for the rest of his career. He was hard driving and "intense," Dr. Jacob Goldberg, secretary of the Tuberculosis Association, recalled, and he seemed "to be in a permanent nervous ferment—a chain smoker, and black coffee drinker." Hopkins showed up at work in clothing that was in disarray, and often shaved at the office. His focus was on his work.[27]

The October 1929 stock market crash sent shock waves throughout the city, including the charitable community. The ranks of the unemployed were growing rapidly, and the federal and state governments were doing little to provide them relief. A former colleague of Hopkins's from AICP, William Matthews, obtained a $75,000 grant from the Red Cross to help the city's unemployed. Matthews, Hopkins, and Dr. Goldberg used the money to develop a public works program that put jobless men to work keeping up the city parks. Hopkins worked on it every night after he was done at the Tuberculosis Association, helping to match unemployed people with work assignments. When the initial $75,000 ran out, the men raised more money. Well-meaning as the effort was, it could help only a very small fraction of New Yorkers in desperate need of work.[28]

While the economy was in turmoil, Hopkins's private life was also in crisis. His marriage, which had produced three sons—David, Robert, and Stephen, who had been born in 1925—was unraveling. Hopkins had begun an affair with Barbara Duncan, a secretary at the Tuberculosis Association, who was a decade his junior. Hopkins began psychoanalysis in an attempt to work out his difficulties, and went to Paris with Kingsbury to study social work, hoping the break might help him to save his marriage. The Hopkinses divorced, however, in May 1931. A month later, Hopkins and Duncan were married.[29]

Hopkins's life was set on a new course in August 1931, when Governor Roosevelt spoke to a special session of the New York legislature. After making his famous "What is the State?" speech, in which he declared that it was the state's duty to care for those who could not care for themselves, Roosevelt created the Temporary Emergency Relief Administration, with a budget of $20 million to be spent on relief and public works. He appointed his friend and political supporter R. H. Macy & Co. president Jesse Isador Straus to head the three-member board. When the board failed to get its first choice, New York City Welfare Council director William Hodson—who would later become Hopkins's partner in developing a federal relief plan—it hired Hopkins to be its executive director. Hopkins began work on October 8, 1931.[30]

As director of the TERA, the forty-one-year-old Hopkins faced the greatest challenge of his professional life. The Depression was causing human suffering on an unprecedented scale from one end of the state to the other. According to the New York State Department of Labor, there were 750,000 unemployed people in New York City alone, and many were facing homelessness and malnutrition. Lines outside of soup kitchens stretched for blocks. Hodson warned Congress that "the specter of starvation faces millions who never were out of work before." In an eight-month period in 1932, 185,794 families received eviction notices. It was common to see evicted families sitting on the sidewalk surrounded by their furniture. Hopkins tried to move the $20 million out to those in need as quickly as possible. Within three months, the TERA was providing relief to almost 10 percent of all New Yorkers. Hopkins tried to spend the money in innovative ways. One TERA-funded program hired unemployed garment workers to make overcoats for poor children. Hopkins also lobbied in favor of relief, urging local officials to keep up their own spending. "The desire to cut down expenses cannot be matched against the tragic hunger and distress" of the state's citizens, he told a conference of mayors. "There is no question of taxes versus life." In March 1932, Straus resigned to devote more of his time to Macy's. Roosevelt appointed Hopkins to take his position as head of the TERA, and extracted another $5 million in relief funds from the legislature.[31]

The economy continued to spiral downward. Hoovervilles were springing up, including in Manhattan, where there were now large encampments of the unemployed along the Hudson and East rivers, and in Central Park. The Hooverville on the East River at Tenth Street had about one hundred "dwellings, each the size of a doghouse or chicken coop, often constructed with much ingenuity out of wooden boxes, metal cans, strips of cardboard or old tar paper," journalist Matthew Josephson observed. The occupants "lived on the margin of civilization by foraging for garbage, junk, and waste lumber." Twenty percent of the city's schoolchildren were found to be malnourished. Health authorities warned that rickets, scurvy, anemia, and other diseases were likely to follow. "The situation here is very bad," Hopkins wrote his brother Lewis in the fall. "[I]n spite of the 'pollyannish' announcements that are coming from Washington," he said, "there is a steady decline in employment and an increase in the number of those in need of relief." Hopkins believed more money was needed, and the voters agreed. On November 8, 1932, the same day Roosevelt was elected president, New Yorkers voted in favor of a bond issue giving Hopkins another $30 million to disburse.[32]

Hopkins had come to see the TERA not as a temporary state initiative, but as a new model for government-run relief that should be taken to the national level. In January 1933, he had the chance to make the case to Congress. In an effort to build support for federal relief legislation, Senator La Follette was holding hearings at which social workers and others with direct knowledge of the unemployment crisis were invited to testify. Hopkins talked about how dire conditions were even in New York, the first state with a substantial relief program. He predicted that 10 percent of the nation, or three million families, would require relief in 1933, at a cost of over $1 billion. The only place that money could come from, he said, was the federal government. Hopkins laid the groundwork for the Federal Emergency Relief Act that Congress would soon pass. He urged that federal funds be given in grants not loans, so states that needed money the most would get it. He also argued for a truly federal program, not just a mechanism for distributing money to the states.[33]

When Roosevelt chose people for his administration, he did not seriously consider Hopkins. Although he had performed well at the TERA and had done his part for Roosevelt's campaign, organizing a campaign committee of social workers, Hopkins was just one of thousands in the Roosevelt orbit. He had not been part of the Brain Trust or the campaign apparatus, and he lacked close connections to Roosevelt or his inner circle. Hopkins accepted Governor Herbert Lehman's invitation to continue heading up the TERA, but he could not resist the pull to be part of the new administration forming in Washington. "Particularly in the weeks following the Inauguration, when the New Deal was bursting out in a series of bewildering pyrotechnic explosions, he felt that he must be part of this historic show," Hopkins's biographer, the Pulitzer Prize–winning playwright Robert Sherwood, observed.

This was when Hopkins and his friend William Hodson developed a plan for federal relief and presented it to Perkins. After Roosevelt accepted the plan, Hopkins began working with Wagner on drafting the Federal Emergency Relief Act. When the law passed, and Roosevelt offered him the administrator's job, Hopkins had his ticket to the historic show.[34]

CHAPTER NINE

"People Don't Eat in the Long Run— They Eat Every Day"

On Sunday, May 21, after accepting the position of federal relief administrator, Hopkins took the train down to Washington. Hopkins's appointment was widely praised when it was announced. Progressives were impressed by Hopkins's relief experience, and by his background in the settlement house and social work movements. The centrist *New York Times* was pleased that Roosevelt had not chosen one of the Brain Trust professors he was so enamored of and had instead named a "practical man." Hopkins arrived in Washington with as much knowledge as anyone in the nation about how to administer relief. He also brought with him a philosophy that Roosevelt's personal secretary, Grace Tully, described as "a profound distaste for a laissez-faire system that reduced men of intelligence and virtue to selling apples while others took to their ermine-lined economic storm cellars." On Monday morning, Hopkins was sworn in. He spoke briefly with Roosevelt, who offered him two guiding principles: distribute adequate relief to those in need, and do not worry about the politics. On day 79 of the Hundred Days, Hopkins went to work.[1]

Hopkins faced a relief crisis that was breathtaking in scope. Since 1929, national income had fallen by more than 50 percent. On May 1, the Commerce Department had reported that unemployment had reached an "all-time peak." As many as 16 million people were jobless, representing about one-quarter of the workforce, and each unemployed worker had an average of three dependents relying on him for support. Even in New York, conditions were bleak. The week Hopkins left for Washington, a committee of clergymen and social workers held hearings that called attention to the inadequacy of the state's cutting-edge relief program. Joseph Felbinger, a seventy-one-year-old jeweler laid off from Tiffany & Co., testified that he and his disabled wife received $7 in food aid every two weeks but nothing for rent, and he worried that if they were evicted it would kill his wife. Charles Holden, an unemployed black man from Harlem, told the hearing tearfully that he could not afford to feed his five children, including three-month-old twins, and his utilities had been shut off. Reports from the rest of the country were even more desperate. "We have unemployment in every third house," J. Prentice Murphy of the Children's Bureau of Philadelphia reported. "It is almost like a visitation of death to the households of the Egyptians at the time of the escape of the Jews from Egypt." In many places, local resources were completely exhausted. Detroit had been paying out a woeful 15 cents per person a day until it ran out of money. In Chicago, teachers who had gone for months without paychecks were drawing on their own meager resources to feed eleven thousand students who had no other source of food.[2]

After his meeting with Roosevelt, Hopkins rushed to the Federal Emergency Relief Administration's headquarters in the Walker-Johnson Building, a run-down yellow-brick building on New York Avenue. The FERA was moving into offices that had been occupied by the Reconstruction Finance Corporation's unemployment relief office, and boxes filled with outgoing employees' belongings were everywhere. When the wiry, chain-smoking Hopkins showed up he was, as one observer noted, a "slender bundle of ideas and nervous energy." His desk was still in a hallway, but he simply sat down at it and got to work. Hopkins treated the applications that states had submitted to the Reconstruction Finance Corporation as FERA applications, which allowed him to start handing out money right away. He sent $2,500,000 to Illinois, $1,630,540 to Michigan, $611,865 to Texas, and more money to Ohio, Colorado, Georgia, Iowa, and Mississippi. "The money will be made available immediately," Hopkins promised Governor Miriam A. "Ma" Ferguson of Texas in a telegram. In his first two hours, Hopkins dispensed more than $5 million to eight states that had run out of money and were on the brink of shutting down their relief programs. Hopkins's pace astonished a nation used to the Hoover administration's dilatory ways. In a story headlined "Money Flies," *The Washington Post* reported that "the half-billion dollars for direct relief of States won't last a month if Harry L. Hopkins, new relief administrator, maintains the pace he set yesterday." Hopkins kept the money coming. On June 3, he handed out another $2,747,426 to five states and the District of Columbia.[3]

Hopkins quickly became a national ambassador for an expansive federal relief program. He traveled extensively, speaking out about the importance of helping victims of the economic crisis. Despite his message of compassion, Hopkins did not come across as a typical do-gooder social worker. A *Chicago Daily News* columnist noted, with admiration, that Hopkins defended his mission to a parade of reporters in language that was "forceful, salted with slang and masculinity." Journalist Ernest K. Lindley concurred, noting that Hopkins had the virtue of being "direct," and that "when he means 'lousy,' he says 'lousy.'" Hopkins was an advocate not only for relief, but for the people who relied on it. Drawing on his own years of experience working with the poor, he tried to dispel stereotypes about what sort of people accepted government aid. "Are they hobos?" he asked a conference of mayors. "Are they unemployables? Are they a bunch of people who are no good and who are incompetent?" They were not, Hopkins insisted. "Take a look at them if you have not and see who they are...carpenters, bricklayers, artisans, architects, engineers, clerks, stenographers, doctors, dentists, ministers," he said. "I think there are the best people in the United States on these relief rolls."[4]

Critics were quick to attack the FERA as a waste of taxpayers' money, and a gravy train for the shiftless and the lazy. Hopkins responded sharply, often with his standard retort: "Some people just can't stand seeing others make a decent living." When someone told Hopkins things would work out for the unemployed "in the long run," he responded, "People don't eat in the long run—they eat every day." Faced with charges that the relief program was wasting tax money, *Fortune* magazine noted, "Mr. Hopkins is likely to return merely a sarcastic jab." He did not hesitate to take the critics on personally. When Eugene Talmadge, the Georgia governor who would become an outspoken New Deal critic, attacked the FERA, Hopkins attacked back. "All that guy is after is headlines," he said. "He doesn't contribute a dime, but he's always yapping." The most valid criticism of the FERA, Hopkins insisted, was the one that was almost never made: that it was not giving enough relief.[5]

Hopkins wasted little money on the FERA's headquarters, preferring to put funds directly into the hands of the unemployed. The paint on the walls of the Walker-Johnson Building "was peeling," one visitor noted, and "the corridors reeked of disinfectant." Hopkins's own office was "terrible," journalist Ernie Pyle noted in a column. "It's so little in the first place, and the walls are faded and water pipes run up the walls and your desk doesn't even shine," he observed. "Maybe it wouldn't look right for you to have a nice office anyway," Pyle added, "when you're dealing in misery all the time." Hopkins would later turn down the chance to move into the ornate, new marble Post Office on Pennsylvania Avenue to remain in what *Collier's* dubbed "the shabbiest building in Washington." Hopkins's frugality about operating expenses would become legendary, and it extended well beyond FERA headquarters. In its first year, the FERA would support 17 million people with a staff of just 121, who earned a combined $22,000 a month. "Our job is to relieve the unemployed, not to develop a big social-work organization," he insisted.[6]

Despite the low pay scale, the FERA attracted a first-rate staff. Hopkins sought out people who shared his philosophy of relief, and he valued real-world experience. One of the first people he brought in as an adviser was Frank Bane, whom he had met during his Red Cross days. Bane, who had organized the American Public Welfare Association, was a strong believer that relief was the responsibility of government, and as a consultant to Hoover's President's Organization on Unemployment Relief, he had urged it to abandon its reliance on private agencies. Hopkins later brought on Aubrey Williams, another American Public Welfare Association social worker, who would become his most important deputy. Williams, who had grown up in poverty in Alabama, had traveled through small-town Mississippi, helping to set up local public welfare departments. He had faced fierce resistance when he encouraged county officials to give the breadwinners in poor families $3 worth of work a week. Hopkins had no patience with bureaucracy or bureaucrats. When Lewis Douglas sent someone to ask for an "organizational chart," he was told that there was none, because Hopkins did not believe in them. "I don't want anybody around here to waste any time drawing boxes," Hopkins told his staff. "You'll always find that the person who drew the chart has his own name in the middle box."[7]

Although he had backed the FERA, Roosevelt remained ambivalent about the new role the federal government was assuming for relief. When he signed the bill into law, he again emphasized that the "first obligation" to provide relief remained "on the locality." That Roosevelt continued to minimize the federal role in relief greatly troubled progressives. Edith Abbott, writing in *The Nation*, called Roosevelt's emphasis on local responsibility "probably the most reactionary pronouncement that has come from the White House since the New Deal was inaugurated." His hesitancy was based partly on his long-standing feelings about the role of states in the federal system, but it was also pragmatic. He was concerned that with the FERA in place state and local governments would stop their own relief efforts, putting the entire burden of caring for the nation's poor on him.[8]

Hopkins stood by his boss on the question of local responsibility. In his public statements and his management decisions, he was vigilant about pressing the states and localities to do their part. "Every department of government that has any taxing power left has a direct responsibility to help those in distress," he insisted. All of the money Hopkins gave out on his first day was in the form of matching grants, which required the states to put in $3 for every $1 in federal funds. When states pled poverty and asked Hopkins to send them money that they would not have to match, he often ordered them to try harder. Hopkins told Governor Ruby Laffoon of Kentucky that his state would be cut off unless he came up with an appropriate share of relief costs. When West Virginia's governor insisted that his state had no more money for relief, Hopkins investigated and announced that the governor "simply does not want to face the music."[9]

Hopkins's immediate goal, besides quickly getting money to those in need, was to build a professional relief organization. The Hoover administration's relief program had simply functioned as a bank, lending money to the states to use as they wished. The FERA—as the statute that Hopkins helped to write established—was to be a single national program. To ensure that it was, Hopkins issued Regulation No. 1, directing that all federal relief money had to be administered by units of government. If private welfare agencies wanted to be involved, their staff had to become public employees. It was in some ways a surprising edict, since it was a rebuff to the sort of charities, like AICP and the Tuberculosis Association, in which he had spent much of his career. But Hopkins was intent on establishing that providing relief to the poor was a government responsibility. He also wanted to ensure that FERA workers, whether in Washington or in the states, would have to follow whatever rules he put in place.[10]

Hopkins was especially eager to establish national standards for benefit levels. The tradition of local responsibility for welfare programs meant that levels of support varied greatly across the country. The average monthly grant for a family in New York was $33.22. In Mississippi, it was $3.86. In Illinois, the standard for relief was the amount necessary to "prevent suffering," which, as Samuel Goldsmith of the Jewish Charities of Chicago told the La Follette Committee, meant that the poor were often denied money for clothing and other necessities. The registration forms that marchers submitted for the national hunger march of December 1932 revealed how inadequate relief was. One marcher from Oregon, M. J. Somers, a twenty-four-year-old unemployed laborer, reported that he was receiving $2.50 a month from county welfare. Another, Oscar Ruutul, said he was receiving $4 a month in scrip from the Salvation Army. Now that relief was a national program, Hopkins had the leverage to force states and localities to do better. "We are not going to allow relief agencies to starve people to death with our money," he declared. In his first month, Hopkins instructed the states that they had to provide for the recipients' basic needs—including food, shelter and utilities, and medical care—and he vowed to cut off aid to states whose benefit levels were "so low as to degrade the recipients." Southern states, in particular, objected that Hopkins was meddling with their local decisions, but he held firm. After Hopkins took charge of the FERA, average benefits began rising steadily. By January 1935, they had doubled.[11]

On June 14, Hopkins convened a conference of governors and state relief executives at the Mayflower Hotel. Forty-five states sent representatives, along with the territories of Alaska, Hawaii, the District of Columbia, and Puerto Rico. The group discussed federal relief, and then visited the White House, where Roosevelt spoke to them extemporaneously. He emphasized again that localities and states had to do their "fair share." Although the FERA had just sent out its first relief checks, Roosevelt made clear that the administration's focus had already shifted to public works. He spoke warmly of the CCC, boasting that there were now more than 235,000 men in camps, and that soon there would be 275,000 unemployed people out working in nature. He also noted that the National Industrial Recovery Act, which had passed Congress a day earlier, would usher in far larger public works programs. Roosevelt had officially gone from skeptic to booster. The new public works program would, he said, "provide a bridge by which people can pass from relief status over to normal self-support."[12]

Putting in place a program to provide relief to 15 million people proved to be hard work. "We did not have a single chart to go by," Hopkins later recalled. "It was almost as if the Aztecs had been asked suddenly to build an aeroplane." Hopkins started out simply dispensing funds to the states, which in turn gave it to the unemployed to meet basic needs. He was, however, an innovator by nature, and he quickly found ways to spend the money more creatively. He hired unemployed teachers to teach adult literacy and vocational training classes and sent them to work in financially strapped rural schools. By the end of 1933, ten thousand teachers had signed up. Another program targeted college and graduate students who were at risk of dropping out, offering them jobs in laboratories, libraries, and museums. A "rural rehabilitation" program provided poor farm families with seed, fertilizer, and livestock so they could produce their own food. Another program encouraged nonfarm families to grow vegetables in "subsistence gardens," both to save money and to promote better nutrition. Hopkins authorized state relief administrators to provide lunches in the schools for children of relief families, many of whom were suffering from malnutrition. These lunches, which were often prepared and served by women on work relief, were a forerunner to the federal school lunch program.[13]

Ever the social worker, Hopkins was particularly concerned about two of the nation's most overlooked groups, transients and the homeless. The hard times had thrown hundreds of thousands of Americans off the land. Many rode the rails or trekked from town to town in search of work. In 1932, Southern Pacific, a single railroad, ejected 683,457 people from its trains. These transients "were not bums, although in many communities they inherited the opprobrium that attaches to bums," Hopkins said. The towns they stopped in, which were struggling themselves, generally offered little in the way of assistance. "A bowl of soup grudgingly given, a place to sleep on the jail floor, and an urgent invitation to be out in the morning, was about as far as they could customarily go," Hopkins observed. The FERA issued grants, through a program called Transient and Homeless Relief, to provide direct aid to transients and to build camps around the country where they could spend the night. Urban homelessness was an even bigger problem. A nationwide survey in early 1933 estimated that there were 1.5 million Americans without homes. Many were living in Hoovervilles or sleeping on streets or in open fields. Hopkins used FERA money to encourage localities to provide them with a place to stay. He significantly improved conditions in homeless shelters, which had long been among the grimmest parts of the relief network. To receive federal funds, shelters had to meet standards for beds, food, health care, recreation, bathing facilities, and laundry.[14]

Almost as soon as he set up the federal relief program, Hopkins was looking to make it obsolete. Although he insisted that cash benefits were often necessary, Hopkins believed that they were a poor substitute for work. "There is nothing nice about this relief business from beginning to end," he said. "None of the relief officials like it, but you may bet the unemployed like it a lot less." Even though it was more costly and more administratively difficult,

Hopkins was committed to finding ways to provide the unemployed with the dignity of earning their own living. Perkins would later say that he "understood intuitively the moral gain" of providing jobs to people on relief. "Yes, work relief was more expensive than cash relief," she observed. "Yes, both were more expensive than soup kitchens and barracks. But Harry Hopkins thought it was the people that mattered." Once the FERA was up and running, Hopkins began pushing to transform it into a work relief program. In this effort, he had the strong support of Roosevelt, who had always preferred relief programs that put the recipients to work. By the fall, Hopkins had won Roosevelt's approval for the Civil Works Administration, which put onetime relief recipients to work on a wide array of government projects. Hopkins's conviction that people wanted to work proved correct. When he made two million jobs available through the CWA, nine million people applied.[15]

Hopkins tried to give people more to do than wield a rake or a shovel. Millions of white-collar workers were unemployed, including large numbers of artists and writers. The American Federation of Musicians surveyed its members and found that two-thirds were without work. Ninety percent of architects, according to a Columbia University study, were unemployed. Hopkins supported projects that used their talents. He used CWA funds to hire architects and draftsmen to work on the Historic American Buildings Survey. He put painters, musicians, and writers to work on artistic and literary projects, forerunners of the public art programs the Works Progress Administration would later sponsor. Relief funds were used to pay actors in New York, through a project sponsored by the Actors Equity Association, to put on plays in hospitals, libraries, and schools. In communities nationwide, the CWA paid musicians to put on public performances. "In Missouri," *Time* magazine reported, "a group of professional singers headed by Miss Edna Haseltine was hired at 35¢ an hour, sent out into the Ozark hills to give grand opera—only it was not called that for fear the natives would not attend."[16]

Critics charged that FERA money was being wasted on "leaf-raking" or dispensed as patronage, and some of it was poorly spent. Most of it, however, went where it was intended to go, and it made an enormous difference in people's lives. Not long after the FERA began, Hopkins hired veteran journalist Lorena Hickok, Eleanor Roosevelt's close friend, to travel the country reporting on how relief was working. Hickok did not hesitate to tell Hopkins when she saw bureaucratic ineptitude, political infighting, or needy people who were not being served. "All I can say is that these people have GOT to have clothing—RIGHT AWAY," she wrote in one dispatch from North Dakota. "It may be Indian Summer in Washington, but it's Winter up here." At the same time, Hickok collected examples of what federal relief was doing for ordinary Americans. In West Virginia, she found nearly four thousand undernourished children being cared for in two National Guard camps staffed by men and women on relief. She discovered that the infusion of relief funds had increased the prosperity in cities and towns across the South. The proprietor of one country store told her business was more than twice what it had been a year earlier. A white Baptist minister in Augusta, Georgia, said that before federal relief arrived, as many as fifteen beggars had come to his study each day. In the past month, he said, almost none had. Hickok found that some of the best programs were in New York, where Hopkins's TERA work had laid the groundwork. The relief in Corning, Rochester, and Syracuse was "what the Federal Emergency Relief Administration is aiming at for the rest of the country," she wrote.[17]

Other observers brought back similar reports. Roosevelt had Frank Walker, a friend who would later become postmaster general, examine Hopkins's early efforts. Walker did his own relief tour and came back with a glowing report. "I saw old friends of mine—men I had been to school with—digging ditches and laying sewer pipe," Walker related of a trip to his home state of Montana. "They were wearing their regular business suits as they worked because they couldn't afford overalls and rubber boots. If I ever thought, 'There, but for the grace of God—' it was right then." One of his old friends told him: "I hate to think what would have happened if this work hadn't come along. The last of my savings had run out. I'd sold or hocked everything I could. And my kids were hungry. I stood in front of the window of the bake-shop down the street and I wondered just how long it would be before I got desperate enough to pick up a rock and heave it through that window and grab some bread to take home."[18]

Statistics about how much money was dispensed and how many millions of people were helped could not convey what the FERA and other relief programs meant to people who had been beaten down by the Depression. In her memoir *The Roosevelt I Knew*, Frances Perkins told of what a relief job had done for an "almost deaf, elderly lawyer" she knew, a Harvard graduate whose legal practice had failed. He had been hired as an assistant caretaker at a small seaside park. The lawyer did "double the work anyone could have expected of him," Perkins recalled. "He made little extra plantings, arranged charming paths and walks, acted as guide to visitors, supervised children's play, and made himself useful and agreeable to the whole community." When Perkins saw him, she said, "he would always ask me to take a message to the President—a message of gratitude for a job which paid him fifteen dollars a week and kept him from starving to death. It was an honorable occupation that made him feel useful and not like a bum and derelict, he would say with tears in his eyes."[19]

The position of federal relief administrator agreed with Hopkins, as his friends were quick to recognize. "He is a bigger, better and more serious man," said his old mentor John Kingsbury, who had employed him two decades earlier at the Association for Improving the Condition of the Poor at a salary of $40 a month. "I don't mean that he seems cocky, but he has the air of a man who has great power, who is enjoying it." One reason for Hopkins's good spirits was that, despite all of the opposition and criticism, he was making real progress. Millions of people were benefiting from his work and, as Hopkins saw it, something larger was happening. "A new standard of public decency was being set," he would later write.[20]

Hopkins approached his job with the manic energy of someone who thought it might be taken away at any minute. He knew that Roosevelt had only hired him provisionally. He also understood that by aggressively championing relief, he was making himself a lightning rod for the New Deal's critics. Hopkins warned an economist who applied to the FERA that he was signing on to an unpopular mission. "One of the disagreeable things I will have to do," he said, "will be to keep reminding the American public of the serious problem of unemployment and destitution and they won't want to hear it." Hopkins "was determined to do what he could as long as he lasted," Rexford Tugwell noted in his diary. "This, he always said, would not be long."[21]

Hopkins's fears of an early dismissal did not come to pass. He not only kept his position as federal relief administrator; he expanded it greatly. Between May 1933 and the end of 1935, Hopkins would hand out more than $3 billion in grants. At the FERA's peak, in January 1935, more than 20 million people, fully 16 percent of the population, were being helped by it. "A curious person," *Collier's* observed, "this Harry Hopkins, who has spent more money personally than any other man in history." He "is heart and soul in the New Deal," journalist John Franklin Carter declared. "If the New Deal achieves the conquest of poverty through the conquest of unemployment," Carter predicted, "Harry Hopkins will be one of the men who did the most to make possible the final victory."[22]

As the Hundred Days began to wind down, there was still work to be done on the banking system. Walter Lippmann had written in March that "there are good crises and there are bad crises." The banking crisis was a good crisis, he said, because Roosevelt was prepared to use it to push for fundamental reforms. That had not happened in the administration's first frenzied days, when the focus had simply been on passing emergency legislation to get the banks up and running again. There was strong sentiment now for doing more. The public put much of the blame for the Crash of 1929 on the banks, both for their own stock speculation and because they pushed unsophisticated depositors into buying overpriced stocks. This popular anger was fanned in early 1933 by Senate hearings into the financial industry, led by former New York prosecutor Ferdinand Pecora. The picture of Wall Street that emerged from the Pecora hearings was as unsavory, one journalist noted, as "the inside of Tammany Hall." The hearings put a particular spotlight on National City Bank, among the nation's largest, which had blurred the line between commercial and investment banking. National City, as the hearings made abundantly clear, had profited handsomely by pushing its customers into reckless stock purchases. One victim, Edgar Brown of Pottsville, Pennsylvania, tes-tified that his portfolio had fallen from $225,000 to $25,000, leaving him indigent. "If you steal $25, you're a thief," *The Nation* explained. "If you steal $250,000, you're an embezzler. If you steal $2,500,000 you're a financier."[23]

At long last, the time was right for reform. Senator Glass had been try-ing for several years to get a banking bill through Congress, but Hoover had opposed it and it had stalled in the House. With Roosevelt in office, lop-sided Democratic majorities in Congress, and the headlines generated by the Pecora hearings, Glass saw an opportunity. The bill he introduced on May 10, and the companion House bill from Representative Steagall, took on an array of abuses. It raised minimum capital requirements for new banks, and it provided that bank officers could be removed and imprisoned for up to five years for engaging in unsound practices. Banks would be barred from lending to their officers, a common cause of bank insolvency. The bill also included a provision separating deposit banking from investment banking, so banks could never again be, as one contemporary account put it, "the chief tom-tom beaters for the speculative frenzy." This separation, which Moley had recom-mended in his May 1932 Brain Trust memo, had long been popular with pro-gressives. Wall Street had opposed it, but after the revelations of the Pecora hearings the opposition waned. The bill also gave large banks more leeway to open branches that competed with small, state-chartered banks. Glass, who viewed undercapitalized, poorly managed banks as the system's greatest vul-nerability, would have gone further, but he faced stiff resistance from South-ern and Western senators, who championed their home-state banks.[24]

The most controversial reform being proposed was federal deposit insur-ance. Progressives strongly supported deposit insurance, which they saw as the best way to guard against runs on banks and bank failures. It was also being pushed by the small-bank lobby, which considered it a way of helping small banks to hold off competition from larger banks. Steagall, who supported federal deposit insurance for fifteen years, included it in his House bill. But deposit insurance also had some powerful enemies, including the American Bankers Association and many large Eastern banks. They argued that it would unfairly require healthy banks to bail out struggling ones, and in the process put a strain on the entire system. Opponents of deposit insurance also insisted that it would encourage bankers to act recklessly, since they would know their mistakes would be covered. New York banks were among the most outspoken critics. With one-quarter of the nation's deposits, they would end up paying a large portion of the insurance fees.[25]

The administration did not take a strong stand for or against the Glass-Steagall bill, which was formally called the Banking Act of 1933, but Roosevelt made clear his opposition to federal deposit insurance. Vice President Garner, who supported it, had raised the issue with Roosevelt before the inauguration and had gotten nowhere. "It won't work, Jack," Roosevelt replied. "The weak banks will pull down the strong." William Woodin told Congress of the administration's opposition, but deposit insurance had enormous support in both the House and Senate. Roosevelt spoke out against deposit insurance at a May 23 Cabinet meeting and threatened to veto the whole banking reform bill if it stayed in. Support in Congress, however, remained overwhelming, and Huey Long declared that if the bill was vetoed there were enough votes in Congress to override. In the end, Roosevelt yielded to congressional sentiment and agreed to sign a bill with deposit insurance.[26]

The Glass-Steagall Act "was not written to please the bankers," Steagall said, and for the most part it did not. The big banks deeply resented the insurance provision. *Time* magazine, which spoke for this group, lamented that the most responsible banks would see "their deposits which they had spent a lifetime to build up and protect with their good names confiscated by the Government to pay for the mistakes and dishonesty of every small-town bankster." Small banks worried that the law would open the door to greater incursions by large banks. Glass-Steagall was, however, popular with the public, who could now feel more secure about the safety of their deposits. The Federal Deposit Insurance Corporation, the agency set up by the law, would be one of the New Deal's most important creations. In their history of American monetary policy, the economists Milton Friedman and Anna Schwartz called federal deposit insurance "the structural change most conducive to monetary stability since state bank notes were taxed out of existence immediately after the Civil War." In later years, few people would remember where Roosevelt had stood. "Roosevelt at first endured and then embraced it," Moley wrote. "I am convinced that finally he made himself believe he had favored it from the beginning."[27]

Roosevelt had been eager to keep Congress in special session as long as it kept passing his initiatives. By mid-June, however, the legislative storm had died down. Banking reform, government economy, agricultural and industrial recovery, and unemployment relief had all passed Congress, and the focus had turned to implementing them. Several other lower-profile bills had also passed in recent days. On June 5, Roosevelt had signed a joint resolution that abrogated the gold payment clauses in public and private contracts, an extension of what had been done when he took the nation off the gold standard. The Farm Credit Act formalized Roosevelt's executive order of March 27, creating a new system of farm credit to make loans more readily available to farmers. Roosevelt had also gotten his Emergency Railroad Coordination Act through Congress, which established a federal coordinator to help improve efficiency among the nation's troubled railroads. Roosevelt had other reasons for wanting to bring the session to a close, beyond the fact that his immediate legislative agenda was nearing completion. Over the previous few weeks, with the uprisings over the Agricultural Adjustment Act and the National Industrial Recovery Act, Roosevelt had begun to worry that the tide on Capitol Hill was shifting against him. "He is becoming frankly nervous about Congress staying on much longer," Ickes wrote in his diary after a visit to the White House. "The situation on the Hill is really dangerous, although so far he has kept Congress within reasonable bounds." The World Economic Conference was also about to convene in London to discuss international monetary policy. The United States was sending a high-level delegation led by Cordell Hull, and Roosevelt did not want congressional work to interfere. In any case, summer was only days away and many people, Roosevelt included, were ready to flee Washington in search of cooler climates and a break from more than three months of frenetic activity.[28]

There was one last thorny issue to be resolved, and it was Lewis Douglas's doing. The reductions in veterans' pensions that he had been eagerly carrying out had been deeper than expected. The cuts, which had been projected to total $383 million, had reached $460 million. The "presumptive" cases, the veterans whose injuries had manifested themselves after their service, were being cut off completely, including some who may have had a valid claim to benefits. There were reports that even soldiers who had been wounded in combat had seen their pensions reduced by 60 percent or more. "Down many Main Streets go armless veterans who used to get $94 a month from the government and now get $36," *The New York Times* reported. At a meeting with the American Legion on May 10, Roosevelt and Douglas had admitted the cuts were excessive, and Roosevelt had promised a review. Congress still had to appropriate Veterans Administration funds for the next fiscal year, and the veterans' lobby was pushing hard to use the appropriation to restore the cuts. It was backing up its campaign with stories of disabled veterans who had been left in dire straits. Roosevelt met with one of them, a double-amputee whose benefits had been slashed. Even if some of the veterans' lobby's stories were overstated, it seemed clear that the cuts were too deep.[29]

Roosevelt issued executive orders restoring $50 million in benefits, but he wanted to hold the line there. Progressives in Congress, led by Senator Thomas Connally, a Texas Democrat, were insisting on restoring $170 million in cuts. On June 10, Roosevelt and Congress reached a compromise, to restore $77 million or more. The administration agreed to keep making payments to 154,000 veterans with "presumptive" disabilities until review boards could investigate their claims, and to keep widows and children of "presumptives" on the rolls indefinitely. It also put on hold plans to close regional Veterans Administration offices. The veterans' lobby wanted more, including a commitment that all veterans with "presumptive" injuries would receive benefits permanently, but Roosevelt said that if Congress demanded any more concessions he would issue a veto and broadcast his veto message to the nation. Congressional progressives pushed to restore more of the cuts, but in the end the compromise held. "President Roosevelt was master of Congress until the end," *Time* magazine declared. Douglas had not gotten all of his veterans' benefits cuts, but he had gotten most of them. With the number of veterans receiving benefits dropping from nearly one million to 581,000, the veterans' supporters felt that an injustice had been done. In a letter home, Senator Hiram Johnson, a progressive California Republican, complained that the Budget Bureau had acted "in the most shameful, outrageous, and cruel manner," and that Douglas had "a heart of stone."[30]

On June 16, 99 days after the start of the special session, and 105 days into the new administration, Roosevelt held a midday signing ceremony at the White House. Flanked by members of Congress, reporters, and aides, he signed the Glass-Steagall Act, handing the pens he used to Glass and Steagall. He joked that the banking reform bill had more lives than a cat, pointing out that it had been killed "fourteen times in this session," a good-natured admission of his ultimate defeat on deposit insurance. Roosevelt declared himself a believer in the new law, which he called the "second most important banking legislation in the history of the country."[31]

The centerpiece of the signing ceremony was the National Industrial Recovery Act, which Roosevelt said history would probably judge to be "the most important and far-reaching legislation ever enacted by the American Congress." The law included a new conception of government-industry cooperation, he said, one that would allow corporations to "act in unison" for "the general good" in a way that antitrust laws had until then prohibited. Roosevelt enumerated the good things the NIRA would do. It would free up industry to set new standards of workers' rights that had been impossible when there was cutthroat competition. It would also establish a "vast program of public works" that would put up to a million people to work by October 1. Most important, Roosevelt said, it would restore American industry to health, which Roosevelt anticipated would "put millions of men back in their regular jobs this summer."[32]

Roosevelt's great hopes for the NIRA never came to pass. The American people rallied to the National Recovery Administration, the agency created by the new law. The Blue Eagle, the NRA symbol, became ubiquitous, appearing on store windows, billboards, and clothing labels. Two million employers signed NRA pledges, and 250,000 New Yorkers marched down Fifth Avenue to show their support. Under Hugh Johnson's leadership, the NRA helped industry and labor to adopt some 750 codes of fair competition, covering everything from the oil industry to the dog food industry and shoulder pad manufacturing. But the results were disappointing. Consumers complained that the codes were slanted toward industry and drove up prices. Small business complained that they were slanted in favor of big business. Big business complained that the codes gave labor unions too much power. The NIRA modestly stimulated the economy, but nowhere near as much as Tugwell, Moley, and Wagner had led Roosevelt to believe it would. By the time the Supreme Court ruled the law unconstitutional in 1935, it had already been dismissed as a failure.[33]

While the main element of the NIRA did not work out, the other parts of the law—the workers' rights and public works provisions—were notable successes. The codes of fair competition hammered out by industry, government, and labor included minimum wages and maximum hours for both men and women. That marked a major advance, since the limited number of states that had such laws covered only women and children, and the protections they offered were not what they should have been. Some allowed women to be put to work twelve hours a day. The Cotton Textile Code, the first one to be approved, established a forty-hour week, set a minimum wage of $13 a week in the North and $12 a week in the South, and prohibited the employment of children, which had been common in the industry. Although the codes of fair competition would be lost when the NIRA was struck down, they set a precedent for the federal government to regulate working conditions. Under Perkins's guidance, these principles would reemerge in the Fair Labor Standards Act, which imposed mandatory national minimum wages and maximum hours. Section 7(a)'s guarantee of the right of workers to organize would be revived in the National Labor Relations Act of 1935.[34]

The NIRA's $3.3 billion in public works had an equally lasting impact. The Public Works Administration, which the law established, created one of the greatest building drives in history. Under Ickes's leadership, it undertook massive projects like New York's Triborough Bridge, and many smaller ones, including school buildings and courthouses across the country. The federal commitment to large-scale public works that the NIRA established led to other major public works programs, including the Civil Works Administration and the Works Progress Administration. Public works would be perhaps the New Deal's single best-known undertaking, one that would make a crucial difference in the lives of the unemployed and the millions of family members who relied on them to survive.[35]

The signing of the NIRA was a fitting conclusion to the Hundred Days. The law had been put together quickly by government officials motivated, above all, by Roosevelt's inauguration-address injunction of "action, and action now." Although much of it failed, it still changed America. The workers' rights and public works provisions not only improved the lives of millions of destitute Americans—they marked a triumph for one faction of the administration, led by Perkins, Wallace, and Hopkins, and a defeat for another, led by Douglas. Taken together, these provisions stood for something fundamental: a recognition of the federal government's responsibility to look after its citizens. The NIRA was the ultimate sign that the old America—of citizens struggling as individuals while their government looked on indifferently—was drawing to a close. Roosevelt was wrong about many of the things he expected the law to accomplish, but he was right about its larger significance. "As in the great crisis of the World War, it puts a whole people to the simple but vital test—," he declared: *"Must we go on in many groping, disorganized, separate units to defeat or shall we move as one great team to victory?"*[36]

"A Lot Happened Out of That Determination of a Few People, Didn't It?"

The explosion of new legislation* during the Hundred Days transformed vast swaths of American life, from banking to agriculture to public welfare. These laws created the first "alphabet soup" agencies—the CCC, the AAA, the NRA, the FERA—government entities that would have enormous influence in the New Deal, and in some cases long afterward. The Hundred Days' greatest impact, though, was one of national philosophy. In just over three months, the federal government changed from being a nearly passive observer of its citizens' problems to an active force in solving them. From this point on, it would be a matter of concern to Washington when farmers were unable to support themselves, when depositors lost their life savings in failed banks, and when parents could not afford to feed their children. The relationship between the American people and their government would never

---

*The legislation passed during the Hundred Days includes: the Emergency Banking Act, March 9; the Economy Act, March 20; the Civilian Conservation Corps, March 31; abandonment of the gold standard, April 19; the Federal Emergency Relief Act, May 12; the Agricultural Adjustment Act, May 12; the Emergency Farm Mortgage Act, May 12; the Tennessee Valley Authority Act, May 18; the Truth in Securities Act, May 27; the abrogation of the gold clause in public and private contracts, June 5; the Home Owners' Loan Act, June 13; the National Industrial Recovery Act, June 16; the Glass-Steagall Banking Act, June 16; the Farm Credit Act, June 16; and the Railroad Coordination Act, June 16.

be the same again. "We have had our revolution," *Collier's* declared, "and we like it."[1]

The accomplishments of the Hundred Days were in large part a matter of timing. Roosevelt took office at a moment of unprecedented national crisis. The journalist Ernest K. Lindley spoke for many when he warned that Roosevelt had less than a year to save the country from complete collapse. The desperate economic conditions made the American people rethink their fundamental values. They were willing to consider things when there was 25 percent unemployment that they would not have contemplated in better times. The 1932 election put Roosevelt in a strong position to deliver on this clamoring for change. He took office with vast reservoirs of political capital after his landslide victory. He also had a new Congress with lopsided Democratic majorities—and a good number of Republicans who were inclined to follow his lead. Congress was not a rubber stamp. It fought him on some issues and prevailed on a few. Still, *The New Republic* was not far off when it declared that "no legislature in modern history, ever yielded more completely to the wishes of the head of state than did the Seventy-third Congress."[2]

Roosevelt arrived in Washington prepared to seize the moment. The Hundred Days has been called a hodgepodge—as thrown together, Moley said, as the stuffed snakes, baseball pictures, chemistry sets, and other things in a boy's bedroom. It was improvised, and often chaotic, but as Tugwell observed, "a bright thread of intention ran through the confusions and contradictions." That intention was to bring an end to the national philosophy of "rugged individualism," and to replace it with one of mutual responsibility. The Hundred Days created an affirmative government duty to protect workers and help the needy that would be expanded on repeatedly throughout the New Deal. The spirit of the Federal Emergency Relief Act would animate Social Security, Aid to Families with Dependent Children, and the federal unemployment insurance program. The Civilian Conservation Corps and the Public Works Administration would lead to the other important public works programs, including the Works Progress Administration. The voluntary minimum wage, maximum hour, and anti-child-labor provisions of the National Industrial Recovery Act codes of fair competition would evolve into the mandatory workers' rights standards of the Fair Labor Standards Act.[3]

The Hundred Days also established the principle that laissez-faire capitalism could not be relied on to protect the public interest. The Truth in Securities Act laid the groundwork for the creation of the Securities and Exchange Commission in 1934 and the broader regulation of capital markets that followed. Section 7(a) of the National Industrial Recovery Act would be expanded into the National Labor Relations Act of 1935 and the National Labor Relations Board, which enforced workers' rights to organize and bargain collectively. With the Agricultural Adjustment Act, the federal government took responsibility for sustaining the nation's farmers and protecting them from the vagaries of the free market. The system of government price supports, which was supposed to be an emergency measure, lasted into the twenty-first century, doing considerable damage along with the good.[4]

Another American tradition was born during the Hundred Days: opposition to the New Deal. Conservatives, whose most cherished ideals were under attack, started to speak out, objecting that Roosevelt was trying to become a dictator, and that his programs were un-American. The more time passed, the more outspoken these critics became. "Private fulminations and public carpings against the New Deal have become almost a routine of the business day," *Time* magazine declared in the fall of 1934. H. L. Mencken, who frequently railed against the New Deal, insisted that it had done nothing of value. The Brain Trust was "the sorriest mob of mountebanks ever gathered together at one time," he insisted. The best of them were merely "uplifters and do-gooders," while the rest were "a miscellaneous rabble of vapid young pedagogs, out-of-work Y.M.C.A. secretaries, third-rate journalists, briefless lawyers and soaring chicken-farmers." As the 1936 election approached, William Randolph Hearst mobilized his twenty-eight newspapers, thirteen magazines, and eight radio stations against Roosevelt. "MOSCOW BACKS ROOSEVELT," blared one headline that ran in all of the Hearst papers. Roosevelt was frequently denounced as a "traitor to his class." He did not, however, let the denunciations deter him. "Never before in all our history have these forces been so united against one candidate as they stand today," he declared on the eve of the 1936 election. "They are unanimous in their hate for me—and I welcome their hatred."[5]

There was also disaffection on the left. To Norman Thomas, the perennial Socialist presidential candidate, the New Deal was an attempt "to cure tuberculosis with cough-drops." Advocates for sharecroppers protested that too much was being done for wealthy farmers and not enough for poor ones. African Americans were frustrated that the New Deal did not challenge racial discrimination, largely because Roosevelt was reluctant to upset the white Southerners who were an important part of his electoral coalition. Leftists constantly called on the administration to take more radical steps—to nationalize the banks and industry or raise taxes on the wealthy. Some opposed the New Deal on a fundamental level, arguing that it sugarcoated the working class's problems. "The unemployed," insisted Abe Bluestein, a polemicist who opposed the NIRA, "must not suffer from any illusions of genuine relief from their heavy burdens under capitalism." At the same time, many leftists worried that the New Deal was stealing their issues and their support. When Thomas saw his share of the popular vote fall sharply in 1936, he joked that the Socialist Party platform was being carried out by Roosevelt—"on a stretcher."[6]

The majority of Americans, though—those who were neither far right nor far left—embraced the New Deal wholeheartedly. Its popularity was evident at the ballot box. In 1934, Democrats added twelve seats to their House majority and nine to their Senate majority, a rare case of the party in power gaining seats in an off-year election. "Boys—this is our hour," a newly energized Harry Hopkins told his staff. "We've got to get everything we want—a works program, social security, wages and hours, everything—now or never." A major reason the voters rallied around the New Deal was simply that it worked. With the launch of relief and public works, breadlines and Hoovervilles became more rare. At the end of Roosevelt's first term, even Walter Lippmann acknowledged the progress:

> There are still grave problems. But there is no overwhelming dangerous crisis. The mass of the people have recovered their courage and their hope.

They are no longer hysterically anxious about the immediate present. They have recovered not only some part of their standard of life but also their self-possession.

Roosevelt's critics like to point out that the New Deal did not end the Great Depression. Although it took World War II to restore the unemployment rate to where it had been before the Great Crash, the New Deal did produce steady economic improvement. The nation's total production increased significantly between 1934 and 1936. By 1937, the gross national product reached 1929 levels. Unemployment had fallen to 14 percent in 1937, still high, but far below the rate of March 1933. Just as important, for people who remained unemployed, New Deal programs were providing a safety net. Most of the 20 million Americans who received relief from the FERA at its height, and the millions who took CCC, CWA, or WPA jobs, would have been destitute if the nation had stuck by its Hoover Era principles.[7]

The New Deal evolved. Roosevelt moved to the left in 1934 and 1935, prodded by the persistence of the hard times and the demands for greater reform made by three outspoken populists: Senator Huey Long, whose "Share the Wealth" movement called for the government to provide poor Americans with the funds to buy a home, an automobile, and a radio; Father Charles Coughlin, the radio priest who railed against financial elites; and Dr. Francis Townsend, a retired California physician who was leading a campaign for old-age pensions. In 1935, Roosevelt embarked on the so-called "Second New Deal," more liberal and more critical of big business than the first. This was the era that ushered in the Works Progress Administration, the National Labor Relations Act, and Social Security. The voters continued to support the New Deal in its new incarnation. In 1936, Roosevelt would win reelection against Alfred Landon—an anti–New Deal Republican who attacked Social Security as a "cruel hoax"—taking 61 percent of the vote. In his second inaugural address, Roosevelt declared that he saw "one-third of a nation ill-housed, ill-clad, ill-nourished," and insisted that "the test of our progress is not whether we add more to the abundance of those who have much; it is whether we provide enough for those who have too little."[8]

There were rough spots along the way. In 1937, Roosevelt decided—in a return to the ideas of the Economy Act—to slash spending. He ordered cuts in New Deal programs, including such popular ones as the CCC. It was a reassertion of his inherent fiscal conservatism—Tugwell observed that even when Roosevelt was engaging in deficit spending "he had a secret longing to balance the national accounts." As historian Alan Brinkley has written, "disaster followed." In the "Roosevelt recession" of 1937 and early 1938, the Dow Jones Industrial Average fell 48 percent in seven months. Roosevelt eventually reversed the cuts and resumed deficit spending. He had other setbacks, notably his misguided effort to pack the Supreme Court in 1937 after the conservative Court overturned many of his New Deal initiatives. Opposition to the New Deal grew in these later years, but even so, the Fair Labor Standards Act, one of its greatest achievements, passed Congress in June 1938. Despite the setbacks, the American people continued to believe in Roosevelt and his agenda. The Republican Party had spent years running against the New Deal, but in the 1940 presidential election, its nominee, Wendell Willkie, was far more sympathetic. When Frances Perkins read the Republican Party platform that year she discovered to her delight that, as she put it, "every single New Deal thing that we had done was mentioned" in it. "Well, God's holy name be praised," she exclaimed to an aide. "No matter who gets elected we've won."[9]

Raymond Moley, the adviser who was closest to Roosevelt during the Hundred Days, was also the first to leave. At the end of the special session, sixty-six nations gathered in London for the World Economic Conference. Conservatives had high hopes that if the gathering could reach an agreement to stabilize world currencies, and if nations like England and Germany could be persuaded to restore the gold standard, the conference could bring the global depression to an end. Roosevelt did not share these views, but he thought the meeting could be valuable if its focus were expanded to include issues beyond currency, such as tariffs and stimulating international trade. He named Secretary of State Cordell Hull to lead a delegation of congressmen, businessmen, and other prominent people. A week later, Roosevelt sent Moley to London to join the delegation.[10]

Moley's trip was a disaster. During the Hundred Days, he had developed a reputation for haughtiness with some members of the administration, and his relations with Hull, his nominal boss, were especially strained. Moley "treated all his associates in the State Department from Hull down to the desk officers off-handedly," Herbert Feis, an economic adviser in the State Department, said. It did not help that Moley was being publicly credited with having more influence with Roosevelt than his top Cabinet members. In May, *Time* magazine had put Moley on its cover, just weeks after Hull had received the same honor. It was Moley, though, who was described as "Roosevelt's closest, most intimate advisor," and who was portrayed as the key strategist of the World Economic Conference. When Moley arrived in London, it appeared to many observers that he, not Hull, really represented Roosevelt. That impression was underscored when Prime Minister Ramsay MacDonald asked Hull to send Moley over on his arrival, adding, "You can come too, if you like." Moley took charge of the currency stabilization negotiations and signed on to an innocuous agreement whose terms were generally favorable to the dollar. Roosevelt, who had become wary of tying his hands on monetary policy, sent word that the conference should stop trying to reach an agreement to stabilize world currencies and should focus instead on its main purpose, "to better and perhaps to cure fundamental economic ills." Roosevelt's "bombshell" message, as it came to be known, blew up the conference.[11]

Moley, who was wounded by the president's rejection of his efforts, returned to Washington in defeat. He also came back to an irreparably damaged relationship with his direct boss. In London, Hull had come across a confidential cable that Moley sent Roosevelt disparaging his abilities. "That piss-ant Moley," Warburg quoted Hull as saying, "here he curled up at mah feet and let me stroke his head like a huntin' dog and then he goes and bites me in the ass!" Moley's fears about accepting the position of assistant secretary of state had been realized. Hull, who was insecure from the beginning about having a subordinate who saw the president more than he did, was now convinced that Moley was an enemy. He suspected, as he and Moley discussed in an awkward phone call, that Moley was really after his job.[12]

The end for Moley did not come right away. Roosevelt was cordial at first, but within weeks he tried to get Moley to undertake a criminal justice investigation in Hawaii. Moley recognized the offer as an attempt to get him out of Washington and turned it down. He reluctantly agreed to take a position as a special assistant in the Justice Department, where he would work on reforming kidnapping laws, but he could not accept his growing distance from Roosevelt. In late August, Moley resigned. The departure of the man who was, until recently, Roosevelt's closest aide mystified other members of the administration. Grace Tully, Roosevelt's secretary, thought Hull had been the driving force. "Moley faded out after trying unsuccessfully to climb over the top of Cordell Hull," she said. "As always in such cases, the President supported his Cabinet officer and Moley went off to sell his wares elsewhere." Tugwell was convinced that Roosevelt's decision had been guided by electoral politics. "Hull, as a conservative Southerner, was indispensable," he argued. "Moley was expendable."[13]

Moley was, in any case, already thinking about leaving the administration. As early as May, he had been talking with Mary Rumsey and Averell Harriman, daughter and son of the railroad magnate E. H. Harriman, about their buying *The Washington Post*, and Moley becoming editor. More recently, he had been making plans to found a weekly magazine with Harriman and Vincent Astor. When Moley left the administration, he helped launch *Today*, which merged into *Newsweek* in 1937. The magazine was originally promoted as a vehicle for explaining the New Deal. Moley started out defending Roosevelt against the charges that were being lobbed at him from the right. He also spoke out against Nazism and argued for helping refugees from Fascism. Moley's relations with Roosevelt remained good, and he traveled frequently to Washington to serve as an adviser and speechwriter. Before the 1934 election, Moley insisted that "the Republican party will have to accept the general principles of the New Deal" and that the Democratic Party would be the nation's main party "for many years to come."[14]

Even during the Hundred Days, liberals like Tugwell had observed that

Moley was drifting rightward. That movement gained force after he left the administration. Samuel Rosenman recalled a dinner at the White House at which Roosevelt had begun "twitting Moley about his new conservatism and about the influence of his 'new, rich friends' on his recent writings." From that night on, Rosenman said, there was a rift between the two men. In the 1936 presidential campaign, Moley seized on a Gallup poll and predicted that Republican Alf Landon would win. It was an indication, he said, that the "continuance of Leftist reform" was a mistake. In 1937, Moley spoke out against Roosevelt's plan to pack the Supreme Court with additional justices so it would uphold New Deal legislation. The court-packing plan, he said, "strikes at the heart of democratic government." By the following spring, Moley was speaking out against the New Deal itself. When Roosevelt prepared to seek an unprecedented third term, Moley publicly argued against it. Debating Tugwell, his onetime Brain Trust colleague, at a forum at the Waldorf-Astoria Hotel, he declared that "the thirst for power is the original sin of rulers."[15]

The final break came in 1939, when Moley published *After Seven Years*, which *The New York Times* called "a long and hostile analysis not only of" Roosevelt's "policies but of his motives and intelligence." Moley said that when he first got to know Roosevelt he liked him "for the same elemental reasons that millions of other people were soon to like him—for his vibrant aliveness, his warmth, his sympathy, his activism." But Moley presented Roosevelt as someone who had grown power-hungry from "a kind of mental autointoxication." Many people who remained loyal to Roosevelt agreed with Tugwell, who called *After Seven Years* "one of the cruelest books I know of." When a Cabinet member asked Roosevelt what he thought of it, according to gossip columnist Walter Winchell, he responded simply, "I trusted him." When Willkie challenged Roosevelt in 1940, Moley was caustic about his old boss. He argued that Roosevelt had embarked on a four-phase drive to expand his power—the passage of sweeping New Deal bills; the attempt to pack the Supreme Court; his drive to defeat Democrats who did not agree with him in the 1938 congressional elections; and his campaign for a third term. Moley declared them, in a bitter twist on the image Roosevelt had used against Hoover, "the four horsemen of autocracy." In 1948, Moley supported Dewey over Truman, and four years later he published *How to Keep Our Liberty: A Program for Political Action*, which argued that America was in danger of lapsing into "statism" and socialism. In 1954, Moley retired from the Columbia faculty, to concentrate on his writing. By the 1960s, he had become a Goldwater Republican.[16]

Moley had one more memoir in him, which he published in 1966. *The First New Deal* added substantially to the historical record. Moley associated himself with the first New Deal, but not with the more progressive Second New Deal that followed. The book was less harsh than *After Seven Years*, but its tone was still negative. "Lives sometimes focus not on a major triumph, but on a major disappointment," *Time* observed in its review. "Raymond Moley, now 80, has chosen to linger in a departed yesterday that let him down." Moley died eight years later, in February 1975.[17]

People who knew the young Moley had trouble making sense of his trajectory. He and Roosevelt had been close, and they accomplished a great deal together. Moley was unhappy with his position in the new administration, and felt badly treated when he was eased out, but he continued to work with Roosevelt afterward. He strongly disagreed with the court-packing plan, but many people in the administration, including Frances Perkins, felt the same way, and still remained loyal to Roosevelt. To his fellow New Dealers, Moley's decision to publish a caustic memoir in 1939, when Roosevelt was preparing to run for a third term, was the hardest to understand. Tugwell pondered the question in his own, more laudatory memoir. "I could not say how many times since 1939 I have been asked: 'What happened to Ray Moley?'" he wrote in *The Democratic Roosevelt*. "I do not yet know how to answer."[18]

Lewis Douglas would be the next to go. By the end of the Hundred Days, his relationship with Roosevelt—who had once called his budget director "in many ways the greatest 'find' of the administration"—had deteriorated badly. Douglas could not forgive Roosevelt for going off the gold standard, which he believed would ruin the economy and put the nation at risk. He was also bitter about the administration's efforts to help the Depression's victims. Years later, economists would conclude that Roosevelt had been right on both counts. Nations that went off the gold standard recovered from the Depression faster than those that remained on it. John Maynard Keynes would later show that increased government spending of the sort Roosevelt approved was the best antidote to a depression.[19]

Had Douglas been less emphatic in his views, he might have accepted Roosevelt's priorities. Instead, he continued to resist, even after the National Industrial Recovery Act made large-scale public works the law of the land. On July 1, 1933, at a meeting of the Special Board for Public Works, the committee created to oversee NIRA public works, Douglas argued against spending all of the money that had been allocated. It was unnecessary, he insisted, because the economy was improving at a "very rapid rate." At the same time, Douglas argued that going forward with the spending that had been agreed to would increase the deficit to the point where it would be "very questionable as to whether or not the credit of the United States government will stand it." Douglas was outvoted on the committee. Harold Ickes, the chairman, said simply that "the Act has been passed and we are called upon to administer it."[20]

As the year wore on, Douglas became more frustrated. It was increasingly clear that the budget would not be balanced, and that federal spending would continue to grow. Henry Morgenthau witnessed one clash, when Douglas chided Roosevelt for breaking his pledge to the voters to be fiscally conservative. It was, Morgenthau later recalled, one of the few times he had ever seen Roosevelt angry. Douglas was also troubled by other parts of the NIRA, especially the codes of fair competition that Hugh Johnson had been developing with leaders of business and labor. The rules being imposed on private enterprise made his "blood boil." In the Douglas family tradition, he was distraught that the codes made it easier for unions to organize. In December, Roosevelt and Douglas found themselves at loggerheads when they were working on a budget for the upcoming fiscal year. Douglas wanted to cap relief spending at $1 billion, although he was willing to accept as much as $2 billion. Roosevelt would not agree to either figure.[21]

On December 30, Douglas presented Roosevelt with a sharply written ten-page memo in which he made a "last plea" to slash spending. Attempts to "prime the pump" through deficit spending, he argued, would "cause infinitely more harm through the consequent paper inflation than any amount of good which might flow from them." Douglas took direct aim at Roosevelt's favorite program, the CCC. "Desirable as this activity may be," he said, because of its inflationary impact "it falls naturally within the category of those things which we might like to do but which in the public interest we cannot and should not do." Douglas argued that if Roosevelt stuck to his high-spending ways, "I prophesy many years of intense suffering on the part of millions—many, many millions of American citizens." Roosevelt was not persuaded, and the memo troubled him. He wondered "whether the man writing such a memorandum wasn't trying to make a written record."[22]

The following year brought more defeats. In March of 1934, Congress rebelled over the Economy Act. Given the enormous increase in federal spending, members of Congress argued that it was unfair to stick with the cuts that had been imposed on veterans and federal workers. Congress passed a bill restoring $228 million in funding for veterans' benefits and federal workers' salaries. When Roosevelt issued a veto, Congress overrode it. The override "entirely changed the President's attitude toward economy measures," Senator James F. Byrnes, one of the Economy Act's biggest supporters, wrote in his memoirs. Roosevelt concluded, according to Byrnes, that "whatever may have been the wish of the Congress in 1933, it was no longer willing to support him in his efforts to economize." At the same time, Douglas was forced to look on as New Dealers expanded the government's regulatory power. He opposed the Securities Act of 1934, and the creation of the Securities and Exchange Commission, which he saw as the "Tugwellians" making further inroads toward a centrally planned economy. Douglas's declining influence was clear even to people outside the administration. "No man in Washington has been so unhappy as Douglas, who sees disaster at every turn," one journalist observed. "Why Douglas remains in the New Deal is something of a mystery." Douglas became increasingly embittered. In a March 2 letter to his father, Douglas called Henry Wallace "absolutely financially irresponsible" and Secretary of the Navy Claude Swanson "a man of no mental fiber at all." Douglas was most contemptuous of Tugwell, whom he called "cunning" and "a Communist at heart." Douglas had also found a larger force to blame for the New Deal's excesses. Jews "as a race," he decided, were pulling Roosevelt astray. "The Hebraic influence in the Administration is very strong," he told his father. "Most of the bad things which it has done can be traced to it."[23]

Douglas and Roosevelt had another confrontation in June over Roosevelt's plan to ask Congress for a multibillion-dollar "kitty" that he could use for various relief projects. After this heated encounter, Roosevelt would not meet with Douglas for two weeks. At the end of the summer, Douglas traveled to Hyde Park to offer his resignation. Roosevelt did not want to lose Douglas, and he worried about the political fallout of having the administration's best-known fiscal conservative leave in a fit of pique. He insisted that in ten years Douglas would regret his decision, but Douglas was resolute. "I have a deep conviction that the Budget must be balanced," he wrote to Vice President Garner. "I could not find evidence of the same conviction elsewhere, so I did what I thought was right as courteously as I know how to do it." Appealing to party loyalty, Roosevelt asked Douglas to stay through December so his resignation would not affect the midterm congressional elections, but Douglas insisted on announcing his departure right away.[24]

Douglas's departure was a victory for the administration's progressives, but they were not all celebrating. Perkins, for one, had tried to convince him to stay. She did not hold his opposition to spending programs against him, and she thought Douglas had done an impressive job of overhauling the badly disorganized budget office he inherited, and of helping individual departments to prepare their budgets in a professional way. When Perkins talked to him about staying, Douglas was cordial, and noted that "you have been more persuasive than I have on some occasions." Douglas felt his losses on policy matters deeply. He left the administration, he would later say, not because he had lost influence, but because he did not want to "destroy myself inside."[25]

Douglas's resignation did not prevent the Democrats from winning the

1934 midterm election handily. He considered running for governor or senator back in Arizona, but his fears that his budget cutting would doom his political career proved correct. Douglas received high-level job offers from several major companies, including Paramount Pictures, as well as from Harvard University, where President James Conant wanted to make him vice president. Douglas instead accepted a position with American Cyanamid, the large chemical company. He was at first reluctant to criticize Roosevelt, but by 1935, he was more willing to speak out. In a series of lectures at Harvard, Douglas attacked, as *The New York Times* put it, "nearly every economic measure the Roosevelt Administration has adopted since" the Economy Act. He had actually gone further, declaring that he regretted that as a member of Congress he had voted for the Reconstruction Finance Corporation, the anemic relief measure adopted by Hoover. When the lectures were published in book form, Douglas wrote a preface that attacked the Roosevelt administration for promoting a "collective system" of government.[26]

In the 1936 election, Douglas publicly opposed Roosevelt and offered himself to Republican nominee Alf Landon as a vice presidential candidate. With each passing year, Douglas's opposition to the administration became more determined. In 1937, he helped organize a group of senators to challenge New Deal legislation. In 1940, Douglas, who had become president of Mutual of New York Life Insurance, helped found "Democrats for Willkie." Roosevelt felt bad about his onetime protégé's opposition, but whether out of respect for Douglas's abilities, lingering affection, or simply a desire to co-opt an influential opponent, he allowed his former budget director to return to the administration as deputy to Averell Harriman, the Lend-Lease representative in London. In 1942, Roosevelt appointed Douglas deputy war shipping administrator, giving him a large role in ensuring that the American military had the supplies it needed to win World War II.[27]

Douglas ended his career in public service with a much-coveted position. In 1947, President Truman appointed him ambassador to the Court of St. James's. In his four years in London, Douglas supported the Marshall Plan and opposed the creation of the state of Israel. He had done his best, he assured the British government, to clamp down on the "subversive activities" of American Jews who were working for a Jewish state. In 1949, he lost the use of an eye in a fishing accident, and he resigned as ambassador the following year. Douglas, who wore an eye patch for the rest of his life, returned to private life, splitting his time between New York and Arizona, where he became chairman of a bank. He backed Republican Dwight D. Eisenhower over Adlai Stevenson in 1952 and, two years later, denounced *Brown v. Board of Education*, the Supreme Court case that declared segregated public schools unconstitutional. Douglas would go on to oppose the civil rights movement as an infringement on states' rights. Until his death in March of 1974 he remained "a bit of a tragedy," as John Franklin Carter had observed back in 1934. "With a wider social outlook and a greater knowledge of economics…he would be one of the mainstays of the New Deal," Carter argued. "As it is, he is a man who has confused the principle of laissez-faire with the Word of God."[28]

Unlike Moley and Douglas, Henry Wallace settled comfortably into the new administration. The Agricultural Adjustment Act presented him with a vast administrative challenge: translating the law's bold promises into a practical system of agricultural incentives and aid to needy farmers. His first major undertaking was paying farmers to produce less cotton, and his success in getting a quarter of the nation's crop plowed under showed not only that domestic allotment could work, but that it was a force to be reckoned with. Wallace, the passionate lover of plants, thought having "to destroy a growing crop" was "a shocking commentary on our civilization." He was able to accept it, however, "as a cleaning up of the wreckage from the old days of unbalanced production."[29]

Wallace had a bigger problem with hogs and corn. There were six million excess hogs, and hog farmers did not want to wait another year to get rid of the surplus. They lobbied Wallace to call for the slaughter of pigs that weighed less than one hundred pounds, to cut down on the pork supply and reduce the need for corn feed. Wallace was not enthusiastic, but he went along. His decision to slaughter "six million baby pigs," as the press invariably put it, caused a national uproar and led to furious personal attacks on him. Wallace could never see why the public was so up in arms. "Doubtless it is just as inhumane to kill a big hog as a little one, but few people would appreciate that," he said. "They contended that every little pig has the right to attain before slaughter the full pigginess of his pigness."[30]

Wallace had warned that if the AAA did not pass until after the spring crop was planted, it would not have a significant impact in its first year, and he was right. Agricultural prices moved up modestly in the first few months, largely due to speculation, but they slid back down. The Farmers' Holiday Association was soon protesting again. The processors, who had been the fiercest opponents of the AAA, had the fewest grievances. They found that they had no trouble passing the processing taxes, and more, on to consumers. Wallace was soon flooded with complaints about the rising price of textiles and other goods made from processed crops. When he investigated and found that textile operators had "increased their margins as well as their prices," he made sure the public knew that the processing taxes were responsible for only a small part of the increase.[31]

The hostility in the Agricultural Adjustment Administration had by now broken out into full-scale civil war. Peek was using his position to promote McNary-Haugenism, and he was still bitter that he was not agriculture secretary. "I think that Fort Sumter was when he said to me, 'I want you to understand that Wallace doesn't mean anything here,'" recalled Jerome Frank, the AAA's general counsel. Peek, who had tried to block Frank's appointment in large part because he was Jewish and from a big city, was more frustrated than ever by the "urban liberals" in his agency, who he thought were more interested in remaking the world than in helping farmers. After Peek and Tugwell clashed over a proposal to dump butter overseas, Roosevelt replaced Peek with Chester Davis, Peek's first lieutenant, who had warmer feelings toward domestic allotment and closer ties to Wallace. Peek's departure did not end the schism between the agrarians and the urban liberals. Davis, a onetime farm leader from Iowa, clashed as sharply with Jerome Frank as Peek had. Frank stood up for consumers and took on powerful business interests like the meatpackers and the tobacco industry. He also pushed the AAA, which had done so much for rich landowners, to do more for tenant farmers, many of whom were being thrown off the land by domestic allotment. Davis and Frank's final clash was over an order Frank sent out to administrators in the South defending sharecroppers' right to remain on the land. Davis demanded that Frank and other leading liberals be purged from the agency, and Wallace—to the bitter disappointment of progressives—reluctantly agreed to put an end to the hostilities. "The farm people," Wallace was said to have told Frank sadly, "are just too strong."[32]

Although it got off to a slow start, the AAA had a dramatic impact on the prices of wheat, cotton, corn, and hogs, and on the income of the farmers who produced them. From 1932 to 1936, farm income increased 50 percent. The AAA also began moving the Farm Belt toward the long-elusive goal of "parity." By the end of the New Deal, the ratio of farm to city income, which had fallen to 48 percent in 1932, would rise to 79 percent. The AAA did not instantly end the farm crisis, but it brought a badly needed infusion of money into the Farm Belt, made it possible once again to farm profitably, and defused the radicalism that had been sweeping the region. Relief came to the Farm Belt more quickly than to the industrial economy, where conditions were still dire.[33]

In January 1936, the Supreme Court ruled that the AAA was unconstitutional, holding that the processor tax was an abuse of the government taxing authority. Wallace, who had anticipated the possibility, was already at work on a substitute that funded domestic allotment directly out of the Treasury. On March 1, Roosevelt signed the Soil Conservation and Domestic Allotment Act, a new version of the AAA that did not rely on a processor tax. In 1937, after taking a lengthy and eye-opening trip through the South— "Two thousand miles of Tobacco Road!" one member of his contingent declared— Wallace belatedly turned his attention to the problems of tenant farmers. With his backing, Congress passed the Farm Tenancy Act, which offered government loans to help sharecroppers buy land and acquire farm equipment. The law ended up helping fewer than 50,000 of the nation's 1.8 million tenant farmers.[34]

The biggest problem with the New Deal farm programs was that once in place they proved impossible to dismantle. The AAA was supposed to end when "the national economic emergency in relation to agriculture" was over. The agricultural emergency ended when the Depression did, but the farm programs never went away. They continued to dispense subsidies as family farms gave way to agribusinesses, and an ever-shrinking percentage of Americans made their living through farming. At the start of the twenty-first century, more than 70 percent of the subsidies were going to large farms. The farm programs that emerged from the New Deal would frequently be criticized for wasting taxpayer money and artificially increasing food prices. According to one government study, as much as 30 percent of the $26 billion in agricultural subsidies the government handed out in a single year went to people ineligible to receive them. With the rise of globalism, it became clear that the farm programs were harming third-world farmers, who were unable to compete with highly subsidized American crops. Congress, under pressure from farm state representatives, continued to block even modest reforms in the subsidy programs.[36]

While Wallace was administering the agricultural programs he also become one of the administration's greatest roving ambassadors. In 1934 alone, he traveled more than forty thousand miles, visiting each of the forty-eight states, and published two books and twenty articles. Wallace was so highly regarded that his name was mentioned frequently as a successor to Roosevelt. When Roosevelt decided to run for an unprecedented third term in 1940, Wallace became his running mate, replacing Vice President Garner, who had challenged Roosevelt for the Democratic nomination. Many conservative Democrats opposed the choice, but Roosevelt had great respect for Wallace, who he thought would make a good vice president and a worthy successor. Not insignificantly, Roosevelt also thought that Wallace would help him carry the Farm Belt. Wallace stepped down as agriculture secretary for the campaign, leaving behind a department that had grown from 40,000 employees when he took office to more than 146,000.[37]

After Roosevelt was reelected, without carrying Iowa, he named Wallace chairman of the Economic Defense Board, giving him a key role in war mobilization. Wallace became a major liberal voice in foreign policy. In a famous

1942 speech, he declared it "The Century of the Common Man," a phrase he would long be associated with, and argued passionately against colonialism and fascism. He became increasingly outspoken, railing against greedy businessmen, isolationists, and "American fascists." When it came time for Roosevelt to run again, Wallace had become a liability with urban bosses and southern Democrats. With Roosevelt's quiet support, the 1944 Democratic National Convention dumped Wallace from the ticket and nominated the more moderate Senator Harry Truman of Missouri for vice president.[38]

Wallace felt betrayed, but he campaigned across the Farm Belt for the Roosevelt-Truman ticket. Roosevelt rewarded him after the election by naming him secretary of commerce. Roosevelt died in April 1945, which meant Wallace had only narrowly missed becoming president. Wallace was one of the few Cabinet members asked to stay on by Truman, but he did not last long. In the fall of 1946, he gave a speech in Madison Square Garden that conflicted with the administration's tough approach toward the Soviet Union. When conservatives inside and outside the administration attacked the speech, and Wallace, Truman asked for Wallace's resignation. Wallace went on to become editor of *The New Republic* and threw himself into progressive politics. As liberals splintered over their responses to communism, Wallace sided with those who worried that the anti-Communists were going too far. His critics charged that he was sounding like a Communist himself.[39]

In 1948, Wallace waged a third-party run for president. As the Progressive Party nominee, he ran on a platform of freedom and international cooperation abroad and civil rights and civil liberties at home. On a southern campaign swing, he broke with tradition and refused to appear anywhere that was not open to blacks on an equal basis. Wallace was strongly attacked from the right, however, and he spent much of his time trying to dispel charges that he was a Communist or a fellow traveler, and hopelessly naïve about the Soviet threat. He was not entirely successful—51 percent of the respondents in a Gallup poll said they believed the Progressive Party was Communist-controlled. With the race between Truman and Dewey a dead heat, many of Wallace's supporters cast their ballots for Truman in the end. Wallace won

2.4 percent of the vote, and finished fourth behind Truman, Dewey, and Dixiecrat Strom Thurmond.[40]

After his defeat, Wallace retreated to upstate New York, where he and Ilo had a sprawling farm. He broke with the Progressive Party in 1950, supporting the United States's response to Soviet-backed aggression from North Korea. In the McCarthy Era, Wallace was frequently red-baited. He defended himself in an appearance before a Senate subcommittee and in public statements. More and more, Wallace dropped from sight and devoted himself to farming. When *The New York Times* checked in on him in 1960, it found Wallace enjoying life on the farm, "where he hybridizes strawberries, gladioli and chickens, some of which lay brown eggs and others—a Chilean strain—green eggs." Wallace died of ALS, Lou Gehrig's disease, on November 18, 1965, at the age of seventy-seven.[41]

When the Hundred Days were over, Frances Perkins played a key role in implementing the NIRA. At meetings of the Special Board for Public Works—which included the secretaries of labor, interior, agriculture, war, the Treasury, and commerce, and the budget director—she helped ensure that the public works programs began on the right footing. Perkins was one of the board members who overruled Douglas's suggestion that not all of the money allocated by Congress had to be spent. At the same time, she opposed board members who argued that the important thing was putting people to work right away, regardless of what they did. Perkins insisted that public works money be spent on socially useful projects like schools and housing, a position the board adopted. "Fortunately, she won the argument and transformed the face of America," one study of public works noted. New Deal public works programs would go on to build thousands of schools, tens of thousands of miles of roads, highways, and sidewalks, major housing developments for the poor, post offices, and key parts of the nation's infrastructure. In significant part because of NIRA public works, as many as one and a half to two million more Americans had jobs in 1934 as in 1933.[42]

Perkins also played a role in drawing up the NIRA codes of fair competition, which gave workers rights that had never been recognized before in America. There were no federal minimum wage and maximum hours laws, and the few state laws that existed applied only to women, and offered relatively little protection. The industry-by-industry codes adopted under the NIRA dramatically altered the landscape of American labor. Most included forty-hour maximum workweeks, and about one quarter imposed limits of eight hours of work a day. In the Department of Labor's Annual Report for 1934, Perkins declared that one of her lifelong goals had been achieved: "We have come practically to a 5-day, 40-hour week as the standard of working time in the United States of America." The codes also banned child labor, imposing a sixteen-year-old minimum age requirement that was higher than the laws of all but three states. The child labor provisions were a major reform—especially the one that took children out of the cotton mills—though, as Perkins noted in the 1934 report, child labor still existed in agriculture, domestic service, and factory homework, so the struggle was not yet over. The codes included provisions guaranteeing unions the right to organize and to bargain collectively, as Section 7(a) required. Under the new rules, and the even stronger ones that would be instituted in 1935, union membership would increase sharply—from 2,689,000, or 6.9 percent of the workforce in 1933, to 8,763,000, or 19.2 percent of the workforce, in 1939.[43]

In 1934, Perkins began drafting an unemployment insurance bill. Rather than make it a federal program, she envisioned the states running unemployment insurance according to federal guidelines. Perkins made it a state-managed program partly because, as a committed Brandeisian, she was skeptical of putting too much power in the federal government, and partly because she believed a state program would have a better chance of being upheld by the Supreme Court. While Perkins was working on unemployment insurance, public support was building for old-age insurance, which was being promoted by Dr. Francis Townsend and his popular Townsend Clubs. Roosevelt announced that he was appointing a committee to consider a broader social insurance program that would include old-age benefits. He named Perkins to chair the Committee on Economic Security, which also included Wallace; Secretary of the Treasury Morgenthau; Attorney General Cummings; and Hopkins. Perkins asked Roosevelt if it wouldn't make sense for someone other than her to serve as chair, since she was known to be such a strong supporter of social insurance. "No, no," Roosevelt responded. "You care about this thing. You believe in it. Therefore I know you will put your back to it more than anyone else, and you will drive it through."[44]

The committee's final recommendations went beyond unemployment and old-age insurance. Along with those insurance programs, which would be paid for by employer and employee contributions, it called for relief programs to cover categories of needy individuals who could not pay premiums: dependent children, the disabled, and the unemployed elderly. The committee nearly included national health insurance, but it backed down. "Its inclusion would have aroused such vehement opposition, sparked by the American Medical Association, that the whole bill, even the simple grants to the states, would have gone down the drain," said Thomas Eliot, a Labor Department lawyer who worked on the bill. Perkins drew up much of the Social Security Act in the Department of Labor, using department staff.[45]

Perkins testified for the bill in Congress and spoke out publicly at every opportunity. It was passed much as the committee recommended, with one significant exception. The committee had called for the Department of Labor to administer social security and unemployment insurance, and for the FERA to manage the programs for dependent children, the disabled, and the unemployed elderly. Congress instead created an independent Social Security Board to run them all. Perkins thought Congress considered the Labor Department "too soft on workers" and wanted the programs in more skeptical hands. At least some members of Congress, however, were trying to prevent Perkins from taking control of large new bureaucracies, because they resented her reform-minded management style. Perkins was "an articulate, intelligent woman," said Arthur Altmeyer, an assistant secretary of labor, but she was "not sufficiently amenable to patronage needs." Roosevelt signed the Social Security Act on August 14, 1935. On her way to the White House for the signing ceremony, Perkins got a call from Paul Wilson's nurse saying he had disappeared. She went to the ceremony to avoid calling press attention to the situation, and when it ended took a train to New York, where she helped locate her husband.[46]

The National Recovery Administration, which Tugwell and Moley had hoped would steer the economy toward prosperity, was the least successful part of the NIRA. The public initially rallied to the NRA, but it soon came to regard the program mainly as a vehicle for big business to raise prices and stifle competition. There was little protest when the Supreme Court held the NIRA unconstitutional in May 1935. The right to organize contained in Section 7(a) had, however, proven valuable, and organized labor rushed to rescue it. Senator Wagner introduced the National Labor Relations Act, which guaranteed workers' right to organize and bargain collectively, outlawed company unions, and declared firing workers for union membership to be an unfair labor practice. Roosevelt and Perkins worried that the bill contained so many protections for organized labor that it had crossed the line to being antibusiness, and that it would energize labor's opponents. Perkins's old social worker instincts also made her skeptical of a bill that saw unions as the full answer to workers' problems. The Wagner Act, which became law on July 5, 1935, put the power of the federal government behind organizing drives. The National Labor Relations Board was given authority to go after employers who engaged in what the act defined as unfair labor practices. Union membership soared, but as Perkins feared, it produced a backlash, culminating in 1947 with the passage of the antiunion Taft-Hartley Act.[47]

When the NIRA was struck down, Perkins's greatest concern was ensuring that its workers' rights provisions lived on. In anticipation of the ruling, she had asked the Labor Department's lawyers to draw up a pair of bills to reauthorize the codes' protections. The more constitutionally cautious bill applied only to government contracts. The Walsh-Healey Act, which passed in June 1936, required that the government buy all goods and services that cost more than $10,000 from manufacturers who observed an eight-hour day and a forty-hour week, with overtime pay for anything over; paid a minimum wage set by the secretary of labor; and banned child labor. Perkins later put forward a more sweeping bill, the Fair Labor Standards Act, which became law in 1938. It called for the secretary of labor to set minimum wages and maximum hours, based on the recommendations of an appointed board. The version that passed authorized Congress, rather than the labor secretary, to set the minimum wage, which began at twenty-five cents an hour, rising to forty cents in two years, and maximum hours, which were set at forty-four hours a week, declining over time to forty hours. It also barred goods made by children under sixteen from interstate commerce. The act gave raises right away to hundreds of thousands of workers, and promised eventual relief to millions of workers who earned less than forty cents an hour.[48]

The Fair Labor Standards Act was the New Deal's last great accomplishment. It also marked, for Perkins, the start of a dark period. There was labor unrest, and Perkins found herself in the middle of it. She came under pressure to deport the leader of the longshoreman's union, Harry Bridges, who was being attacked as a Communist, but she refused. Perkins was right on the law, but was attacked by conservatives in Congress. In early 1938, the House Special Committee on Un-American Activities, chaired by Martin Dies of Texas, introduced an impeachment resolution. Perkins was not fond of Bridges, but since she did not believe he was deportable she would not deport him. "Nothing but her concept of what was right affected her," her counsel, Charles Wyzanski, said. In the 1940 election, Willkie made Perkins an issue. He would appoint a secretary of labor from the labor movement, he promised a union crowd in Pittsburgh, adding, "and it won't be a woman, either." After the election, Perkins submitted her resignation, but Roosevelt would not accept it.[49]

Perkins's influence declined in Roosevelt's final years in office, when labor issues took a backseat to the all-consuming focus on winning World War II. She made it her mission to keep the labor peace, so wartime production would not be interfered with. At the same time, she tried to ensure that defense contractors did not erode the labor standards she had fought for simply by pleading national defense. When contractors tried to get state and federal maximum hour, minimum wage, and child labor laws repealed, Perkins

enlisted Roosevelt's help in resisting. Particular laws were suspended tempo-
rarily when absolutely necessary but, as Perkins recalled, "we came through
the war with basic labor legislation intact."[50]

Perkins again offered her resignation after Roosevelt was reelected to his
fourth term, but he refused again. "I can't think of anybody else, and I can't
get used to anybody else," he said. She remained in office until Roosevelt's
death on April 12, 1945. Perkins was one of only two Cabinet members—
Ickes was the other—to serve for Roosevelt's entire presidency. Counting
her four years as his industrial commissioner, no one had worked for him
longer. When Truman became president she submitted her resignation, and
he accepted it. Perkins received a warm send-off from 1,800 Labor Department employees. She dispensed with her trademark tricorn for the occasion,
wearing a sailor hat instead. "This is in honor of my new life," she said. "It's
my private hat." To ensure that her successor did not go through what she
had thirteen years earlier, she met him at the train station and brought along
a department car for his use.[51]

At the end of her career, Perkins's standing with the public was not high.
She received little credit for her two decades of accomplishments, many of
which were simply attributed to Roosevelt, or to the New Dealers as a group.
At the same time, the Bridges affair, and the impeachment charges, had
taken a toll. Perkins's antagonism toward the press had made matters worse,
resulting in years of unflattering, and often antagonistic, coverage. *Collier's* ran a profile in 1944 that began, "A major Washington mystery is how
Frances Perkins has managed to hang onto her job as Secretary of Labor
for twelve long years." It went through a litany of her failings, and reported
that "correspondents have voted her 'the most useless' of Washington officials." *Collier's* acknowledged, however, that before she agreed to be labor
secretary, Perkins had asked Roosevelt to support her on a wide-ranging
social agenda, and that twelve years later she had checked off every item on
it. She had wanted immediate federal aid to states and local governments for
unemployment relief, which became the FERA and the CWA. The large-
scale public works program she sought became the WPA. Federal minimum
wage and maximum hours laws and a ban on child labor were guaranteed in

the Walsh-Healey and Fair Labor Standards acts. Old-age and unemploy-ment insurance were established by the Social Security Act. Despite her cur-rent unpopularity, *Collier's* predicted that "when the definitive history of this Administration is written, it is quite likely that Miss Perkins will be hailed as the most successful of the New Dealers, for the Roosevelt pattern of govern-ment contains more of her ideas than those of any other of the President's fol-lowers." It could be said, *Collier's* concluded, that "what this country has been operating under for the past twelve years is not so much the Roosevelt New Deal as it is the Perkins New Deal."[52]

For all of her career success, Perkins led a life filled with challenges and unhappiness. Mary Rumsey, her good friend and Washington housemate, died in December 1934 after a horseback riding accident. Paul Wilson never recovered his health. In his final years, after Perkins was out of the Cabi-net, he moved in with her in Washington, but he remained troubled and depressed and avoided interacting with people. Hardest of all for Perkins was her relationship with her daughter. Susanna, who lived apart from her mother for much of her youth, was a difficult child and a troubled adult. Per-kins and Susanna clashed frequently, and in her old age Susanna would call her mother a "dragon lady" and make wild charges against her. The intensely private Perkins spoke as little about Susanna's problems as she did about her husband's. At the end of her life, Perkins expressed doubts about the choices she had made, and said frequently that a woman should put family ahead of career. "There is no question that this was a summing up time of her life," said Allan Bloom, a Cornell University English professor who befriended her in the early 1960s, "and she wasn't the least bit sure that she had handled it right."[53]

When she left the Department of Labor, Perkins wrote a book about the late president, at the urging of a friend who was a literary agent. *The Roosevelt I Knew,* which her publisher rushed out in 1946, was an instant best seller. Perkins hoped Truman would name her to the Social Security Board so she could work with the program of which she was most proud. Instead, in the fall of 1946, he appointed her to the Civil Service Commission. When Dwight Eisenhower was elected, she gave up her position on the commission and returned to New York. Perkins was happy to make the move. "I felt much more at home in New York," she said. "I could never crack Washington. In New York I could see a fire escape someplace and say: I did that."[54]

In her final years, Perkins accepted an invitation to teach at Cornell University's School of Industrial and Labor Relations. She was by now a bit more conservative than she had once been. She still strongly supported relief for those who needed it, but she worried about it sapping the work ethic of those who could find gainful employment. At the same time, Perkins remained the guardian of the New Deal flame, and she talked about ways the New Deal legacy could be expanded and improved upon. In the years before Medicare was created, she advocated a federal health insurance program for the elderly, which she regarded as "the next step in expanding Social Security." While she was at Cornell, the thirty young men who lived in Telluride House, a residence for high-achieving students, invited her to move in. "I feel like a bride on her wedding night," she told a colleague before accepting. Perkins helped out in the garden, attended house meetings, and showed up at parties. To the students, she was a wise counselor, and a living piece of history—the "last leaf," she used to say, of the New Deal. She remained at Cornell until her death on May 14, 1965, at the age of eighty-five.[55]

In late 1962, at the urging of her students, Perkins invited Henry Wallace, another "last leaf," to Cornell for the weekend. She was not sure that her old Cabinet colleague, who was not venturing out much, would accept the invitation, but he did. Wallace's hair had turned white, but he otherwise looked much as he had in his younger days. Perkins's students, who expected to meet the fiery left-wing presidential candidate of 1948, were surprised to see an earlier version of Wallace, one who talked about his love of plants and his hope of developing a strain of corn that could be grown in the Caribbean and withstand tropical storms.[56]

The two New Deal veterans led a pair of undergraduate seminars. In the first, Wallace talked about the agricultural policies he had helped establish. The Roosevelt administration had been able to do a lot for struggling farmers, he said, but it had not managed to slow the flight of farmers from the land. Wallace cited projections that in two decades less than 5 percent of

Americans would be living on farms. If he were a younger man, he said, he would consider leaving this fast-urbanizing United States. When Perkins's expression indicated that she did not share his sense of loss, one student who was there recalled, Wallace joked that the two of them had never agreed on the advantages and disadvantages of growing up in a city like New York."[57]

Perkins led the second seminar, on conditions in the cities during the Great Depression. She talked about the kind of inspired improvisation that had guided the New Deal. The CCC was, she said, a good example. It had begun as an idea of Roosevelt's that sounded completely impractical, but the Cabinet departments stepped in and made it practical. Labor put together a system for recruiting and selecting workers. The army developed a plan for provisioning the corps with uniforms and tents. The Forest Service supervised the workers. It was how many New Deal programs had become a reality.[58]

To the Cornell undergraduates, the Great Depression was ancient history—they had not been born when Perkins and Wallace arrived in Washington in March 1933 and ran through the mud to get to the inauguration before Roosevelt's address was over. The students could not appreciate how bad things had been, or how much the two elderly former government officials in their midst had accomplished. Perkins told the students the animating spirit of the New Deal, as she saw it. The goal—hers, Wallace's, and Roosevelt's—was a simple one, she said: "to take the edge off human misery."[59]

Harry Hopkins was only in the administration for the last twenty-one of the Hundred Days, but he more than made up for his late start. Even before he joined, Hopkins had played an important role in shaping the Federal Emergency Relief Act. Once he became relief administrator, he put together one of the most dynamic departments in the federal government. Hopkins was not only passionate and fast-moving; he was thoughtful and innovative. The new relief law had established for the first time the principle that providing destitute people with food, clothing, and other necessities was a federal responsibility, not something that could be left to the states, localities, or private charities. In administering the program, Hopkins took this principle a step further and created a social welfare system that operated by a single set of national standards. For the first time, destitute people in South Carolina and Mississippi could have the same hope of having their basic needs met as poor people in New York City or Philadelphia.[60]

Once he had the relief system in place, Hopkins pushed to create public works jobs—real jobs that paid prevailing wages, not assignments to relief recipients to work off the value of the benefits they received. The NIRA public works program, the Public Works Administration, got off to a slow start under Ickes, who was extremely cautious about spending government money. "Ickes insisted on almost extravagant safeguards against waste and corruption," Tugwell noted. "This earned him the title of Honest Harold; but it did not relieve unemployment." Hopkins worried that the unemployed would not make it through the winter of 1933–34, and insisted on doing something about it. In the fall of 1933, he persuaded Roosevelt to let him start a new public works program, the Civil Works Administration. It would focus on smaller projects than the massive undertakings of the PWA, ones that could be started up quickly. Hopkins transferred the FERA work relief recipients into the CWA and also began hiring unemployed workers directly into the program. As usual, Hopkins spent with abandon. He was "aware a certain amount would be wasted—because it was more important to get the non-wasted ninety percent than to avoid the wasting of ten percent," recalled Jerome Frank, who served as counsel to the FERA. Hopkins "knew he was taking chances, very personal chances," Frank said, but he also believed that getting immediate help to the unemployed "mattered terribly." When the CWA began, 814,511 workers were on the payroll. "He was not priming the pump," Ickes complained. "He was turning on the fire plug." Adding to Ickes's unhappiness, Hopkins was doing it with his money, because the CWA's $400 million budget came from Ickes's Public Works Administration. In early 1934, when the CWA was disbanded, it was putting more than four million people to work. After being criticized for assigning FERA workers to "leaf-raking" make-work jobs, Hopkins promoted—sharing Perkins's formulation—jobs that were "socially useful." The 200,000 projects CWA

workers undertook ranged from tearing down dilapidated houses in Alabama to extending a municipal sewer system in Texas. Hopkins's workers
rebuilt rural schools, built playgrounds and swimming pools, and engaged in
tick eradication and malaria control.[61]

The CWA was short-lived, but it was the biggest public works program
that had existed in America. It turned the New Deal's focus even more
toward providing the unemployed with jobs and salaries. Later in 1934, Hopkins lobbied Roosevelt to create more public works, and Roosevelt agreed to
a new $4.8 billion program. Ickes and Hopkins both wanted to run it and
Roosevelt divided it between them. Hopkins turned his part into the Works
Progress Administration, and he proved adept at getting control of much of
the available money. In its lifetime, the WPA employed 8.5 million people
and supported 20 million, more than 20 percent of the population. "Hopkins,
who was already the great alms-giver, became the greatest employer," *The
New Republic* noted. In June 1939, federal public works programs still supported almost 19 million people, nearly 15 percent of the population.[62]

In addition to helping millions of American families survive the Depression, the WPA left a rich legacy of socially useful projects. Its workers constructed or repaired more than 125,000 buildings, including 83,000 schools;
800 airports; 950 sewage plants; and 650,000 miles of roads. They built or
improved 78,000 bridges and 25,000 playgrounds; terraced 271,000 acres of
eroded land; and taught two million people to read. They also ran a famous
Federal Art Project, which hired destitute artists to create murals for public buildings, posters, and paintings. The WPA produced a highly regarded
series of state guidebooks and an acclaimed collection of interviews with
former slaves, and it played a major role in building the San Antonio Zoo,
New York City's LaGuardia and Washington's Reagan airports, and the
presidential retreat at Camp David. In 1965, on the program's thirtieth anniversary, *The New York Times* quoted a dispossessed North Carolina tenant farmer living in an abandoned gas station, who had been rescued by a
WPA job. "I'm proud of our United States, and every time I hear 'The Star-
Spangled Banner' I feel a lump in my throat," he said. "There ain't no other
nation in the world that would have the sense enough to think of W.P.A."[63]

Hopkins, predictably, became a lightning rod for the New Deal's opponents. Some of the criticism, especially charges that local administrators were using jobs for political patronage, had merit. Hopkins rooted out such abuse when he learned of it, firing employees who broke the rules. He gave no ground, however, to charges that he presided over boondoggles, a word that quickly came into vogue. As always, he was adept at answering his detractors. "With the smug complacency which apparently goes with the chairmanship of the Republican National Committee, Mr. Fletcher has seen fit to accuse me of playing politics because I am feeding the hungry, clothing the naked, and sheltering the destitute, regardless of their sex, age, creed, color, race or place of residence," Hopkins said in answer to one critic. "If that be politics, I plead guilty, but decline to enter into argument with Mr. Fletcher. Hunger is not debatable."[64]

Hopkins's position seemed precarious. "It is only a matter of time when a 'going out of business' sign will be hung on the shop of Harry L. Hopkins, Tailor to the Existing Order," *The Nation* predicted. The promotion to head the WPA had thrust him into the limelight and, the magazine said, "no man can long survive such eminence in the nation's capital." Against all predictions, Hopkins's rise continued. After Louis Howe's death in April 1936, a bond developed between Roosevelt and Hopkins that rivaled the one that had existed between Roosevelt and Howe. When Barbara Hopkins died of cancer the following year at the age of thirty-seven, the two men grew even closer. "Harry Hopkins is uniquely the President's friend, counselor, confidant," *Time* wrote. "Somewhere within the lean and hungry Hopkins frame, the burning Hopkins mind, the President found a quality and a kinship which he found in no other human being." Roosevelt "was a person who relied on people he sort of chemically got along with," Franklin Delano Roosevelt, Jr., said, and Hopkins was one of them. Perkins believed the friendship was based on a shared outlook. Hopkins "was truly another self for President Roosevelt," she said. "The mutual trust between the two men sprang partly, of course, from personal sympathy and temperamental harmony, but more from a common devotion to the idea that their mission in life was to make things better for the people."[65]

Roosevelt wanted Hopkins to succeed him as president, but that was not to be. He was regarded as too ideological to have broad appeal in a national election. His FERA and WPA work had left him with a reputation as "the world's greatest spender," and one profile noted that he had attracted, along with many admirers, "the frank hatred of many of the President's foes." His divorce would also be a problem, especially since he and Ethel had not ended their marriage on good terms. At the end of 1938, Roosevelt appointed Hopkins secretary of commerce. The final blow to Hopkins's presidential ambitions came the following year when he became seriously ill with a disease that interfered with his ability to digest food. As war spread across Europe, Hopkins became involved in confidential efforts to prepare America's response. He helped Roosevelt plan his campaign for a third term and was his personal representative to the July 1940 Democratic National Convention in Chicago.[66]

A month later, Hopkins resigned as secretary of commerce and moved to New York. He played a major role in Roosevelt's reelection and, in the lead-up to World War II, became a key foreign policy aide. Hopkins served as Roosevelt's envoy to the British government and headed up the Lend-Lease program, which ensured that Britain and other allies had the military supplies they needed to defend themselves against Nazi Germany. When the United States entered the war, Hopkins traveled to Moscow and London to discuss strategy. "We came to think of Hopkins as Roosevelt's own, personal Foreign Office," a British official told Hopkins's biographer, Robert Sherwood. The ailing Hopkins had by now moved into a suite in the White House. In 1942, Hopkins married Louise Macy, a former Paris editor of *Harper's Bazaar*, who moved into the White House with him. He suffered a painful blow two years later, when eighteen-year-old Stephen Hopkins, his and Ethel's youngest child, died in battle in the Marshall Islands. At the war's end, Hopkins attended the Yalta Conference, where he took an active role in the negotiations, despite his declining health. In January 1946 Hopkins died, at the age of fifty-five. The nature of the illness that had plagued him for eight years was, the hospital declared, "obscure."[67]

As historic as Hopkins's wartime service was, his leadership of the FERA, the CWA, and the WPA was his most enduring legacy. The relief and public works programs that he set in motion were as important as any part of the New Deal in changing the relationship between the federal government and its citizens. In the summer of 1940, when Hopkins resigned as commerce secretary, apparently leaving government service for good, Perkins wrote him a farewell letter. She thanked him for "putting a decent, reasonable, human relief system into operation," which she called "perhaps the most creative thing that has been done in the whole New Deal." Perkins also indulged in a brief, uncharacteristic moment of nostalgia. "My mind can't help but run back to that evening in March 1933 when you and I and Bill Hodson argued out the urgency of the relief situation and devised ways and means of bringing it to the attention of the President," she told Hopkins. "A lot happened out of that determination of a few people, didn't it?"[68]

By the seventy-fifth anniversary of the start of the Hundred Days, in March 2008, Franklin Roosevelt was firmly entrenched as one of America's greatest presidents. In surveys of historians and of the general public, he regularly ranked in the top three, alongside George Washington and Abraham Lincoln, the two presidents who held office in equally cataclysmic times. The principles of the Hundred Days had not merely survived—they had become integral to American life. Roosevelt's critics had not been able to derail them during his lifetime or in the two decades that followed. In the early 1960s, the spirit of the New Deal seized the country once again. In a 1964 speech at the University of Michigan, Lyndon Johnson unveiled his own progressive agenda, which he called the Great Society. Johnson was consciously attempting to build on the New Deal legacy. Richard Goodwin, the Johnson aide who coined the phrase "Great Society," would later say that his boss's goal had been nothing less than to "out-Roosevelt Roosevelt." This time, the impetus was not to overcome a devastating depression, but to share the wealth in a time of unprecedented prosperity. Some of the Great Society programs, such as Vista and the Job Corps, had a relatively modest impact. Others, such as

Medicare, Medicaid, Head Start, and food stamps, expanded the promise of the New Deal in significant and lasting ways.[69]

There have been repeated efforts over the years to undo the New Deal and its central philosophy of the government's duty to care for its citizens. As the Great Society was being launched, the Republicans nominated Barry Goldwater for president. Goldwater, who had attacked his fellow Republican Dwight Eisenhower for presiding over a "dime store New Deal," ran in 1964 on a platform of shrinking big government. Goldwater lost in a landslide, but his ideas lived on. The modern conservative movement was born out of his failed candidacy, and his successors scored some significant successes in chipping away at the New Deal legacy. Ronald Reagan, who was elected in 1980 on a promise to scale back the welfare state, appointed a budget director, a modern-day Lewis Douglas, who called for "starving the beast," or cutting taxes to force a reduction in government spending. When Republicans took control of the House of Representatives in 1994, under the leadership of Newt Gingrich, Congress passed a welfare reform bill that ended the federal guarantee of cash assistance to poor children that dated back to 1935. A Democratic president, Bill Clinton, signed it into law. Also in the Clinton years, the Glass-Steagall Act's separation of commercial and investment banking, a major reform of the Hundred Days, was repealed. When President George W. Bush took office in 2001, he pushed through tax cuts so tilted toward the rich that when they took full effect, wealthy Americans would pay the lowest taxes since the Hoover years. The Bush administration weakened New Deal–era federal regulations and appointed pro-business agency heads, creating an environment that contributed to corporate scandals and a home foreclosure crisis.[70]

Despite these challenges, the fundamental elements of the New Deal proved resilient. Bush began his second term with an energetic campaign to privatize Social Security. He had to back down, however, in the face of strong bipartisan opposition. He went on to sign a Medicare prescription drug law, sponsored by congressional Republicans, which significantly expanded the scope of the welfare state. The political discussion quickly moved on to health insurance, with a majority of Americans telling poll takers that they supported universal access to health care. Even with the ebbing and flowing of the federal regulatory regime, which varied depending on the administration in power, the idea that government had a duty to protect the public from dishonest stock offerings, unsafe food and drugs, and failed banks, which was revolutionary in 1933, had ceased to be controversial. In the fall of 2008, when a Republican president and a Democratic Congress united to enact a $700 billion bailout of the financial industry, it was clear that the whole country had accepted the fundamental principles of the New Deal.

No serious presidential candidate would run again on Hoover's platform of rugged individualism and laissez-faire economics. After seventy-five years, the principles that emerged during the Hundred Days are still a flashpoint in American politics. At the most basic level, however, the debate has ended. Roosevelt, Perkins, Wallace, Hopkins, and the rest of the New Dealers—like George Washington and the Founders, and Abraham Lincoln and his Cabinet and generals—built something that has become an essential part of America.[71]

ACKNOWLEDGMENTS

One of the pleasures of writing history is the chance to spend time with people from the past. In researching this book, I got to know a group of extraordinary individuals. Frances Perkins's lively intelligence and keen sense of moral purpose come across powerfully in the interviews she gave to the Columbia Oral History Project. Henry Wallace's deep feeling for the nation's beleaguered farmers jumps off the pages of the articles he wrote for *Wallaces' Farmer*. Raymond Moley recounted his triumphs and defeats in absorbing detail in two classic New Deal histories. Harry Hopkins shared his passion for social welfare programs and his compassion for the Depression's victims in his fine memoir, *Spending to Save*. Lewis Douglas expressed himself frankly—at times, too frankly—in handwritten letters home to his father in Arizona. My thanks begin with these four men and one woman for leading such remarkable lives.

As each of these examples suggests, even in this digital age the research for a book like this begins with words on paper—and in libraries. I am grateful to the dedicated staffs of the libraries that hold the papers of the book's protagonists. Columbia University's Rare Book and Manuscript Library is home to Frances Perkins's papers and an array of other important collections, including the papers of the Christodora House, the settlement house at which Harry Hopkins began his social work career. The Columbia Oral History Project has not only Frances Perkins's oral history, but ones from Henry Wallace and early New Dealers Jerome Frank and Charles Wyzanski. Moley, who ended his life a passionate conservative, left his papers to the Hoover Institution at Stanford University, whose staff could not have been more helpful. The same is true of the staff of the University of Arizona library, which holds Lewis Douglas's papers, and of the Georgetown University library, which has some of Harry Hopkins's papers. The staff of the University of Iowa library made spending a week there one summer reading Henry Wallace's papers a delight. My enormous thanks also to the staff of the Franklin D. Roosevelt Presidential Library, in Hyde Park, New York, who do a laudable job of tending to the New Deal flame.

I benefited from the help of three talented students. Mizue Aizeki of Vassar assisted me in mining the files of the Roosevelt Library. Vilja Hulden, at the University of Arizona, uncovered a trove of valuable material on Lewis Douglas. Sara Marcus, a Columbia University graduate student who came to me through a Hertog research fellowship, pored through periodicals from the 1930s and came up with gold.

Tomlin Coggeshall, Frances Perkins's grandson, was generous with his recollections of his grandmother and smoothed the way for my access to restricted portions of the Perkins papers.

An author can have no greater good fortune than to fall under the guidance of the remarkable Ann Godoff. The title publisher does not do her justice. Ann has an extraordinary sense of how to put together a book, from bringing out the important themes, to honing the characters and story arc, to producing a breathtaking cover. The best refutation of the notion that publishing's golden age is over is that Ann is still hard at work.

My editor, Laura Stickney, was a joy to work with. She offered valuable insights about the manuscript and did a superb job of shepherding me through critical stages of the process.

Barbara Campo, the production editor, did an excellent job of smoothing out the text's rough edges and ensuring that the citations were in order.

Kris Dahl has, for the third time now, been not only an extraordinary agent, but a tireless advocate and a wise counselor.

For the book's photos, I am indebted to Phyllis Collazo of *The New York Times,* who helped turn a folder of time-worn prints into shining pieces of history; Jeffrey Roth, who ably guided me through the *Times*'s photo archives; and the ever-helpful Carolyn McGoldrick, of the Associated Press.

Much thanks to my colleagues on *The New York Times* editorial board: Eleanor

Randolph; Dorothy Samuels; Brent Staples; David Unger; Francis X. Clines; Eduardo Porter; Lawrence Downes; Teresa Tritch; Robert Semple; Phil Boffey; Carol Giacomo; Maureen Muenster; Verlyn Klinkenborg; Carolyn Curiel; Elizabeth Harris; Linda Cohn; Juston Jones; Sue Kirby; Gail Collins; Frank Rich; Nick Kristof; Serge Schmemann; Carla Robbins; David Shipley; and the ringmaster of it all, Andrew Rosenthal. Profound appreciation, of course, to Arthur Sulzberger, who makes our work possible.

Family provided encouragement: Beverly Cohen; Stuart Cohen; Harlan Cohen; Noam Cohen; Alan Cohen; Lori Cohen; Ethan Cohen; Gabe Cohen; Seymour Shapiro; and Carl Shapiro.

Friends helped with the book—and provided much-needed distraction from it. Thanks to Elaine Rivera; Elisabeth Benjamin and Daniel Coughlin; Laura Franco and David Kostin; Caroline Arnold and Shan Sullivan; Charles M. Young; Diane Faber; P. J. Posner; Mickey Dubno; Aisha Labi; Gail Ablow; Lavea Brachman; Michael Heller; the fishing crew—Paul Engelmayer, Peter Mandelstam, Jim Rosenthal, Antony Blinken, and Eric Washburn; Kathy Bishop; Loren Eng and Dinakar Singh; Elaine Mandelbaum; Olivia Turner; Bobby Segall; Amy Gutman; Gerald Frug; Lizzie Glazer; and Eileen Hershenov. Tina McGerald Smith offered brilliant insights on leadership, morality, and many other subjects. After two decades, Elizabeth Taylor remains an unending source of advice, support, and friendship.

Nearly seventy years ago, Frances Perkins wrote to Harry Hopkins about their work in the Hundred Days: "A lot happened out of the determination of a few people, didn't it?" The power of a few determined people to do good is as true today as it ever was. My greatest appreciation is to the Perkinses, Wallaces, and Hopkinses of today—who exist in every part of the country and in every walk of life.

NOTES

Introduction

1. Edmund Wilson, *American Earthquake: A Documentary of the Jazz Age, the Great Depression, and the New Deal* (Garden City, N.Y.: Doubleday Anchor Books, 1958), pp. 454–55, 458, 462–63.
2. Harry Hopkins, *Spending to Save* (New York: W. W. Norton & Company, 1936), pp. 18–19; 50–51, 66; Dixon Wecter, *The Age of the Great Depression, 1929–41* (New York: MacMillan Company, 1948), pp. 17, 39; Caroline Bird, *The Invisible Scar* (New York: David McKay Company, Inc., 1966), p. 16; Irving Bernstein, *A Caring Society: The New Deal, the Worker, and the Great Depression* (Boston: Houghton Mifflin Company, 1985); Frances Perkins, "The Return of the Sweatshops," article for Scripps-Howard Syndicate, undated, ca. June 1933, Box 46, Frances Perkins Papers, Columbia University Rare Book and Manuscript Library (hereafter, "Perkins Papers"); *Time*, 2/1/82.
3. Jean Edward Smith, *FDR* (New York: Random House, 2007), p. 287; Hopkins, *Spending to Save*, pp. 62–63; David Burner, *Herbert Hoover: A Public Life* (New York: Atheneum, 1984), pp. 250, 266, 316; Richard Norton Smith, *An Uncommon Man: The Triumph of Herbert Hoover* (New York: Simon and Schuster, 1984), p. 147; Edgar Eugene Robinson and Vaughn Davis Bornet, *Herbert Hoover: President of the United States* (Stanford, Calif.: Hoover Institution Press, 1975), p. 180; Walter I. Trattner, *From Poor Law to Welfare State: A History of Social Welfare in America* (New York: The Free Press, 1994), p. 277.
4. Arthur M. Schlesinger, Jr., *The Coming of the New Deal* (Boston: Houghton Mifflin, 1958), pp. 13, 20–21; *Time*, 1/2/33; *New York Times*, 6/17/33.
5. Ernest K. Lindley, *The Roosevelt Revolution: First Phase* (New York: Viking Press, 1933), p. 166.
6. Schlesinger, *Coming of the New Deal*, pp. 13, 20–21; Lindley, *Roosevelt Revolution*, pp. 272–73; *New York Times*, 6/17/33.
7. Frances Perkins, *The Roosevelt I Knew* (New York: Viking Press, 1946), pp. 166–67; Franklin D. Roosevelt, *The Public Papers and Addresses of Franklin D. Roosevelt*, Vol. II (New York: Random House, 1938), p. 646; Raymond Moley, *After Seven Years* (New York: Harper & Brothers, 1939), pp. 369–70; Lindley, *Roosevelt Revolution*, p. 15; Reminiscences of Frances Perkins, 1961, Pt. 3, p. 575, Columbia University Oral History Research Office Collection (hereafter, CUOHRO), http://www.columbia.edu/cu/lweb/digital/collections/nny/perkinsf/index.html. Also available as printed transcript. *Navigating the Rapids 1918–1971: From the Papers of Adolf A. Berle*, ed. Beatrice Bishop Berle and Travis Beal Jacobs (New York: Harcourt Brace Jovanovich, Inc., 1973), p. 72; Raymond Moley, *The First New Deal* (New York: Harcourt, Brace & World, Inc., 1966), p. 224; Smith, *FDR*, pp. 310–11.

8. Richard Hofstadter, *The American Political Tradition and the Men Who Made It* (New York: Vintage Books, 1973), p. 427; Samuel Rosenman, *Working with Roosevelt* (New York: Harper & Brothers, 1952), p. 55; Perkins, *The Roosevelt I Knew*, pp. 328, 330; Howard Zinn, Introduction, in *New Deal Thought*, ed. Howard Zinn (Indianapolis: The Bobbs-Merrill Company, 1966), pp. xxviii–xxix; Reinhold Niebuhr, "After Capitalism—What?" in Zinn, *New Deal Thought*, p. 16; *New York Times*, 7/28/35; Reminiscences of Frances Perkins, 1961, CUOHRO, Pt. 4, p. 469.

9. Rexford Tugwell, *The Democratic Roosevelt: A Biography of Franklin Delano Roosevelt* (Garden City, N.Y.: Doubleday & Co., 1957), p. 150, Moley, *First New Deal*, p. 224.

10. Berle and Jacobs, *Navigating the Rapids*, p. 72; Frank Freidel, Introduction, *Realities and Illusions 1886–1931: The Autobiography of Raymond Moley* (New York: Garland Publishing Co., 1980), p. vii; "Behind the New Deal," *New Outlook*, March 1933; Moley, *First New Deal*, p. 224.

11. John Gunther, *Roosevelt in Retrospect: A Profile in History* (New York: Harper & Brothers, 1950), p. 127; Moley, *First New Deal*, p. 236; John Franklin Carter, *The New Dealers* (New York: Da Capo Press, 1975), p. 3.

12. Moley, *First New Deal*, p. 237; *Time*, 3/8/33.

13. Franklin D. Roosevelt, *FDR: His Personal Letters, 1928–1945*, ed. Elliott Roosevelt (New York: Duell, Sloan and Pearce, 1950), p. 342.

14. *Saturday Evening Post*, 7/27/40; George Martin, *Madam Secretary: Frances Perkins* (Boston: Houghton Mifflin, 1976); Lillian Mohr, *Frances Perkins: That Woman in FDR's Cabinet* (Croton on the Hudson, N.Y.: North River Press, 1979); Bill Severn, *Frances Perkins: A Member of the Cabinet* (New York: Hawthorn Books, Inc., 1976).

15. John C. Culver and John Hyde, *American Dreamer: The Life and Times of Henry A. Wallace* (New York: W. W. Norton & Co., 2000), p. 83 and n.

16. Carter, *New Dealers*, p. 179; *Washington Post*, 5/23/33.

17. Lindley, *Roosevelt Revolution*, pp. 3–4; Rexford Tugwell, *Roosevelt's Revolution: The First Year, a Personal Perspective* (New York: Macmillan, 1977).

18. Schlesinger, *Coming of the New Deal*, p. 238.

19. Smith, *FDR*, pp. 370–74, George Wolfskill and John A. Hudson, *All but the People: Franklin D. Roosevelt and His Critics* (New York: The MacMillan Company, 1969), p. 152; Rexford Tugwell, "America Takes Hold of Its Destiny," *Today*, 4/28/34, p. 256, quoted in Bernard Sternsher, *Rexford Tugwell and the New Deal* (New Brunswick, N.J.: Rutgers University Press, 1964), p. 151.

Chapter 1: "Action, and Action Now"

1. Works Progress Administration, *Washington: City and Capital* (Washington, D.C.: Government Printing Office, 1937), pp. 56, 157–58; 637; David Herbert Donald, *Lincoln* (New York: Simon & Schuster, 1995), pp. 278–79.

2. Charles Hurd, *When the New Deal Was Young and Gay* (New York: Hawthorne Books Inc., 1965), p. 101; Wilson, *American Earthquake*, p. 560; George Creel, "The Mystery of the Secret Cabinet," *The Elks Magazine*, Murphy File, Box 1, Henry A. Wallace Papers, University of Iowa, Special Collections Department (hereafter, "Wallace Papers"); Benjamin Stolberg, "Madam Secretary: A Study in Bewilderment," *Saturday Evening Post*, 7/27/40.

3. Works Progress Administration, *Washington*, pp. 203–6; Reminiscences of Frances Perkins, 1961, CUOHRO, Pt. 4, pp. 9, 26; Lester V. Chandler, *America's Greatest Depression, 1929–1941* (New York: Harper & Row Publishers, 1970), p. 5; *Time*, 3/13/33; *The New Republic*, 3/15/33; *Newsweek*, 3/4/33; Martin, *Madam Secretary*, pp. 63, 74, 84–90.

4. David Kennedy, *Freedom from Fear: The American People in Depression and War, 1929–1945* (New York: Oxford University Press, 1999), p. 166; *The Great Depression: Opposing Viewpoints*, ed. William Dudley (San Diego: Greenhaven Press, 1994), p. 15; William Brock, *Welfare, Democracy, and the New Deal* (Cambridge: Cambridge University Press, 1988), pp. 164, 166; Anthony J. Badger, *FDR: The First Hundred Days* (New York: Hill and Wang, 2008), p. 3; Wecter, *Age of the Great Depression* p. 13; *Time*, 3/13/33.

5. Bernstein, *A Caring Society*, p. 19; Wecter, *Age of the Great Depression*, p. 13; Harold Mayer and Rich-

ard C. Wade, *Chicago: Growth of a Metropolis* (Chicago: University of Chicago Press, 1973), p. 358; *New York Times*, 6/5/32; *New York Times*, 10/29/32; Arthur Ballantine, "When All the Banks Closed," *Harvard Business Review*, March 1948, Vol. XXVI, No. 2, p. 131; Harold L. Ickes, *The Autobiography of a Curmudgeon* (New York: Reynal & Hitchcock, 1943), p. 282; Dudley, *The Great Depression*, pp. 25, 34–35; James R. McGovern, *And a Time for Hope: Americans in the Great Depression* (Westport, Conn.: Praeger, 2000), pp. 6–11.

6. *Atlantic Monthly*, May 1932; Ballantine, "When All the Bank Closed," p. 131; *Time*, 3/13/33; Matthew Josephson, *Infidel in the Temple: A Memoir of the Nineteen-Thirties* (New York: Knopf, 1967), pp. 75–76, 98; Roger K. Newman, *Hugo Black: A Biography* (New York, Pantheon Books, 1994), p. 144; Dudley, *The Great Depression*, pp. 25, 34–35; McGovern, *And a Time for Hope*, pp. 6–11; *New York Times*, 6/5/32; *New York Times*, 10/29/32.

7. Hopkins, *Spending to Save*, pp. 18–19; Edward L. and Frederick Schapsmeier, *Henry A. Wallace of Iowa: The Agrarian Years, 1910–1940*, (Ames: Iowa State University Press, 1968), p. 146; John L. Shover, *Cornbelt Rebellion: The Farmers' Holiday Association* (Urbana: The University of Illinois Press, 1965), pp. 78; McGovern, *And a Time for Hope*, p. 8.

8. John Dos Passos, "Detroit: City of Leisure," in *The New Republic Anthology, 1915–1935*, ed. Groff Conklin (New York: Dodge Publishing Company, 1936), pp. 424–28; Niebuhr, "After Capitalism—What?" p. 16; *New York Times*, 3/8/33; Alfred B. Rollins, Jr., *Roosevelt and Howe* (New York: Alfred A. Knopf, 1962), p. 15; Wecter, *Age of the Great Depression*, p. 37; Bird, *Invisible Scar*, pp. 140–41; Franklin Folsom, *America Before Welfare* (New York: New York University Press, 1991), p. 268; Shover, *Cornbelt Rebellion*, p. 83.

9. Arthur Schlesinger, *The Crisis of the Old Order, 1919–1933* (Boston: Houghton Mifflin Co., 1957), pp. 474–81.

10. Tugwell, *Roosevelt's Revolution*, p. 24; Sternsher, *Rexford Tugwell and the New Deal*, p. 144.

11. Reminiscences of Frances Perkins, 1961, CUOHRO, Pt. 4, p. 149; Ruth Backes, Interview with Carol Lubin, Box 12, Folder 11, Ruth Backes Papers, Mount Holyoke College Archives and Special Collections; *Saturday Evening Post* 7/27/40.

12. *The Nation*, 3/8/33; *Saturday Evening Post*, 7/27/40; Reminiscences of Frances Perkins, 1961, CUOHRO, Pt. 4, pp. 56–9; Adam Cohen, Interview with Tomlin Coggeshall, 8/10/2007.

13. Reminiscences of Frances Perkins, 1961, CUOHRO, Pt. 4, pp. 10–12; Smith, *FDR*, p. 300.

14. Reminiscences of Frances Perkins, 1961, CUOHRO, Pt. 4, pp. 13–14; Perkins, *The Roosevelt I Knew*, p. 139.

15. Reminiscences of Frances Perkins, 1961, CUOHRO, Pt. 4, p. 15.

16. Works Progress Administration, *Washington*, pp. 465, 491–92; Moley, *First New Deal*, p. 10.

17. James Roosevelt, *Affectionately, F.D.R.: A Son's Story of a Lonely Man* (New York: Harcourt, Brace & Co. 1959), p. 144; Smith, *FDR*, pp. 10, 17, 37–38; Gunther, *Roosevelt in Retrospect*, p. 152; Carter, *New Dealers*, p. 11; Frank Freidel, *Franklin D. Roosevelt: Launching the New Deal* (Boston: Little, Brown & Co., 1973), pp. 6–7; Hofstadter, *American Political Tradition*, pp. 414–16; Samuel and Dorothy Rosenman, *Presidential Style: Some Giants and a Pygmy in the White House* (New York: Harper & Row Publishers, 1976), p. 267; Tugwell, *Democratic Roosevelt*, pp. 42–43, 57; James E. Sargent, *Roosevelt and the Hundred Days: Struggle for the Early New Deal* (New York: Garland, 1981), pp. 13–14.

18. Tugwell, *Democratic Roosevelt*, pp. 68, 71; Smith, *FDR*, pp. 70–78.

19. Smith, *FDR*, pp. 85–89, 123–25; Perkins, *The Roosevelt I Knew*, p.11.

20. Alan Brinkley, *Liberalism and Its Discontents* (Cambridge, Mass.: Harvard University Press, 1998), p. 5; Raymond Moley, "Contemporary National Politics," Lecture to Columbia class, April 29, 1936, Box 189, Moley Papers, Hoover Institution Library and Archives, Stanford University (hereafter, "Moley Papers"); Hofstadter, *American Political Tradition*, p. 417; Smith, *FDR*, pp. 123–25, 150–161; Resa Willis, *FDR and Lucy: Lovers and Friends* (New York: Routledge, 2004), pp. 34–37; Tugwell, *Democratic Roosevelt*, p. 107.

21. Rollins, *Roosevelt and Howe*, p. 184; J. Roosevelt, *Affectionately, F.D.R.*, p. 136.

22. Frank Freidel, Interview with James A. Farley, August 7, 1954, Small Collections Oral History Interviews, in Franklin D. Roosevelt Presidential Library (hereafter, "Roosevelt Library"); Eleanor Roosevelt,

The Autobiography of Eleanor Roosevelt (New York: Da Capo Press, 1992), pp. 149–50; Rexford Tugwell, *FDR: Architect of an Era* (New York: The MacMillan Co., 1967), p. 57; Reminiscences of Frances Perkins, 1961, CUOHRO, Pt. 4, pp. 198–99; Tugwell, *Democratic Roosevelt*, p. 27; *Time*, 1/2/33; Hugh Gregory Gallagher, *FDR's Splendid Deception: The Moving Story of Roosevelt's Massive Disability—And the Intense Efforts to Conceal It from the Public* (St. Petersburg, Fla.: Vandamere Press, 1999); Badger, *FDR*, pp. 14–15.

23. Tugwell, *FDR: Architect of an Era*, p. 60; Rosenman, *Working with Roosevelt*, pp. 13, 16, 26; Smith, *FDR*, pp. 210–12, 245, 272–73; James A. Farley, *Behind the Ballots: The Personal History of a Politician* (New York: Harcourt, Brace and Company, 1938), p. 79; Schlesinger, *Crisis of the Old Order*, p. 376; *New York Times*, 11/5/30; *Franklin D. Roosevelt and the Age of Action*, ed. Alfred B. Rollins, Jr. (New York: Dell Publishing Co., 1960), p. 14; Badger, *FDR*, p. 18; *The Two Faces of Liberalism: How the Hoover-Roosevelt Debate Shapes the 21st Century*, ed. Gordon Lloyd (Salem, Mass.:M&M Scrivener Press, 2007), p. 39; *New York Herald Tribune*, 7/1/24.

24. Perkins, *The Roosevelt I Knew*, p. 144; Roosevelt, *Affectionately, F.D.R.*, pp. 99, 103; Farley, *Behind the Ballots*, p. 208; Thomas Greer, *What Roosevelt Thought* (East Lansing: Michigan State University Press, 1958), p. 4.

25. Reminiscences of Frances Perkins, 1961, CUOHRO, Pt. 4, p. 16; *New York Times*, 3/5/33, p. 3; Martin, *Madam Secretary*, pp. 7–9; Garry Wills, "What Makes a Good Leader?" *Atlantic Monthly*, April 1994.

26. Conrad Black, *Franklin Delano Roosevelt, Champion of Freedom* (New York: Public Affairs, 2003), p. 269; Reminiscences of Frances Perkins, 1961, CUOHRO, Pt. 4, p. 17; *New York Times*, 3/5/33; *New York Herald Tribune*, 3/5/33.

27. Reminiscences of Frances Perkins, 1961, CUOHRO, Pt. 4, pp. 17–19; T. H. Watkins, *Righteous Pilgrim: The Life and Times of Harold Ickes 1874–1952* (New York: Henry Holt & Company, 1990), p. 295.

28. *Time*, 3/6/33.

29. Martin, *Madam Secretary*, p. 12.

30. Reminiscences of Frances Perkins, 1961, CUOHRO, Pt. 4, p. 19.

31. Reminiscences of Henry A. Wallace, 1951, CUOHRO, pp. 203–6; Reminiscences of Frances Perkins, 1961, CUOHRO, Pt. 4, p. 19.

32. Rollins, *Roosevelt and Howe*, p. 40; *New York Herald Tribune*, 3/5/33.

33. *The New Deal: The National Level*, ed. John Braeman et al. (Columbus: Ohio State University, 1975), p. 5; Hofstadter, *American Political Tradition*, pp. 370–71; David Burner, *Herbert Hoover: A Public Life* (New York: Alfred A. Knopf, 1979), p. 253.

34. Herbert Hoover, *American Individualism* (New York: Doubleday, Page & Company, 1922), p. 13; Hofstadter, *American Political Tradition*, p. 387; Burner, *Herbert Hoover*, pp. 193–96; Wecter, *Age of the Great Depression*, p. 42.

35. Burner, *Herbert Hoover*, pp. 295–96; Hopkins, *Spending to Save*, p. 42; Sargent, *Roosevelt and the Hundred Days*, p. 18; Annual Message to the Congress on the State of the Union, December 8, 1931, in Lloyd, *The Two Faces of Liberalism*, pp. 54–65.

36. Burner, *Herbert Hoover*, p. 250; Josephson, *Infidel*, p. 69; Hofstadter, *American Political Tradition*, pp. 372, 398 n.; Joel Seligman, *The Transformation of Wall Street* (Boston: Houghton Mifflin Company, 1982), pp. 53–54; *The Public Papers and Addresses of Franklin D. Roosevelt*, Vol. II (New York: Random House, 1938), p. 93; Freidel, *Launching the New Deal*, p. 6; Dudley, *The Great Depression*, p. 80.

37. Elliot A. Rosen, *Hoover, Roosevelt and the Brains Trust* (New York: Columbia University Press, 1977), p. 287; Hofstadter, *American Political Tradition*, p. 400; Dudley, *The Great Depression*, pp. 27–30, 33; *The Nation*, 7/15/31; Josephson, *Infidel*, p. 52; Edward Ainsworth Williams, *Federal Aid for Relief* (New York: Columbia University Press, 1939), p. 21; Elliot A. Rosen, *Roosevelt, the Great Depression and the Economics of Recovery* (Charlottesville: University of Virginia Press, 2005), pp. 72–73.

38. Hopkins, *Spending to Save*, pp. 62–63; Searle F. Charles, *Minister of Relief: Harry Hopkins and the Depression* (Syracuse: Syracuse University Press, 1963), pp. 10–11; Burner, *Herbert Hoover*,

pp. 263–65; Ernest K. Lindley, *Half Way with Roosevelt* (New York: Viking Press, 1937), p. 48; Williams, *Federal Aid for Relief*, pp. 24–33; Badger, *FDR*, pp. 7–8, 48.

39. Paul Studenski and Herman E. Krooss, *Financial History of the United States: Fiscal, Monetary, Banking, and Tariff, Including Financial Administration and State and Local Finance* (New York: McGraw-Hill Books, 1963), pp. 357–59; Badger, *FDR*, pp. 8, 48; *New York Times*, 6/25/33; *New York Times*, 7/12/33; Joseph Huthmacher, *Senator Robert F. Wagner and the Rise of Urban Liberalism* (New York: Atheneum, 1968), pp. 84, 96; Rollins, *Roosevelt and Howe*, p. 46; *The Hoover Administration: A Documentary Narrative*, ed. William Starr Myers and Walter H. Newton (New York: Charles Scribner's Sons, 1936), p. 63; Brock, *Welfare, Democracy, and the New Deal*, p. 149; Robert D. Leighninger, Jr., *Long-Range Public Investment* (Columbia: The University of South Carolina Press, 2007), pp. 6–7; Bonnie Fox Schwartz, *The Civil Works Administration, 1933–1934: The Business of Emergency Employment in the New Deal* (Princeton, N.J.: Princeton University Press, 1984), p. 21; Hopkins, *Spending to Save*, p. 89–90; Kenneth W. Dam, "From the Gold Clause Cases to the Gold Commission: A Half Century of American Monetary Law," *University of Chicago Law Review* 50 (Spring 1983), pp. 504, 507; Williams, *Federal Aid for Relief*, p. 43.

40. Paul Dickson and Thomas B. Allen, *The Bonus Army: An American Epic* (New York: Walker & Company, 2004), pp. 153–83, 193.

41. Arthur M. Schlesinger, Jr., *The Cycles of American History* (Boston: Houghton Mifflin Company, 1986), pp. 376–80; Amity Shlaes, *The Forgotten Man: A New History of the Great Depression* (New York: HarperCollins, 2007), p. 6.

42. Myers and Newton, *The Hoover Administration*, p. 516; Lindley, *Roosevelt Revolution*, p. 19; *New York Times*, 3/12/33.

43. Smith, *An Uncommon Man*, p. 144; Rosen, *Hoover, Roosevelt*, pp. 298–99; Lindley, *Roosevelt Revolution*, p. 5; Wecter, *Age of the Great Depression*, p. 51.

44. Tugwell, *FDR: Architect of an Era*, p. 75; Moley, *After Seven Years*, pp. 12–13; *New York Times*, 8/29/31.

45. Herbert Hoover, *Addresses Upon the American Road* (New York: Scribner's Sons, 1938), p. 1; *The Public Papers and Addresses of Franklin D. Roosevelt*, Vol. I (New York: Random House, 1938), pp. 625, 659; *FDR Papers*, Vol. II, p. 5; Frank Freidel, *Franklin D. Roosevelt: The Triumph* (Boston: Little, Brown and Company, 1956), p. 315; Perkins, *The Roosevelt I Knew*, p. 166; Rosenman, *Working with Roosevelt*, pp. 61–62.

46. Ronald Steel, *Walter Lippmann and the American Century* (Boston: Little, Brown and Company, 1980), p. 292; Smith, *An Uncommon Man*, p. 147; Rollins, *Age of Action*, p. 43; Lindley, *Roosevelt Revolution*, p. 5.

47. *FDR Papers*, Vol. I, pp. 781, 832.

48. Jordan A. Schwarz, *The New Dealers: Power Politics in the Age of Roosevelt* (New York: Vintage Books, 1994), p. 54; Gunther, *Roosevelt in Retrospect*, p. 272; Schlesinger, *Crisis of the Old Order*, p. 416; Freidel, Interview with James A. Farley; Robert Bendiner, *Just Around the Corner: A Highly Selective History of the Thirties* (New York: E. P. Dutton, 1967), p. 26; Wecter, *Age of the Great Depression*, p. 54.

49. Freidel, *Launching the New Deal*, pp. 26–27, 31–36, 131–33, 198; Schlesinger, *Coming of the New Deal*, p. 4; Lindley, *Roosevelt Revolution*, p. 42.

50. Freidel, *Launching the New Deal*, pp. 26–27, 31–36, 131–33, 198; Rexford G. Tugwell, *In Search of Roosevelt* (Cambridge, Mass.: Harvard University Press, 1972), p. 233; *New York Times*, 3/5/33; *Time*, 3/13/33; *New York Herald Tribune*, 3/5/33.

51. J. Roosevelt, *Affectionately, F.D.R.*, p. 252–53; *Washington Post*, 3/5/33; *New York Times*, 3/5/33; *Time*, 3/13/33.

52. *The New Republic*, 3/22/33; *Time*, 3/6/33; *Time*, 3/13/33; Moley, *After Seven Days*, p. 139; Moley, *First New Deal*, pp. 66–68; *Washington Post*, 2/17/33.

53. *New York Times*, 3/5/33; *New York Times*, 3/4/1933; *Washington Post*, 3/5/30; E. Roosevelt, *Autobiography*, p. 163; Works Progress Administration, *Washington*, pp. 219–20; *Time*, 3/13/33; Letter from Franklin D. Roosevelt to Charles Elmore Cropley, Esq., February 25, 1933, PSF 140, FDR Library; Inaugurations, February 25, 1933; Grace Tully, *F.D.R.: My Boss* (New York: Charles Scribner's Sons, 1949), p. 69.

54. *The New Republic*, 3/8/33; Steel, *Walter Lippmann*, p. 300; *Time*, 3/6/33; Lindley, *Half Way with Roosevelt*, p. 6; *New York Herald Tribune*, 3/4/33.

55. Moley, *First New Deal*, pp. 97–98; Raymond Henle, Interview with Raymond Moley, November 13, 1967, in Raymond Moley Papers, Box 245, Hoover Institution, Stanford University; Raymond Moley, Diary, Moley Papers, Box 1, 2/14/33.

56. Moley, Diary, 2/28/33; Raymond Moley, Inaugural Address 1933 Notes, Moley Papers, Box 289; Moley, *First New Deal*, pp. 96–114; Edward J. Flynn, *You're the Boss: The Practice of American Politics* (New York: Collier Books, 1962), pp. 138–39; Sargent, *Roosevelt and the Hundred Days*, pp. 39–40; Patrick Anderson, *The President's Men* (Garden City, N.Y.: Doubleday & Co., 1968), p. 24.

57. Moley, *First New Deal*, pp. 117–19; Moley, Diary, 2/28/33; Jonathan Alter, *The Defining Moment: FDR's Hundred Days and the Triumph of Hope* (New York: Simon & Schuster, 2006), p. 211; *New York Times*, 2/9/31.

58. Reminiscences of Frances Perkins, 1961, CUOHRO, Pt. 4, p. 26; E. Roosevelt, *Autobiography*, p. 163; Works Progress Administration, *Washington*, pp. 219–20; *Time*, 3/13/33; Wilson, *American Earthquake*, p. 478; Henrietta Nesbitt, *White House Diary* (Garden City, N.Y.: Doubleday & Co., 1948), p. 4.

59. Moley, *First New Deal*, pp. 97–98, 118; Rosenman, *Working with Roosevelt*, pp. 90–91; *Washington Post*, 3/5/33; *Time*, 3/13/33.

60. *FDR Papers*, Vol. II, pp. 11, 13.

61. *FDR Papers*, Vol. II, pp. 12–15; Davis W. Houck, *FDR and Fear Itself* (College Station: Texas A&M University Press, 2002), pp. 135–48; Reminiscences of Frances Perkins, 1961, CUOHRO, Pt. 4, p. 31; *New York Times*, 3/5/33.

62. *FDR Papers*, Vol. II, pp. 13–15; Freidel, *Launching the New Deal*, p. 205; Houck, *FDR and Fear Itself*, pp. 135–48; *New York Times*, 3/5/33.

63. Reminiscences of Frances Perkins, 1961, CUOHRO, Pt. 1, pp. 20–23; Martin, *Madam Secretary*, p. 8.

64. Reminiscences of Frances Perkins, 1961, CUOHRO, Pt. 4, p. 31; Reminiscences of Frances Perkins, 1961, CUOHRO, Pt. 3, p. 195; Reminiscences of Henry A. Wallace, 1951, CUOHRO, pp. 205–6; Martin, *Madam Secretary*, p. 9.

65. Watkins, *Righteous Pilgrim*, p. 297; *New York Times*, 3/5/33; *Washington Post*, 3/5/33; Reminiscences of Frances Perkins, 1961, CUOHRO, Pt. 4, p. 29; *Time*, 3/13/33; Burner, *Herbert Hoover*, pp. 327–28; Steel, *Walter Lippmann*, p. 299.

66. Sargent, *Roosevelt and the Hundred Days*, p. 88; *New York Times*, 3/4/33; *New York Times*, 3/5/33; Houck, *FDR and Fear Itself*, pp. 11–12; Schlesinger, *Coming of the New Deal*, p. 1; Cabell Phillips, *From the Crash to the Blitz, 1929–1939* (New York: Fordham University Press, 2000), p. 107; New York *Daily News*, 3/6/33.

67. Lindley, *Roosevelt Revolution*, p. 80; Rosenman, *Presidential Style*, p. 323; Black, *Roosevelt*, p. 273; *Time*, 3/13/33; Reminiscences of Henry A. Wallace, 1951, CUOHRO, pp. 205–6; Freidel, *Launching the New Deal*, pp. 170–71; 210–11; Smith, *FDR*, pp. 303–4.

68. Smith, *FDR*, pp. 303–4; Freidel, *Launching the New Deal*, pp. 208–12; *New York Times*, 3/5/33.

69. Farley, *Behind the Ballots*, p. 209; Reminiscences of Frances Perkins, 1961, CUOHRO, Pt. 4, pp. 65–66; *Chicago Tribune*, 3/5/33; Molly Dewson, "An Aid to the End," unpublished manuscript, FDR Library, p. 107; Freidel, *Launching the New Deal*, p. 211; Watkins, *Righteous Pilgrim*, p. 301.

70. *Washington Post*, 2/26/33; *New York Times*, 2/26/33; Lindley, *Roosevelt Revolution*, p. 53; Walter Lippmann, "Today and Tomorrow," *The New York Tribune*, 2/28/33; Freidel, *Launching the New Deal*, p. 142.

71. Lindley, *Roosevelt Revolution*, pp. 59–61; Joseph Lash, *Dealers and Dreamers* (New York: Doubleday, 1988), p. 80; *Washington Post*, 3/5/33; *Time*, 3/6/33.

72. Farley, *Behind the Ballots*, p. 209; Reminiscences of Frances Perkins, 1961, CUOHRO, Pt. 4, pp. 65–67, 75; Dewson, "An Aid to the End," p. 107; Freidel, *Launching the New Deal*, pp. 211–12.

73. Lippmann, "Today and Tomorrow," 2/28/33; Freidel, *Launching the New Deal*, pp. 211–12; Reminiscences of Henry A. Wallace, 1951, CUOHRO, pp. 205–6; Reminiscences of Frances Perkins, 1961, CUOHRO, Pt. 4, p. 75; *New York Times*, 3/5/33; *Time*, 3/6/33.

NOTES

CHAPTER 2: "MOLEY! MOLEY! MOLEY! LORD GOD ALMIGHTY!"

1. Thomas H. Eliot, *Recollections of the New Deal: When People Mattered* (Boston: Northeastern University Press, 1992), p. 7; George N. Peek with Samuel Crowther, *Why Quit Our Own* (New York: D. Van Nostrand Company, Inc., 1936), p. 20.

2. Phillips, *Crash to the Blitz*, p. 114; Dewson, "An Aid to the End," p. 108; *The New Republic*, 3/15/33; Eliot, *Recollections*, p. 7; Schlesinger, *Coming of the New Deal*, p. 17; Reminiscences of Jerome Frank, 1960, CUOHRO, pp. 83–84.

3. Eleanor Roosevelt, *This I Remember* (New York: Harper & Brothers, 1949), p. 107; Freidel, *Launching the New Deal*, p. 267; *The Making of the New Deal: The Insiders Speak*, ed. Katie Louchheim (Cambridge, Mass.: Harvard University Press, 1983), p. 121; McGovern, *And a Time for Hope*, p. 22; *New York Times*, 8/11/95; Schlesinger, *Coming of the New Deal*, p. 14.

4. Wecter, *Age of the Great Depression*, pp. 2–4; John Kenneth Galbraith, *The Great Crash* (Boston: Houghton Mifflin, 1972), pp. 44, 54, 57; *Time*, 11/7/49.

5. Wecter, *Age of the Great Depression*, pp. 4–5; J. F. T. O'Connor, *The Banking Crisis and Recovery Under the Roosevelt Administration* (New York: Da Capo Press, 1971), p. 10; F. G. Awalt, Unpublished Manuscript on Banking Crisis, p. 7, Moley Papers, Box 245, Folder 3; Moley, *First New Deal*, p. 129; Rosen, *Hoover, Roosevelt*, p. 279.

6. O'Connor, *The Banking Crisis*, p. 8; Milton Friedman and Anna Jacobson Schwartz, *A Monetary History of the United States, 1867–1960* (Princeton, N.J.: Princeton University Press, 1963), p. 308; Ballantine, "When All the Banks Closed," p. 131; C. C. Colt and N. S. Keith, *28 Days: A History of the Banking Crisis* (New York: Greenberg, Publisher, Inc., 1933), p. 23; Bendiner, *Just Around the Corner*, p. 31; Wecter, *Age of the Great Depression*, pp. 62, 101–2.

7. Freidel, *Triumph*, pp. 186–87; *New York Times*, 12/12/1930; *Time*, 1/18/32; *Time*, 9/12/69; Susan Estabrook Kennedy, *The Banking Crisis of 1933* (Lexington: University of Kentucky Press, 1973), pp. 1–5, 19.

8. Studenski and Krooss, *Financial History of the United States*, p. 371; Schwarz, *The New Dealers*, pp. 51, 88; *Time*, 10/19/31; Kennedy, *Banking Crisis*, pp. 34–35.

9. *New York Times*, 1/23/32; Schwarz, *The New Dealers*, pp. 50–51; Studenski and Kroos, *Financial History of the United States*, pp. 372–75; Friedman and Schwartz, *Monetary History of the United States*, p. 325; Ballantine, "When All the Banks Closed," p. 132; Josephson, *Infidel*, pp. 72–73; Ronald Edsforth, *The New Deal: America's Response to the Great Depression* (Malden, Mass.: Blackwell Publishers, 2000), p. 61; Moley, *First New Deal*, p. 132; Wecter, *Age of the Great Depression*, p. 48; Kennedy, *Banking Crisis*, p. 42.

10. Awalt, Unpublished Manuscript on Banking Crisis, p. 9; *New York Times*, 2/15/33; *Time*, 3/6/33; Kennedy, *Banking Crisis*, pp. 63–64, 80–82.

11. *Time*, 3/6/33; *New York Times*, 2/15/33; Moley, *First New Deal*, p. 138; Jerry Markham, *A Financial History of the United States* (Armonk, N.Y.: M. E. Sharpe, 2001) p. 165.

12. Kennedy, *Banking Crisis*, pp. 77–134; Colt and Keith, *28 Days*, pp. 1, 6; Awalt, Unpublished Manuscript on Banking Crisis, pp. 10–16, 20; *New York Times*, 2/17/33; *New York Times*, 2/15/33; *New York Times*, 2/18/33; *Time*, 3/6/33; *New York Times*, 2/19/33; Ballantine, "When All the Banks Closed," p. 136; Moley, *First New Deal*, p. 138; *New York Times*, 2/15/33; FDR Papers, Vol. II, p. 27.

13. Moley, *After Seven Years*, pp. 141–45; Moley, *First New Deal*, pp. 141–42, 145–46; Badger, *FDR*, p. 32; Studenski and Krooss, *Financial History of the United States*, p. 381.

14. Awalt, Unpublished Manuscript on Banking Crisis, pp. 21–22; Raymond Henle, Oral History Interview with Raymond Moley, November 13, 1967, Moley Papers, Box 245; Studenski and Krooss, *Financial History of the United States*, p. 381; Freidel, *Launching the New Deal*, pp. 189–92; Moley, *First New Deal*, pp. 140–51; Badger, *FDR*, p. 27; Alter, *The Defining Moment*, pp. 178–79; Moley, *After Seven Years*, pp. 139–43.

15. J. Roosevelt, *Affectionately, F.D.R.*, pp. 251–52; Kenneth S. Davis, *FDR: The New Deal Years, 1933–1937* (New York: Random House, 1979), p. 24; Moley, *First New Deal*, pp. 145–46; Letter of Walter

Wyatt to Raymond Moley, March 16, 1966, Moley Papers, Box 245, Folder 11; Sargent, *Roosevelt and the Hundred Days*, pp. 87–88; *FDR Papers*, Vol. II, p. 28; Moley, *After Seven Days*, p. 146.

16. J. Roosevelt, *Affectionately, F.D.R.*, pp. 251–52; Moley, *First New Deal*, pp. 145–48; Tully, *F.D.R.: My Boss*, p. 60; Letter of Walter Wyatt to Raymond Moley, March 16, 1966, Sargent, *Roosevelt and the Hundred Days*, pp. 87–88; *FDR Papers*, Vol. II, p. 28; Moley, *After Seven Days*, p. 146; Lindley, *Roosevelt Revolution*, p. 69; Friedel, *Launching the New Deal*, pp. 192–93.0

17. Moley, *First New Deal*, pp. 81–83; Moley, Diary, 1/27/33, 1/28/33; Lindley, *Roosevelt Revolution*, p. 55; *New York Times*, 3/4/33; *New York Times*, 11/5/32.

18. Carter, *New Dealers*, pp. 283–84; Freidel, *Launching the New Deal*, p. 150; Sargent, *Roosevelt and the Hundred Days*, p. 35; Lindley, *Roosevelt's Revolution*, p. 56; Lewis Douglas, Letter to Samuel Rosenman, Oct. 26, 1972, Box 118, Lewis Douglas Papers, University of Arizona Special Collections (hereafter, "Douglas Papers").

19. Carter, *New Dealers*, p. 284; Moley, *After Seven Years*, p. 122; Moley, *First New Deal*, pp. 84–85.

20. Moley, *After Seven Years*, pp. 121–22; *Newsweek*, 3/4/33; *New York Times*, 2/23/33; *Time*, 3/6/33; *Time*, 3/13/33; James Sargent, Interview with Lewis Douglas, p. 16, Douglas Papers, Box 119, Folder 5; Reminiscences of Walter Wyatt, 1973, CUOHRO, p. 11.

21. *Collier's*, 6/17/33; Wolfskill and Hudson, *All but the People*, p. 53; Tully, *F.D.R.: My Boss*, p. 61; *Time*, 5/8/33; Tully, *F.D.R.: My Boss*, p. 61.

22. *Collier's*, 6/17/33; Moley, *First New Deal*, pp. xi–xii; Schlesinger, *Coming of the New Deal*, p. 182.

23. Moley, *Realities and Illusions*, pp. 1–5, 7–8; Letter of Raymond Moley to Frank Freidel, March 3, 1966, Moley Papers, Box 245, Folder 6; Sargent, *Roosevelt and the Hundred Days*, p. 10.

24. Letter of Raymond Moley to Frank Freidel, March 3, 1966, Moley Biographical Materials, Box 144, Moley Papers; Moley, *First New Deal*, p. 13; Moley, *Realities and Illusions*, pp. 22, 28–29, 52, 60–61; Sargent, *Roosevelt and the Hundred Days*, p. 10; Rosen, *Hoover, Roosevelt*, p. 124; Freidel, Introduction, *Realities and Illusions*, p. viii; Moley, *After Seven Days*, p. 4; Sargent, *Roosevelt and the Hundred Days*, p. 10.

25. Frank Freidel, Introduction in Moley, *First New Deal*, p. ix; Charles A. Beard, *An Economic Interpretation of the Constitution of the United States* (New York: Free Press, 1986); Moley, *Realities and Illusions*, pp. 71, 78–79; Letter of Raymond Moley to Frank Freidel, March 3, 1966; Robert A. McGuire, *To Form a More Perfect Union: A New Economic Interpretation of the United States Constitution* (Oxford: Oxford University Press, 2003); Rosen, *Hoover, Roosevelt*, p. 125; Moley, *Realities and Illusions*, pp. 73–84.

26. Moley, *First New Deal*, pp. xi, 12; *Time*, 3/8/33; Rosen, *Hoover, Roosevelt*, p. 126; Moley, *Realities and Illusions*, pp. 40, 110–31; *Time*, 5/8/33; Sargent, *Roosevelt and the Hundred Days*, pp 11–12; Americanization Pamphlets, Moley Papers, Box 144; *Cleveland Plain Dealer*, 8/27/19.

27. Moley, *First New Deal*, pp. 11–12; Rosen, *Hoover, Roosevelt*, pp. 127–28; *New York Times*, 10/31/28; Moley, Lecture Notes, "Contemporary American Politics," Columbia University, March 11, 1936; Moley, *After Seven Years*, pp. 1–3; Moley, *Realities and Illusions*, pp. 173–75.

28. Tugwell, *The Brains Trust*, pp. 3–6; Smith, *FDR*, p. 245; Moley, *After Seven Years*, p. 6; Lindley, *Roosevelt Revolution*, pp. 23, 26; Rosenman, *Working with Roosevelt*, pp. 56–58.

29. Letter from Samuel Rosenman to Rexford Tugwell, January 16, 1969, p. 3, Box 23, Tugwell Papers, FDR Library; Sternsher, *Rexford Tugwell and the New Deal*, pp. 3, 9–10, 144; Reminiscences of Rexford G. Tugwell, 1951, CUOHRO, pp. 4–5, 12; Moley, *After Seven Years*, p. 15.

30. Jordan Schwarz, *Liberal: Adolf A. Berle and the Vision of an American Era* (New York: The Free Press, 1987), pp. 16, 60–61, 71; Reminiscences of Adolf A. Berle, 1974, CUOHRO, pp. 167–71; Phillips, *Crash to the Blitz*, p. 109; Michael Vincent Namorato, *Rexford G. Tugwell: A Biography* (New York: Praeger, 1988), pp. 14, 45, 60–61; Reminiscences of Adolf A. Berle, 1974, CUOHRO, pp. 173–74; Moley, *After Seven Years*, p. 18.

31. Tugwell, *Brains Trust*, pp. 21–31, 166; Reminiscences of Adolf A. Berle, 1974, CUOHRO, pp. 187–88; Reminiscences of Rexford G. Tugwell, 1951, CUOHRO, p. 7; Lindley, *Roosevelt Revolution*, pp. 23–24; Sternsher, *Rexford Tugwell and the New Deal*, p. 40.

32. Tugwell, *Brains Trust*, pp. 47–49; Tugwell, *Democratic Roosevelt*, p. 218; Moley, *First New Deal*, pp. 15–17; Moley, *After Seven Years*, p. 22–23, 55; Rosen, *Hoover, Roosevelt*, pp. 130–32; *FDR Papers*, Vol. I, pp. 625, 639, 751–52; Schwarz, *Liberal*, pp. 78–79; Sargent, *Roosevelt and the Hundred Days*, p. 13.

33. Raymond Moley, Memorandum of May 19, 1932, Moley Papers, Box 282; Rosen, *Hoover, Roosevelt*, pp. 140–48; Freidel, *Triumph*, pp. 272–73; Moley, *After Seven Years*, pp. 23–24, inset opposite p. 146; Sargent, *Roosevelt and the Hundred Days*, p. 45; Lindley, *Roosevelt Revolution*, p. 34.

34. Lindley, *Roosevelt Revolution*, pp. 54–55; Moley, *First New Deal*, p. 17; Sargent, *Roosevelt and the Hundred Days*, p. 41; Moley, *After Seven Years*, pp. 52–55.

35. Moley, Diary, 3/3/33; Tugwell, *In Search of Roosevelt*, p. 195; Sargent, *Roosevelt and the Hundred Days*, pp. 22–23, 25; Moley, *After Seven Years*, pp. 68, 70–72, 81–83; Anderson, *The President's Men*, p. 23; Moley, *First New Deal*, pp. 21–35, 51–54. *Washington Post*, 11/18/32; *Wall Street Journal*, 11/19/32.

36. Reminiscences of Samuel Rosenman, 1960, CUOHRO, p. 113; *The Diary of Rexford G. Tugwell: The New Deal, 1932–1935*, ed. Michael Vincent Namorato (New York: Greenwood Press, 1992), p. 74; Moley, *After Seven Days*, pp. 79–80; Sargent, *Roosevelt and the Hundred Days*, p. 4; Moley, *First New Deal*, p. xiii; Anderson, *The President's Men*, p. 56; Reminiscences of Frances Perkins, 1961, CUOHRO, Pt. 4, pp. 454–57; Rosenman, *Working with Roosevelt*, pp. 24–25; Reminiscences of Rexford G. Tugwell, 1951, CUOHRO, p. 17; Sargent, *Roosevelt and the Hundred Days*, p. 30; Rollins, *Roosevelt and Howe*; p. 380; *New York Times*, 4/19/36.

37. Moley, Diary, 2/8/33; Carter, *New Dealers*, p. 325; Moley, *After Seven Years*, p. 81; Tugwell, *Roosevelt's Revolution*, p. 40; Sargent, *Roosevelt and the Hundred Days*, p. 32.

38. Moley, Diary, 2/8/33; Moley, *After Seven Years*, pp. 81, 106–8; Reminiscences of Samuel Rosenman, CUOHRO, p. 113.

39. Moley, Diary, 2/8/33, 2/28/33; Adam Cohen, Interview with Mary Mitchell, July 31, 2007; Moley, *After Seven Years*, pp. 115–16, 162; Moley, *First New Deal*, pp. 18, 240–41; Tugwell, *Diary*, p. 74; Sargent, *Roosevelt and the Hundred Days*, p. 30; Carter, *New Dealers*, p. 325.

40. Sargent, *Roosevelt and the Hundred Days*, pp. 44–45; Schlesinger, *Coming of the New Deal*, pp. 181–82; Letter from Lewis Douglas to James Sargent, March 19, 1973, Douglas Papers, Box 119; Letter of Raymond Moley to Frank Freidel, March 3, 1966; *Time*, 5/8/33; Reminiscences of Adolf A. Berle, 1974, CUOHRO, p. 176.

41. Raymond Henle, Oral History Interview with Raymond Moley; Sargent, *Roosevelt and the Hundred Days*, p. 85.

42. Reminiscences of Walter Wyatt, 1973, CUOHRO, pp. 2, 10; Moley, *First New Deal*, p. 216; Sargent, *Roosevelt and the Hundred Days*, p. 87.

43. Moley, *First New Deal*, pp. 148–51; Moley, *After Seven Days*, pp. 146–7; *The Hoover Administration: A Documented Narrative*, ed. William Starr Myers and Walter H. Newton (New York: Charles Scribner's Sons, 1936), p. 366.

44. Awalt, Unpublished Manuscript on Banking Crisis, p. 23; Moley, *First New Deal*, p. 151

45. Moley, Diary, 3/4/33; Moley, *After Seven Years*, pp. 147–48; Freidel, *Launching the New Deal*, pp. 193–94; Tugwell, *Roosevelt's Revolution*, p. 34; Lindley, *Roosevelt Revolution*, p. 80; Moley, *First New Deal*, p. 151; Awalt, Unpublished Manuscript on Banking Crisis, p. 23.

46. *New York Times*, 3/4/33; Moley, *First New Deal*, p. 160.

47. Moley, *First New Deal*, pp. 160–61, 214; Freidel, *Launching the New Deal*, p. 215; Awalt, Unpublished Manuscript on Banking Crisis, p. 26; Lindley, *Roosevelt Revolution*, p. 115.

48. Moley, *After Seven Years*, pp. 149; Freidel, *Launching the New Deal*, p. 219; *Time*, 3/13/33; Sargent, *Roosevelt and the Hundred Days*, p. 91; Letter of Walter Wyatt to Raymond Moley, March 16, 1966, Moley Papers, Box 245, Folder 11; *New York Times*, 3/5/33; Moley, *First New Deal*, p. 170.

49. Harold Ickes, *The Secret Diary of Harold L. Ickes: The First Thousand Days* (New York: Simon & Schuster, 1953), p. 3; Reminiscences of Frances Perkins, 1961, CUOHRO Pt. IV, p. 75; Sargent, *Roosevelt and the Hundred Days*, p. 93; FDR Diary, 3/5/33, PSF 159, FDR Library; Works Progress Administration, *Washington*, p. 302; *Time*, 3/13/33; Roosevelt, *His Personal Letters,* pp. 334–35; Moley, *After Seven Years*, p. 148; Franklin D. Roosevelt, *On Our Way* (New York: The John Day Company, 1934), pp. 4–5; Lindley, *Roosevelt Revolution*, pp. 81–82.

50. Reminiscences of Walter Wyatt, 1973, CUOHRO, pp. 16–18; Letter of Walter Wyatt to Raymond Moley, March 16, 1966; Freidel, *Launching the New Deal*, pp. 215–19; Sargent, *Roosevelt and the First Hundred Days*, pp. 93–95; Roosevelt, *His Personal Letters*, pp. 334–35; *New York Times*, 3/7/33.

51. *FDR Papers*, Vol. II, pp. 24, 26–29, 33–36; Moley, *First New Deal*, p. 161; Freidel, *Launching the New Deal*, pp. 189–90, 217; *Time*, 3/13/33; Awalt, Unpublished Manuscript on Banking Crisis, p. 29; Lindley, *Roosevelt Revolution*, pp. 82, 115.

52. James D. Horan, *The Desperate Years: A Pictorial History of the Thirties* (New York: Crown Publishers, Inc., 1962), p. 99; Moley, *First New Deal*, pp. 163–64; Letter of Walter M. Pierce to Franklin D. Roosevelt of March 18, 1933, OF 230 Banking, Box 1, FDR Library; Bendiner, *Just Around the Corner*, p. 32; Lindley, *Roosevelt Revolution*, pp. 82, 84; *Washington Post*, 3/7/33; Kennedy, *Banking Crisis*, pp. 161, 164–65; *New York Times*, 3/6/33; *Washington Post*, 3/6/33; Davis, *The New Deal Years*, p. 43.

53. Moley, *First New Deal*, p. 164; Lindley, *Roosevelt Revolution*, p. 82; *New York Times*, 3/6/33; *New York Times*, 3/8/33; *Washington Post*, 3/8/33; *FDR Papers*, Vol. II, pp. 24, 26–29; Horan, *The Desperate Years*, pp. 98–99.

54. Horan, *The Desperate Years*, p. 100; Henry F. Ashurst, *A Many-Colored Toga: The Diary of Henry Fountain Ashurst*, ed. George F. Sparks (Tucson: The University of Arizona Press, 1962), p. 333; *Washington Post*, 3/11/33; *New York Times*, 3/10/33, 3/11/33, 3/12/33.

55. Tugwell, *Democratic Roosevelt*, pp. 270–71; Freidel, *Launching the New Deal*, pp. 213–14.

56. Tugwell, *Democratic Roosevelt*, p. 271.

57. Ibid., p. 272; Roosevelt, *On Our Way*, pp. 9, 14; Sargent, *Roosevelt and the Hundred Days*, p. 95; *New York Times*, 3/6/33; *New York Times*, 3/7/33; *Washington Post*, 3/7/33.

58. E. Roosevelt, *This I Remember*, pp. 102–3; Blanche Wiesen Cook, *Eleanor Roosevelt, Vol. II, 1933–38* (New York: Viking, 1999), pp. 40–41, 290; Reminiscences of Frances Perkins, 1961, CUOHRO, pt. 4, pp. 335–36; *New York Times*, 3/7/33; Freidel, *Launching the New Deal*, pp. 294–95; Lindley, *Roosevelt Revolution*, p. 282.

59. Moley, *First New Deal*, pp. 149, 165, 171; Moley, Diary, 3/6/33; Moley, *After Seven Years*, p. 149.

60. Moley, *First New Deal*, pp. 152, 171–73; Moley, *After Seven Years*, pp. 151–52; Awalt, Unpublished Manuscript on Banking Crisis, p. 30; Alter, *The Defining Moment*, p. 324; Schlesinger, *Coming of the New Deal*, p. 6.

61. Letter of Walter Wyatt to Raymond Moley, March 16, 1966; Awalt, Unpublished Manuscript on Banking Crisis, p. 31; *New York Times*, 3/10/33; Lindley, *Roosevelt Revolution*, p. 86; Moley, *First New Deal*, pp. 171–73, 178–79; Moley, *After Seven Years*, pp. 151–53; Freidel, *Launching the New Deal*, p. 227; Sargent, *Roosevelt and the Hundred Days*, pp. 98–99, 109.

62. Anderson, *The President's Men*, p. 59; *FDR Papers*, Vol. II, pp. 30–36; Sargent, *Roosevelt and the Hundred Days*, pp. 100–101.

63. Lindley, *Roosevelt Revolution*, p. 87; Schlesinger, *Coming of the New Deal*, p. 7; Freidel, *Launching the New Deal*, pp. 225–26; Moley, *First New Deal*, p. 177; Sargent, *Roosevelt and the Hundred Days*, pp. 102–3; Reminiscences of Walter Wyatt, 1973, CUOHRO, pp. 28–29; *New York Times*, 3/10/33; Kennedy, *Banking Crisis of 1933*, p. 177.

64. *FDR Papers*, Vol. II, p. 45; Moley, *First New Deal*, pp. 182–84; Letter of Walter Wyatt to Raymond Moley, March 16, 1966; *New York Times*, 3/10/33.

65. Moley, *First New Deal*, pp. 184–88; Letter of Walter Wyatt to Raymond Moley, March 16, 1966; *New York Times*, 3/10/33; Lindley, *Roosevelt Revolution*, pp. 87, 135–37; Ronald L. Feinman, *The Twilight of Progressivism: The Western Republican Senators and the New Deal* (Baltimore: The Johns Hopkins Press, 1981), p. 58; Kennedy, *Banking Crisis of 1933*, p. 176.

66. Moley, Diary, 3/9/33; Moley, *First New Deal*, p. 190; Freidel, *Launching the New Deal*, p. 229; *FDR Papers*, Vol. II, pp. 54–57, 59–60; *New York Times*, 3/10/33; *New York Times*, 3/11/33; Awalt, Unpublished Manuscript on Banking Crisis, p. 37; Roosevelt, *On Our Way*, p. 26; Kennedy, *Banking Crisis of 1933*, p. 177.

67. *FDR Papers*, Vol. II, pp. 64–65; Moley, *First New Deal*, pp. 194–96; *Time*, 3/20/33; Alter, *The Defining Moment*, p. 271; Black, *Roosevelt*, pp. 276–77; Lindley, *Roosevelt Revolution*, p. 91.

68. Schlesinger, *Coming of the New Deal*, p. 13; Sargent, *Roosevelt and the Hundred Days*, p. 116; *New York Times*, 3/14/33; Rosenman, *Presidential Style*, p. 335.

69. Moley, *First New Deal*, pp. 196–97; Freidel, *Launching the New Deal*, p. 234; Letter of Walter Wyatt to Raymond Moley, March 16, 1966; *New York Times*, 3/10/33; *New York Times*, 3/14/33; Moley, *After*

Seven Years, p. 155; Schlesinger, *Coming of the New Deal*, p. 13; Studs Terkel, *Hard Times: An Oral History of the Great Depression*, (New York: Pantheon Books, 1970), p. 272; Alter, *The Defining Moment*, p. 269; Black, *Roosevelt*, p. 278; Lindley, *Roosevelt Revolution*, p. 92.

70. Schwarz, *The New Dealers*, p. 329; Geoffrey C. Ward, *Before the Trumpet: Young Franklin Roosevelt, 1882–1895* (New York: Harper & Row, 1985), p. 325 n. 5; Moley, *First New Deal*, p. 237; Moley, *After Seven Years*, p. 162.

71. Schlesinger, *Coming of the New Deal*, p. 5; Moley, *First New Deal*, pp. 92–93; *The New Republic*, 3/15/33; Moley, *After Seven Years*, p. 155; *New York Times*, 3/12/33; Robert S. McElvaine, *The Great Depression: America 1929–1941* (New York: Crown, 1984), p. 140; Tugwell, *Roosevelt's Revolution*, p. 23; Rosenman, *Presidential Style*, p. 324; Davis, *The New Deal Years*, p. 50; Black, *Roosevelt*, p. 275; Tugwell, *In Search of Roosevelt*, p. 272.

72. Carter, *New Dealers*, p. 329; Moley, *First New Deal*, pp. 214–19; Moley, *After Seven Years*, p. 155; Rosenman, *Working with Roosevelt*, p. 55.

CHAPTER 3: "THE HARDEST-BOILED MAN IN WASHINGTON"

1. *FDR Papers*, Vol. I, pp. 804–5, 811; Moley, *First New Deal*, p. 200; Sargent, *Roosevelt and the Hundred Days*, p. 126.

2. Freidel, *Launching the New Deal*, p. 238; Moley, *First New Deal*, p. 200; Sargent, *Roosevelt and the Hundred Days*, pp. 254–55; Letter of Lewis Douglas to Raymond Moley, May 4, 1964, Douglas Papers, Box 118; Robert Browder and Thomas G. Smith, *Independent: A Biography of Lewis W. Douglas*, (New York: Alfred A. Knopf, 1986), p. 85; Reminiscences of Adolf A. Berle, 1974, CUOHRO, p. 177.

3. *FDR Papers*, Vol. I, pp. 797, 811; *FDR Papers*, Vol. II, pp. 49–52; Julian Zelizer, "The Forgotten Legacy of the New Deal: Fiscal Conservatism and the Roosevelt Administration, 1933–1938," *Presidential Studies Quarterly*, June 2000, pp. 331–33; Moley, *First New Deal*, p. 202; Freidel, *Launching the New Deal*, p. 238; Tugwell, *The Brains Trust*, p. 517; Ronnie J. Davis, "Chicago Economists, Deficit Budgets, and the Early 1930s," *The American Economic Review*, Vol. 58, No. 3, Part 1 (June 1968), 476–81.

4. Letter from Admiral Richard E. Byrd, Chairman, National Economy League, to Raymond Moley, March 17, 1933, Moley Papers, Box 63; Lindley, *Half Way with Roosevelt*, p. 38; Rosen, *Hoover, Roosevelt*, pp. 144–46; William Leuchtenburg, *Franklin D. Roosevelt and the New Deal, 1932–1940* (New York: Harper Colophon Books, 1963), pp. 36–37; Kelly McMichael Stott, "FDR, Lewis Douglas, and the Raw Deal," *The Historian*, Fall 2000; Lindley, *Roosevelt Revolution*, p. 53; Walter Lippmann, "Today and Tomorrow," *The New York Herald Tribune*, 2/28/33; Freidel, *Launching the New Deal*, p. 142; *Time*, 1/2/33. *Washington Post*, 2/26/33; *New York Times*, 2/26/33; *New York Times*, 4/2/33; *New York Times*, 6/21/36; Moley, *First New Deal*, p. 388; *New York Times*, 12/5/32.

5. Reminiscences of Henry A. Wallace, 1951, CUOHRO, pp. 198–99; Gunther, *Roosevelt in Retrospect*, p. 74.

6. Stott, "FDR, Lewis Douglas, and the Raw Deal"; Moley, *First New Deal*, p. 201; Freidel, *Launching the New Deal*, pp. 239–40, 245; *FDR Papers*, Vol. I, pp. 796–97.

7. *FDR Papers*, Vol. II, pp. 17–18; *New York Times*, 3/6/33; Browder and Smith, *Independent*, p. 86.

8. *Washington Star*, 3/3/33; Moley, *First New Deal*, p. 201; *Time*, 3/20/33; *Time*, 3/10/47; Stott, "FDR, Lewis Douglas, and the Raw Deal."

9. Stott, "FDR, Lewis Douglas, and the Raw Deal."; Tugwell, *Roosevelt's Revolution*, p. 8; *Literary Digest*, 7/8/33.

10. Browder and Smith, *Independent*, p. 4; Letter of Lewis Douglas to James Sargent, July 26, 1971, Douglas Papers, Box 119; *New York Times*, 12/22/1890.

11. *New York Times*, 12/22/1890; Browder and Smith, *Independent*, pp. 4–5; *Arizona: The Grand Canyon State: A State Guide*, ed. Henry G. Alsberg and Harry Hansen, revised by Joseph Miller (New York: Hastings House, 1966), pp. 171, 175; James W. Byrkit, *Forging the Copper Collar: Arizona's Labor-Management War of 1901–1921* (Tucson: The University of Arizona Press, 1982), pp. 17–18, 20.

12. Alsberg and Hansen, *Arizona: The Grand Canyon State*, pp. 173–74; Letter of Lewis Douglas to Samuel Rosenman, October 26, 1972, Douglas Papers, Box 118.

13. Browder and Smith, *Independent*, pp. 4–7; Alsberg and Hansen, *Arizona: The Grand Canyon State*, pp. 173–74; *New York Herald Tribune*, 4/16/33; Bykrit, *Forging the Copper Collar*, p. 16.

14. Alsberg and Hansen, *Arizona: The Grand Canyon State*, p. 175; Browder and Smith, *Independent*, pp. 10–12, 14–15; *New York Times*, 1/3/49; Letter of Lewis Douglas to James Sargent, July 26, 1971, Douglas Papers, Box 119; Letter of Lewis Douglas to Samuel Rosenman, October 26, 1972.

15. Browder and Smith, *Independent*, pp. 8–9, 14–15; Byrkit, *Forging the Copper Collar*, pp. xiii–xiv, 28–32 48, 102–3, 110, 116–17, 158; Letter of Lewis Douglas to James Sargent, July 26, 1971.

16. Byrkit, *Forging the Copper Collar*, pp. 1–2, 28, 158–60; Browder and Smith, *Independent*, pp. 8–9, 14–15; *New York Times*, 5/29/18; *New York Times*, 7/4/17; *New York Times*, 7/13/17; *New York Times*, 7/14/17; *New York Times*, 6/29/17.

17. Byrkit, *Forging the Copper Collar*, pp. 1–2, 107, 162, 184, 204, 211–15, 290; Browder and Smith, *Independent*, pp. 8–9, 14–15; *New York Times*, 5/29/18; *New York Times*, 7/4/17; *New York Times*, 7/13/17; *New York Times*, 7/14/17.

18. *United States v. Wheeler*, 254 U.S. 281 (1920); *Hitchman Coal & Coke Co. v. Mitchell*, 245 U.S. 229 (1917); Michael E. Parrish, *Felix Frankfurter and His Times: The Reform Years* (New York: The Free Press, 1982), pp. 88, 93–94; Liva Baker, *Felix Frankfurter* (New York: Coward-McCann, Inc., 1969), pp. 66–67; Byrkit, *Forging the Copper Collar*, pp. 7, 249–50, 260, 290.

19. Letter of Lewis Douglas to Samuel Rosenman, October 26, 1972; Letter of Lewis Douglas to James Sargent, July 26, 1971; "Douglas, Lewis," *Current Biography*, March 1947; Browder and Smith, *Independent*, pp. 10–15, 17–19.

20. Ibid. pp. 19–24.

21. Thomas G. Smith, "Lewis Douglas, Arizona Politics and the Colorado River Controversy," *Arizona and the West* 22 (Summer 1980), pp. 125–26; Charles G. Ross, "A Man Who Can Say No with a Smile," *The Literary Digest*, 7/8/33; Stott, "FDR, Lewis Douglas, and the Raw Deal"; Letter of Lewis Douglas to James Sargent, July 26, 1971; Browder and Smith, *Independent*, pp. 22–23.

22. Smith, "Colorado River Controversy," pp. 126–27; Letter of Lewis Douglas to James Sargent, July 26, 1971; Browder and Smith, *Independent*, pp. 32–34; Byrkit, *Forging the Copper Collar*, pp. 82–84; "Douglas, Lewis," *Current Biography*, March 1947.

23. Browder and Smith, *Independent*, p. 35.

24. Ibid., pp. 40–48; *New York Times*, 9/7/26.

25. Browder and Smith, *Independent*, pp. 49–53; Ross, "A Man Who Can Say No with a Smile," p. 3; *Collier's*, 7/29/33; *New York Times*, 3/8/74.

26. Browder and Smith, *Independent*, pp. 59, 63, 65. Letter of Lewis Douglas to James S. Douglas, May 28, 1932, Douglas Papers, Box 239.

27. Huthmacher, *Senator Robert F. Wagner*, p. 77; Browder and Smith, *Independent*, p. 65; Schlesinger, *Coming of the New Deal*, p. 9; Letter of Lewis Douglas to W. R. Mathews of December 29, 1932, Douglas Papers, Box 238; Letter of Lewis Douglas to Franklin Roosevelt of January 19, 1933, Douglas Papers, Box 238.

28. Letter from Lewis Douglas to James Douglas, January 25, 1931, Douglas Papers, Box 239, Folder 4; Letter from Lewis Douglas to James Douglas, January 16, 1932, Douglas Papers, Box 239, Folder 4; Letter from Lewis Douglas to James Douglas, March 1, 1932, Douglas Papers, Box 239, Folder 4; Letter from James Douglas to Lewis Douglas, November 24, 1932, 1932, Douglas Papers, Box 239, Folder 4; Letter from Lewis Douglas to Raymond Moley, May 4, 1964, Douglas Papers, Box 118; Letter from Senator James Byrnes to Raymond Moley, February 24, 1933, Moley Papers, Box 63; Browder and Smith, *Independent*, pp. 65–66; *New York Times*, 12/10/32; *New York Times*, 3/30/32.

29. Browder and Smith, *Independent*, pp. 65–66; Moley, *First New Deal*, p. 202; *New York Times*, 3/30/32, 4/24/32, 12/10/32.

30. Letter from Lewis Douglas to Raymond Moley, May 4, 1964; Browder and Smith, *Independent*, pp. 66–67, 87; Ross, "A Man Who Can Say No with a Smile"; Letter from Judge William Clark to Raymond Moley, March 13, 1933, Moley Papers, Box 65; Robert Cruise McManus, "Best Apple in

the Barrel," *The North American Review*, September 1932; Lindley, *Roosevelt Revolution*, pp. 88–90; Dickson and Allen, *Bonus Army*, pp. 29–38, 88–90; *Time*, 3/20/33; *New York Times*, 12/25/32; *New York Times*, 5/4/32, 5/5/32.

31. *New York Times*, 5/29/32.

32. Browder and Smith, *Independent*, pp. 73–77; *New York Times*, 9/27/32; Schlesinger, *Crisis of the Old Order*, pp. 285–87; Sargent, *Roosevelt an the Hundred Days*, pp. 69–70; Telegram of Lewis Douglas to Franklin D. Roosevelt, November 21, 1932, Douglas Papers, Box 174; Letter of Lewis Douglas to James Sargent, July 26, 1971, Douglas Papers, Box 119.

33. Tugwell, *In Search of Roosevelt*, p. 216; Letter of Lewis Douglas to W. R. Matthews, December 29, 1932, in Douglas Papers, Correspondence File, Folder 1; Tugwell, *Diary*, pp. 31–33; Letter of Guernsey T. Gross to Lewis Douglas, December 10, 1932, Douglas Papers, Box 174; Letter of Lewis Douglas to Raymond Moley, May 4, 1964.

34. Letter of Lewis Douglas to W. R. Matthews, December 29, 1932, Lewis Douglas, "The Budget Years," unpublished draft manuscript, Douglas Papers, Box 119; *New York Times*, 2/24/33; *New York Times*, 2/24/33; Browder and Smith, *Independent*, p. 81; Moley, *After Seven Years*, p. 84. Letter of Lewis Douglas to James S. Douglas. March 12, 1933, Douglas Papers, Box 239.

35. Letter of Lewis Douglas to James Sargent, July 26, 1971, "Memorandum of Mr. Douglas Re Present Banking Situation," Douglas Papers, Box 118; Letter from Lewis Douglas to Raymond Moley, May 4, 1964; *Washington Daily News*, 1/5/33; Browder and Smith, *Independent*, pp. 82–83; Sargent, *Roosevelt and the Hundred Days,* pp. 72–73.

36. Browder and Smith, *Independent*, pp. 82–83; Carter, *New Dealers*, p. 125; Letter from Lewis Douglas to Arthur Curless, February 24, 1933, Douglas Papers; Letter from Lewis Douglas to Raymond Moley, May 4, 1964; Sargent, *Roosevelt and the Hundred Days,* pp. 72–73; Letter of Lewis Douglas to James Sargent, July 26, 1971; *New York Times*, 2/24/33.

37. Letter from Robert G. Simmons to Lewis Douglas, March 2, 1933, Douglas Papers; Letter of Mrs. Robert Lincoln Hoyal to Lewis Douglas, March 4, 1933, Douglas Papers; Shields & Company, "Stock Market Comment," February 25, 1933, Douglas Papers; Letter from H. N. Conant to Lewis Douglas, February 25, 1933, Douglas Papers; Letter from Lewis Douglas to Raymond Moley, May 4, 1933, in Moley, *First New Deal*, pp. 201–2; *New York Times*, 2/24/33; Ross, "A Man Who Can Say No with a Smile," p. 3. *New York Herald Tribune*, 4/16/33.

38. Ross, "A Man Who Can Say No with a Smile," p. 3; Letter from Lewis Douglas to Raymond Moley, May 4, 1964; Sargent, *Roosevelt and the Hundred Days*, p. 103.

39. Letter from Lewis Douglas to James Douglas, March 12, 1933, Douglas Papers, Box 239, Folder 4, *FDR Papers*, Vol. II, pp. 49–50; Moley, *First New Deal*, pp. 202–3.

40. Letter from Lewis Douglas to Turner Catledge, April 12, 1969, Douglas Papers, Box 118; Browder and Smith, *Independent*, p. 87; Stott, "FDR, Lewis Douglas, and the Raw Deal"; Moley, *First New Deal*, pp. 202–3; *FDR Papers*, Vol. II, p. 52; Sargent, *Roosevelt and the Hundred Days*, p. 111; *Washington Post*, 4/2/33.

41. Letter from Lewis Douglas to Raymond Moley, May 4, 1964; Moley, *First New Deal*, pp. 202–3; Moley, *Diary*, 3/8/33; James Sargent, "Oral History, Franklin D. Roosevelt and the New Deal: Some Recollections of Adolf A. Berle, Jr., Lewis Douglas, and Raymond Moley," *Oral History Review*, September 1973, p. 102; *FDR Papers*, Vol. II, pp. 49–50; Sargent, "Oral History," p.103.

42. Schlesinger, *Coming of the New Deal*, p. 10; Sargent, *Roosevelt and the Hundred Days,* p. 109; Freidel, *Launching the New Deal*, p. 243.

43. Three Phonotapes of Interviews of Raymond Moley, 1970, Moley Papers, Tape Cabinet, Sargent, *Roosevelt and the Hundred Days*, pp. xx–yy, 110–111; Letter; Lewis Douglas, Interview with James Sargent, pp. 55–56, Douglas Papers, Box 119; Freidel, *Launching the New Deal*, pp. 274–75; Carter, *New Dealers*, p. 125.

44. Cook, *Eleanor Roosevelt*, Vol. II, pp. 70–71; Sargent, *Roosevelt and the Hundred Days,* p. 128; Stott, "FDR, Lewis Douglas, and the Raw Deal"; Moley, *First New Deal*, p. 203; Freidel, *Launching the New Deal*, pp. 234, 245; *New York Times*, 3/12/33; *New York Times*, 3/13/33; *New York Times*, 4/11/33; *Time*, 3/20/33; *Time*, 10/5/36.

45. *Congressional Record*, 3/11/33; Stott, "FDR, Lewis Douglas, and the Raw Deal"; Badger, *FDR*, p. 74; Sargent, *Roosevelt and the Hundred Days*, p. 112; Moley, *First New Deal*, pp. 203–4; Lindley, *Roosevelt Revolution*, pp. 89–91; Moley, *After Seven Years*, p. 153; *The New Republic*, 6/28/33; *New York Times*, 3/12/33; *Time*, 5/16/32; Sargent, *Roosevelt and the Hundred Days*, p. 112.

46. *Congressional Record*, 3/11/33.

47. Ibid.; Stott, "FDR, Lewis Douglas, and the Raw Deal"; Dickson and Allen, *Bonus Army*, pp. 30–31; *New York Times*, 3/12/33; *New York Times*, 3/16/33.

48. *Congressional Record*, 3/11/33; Leuchtenburg, *Franklin D. Roosevelt and the New Deal*, p. 45; *New York Times*, 3/12/33.

49. Anne O'Hare McCormick, *The World at Home: Selections from the Writings of Anne O'Hare McCormick*, ed. Marion Turner Sheehan (Salem, N.H: Ayer Publishing, 1970), p. 182; Moley, *First New Deal*, p. 204; *Congressional Record*, 3/11/33; Sargent, *Roosevelt and the Hundred Days*, pp. 1–2, 112–13; Lindley, *Roosevelt Revolution*, p. 91; *New York Times*, 3/12/33; *Washington Post*, 3/12/33.

50. Letter of Lewis Douglas to James Douglas, March 12, 1933; *Congressional Record*, 3/11/33; Moley, *First New Deal*, p. 205; Freidel, *Launching the New Deal*, p. 244; *New York Times*, 3/15/33; Huthmacher, *Senator Robert F. Wagner*, p. 139; Alan Brinkley, *Voices of Protest: Huey Long, Father Coughlin, and the Great Depression* (New York: Alfred A. Knopf, 1982), p. 59; *Time*, 11/12/34.

51. *Congressional Record*, 3/11/1933; Moley, *First New Deal*, p. 205; Freidel, *Launching the New Deal*, p. 144; *New York Times*, 3/11/33; *New York Times*, 3/15/33; *New York Times*, 3/16/33; Huthmacher, *Senator Robert F. Wagner*, p. 139; Sargent, *Roosevelt and the Hundred Days*, p. 118; *Washington Post*, 3/16/33.

52. Lindley, *Roosevelt Revolution*, p. 91; Leuchtenburg, *Franklin D. Roosevelt and the New Deal*, p. 46; Freidel, *Launching the New Deal*, pp. 245–46; Schlesinger, *Coming of the New Deal*, p. 11; *Time*, 3/27/33; *New York Times*, 3/20/33.

53. Letter of Franklin D. Roosevelt to Edward House, April 5, 1933, in Moley Papers, Roosevelt, Pres. Franklin D., 1933–38, House Drawer 16, Folder 47a; Schlesinger, *Coming of the New Deal*, p. 10; *New York Times*, 6/1/33; *New York Times*, 3/11/33; *New York Times*, 3/21/33; *Washington Post*, 3/17/33; *Washington Post*, 3/21/33; Sargent, *Roosevelt and the Hundred Days*, pp. 117–18; Browder and Smith, *Independent*, pp. 85–87; Lindley, *Roosevelt Revolution*, p. 91.

54. Lewis Douglas, Interview with James Sargent, p. 42; Roosevelt, *FDR: His Personal Letters*, p. 342; Browder and Smith, *Independent*, pp. 85, 420; Moley, *First New Deal*, p. 352; *New York Times*, 5/19/33; Schlesinger, *Coming of the New Deal*, pp. 10–11.

55. Sargent, *Roosevelt and the Hundred Days*, p. 130; Letter of Lewis Douglas to Charles M. Mills, March 29, 1933, Douglas Papers, Box 245, Folder 6.

56. "Speech of Hon. Park Trammell in the Congressional Record," in Douglas Papers, Box 293; Letter of Lewis Douglas to John Gaus, April 8, 1933, Douglas Papers, Box 10, Folder 10; Letter of Lewis Douglas to James Sargent, March 19, 1973, Douglas Papers, Box 119; Browder and Smith, *Independent*, pp. 87–88.

57. *FDR Papers*, Vol. I, p. 625; Terkel, *Hard Times*, p. 252.

CHAPTER 4: "GOOD FARMING; CLEAR THINKING; RIGHT LIVING"

1. Reminiscences of Henry A. Wallace, 1951, CUOHRO, pp. 208, 216, 221; Press Release, Agriculture Department, March 3, 1933, in Wallace Papers, Speeches Box S1; Culver and Hyde, *American Dreamer*, p. 111–13; Schapsmeier and Schapsmeier, *Henry A. Wallace*, p. 163; The Official Record, United States Department of Agriculture, March 11, 1933, in Wallace Papers, Series II: Clippings, Box 1; Russell Lord, *The Wallaces of Iowa*, (New York: Da Capo Press, 1972), p. 337; *Life*, 9/2/40.

2. *Wallaces' Farmer and Iowa Homestead*, 3/4/33; Schapsmeier and Schapsmeier, *Henry A. Wallace*, p. 163; Lord, *Wallaces of Iowa*, pp. 332–33; *Time*, 11/26/65; Herbert Feis, *1933: Characters in Crisis* (Boston: Little, Brown, 1966), p. 105; George Creel, "The Mystery of the Secret Cabinet," *The Elks Magazine*, in Wallace Papers, Murphy File, Box 1; Schlesinger, *Coming of the New Deal*, p. 34; Tugwell, *Roosevelt's Revolution*, p. 20; *Life*, 9/2/40.

3. Shover, *Cornbelt Rebellion*, pp. 72, 77–79, 87–88; *New York Times*, 1/22/33; Schlesinger, *Coming of the New Deal*, p. 27; Bernstein, *A Caring Society*, p. 4; Schapsmeier and Schapsmeier, *Henry A. Wallace*, pp. 145–46; *FDR Public Papers*, Vol. II, p. 75; "Henry Wallace and the Farm Crisis of the 1920s and 1930s," *The Annals of Iowa*, Fall 1983; Theodore Saloutos, *The American Farmer and the New Deal* (Ames: The Iowa State University Press, 1982), p. 48; Lord, *Wallaces of Iowa*, p. 332.

4. Reminiscences of Henry A. Wallace, 1951, CUOHRO, pp. 213, 216–21; Moley, *First New Deal*, p. 356; Culver and Hyde, *American Dreamer*, p. 113; Lord, *Wallaces of Iowa*, pp. 332–33; Tugwell, *Diary*, pp. 82–83; Sargent, *Roosevelt and the Hundred Days,* pp. 56–57; Namorato, *Tugwell*, pp. 2, 39; Lindley, *Roosevelt Revolution*, pp. 304–7.

5. Freidel, *Launching the New Deal*, p. 308; Reminiscences of Henry A. Wallace, 1951, CUOHRO, pp. 208–9; Tugwell, *Diary*, pp. 88–91; Tugwell, *Roosevelt's Revolution*, pp. 36, 69; Culver and Hyde, *American Dreamer*, p. 114.

6. Raymond Moley, "Contemporary National Politics," Lecture to Columbia class, April 29, 1936, in Moley Papers, Box 189; Freidel, *Launching the New Deal*, p. 308; Reminiscences of Henry A. Wallace, 1951, CUOHRO, pp. 208–9; Tugwell, *Roosevelt's Revolution*, pp. 36, 69; Culver and Hyde, *American Dreamer*, p. 114; Tugwell, *Diary*, pp. 63–64, 88–89; Tugwell, *Democratic Roosevelt*, p. 275; Moley, *After Seven Years*, p. 165; Rosenman, *Working with Roosevelt*, p. 43; Rosenman, *Presidential Style*, p. 297; *FDR Papers*, Vol. I, p. 82; Badger, *FDR*, p. 63.

7. Tugwell, *Roosevelt's Revolution*, p. 69; Culver and Hyde, *American Dreamer*, p. 114; Tugwell, *Diary*, pp. 63–64, 88–89.

8. *FDR Papers*, Vol. II, pp. 74–79; Tugwell, *Roosevelt's Revolution*, p. 36.

9. "Genealogical Charts," p. 32, Wallace Biographical Materials, Wallace Papers; Culver and Hyde, *American Dreamer*, pp. 5–8; Murphy Diary, pp. 1–2, Wallace Papers, Murphy Files, Box 7; "Biography of Henry Wallace," in Wallace Biographical Materials, Wallace Papers; Lord, *Wallaces of Iowa*, 5–6, 21–23, 41–42, 51, 57, 78–79, 81, 107; Schapsmeier and Schapsmeier, *Henry A. Wallace*, pp. 3–4, 6; *Des Moines Register*, 3/28/33; "Henry Wallace Birthplace" pamphlet, Wallace Papers, Box WF1; Murphy Diary, *Wallaces' Farmer*, 2/17/28.

10. Biography of Henry C. Wallace, pp. 1–4, Wallace Papers, Murphy Diary, p. 1–2; Lord, *Wallaces of Iowa*, pp. 7, 12; Culver and Hyde, *American Dreamer*, pp. 9, 15; Reminiscences of Henry A. Wallace, 1951, CUOHRO, pp. 7, 12, 16; *Des Moines Register*, 3/28/33; Ben James, "The Wallaces—A Saga of the Soil," *New York Herald Tribune*, 10/8/33; Lord, *Wallaces of Iowa*, p. 131.

11. "Three Generations," booklet on *Wallaces' Farmer*, undated, Wallace Papers, Murphy Files, Box 1, "Genealogical Charts," pp. 5–9; Schapsmeier and Schapsmeier, *Henry A. Wallace*, p. 10; Dwight Macdonald, *Henry Wallace: The Man and the Myth* (New York: The Vanguard Press, 1948), p. 40; "From the Vice President of the United States…Henry A. Wallace," Wallace Papers, Murphy Files, Box 1.

12. *Wallaces' Farmer*, 3/4/16; "Uncle Henry," Scrapbooks, *Wallaces' Farmer*; Reminiscences of Henry A. Wallace, 1951, CUOHRO, p. 29; Culver and Hyde, *American Dreamer*, p. 43.

13. *Wallaces' Farmer*, 11/7/24; Edward L. Schapsmeier and Frederick H. Schapsmeier, "The Wallaces and Their Farm Paper: a Story of Agrarian Leadership," pp. 290–91, in Wallace Papers; Culver and Hyde, *American Dreamer*, pp. 24, 47–50; Schapsmeier and Schapsmeier, *Henry A. Wallace*, pp. 40–44; Letter from Don Murphy to W. W. Waymack, April 11, 1939, Wallace Papers, Box of Personal Biographical Materials; Lord, *Wallaces of Iowa*, p. 4; Reminiscences of Henry A. Wallace, 1951, CUOHRO, p. 4; Macdonald, *The Man and the Myth,* p. 41.

14. Culver and Hyde, *American Dreamer*, pp. 54–55, 61–64, 78–79; Gilbert Fite, *George N. Peek and the Fight for Farm Parity* (Norman: University of Oklahoma Press, 1954), p. 3; Saloutos, *American Farmer and the New Deal*, p. 3; Reminiscences of Henry A. Wallace, 1951, CUOHRO, pp. 9, 47–49; Schapsmeier and Schapsmeier, *Henry A. Wallace*, pp. 71–78; J. Samuel Walker, "Henry A. Wallace as Agrarian Isolationist, 1921–1930," *Agricultural History* 49 (July 1975), p. 539; Henry A. Wallace, *New Frontiers* (New York: Reynal & Hitchcock, 1934), pp. 145–49; Macdonald, *The Man and the Myth,* p. 44; Edwin G. Nourse, Joseph S. Davis, and John Black, *Three Years of the Agricultural Adjustment Administration* (New York: Da Capo Press, 1971), p. 6.

15. Schapsmeier and Schapsmeier, *Henry A. Wallace*, pp. 63–64, 94–95; Culver and Hyde, *American Dreamer*, pp. 58–59; Fite, *George N. Peek* pp. 62–63; Harold F. Breimyer, "Agricultural Philosophies and Policies in the New Deal," *Minnesota Law Review* 68 (December 1983), pp. 333, 337; Tugwell, *The Democratic Roosevelt*, p. 158.

16. Wallace, *New Frontiers*, pp. 145–49; Culver and Hyde, *American Dreamer*, pp. 63–64; Schapsmeier and Schapsmeier, *Henry A. Wallace*, pp. 71–78; Walker, "Wallace as Agrarian Isolationist," p. 539; Macdonald, *The Man and the Myth*, p. 44; Nourse et al., *Three Years*, pp. 5–6; Lindley, *Roosevelt Revolution*, p. 13; *New York Times* 6/3/24.

17. Lord, *Wallaces of Iowa*, pp. 107, 118, 124; Reminiscences of Henry A. Wallace, 1951, CUOHRO, pp. 4, 15, 25–29, 34; Culver and Hyde, *American Dreamer*, p. 13; "Seeds and Science: Henry A. Wallace on Agriculture & Human Progress," lecture by Senator John C. Culver, May 14, 1996, Carnegie Institution of Washington, Washington, D.C., pp. 2–5.

18. Culver, "Seeds and Science," p. 7; Reminiscences of Henry A. Wallace, 1951, CUOHRO, p. 4; Schapsmeier and Schapsmeier, *Henry A. Wallace*, pp. 30–31; Reminiscences of Henry A. Wallace, 1951, CUOHRO, pp. 2–4; Untitled, undated newspaper article about Wallace address at Tuskegee University, Wallace Papers, Series II Clippings, Box 1; *Wallaces' Farmer*, 12/23/21.

19. Reminiscences of Henry A. Wallace, 1951, CUOHRO, pp. 70–71, 84–85: Lord, *Wallaces of Iowa*, pp. 143–45, 150; Henry A. Wallace, "Pioneer Kernels," December 1965, Wallace Papers, Box WF1, "Wallace Hi-Bred Seed Corn: Larger Yields from Smaller Fields," undated paper from the Hi-Bred Corn Company, in Wallace Papers, Box WF1.

20. Reminiscences of Henry A. Wallace, 1951, CUOHRO, pp. 52, 56–57; Culver and Hyde, *American Dreamer*, pp. 33–34, 52, 72; *Des Moines Register*, 3/28/33; Wallace, "Pioneer Kernels," December 1965.

21. Reminiscences of Henry A. Wallace, 1951, CUOHRO, pp. 74, 78–84, 86, 94; Culver and Hyde, *American Dreamer*, pp. 36–39; Schapsmeier and Schapsmeier, *Henry A. Wallace*, p. 21.

22. Reminiscences of Henry A. Wallace, 1951, CUOHRO, pp. 90–98; Culver and Hyde, *American Dreamer*, pp. 51–52; Schapsmeier and Schapsmeier, *Henry A. Wallace*, pp. 24, 35, 122–23; Richard S. Kirkendall, "Henry A. Wallace's Turn Toward the New Deal, 1921–1924," *The Annals of Iowa*, Winter/Spring 1988, p. 222; Frank Freidel, Interview with Henry A. Wallace, p. 14; Lord, *Wallaces of Iowa*, pp. 209–10.

23. *Wallaces' Farmer*, 5/1/25; Dorothy Schwieder, "Rural Iowa in the 1920s: Conflict and Community," in Wallace Papers, Box 1; *Wallaces' Farmer*, 3/6/25; *Wallaces' Farmer*, 11/5/26; Richard S. Kirkendall, "The Mind of a Farm Leader," pp. 148–50, in Wallace Papers, Box 1; T. H. Watkins, *The Hungry Years: A Narrative History of the Great Depression in America* (New York: Holt, 2000), p. 341; Don. S. Kirschner, "Henry A. Wallace as Farm Editor," *American Quarterly*, Vol. 17, No. 2, Part I (Summer 1965), pp. 188, 197; Fite, *George N. Peek*, p. 5.

24. Wallace, "Pioneer Kernels," December 1965, pp. 1–3; William L. Brown, "H. A. Wallace and the Development of Hybrid Corn," p. 167, in Wallace Papers; *Wallaces' Farmer*, 8/30/26, p. 67; Culver and Hyde, *American Dreamer*, pp. 82–83; Schapsmeier and Schapsmeier, *Henry A. Wallace*, pp. 27–28; *New York Times*, 3/16/99.

25. Carroll P. Streeter, "We've Never Seen This Before!" *Farmer's Wife*, January 1934; Badger, *FDR*, p. 67; Reminiscences of Henry A. Wallace, 1951, CUOHRO, pp. 47–49; Culver and Hyde, *American Dreamer*, pp. 78–79; 96–99.

26. *Wallaces' Farmer*, 3/16/28; Glenda Riley and Richard Kirkendall, "Henry A. Wallace and the Mystique of the Farm Male, 1921–1933," *Annals of Iowa* 48 (Summer–Fall 1985); Reminiscences of Henry A. Wallace, 1951, CUOHRO, pp. 121, 130; *Wallaces' Farmer*, 5/30/24; Schapsmeier and Schapsmeier, *Henry A. Wallace*, pp. 48–49; Macdonald, *The Man and the Myth*, p. 43; Henry A. Wallace, "Agriculture Recognized at Last," *The Jeffersonian*, June 1933, p. 4; Leland L. Sage, "Rural Iowa in the 1920s and 1930s: Roots of the Farm Depression," in "Henry A. Wallace and Iowa Agriculture," *The Annals of Iowa*, Fall 1983; Frank Freidel, "Notes of an Interview with Henry A. Wallace," Small Collections Oral History, FDR Library; Wallace, *New Frontiers*, p. 142.

27. Reminiscences of Henry A. Wallace, 1951, CUOHRO, pp. 121–22, 130; Letter from Don Murphy to W. W. Waymack, April 11, 1939, in Wallace Papers, Personal Biographical Materials Box; Schapsmeier and Schapsmeier, *Henry A. Wallace*, p. 148; *Wallaces' Farmer*, 4/11/31.

28. Reminiscences of Henry A. Wallace, 1951, CUOHRO, pp. 123–28; Schapsmeier and Schapsmeier, *Henry A. Wallace*, p. 68; Kirkendall, *Wallace's Turn Toward the New Deal*, p. 230; Freidel, Notes of an Interview; Fite, *George N. Peek*, pp. 131–32; Culver and Hyde, *American Dreamer*, p. 56.

29. Fite, *George N. Peek*, pp. 175–79; Schapsmeier and Schapsmeier, *Henry A. Wallace*, pp. 63–64, 75, 99–107, 108; *Wallaces' Farmer*, 6/1/28, 6/8/28; Schapsmeier and Schapsmeier, "The Wallaces and Their Farm Paper," pp. 291–92; Walker, "Wallace as Agrarian Isolationist"; Reminiscences of Henry A. Wallace, 1951, CUOHRO, pp. 130–38; Fite, *George N. Peek*, pp. 175–79, 192–96.

30. Henry A. Wallace, "Statement Before Cosmos Club, April 19, 1933," p. 7, in Wallace Papers, Box S1; Reminiscences of Henry A. Wallace, 1951, CUOHRO, pp. 138–39, 152; Culver and Hyde, *American Dreamer*, p. 84; Freidel, "Notes of an Interview"; Schlesinger, *Coming of the New Deal*, p. 29; Schapsmeier and Schapsmeier, *Henry A. Wallace*, p. 108–14; *Wallaces' Farmer* 6/1/28.

31. Macdonald, *The Man and the Myth*, p. 43; Culver and Hyde, *American Dreamer*, pp. 88–89, 92–93, 99; "Wallace, Henry A.," *Current Biography*, January 1947; Schapsmeier and Schapsmeier, *Henry A. Wallace*, pp. 116–121; Saloutos, *American Farmer and the New Deal*, pp. 28–29; Nourse et al., *Three Years*, pp. 7–12; Breimyer, "Agricultural Philosophies," p. 339; John Morton Blum, *From the Morgenthau Diaries: Years of Crisis, 1928–1938* (Boston: Houghton Mifflin, 1959), pp. 36–37; Reminiscences of Henry A. Wallace, 1951, CUOHRO, pp. 121–22, 156; Henry A. Wallace, "Causes of the World Wide Depression of 1930," p. 7, in Wallace Papers, Box A1; Lauren Soth, "Henry A. Wallace and the Farm Credit Crisis of the 1920s and 1930s," p. 198, in Wallace Papers, Articles About Wallace, Box 1; Shover, *Cornbelt Rabellion*, p. 11; Walker, "Wallace as Agrarian Isolationist," p. 545; Smith, *FDR*, p. 252; Schlesinger, *Crisis of the Old Order*, p. 164; *New York Times*, 5/5/30.

32. Reminiscences of Henry A. Wallace, 1951, CUOHRO, pp. 143–48; Walker, "Wallace as Agrarian Isolationist," p. 545; Macdonald, *The Man and the Myth*, p. 44; Schlesinger, *Coming of the New Deal*, p. 37; Saloutos, *American Farmer and the New Deal*, pp. 126–27; Schapsmeier and Schapsmeier, *Henry A. Wallace*, pp. 127–30.

33. Soth, *Farm Credit Crisis*, p. 205; Hofstadter, *American Political Tradition*, p. 243; Schapsmeier and Schapsmeier, *Henry A. Wallace*, p. 148; *Wallaces' Farmer*, 4/11/1931; Henry A. Wallace, "The Honest Dollar Fight," speech to the Iowa Bankers Association, June 22, 1932, Wallace Papers, Box S1.

34. Schapsmeier and Schapsmeier, *Henry A. Wallace*, pp. 149–51; Reminiscences of Henry A. Wallace, 1951, CUOHRO, pp. 170–71; William D. Rowley, *M. L. Wilson and the Campaign for the Domestic Allotment* (Lincoln: University of Nebraska Press, 1970), pp. 135–36; Freidal, *Roosevelt: The Triumph*, p. 273; Sternsher, *Rexford Tugwell and the New Deal*, p. 183.

35. Shover, *Cornbelt Rebellion*, pp. 36–37, 72, 77; *New York Times*, 1/22/33; Schlesinger, *Coming of the New Deal*, p. 27; Lawrence Meir Friedman, *American Law in the 20th Century* (New Haven: Yale University Press, 2004), p. 176; Schapsmeier and Schapsmeier, *Henry A. Wallace*, pp. 147–80; William Allen White, "The Farmer Takes a Holiday," *Saturday Evening Post*, 11/26/32.

36. Kirkendall, "Henry A. Wallace's Turn Toward the New Deal," pp. 224–25; Reminiscences of Henry A. Wallace, 1951, CUOHRO, pp. 152–56; Macdonald, *The Man and the Myth*, p. 47; Letter of Henry Wallace to Raymond Moley, May 27, 1965, Moley Papers, Box 245, Folder 10.

37. Schapsmeier and Schapsmeier, *Henry A. Wallace*, pp. 149–51; Reminiscences of Henry A. Wallace, 1951, CUOHRO, pp. 165, 170–71; Rowley, *M. L. Wilson*, pp. 135–36; Freidel, *Triumph*, p. 273; Sternsher, *Rexford Tugwell and the New Deal*, p. 183; Culver and Hyde, *American Dreamer*, p. 99; Freidel, "Notes of an Interview"; Sargent, *Roosevelt and the Hundred Days*, p. 58; Reminiscences of Rexford G. Tugwell, 1951, CUOHRO, pp. 20–24; *Time*, 4/3/33.

38. Lord, *Wallaces of Iowa*, pp. 319–21; Culver and Hyde, *American Dreamer*, p. 100; Reminiscences of Henry A. Wallace, 1951, CUOHRO, pp. 166–67, 170–71; Schapsmeier and Schapsmeier, *Henry A. Wallace*, pp. 153–56; Freidel, "Notes of an Interview"; Letter from Henry Wallace to Henry Morgenthau, September 19, 1932, Wallace Papers, Reel 16, Frame 238; *Wallaces' Farmer*, 9/13/32.

39. Bernard Bellush, *Franklin D. Roosevelt as Governor of New York* (New York: Columbia University Press, 1955) p. 76–77; *FDR Papers*, Vol. I, p. 625; Moley, *First New Deal*, p. 251.

40. Memorandum to Judge Samuel Rosenman from Raymond Moley and Rexford G. Tugwell, July 11, 1932, Moley Papers, Box 283; *FDR Papers*, Vol. I, pp. 693–711; Moley, *First New Deal*, p. 250; Saloutos, *American Farmer and the New Deal*, pp. 40–41; Moley, *After Seven Years*, pp. 44–45.

41. Letter from Don Murphy to W. W. Wymack, April 11, 1939, in Wallace Papers, Murphy Files, Box 1; Letter from Henry Wallace to Edward Bernays, December 14, 1932, Wallace Papers, Reel 18, Frame 106; Letter from Henry A. Wallace to Franklin Delano Roosevelt, September 22, 1932, Moley Papers, Box 69; Culver and Hyde, *American Dreamer*, pp. 99–100, 103; Schapsmeier and Schapsmeier, *Henry A. Wallace*, p. 122, 145–56, 158; *Time,* 8/29/32; Moley, *After Seven Years*, p. 42; Reminiscences of Henry A. Wallace, 1951, CUOHRO, pp. 166–67; Letter of Henry Wallace to Dante Pierce, November 30, 1932, Wallace Papers, Reel 59, Frame 577; *Des Moines Register*, 10/4/32; Watkins, *The Hungry Years*, pp. 350–51; Shover, *Cornbelt Rebellion*, pp. 3, 36–37; Michael W. Schuyler, "The Hair-Splitters: Reno and Wallace, 1932–1933," *Annals of Iowa* 43 (Fall 1976), pp. 403–4; Wallace, *New Frontiers*, pp. 151, 165; Edsforth, *New Deal*, p. 102; Saloutos, *American Farmer and the New Deal*, pp. 40; *Wallaces' Farmer*, 10/9/32.

42. Letter of George Peek to Henry Wallace, November 21, 1932, Wallace Papers, Reel 17, Frame 710; Tugwell, *Diary*, p. 32; *The Nation*, 8/14/35, p. 83; Saloutos, *American Farmer and the New Deal*, p. 44.

43. Letter of Henry Wallace to Franklin Roosevelt of November 17, 1932, Wallace Papers, Reel 17, Frame 614; Letter of Edward L. Bernays to Henry Wallace, November 10, 1932, Wallace Papers, Reel 17, Frame 434; Letter of Henry Wallace to Dante Pierce, November 30, 1932; Freidel, "Notes of an Interview"; Reminiscences of Henry A. Wallace, 1951, CUOHRO, pp. 179–82; Wallace, *New Frontiers*, p. 158; Sargent, *Roosevelt and the Hundred Days*, pp. 51, 60.

44. Letter of Henry Wallace to Dante Pierce, November 30, 1932; Reminiscences of Henry A. Wallace, 1951, CUOHRO, pp. 179–82; Wallace, *New Frontiers*, p. 158; Tugwell, Interview of Henry A. Wallace, FDR Library; Telegram from Raymond Moley to Henry Wallace, Nov. 29, 1932, Wallace Papers, Reel 17, Frame 818; Lord, *Wallaces of Iowa*, p. 324.

45. Saloutos, *American Farmer and the New Deal*, p. 42; Freidel, *Launching the New Deal*, pp. 96–98; Reminiscences of Henry A. Wallace, 1951, CUOHRO, pp. 184–85; Tugwell, *In Search of Roosevelt*, p. 192; Nourse et al., *Three Years*, pp. 14–15; Blum, *Morgenthau Diaries,* pp. 39–42; Tugwell, *Diary*, pp. 88–91; Sargent, *Roosevelt and the Hundred Days,* p. 61.

46. Reminiscences of Henry A. Wallace, 1951, CUOHRO, pp. 185–90; Wallace, *New Frontiers*, p. 165; Letter from John R. Kirk to Franklin Delano Roosevelt, January 23, 1933, Letter from Henry A. Wallace to H. E. Mile, February 2, 1933, Letter from Henry A. Wallace to Franklin Delano Roosevelt, January 26, 1933, Wallace Papers, Correspondence, Box 13; Sternsher, *Rexford Tugwell and the New Deal* p. 86; Moley, *After Seven Years*, p. 124 n. 12; Bellush, *Roosevelt as Governor of New York*, p. 78; Letter from Robert A. Allen to Raymond Moley, January 8, 1933, Moley Papers, Box 63; Moley, *First New Deal*, p. 252.

47. Letter from Franklin D. Roosevelt to Henry A. Wallace, February 3, 1933, Wallace Papers, Correspondence, Box 13; Reminiscences of Henry A. Wallace, 1951, CUOHRO, pp. 189–91; *Des Moines Register*, 2/27/33; Lord, *Wallaces of Iowa*, p. 332; Moley, *After seven Years,* p. 124 n. Moley, *First New Deal*, p. 78.

48. Reminiscences of Henry A. Wallace, 1951, CUOHRO, pp. 193–95, 198; Brinkley, *Voices of Protest*, pp. 45–47.

49. Reminiscences of Henry A. Wallace, 1951, CUOHRO, pp. 195–96.

50. Reminiscences of Henry A. Wallace, 1951, CUOHRO, pp. 143–48; Lord, *Wallaces of Iowa*, pp. 332, 346; *Wallaces' Farmer*, 3/4/33; *Des Moines Register*, 3/1/33; Tugwell, *Roosevelt's Revolution*, p. 54; "Wallace, Henry A.," *Current Biography*, January 1947; *New York Times*, 4/2/33.

Chapter 5: "Good Lord! This Is a Revolution"

1. Press Release, Agriculture Dept., March 8, 1933, Wallace Papers, Box S1; Press Release, Agriculture Dept., March 10, 1933, Wallace Papers, Box S1; Hearing, United States Senate Committee on

Agriculture and Forestry, *Congressional Record*, 73rd Session, pp. 8–9; *Saturday Evening Post*, July 3, 1937; Henry Wallace, *Democracy Reborn* (New York: Reynal and Hitchcock, 1944), p. 41; Tugwell, *Roosevelt's Revolution*, pp. 69–70; Saloutos, *American Farmer and the New Deal*, pp. 44–45; Reminiscences of Henry A. Wallace, 1951, CUOHRO, p. 209; *New York Times*, 3/9/1933; Culver and Hyde, *American Dreamer*, p. 115; Schapsmeier and Schapsmeier, *Henry A. Wallace* p. 169.

2. Henry A. Wallace, Radio Address, May 1, 1933, Wallace Papers, Box S1; Tugwell, *Democratic Roosevelt*, pp. 275–76; Schapsmeier and Schapsmeier, *Henry A. Wallace*, p. 168; Sternsher, *Rexford Tugwell and the New Deal*, p. 188; Lord, *Wallaces of Iowa*, p. 328; Tugwell, *Roosevelt's Revolution*, p. 73; Shover, *Cornbelt Rebellion*, pp. 38–39.

3. Tugwell, *Diary*, p. 319; Tugwell, *Roosevelt's Revolution*, p. 73; Schapsmeier and Schapsmeier, *Henry A. Wallace*, p. 168; Freidel, *Launching the New Deal*, pp. 308–9.

4. Reminiscences of Henry A. Wallace, 1951, CUOHRO, pp. 210–11, 225; Press Release, Agriculture Dept., March 10, 1933; Schapsmeier and Schapsmeier, *Henry A. Wallace*, p. 169; Culver and Hyde, *American Dreamer*, p. 115; *New York Times*, 3/11/33; Freidel, *Launching the New Deal*, pp. 308–9; Radio Address by Henry A. Wallace, *National Farm and Home Hour*, March 10, 1933, Wallace Papers, Speeches Box S1; Wallace, *Democracy Reborn*, p. 41; Sargent, *Roosevelt and the Hundred Days*, pp. 114–15; Telegram from Henry Wallace to William Seaver Woods, December 20, 1932, Wallace Papers, Reel 18, Frame 265; Charles O. Gridley, "Henry A. Wallace," reprinted from the *Rainbow* of Delta Tau Delta, in Wallace Papers, Murphy Files, Box 1.

5. Press Release, Agriculture Dept., March 10, 1933; Charles O. Gridley, "Henry A. Wallace"; Schapsmeier and Schapsmeier, *Henry A. Wallace*, p. 169; Culver and Hyde, *American Dreamer*, p. 115; *New York Times*, 3/11/33; Freidel, *Launching the New Deal*, pp. 308–9; Radio Address by Henry A. Wallace, *National Farm and Home Hour*, March 10, 1933, Wallace Papers, Speeches Box S1; "Statement Submitted to Secretary of Agriculture Henry A. Wallace By National Farm Leaders," March 11, 1933, Wallace Papers, Speeches Box S1; Peek and Crowther, *Why Quit Our Own*, p. 80; Letter of Rexford Tugwell to Raymond Moley, October 29, 1965, Moley Papers; Tugwell, *Diary*, pp. 320–21; Reminiscences of Henry A. Wallace, 1951, CUOHRO, pp. 210–11, 225; Wallace, *New Frontiers*, p. 164; Sargent, *Roosevelt and the Hundred Days*, p. 114; Tugwell, *Roosevelt's Revolution*, pp. 75–76; Sternsher, *Rexford Tugwell and the New Deal*, p. 181; *New York Times*, 3/11/33.

6. Tugwell, *Democratic Roosevelt*, p. 276; Schapsmeier and Schapsmeier, *Henry A. Wallace*, pp. 169–71; Peek and Crowther, *Why Quit Our Own*, pp. 80–81; Hearing, United States Senate Committee on Agriculture and Forestry, *Congressional Record*, 73rd Session, p. 7; Wallace, *New Frontiers*, p. 164; Schlesinger, *Coming of the New Deal*, p. 39; Saloutos, *American Farmer and the New Deal*, p. 45; Stanley High, "Will It Be Wallace?" *Saturday Evening Post*, 7/3/37.

7. Letter of Henry Wallace to Raymond Moley, May 27, 1965, Moley Papers, Box 245, Folder 10; Reminiscences of Rexford G. Tugwell, 1951, CUOHRO, p. 44; Schapsmeier and Schapsmeier, *Henry A. Wallace*, pp. 169–71, 191; *Time*, 3/27/33; Wallace, *New Frontiers*, pp. 164–65, 275; Nourse, et al., *Three Years*, pp. 18, 42, 70; Fite, *George N. Peek*, p. 252; Sargent, *Roosevelt and the Hundred Days*, p. 114.

8. Shover, *Cornbelt Rebellion*, pp. 95–96; Lord, *Wallaces of Iowa*, p. 331; Hearing, United States Senate Committee on Agriculture and Forestry, *Congressional Record*, 73rd Session, p. 106; Schuyler, "The Hair Splitters"; Tugwell, *Roosevelt's Revolution*, p. 36.

9. Press Release, Agriculture Dept., March 14, 1933, Wallace Papers, Speeches Box S1; Moley, *First New Deal*, pp. 253–54; Peek and Crowther, *Why Quit Your Own*, p. 82; Moley, Diary, 3/9/33; Tugwell, *Democratic Roosevelt*, p. 276; Freidel, *Launching the New Deal*, p. 311; Tugwell, *Diary*, pp. 88–91; Browder and Smith, *Independent*, pp. 90–91; Sargent, *Roosevelt and the Hundred Days*, p. 83; Lord, *Wallaces of Iowa*, p. 338.

10. *FDR Papers*, Vol. II, p. 74; Reminiscences of Henry A. Wallace, 1951, CUOHRO, p. 221; "Statement by Secretary Wallace," March 17, 1933, Wallace Papers, Speeches Box S1; Freidel, *Launching the New Deal*, p. 311; Moley, *First New Deal*, p. 254; Sargent, *Roosevelt and the Hundred Days*, p. 161.

11. "Address on the Farm Bill by Henry A. Wallace," March 18, Wallace Papers, Box S1; Freidel, *Launching the New Deal*, p. 312; Tugwell, *Diary*, pp. 89–90; Hearing, United States Senate Committee on Agriculture and Forestry, *Congressional Record*, 73rd Session, pp. 7–9, 36; *New York Times*, 3/19/33;

New York Times, 3/23/33; Lindley, *Roosevelt Revolution*, p. 97; *Congressional Record*, January 10, 1933, pp. 1489–93, in Zinn, *New Deal Thought*, p. 228.

12. Shover, *Cornbelt Rebellion*, p. 103; Freidel, *Launching the New Deal*, p. 313; Lindley, *Roosevelt Revolution*, p. 97; *New York Times*, 3/22/33; *New York Times*, 3/23/33; *Washington Post*, 3/22/33.

13. "Statement by Secretary of Agriculture Henry A. Wallace Before the Senate Committee on Agriculture and Forestry," March 25, 1933, Wallace Papers, Box S1; Letter of Henry Wallace to Dante Pierce, March 1933, Wallace Papers, Reel 118, Frame #808; Hearing, United States Senate Committee on Agriculture and Forestry, *Congressional Record*, 73rd Session, pp. 248, 250; Tugwell, *Diary*, pp. 89–90; 322; Freidel, *Launching the New Deal*, p. 314; *The Boston Globe*, 3/26/33; *New York Times*, 3/23/33.

14. Hearing, United States Senate Committee on Agriculture and Forestry, *Congressional Record*, 73rd Session, p. 116.

15. Letter from Wallace to Dante Pierce, March [undated] 1933, Wallace Papers, Correspondence, Box 13; Tugwell, *Diary*, pp. 58–59; Freidel, *Launching the New Deal*, pp. 316–18; Reminiscences of Henry A. Wallace, 1951, CUOHRO, p. 222.

16. Schapsmeier and Schapsmeier, *Henry A. Wallace*, p. 175; Freidel, *Launching the New Deal*, pp. 309–16; Lindley, *Roosevelt Revolution*, pp. 108–9; "Radio Address by Secretary of Agriculture Henry A. Wallace," April 1, 1933, Wallace Papers, Speeches Box S1; Wallace, *New Frontiers*, p. 168; Peek and Crowther, *Why Quit Our Own*, pp. 14–15; Sargent, *Roosevelt and the Hundred Days*, p. 166.

17. "Radio Address by Secretary of Agriculture Henry A. Wallace," April 1, 1933, Wallace Papers, Speeches Box S1; Wallace, *New Frontiers*, p. 168; Peek and Crowther, *Why Quit Our Own*, pp. 14–15; Moley, *First New Deal*, p. 253; Fite, *George N. Peek*, p. 253; Letter from Henry A. Wallace to Dante Pierce, April 1933, Wallace Papers, Reel 18, Frame 852; Tugwell, *Diary*, p. 328.

18. Shover, *Cornbelt Rebellion*, p. 103; Culver and Hyde, *American Dreamer*, p. 117; *New York Times*, 4/14/33; *Time*, 4/10/33.

19. Moley, *First New Deal*, p. 257; Smith, *FDR*, p. 326; Kennedy, *Freedom from Fear*, p. 369; Anthony Badger, *The New Deal: The Depression Years, 1933–1940* (New York: Ivan R. Dee, 2002), p. 239; Schlesinger, *Coming of the New Deal*, pp. 297–98; Sargent, *Roosevelt and the Hundred Days*, p. 147; *New York Times*, 4/14/33; *New York Times*, 6/13/33; *New York Times*, 6/17/33.

20. *New York Times*, 4/15/33; William G. Shepherd, "Why the Farmer Doesn't Like Our Dollar," *Collier's*, 4/1/33, in Wallace Papers, Series II: Clippings, Box 1; Wolfskill and Hudson, *All but the People*, p. 208; Feis, *1933: Characters in Crisis*, pp. 122–23, 126; Freidel, *Launching the New Deal*, pp. 322–23; Schlesinger, *Coming of the New Deal*, pp. 40–42; Lindley, *Roosevelt Revolution*, p. 114.

21. Browder and Smith, *Independent*, p. 91; Berle and Jacobs, *Navigating the Rapids*, p. 72; Feis, *1933: Characters in Crisis*, pp. 114–15; Lindley, *Roosevelt Revolution*, p. 19; Roosevelt, *FDR: His Personal Letters*, pp. 342; Steel, *Walter Lippmann*, p. 304.

22. Walter Lippmann, "Today and Tomorrow," *New York Herald Tribune*, 4/19/33; Lindley, *Roosevelt Revolution*, p. 119; Moley, *First New Deal*, pp. 300–302; Moley, *After Seven Years*, p. 157–58; Moley, *Diary*, 4/18/33, 4/19/33; Wolfskill and Hudson, *All but the People*, p. 208; *New York Times*, 1/25/33.

23. Moley, *First New Deal*, pp. 300–302; Moley, *After Seven Years*, p. 157; Sargent, *Roosevelt and the Hundred Days*, p. 177.

24. Memorandum from Adolf Berle, April 24, 1933, p. 1, in Berle 15, Memorandum from Campaign (August 1932–August 1933), FDR Library; Letter from Lewis Douglas to James Douglas, April 23, 1933, Douglas Papers, Box 239; Letter from Lewis Douglas to James Sargent, March 19, 1973, Douglas Papers, Box 119; Feis, *1933: Characters in Crisis*, pp. 125–31; John Brooks, *Once in Golconda: A True Drama of Wall Street 1920–1938* (New York: Harper & Row, 1969), pp. 154–55; Moley, *First New Deal*, pp. 301–2; Moley, *After Seven Years*, p. 159; Browder and Smith, *Independent*, pp. 91–92; Schlesinger, *Making of the New Deal*, pp. 41–42; *New York Times*, 11/5/32.

25. Lindley, *Roosevelt Revolution*, pp. 120–21; Moley, *First New Deal*, pp. 303–4; Browder and Smith, *Independent*, pp. 92–93; Wolfskill and Hudson, *All but the People*, pp. 208–9; Kennedy, *Freedom from Fear*, pp. 143–44; Dam, "Gold Clause Cases," p. 512; Schlesinger, *Coming of the New Deal*, p. 44; *New York Herald Tribune*, 4/19/33.

26. Terkel, *Hard Times*, pp. 221–22; Shover, *Cornbelt Rebellion*, pp. 118–19; Smith, *FDR*, p. 327 n.; *Time*, 4/17/33, 5/8/33.

27. Freidel, *Launching the New Deal*, p. 337; *The New Republic*, 3/15/33; *New York Times*, 5/11/33.

28. "Henry A. Wallace Address to the US Chamber of Commerce," May 5, 1933, Wallace Papers, Speeches Box S1; William G. Shepherd, "Why the Farmer Doesn't Like Our Dollar," *Collier's*, 4/1/33, in Wallace Papers Series II: Clippings, Box 1; Lord, *Wallaces of Iowa*, p. 332; Henry Wallace, "A Declaration of Interdependence" in Wallace, *Democracy Reborn*, p. 43; *New York Times*, 5/13/33.

29. Roosevelt Presidential Press Conferences, March 17, 1933, *Complete Presidential Press Conferences of Franklin D. Roosevelt*, Vols. 1–2, 1933, (New York: Da Capo Press, 1972); Sargent, *Roosevelt and the Hundred Days*, p. 122.

30. Harold Koontz and Richard Gable, *Public Control of Economic Enterprise* (New York: McGraw-Hill Book Co., 1956), pp. 688–89; Schlesinger, *Crisis of the Old Order*, pp. 121–24; Moley, *First New Deal*, p. 324; Tugwell, *The Democratic Roosevelt*, p. 286; Badger, *The New Deal*, p. 171, *Time*, 11/17/41.

31. Kenneth S. Davis, FDR, *The New York Years*, 1928–1933 (New York: Random House, 1985), pp. 99–100; Moley, *First New Deal*, pp. 325–29; Schlesinger, *Crisis of the Old Order*, p. 124; Smith, *FDR*, p. 237; Freidel, *Triumph*, p. 106; Rosenman, *Working with Roosevelt*, p. 35; Reminiscences of Samuel Rosenman, 1960, CUOHRO, pp. 57–58.

32. Tugwell, *The Democratic Roosevelt*, p. 287; *FDR Papers*, Vol. I, pp. 738–9 *FDR Papers*, Vol. II, pp. 123, 738–39; Badger, *New Deal*, pp. 171–72; Freidel, *Launching the New Deal*, pp. 350–51; Eric F. Goldman, *Rendezvous with Destiny* (New York: Alfred A. Knopf, 1952), p. 263; Moley, *First New Deal*, pp. 326–27; Freidel, *Triumph*, pp. 106, 332–33.

33. *FDR Papers*, Vol. II, p. 123; Moley, *First New Deal*, pp. 325–29; Koontz and Gable, *Public Control*, p. 689; *New York Times*, 4/11/33; Marquerite Owen, *The Tennessee Valley Authority* (New York: Praeger, 1973), p. 19.

34. Moley, *First New Deal*, p. 326; Freidel, *Launching the New Deal*, pp. 350–54; *New York Times*, 1/22/33, 2/3/33.

35. Freidel, *Triumph*, pp. 107, 160; Freidel, *Launching the New Deal*, 350–51; Moley, *First New Deal*, pp. 328–30.

36. Tugwell, *Democratic Roosevelt*, p. 287; Ickes, *Diary*, p. 15; Moley, *First New Deal*, pp. 328–29; *FDR Papers*, Vol. II, pp. 122–23; Reminiscences of Henry A. Wallace, 1951, CUOHRO, p. 247; *New York Times*, 4/2/33; *New York Times*, 4/11/33; *New York Times*, 4/12/33; *New York Times*, 4/14/33; *New York Times*, 4/15/33; *New York Times*, 5/19/33.

37. *FDR Papers*, Vol. II, p. 123; Moley, *First New Deal*, p. 331; Freidel, *Launching the New Deal*, pp. 353–54; *New York Times*, 5/4/33; *New York Times*, 5/20/33; *New York Times*, 5/10/33; *New York Times*, 5/19/33.

38. Memorandum of Adolf Berle, August 5, 1932, Memoranda from Campaign (Aug. 1932–Aug. 1933), Adolf Berle Papers, FDR Library, p. 3; *FDR Papers*, Vol. I, p. 682; Moley, *After Seven Years*, p. 176; Moley, *First New Deal*, p. 307; Sargent, *Roosevelt and the Hundred Days*, p. 141; William Lasser, *Benjamin V. Cohen: Architect of the New Deal* (New Haven: Yale University Press, 2002), p. 71.

39. Lash, *Dealers and Dreamers*, p. 130; Moley, *After Seven Years*, p. 176–78; Moley, *First New Deal*, pp. 308–9; Freidel, *Launching the New Deal*, pp. 341–42; *New York Times*, 7/12/13; *Time*, 4/10/33.

40. Moley, *First New Deal*, p. 309; Moley, *After Seven Years*, pp. 177–78.

41. Moley, *After Seven Years*, p. 178; Freidel, *Launching the New Deal*, p. 343; Sargent, *Roosevelt and the Hundred Days*, pp. 142–43; Lindley, *Roosevelt Revolution*, p. 106.

42. Seligman, *Transformation of Wall Street*, p. 343; Moley, *First New Deal*, pp. 309–10; Seligman, *Transformation of Wall Street*, pp. 54–55; *New York Times*, 4/1/33; Lash, *Dealers and Dreamers*, pp. 130–31.

43. Seligman, *Transformation of Wall Street*, pp. 57, 61–63; Freidel, *Launching the New Deal*, p. 347; Lasser, *Benjamin V. Cohen,* pp. 47–64, 73; Moley, *First New Deal*, p. 312; Wolfskill and Hudson, *All but the People*, p. 53.

44. Works Progress Administration, Washington, p. 664; Lasser, *Benjamin V. Cohen*, pp. 75–79; Seligman, *Transformation of Wall Street*, pp. 63–65; Letter of Felix Frankfurter to FDR, April 17, 1933,

in PPF 140 Frankfurter, Felix, 1932–April 1933, FDR Library; Telegram of Felix Frankfurter to Raymond Moley, April 15, 1933, Moley Papers, Box 68.

45. Seligman, *Transformation of Wall Street*, pp. 65–67; Freidel *Launching the New Deal*, p. 349; Moley, Diary, May 3, 1933; Sargent, *Roosevelt and the Hundred Days*, p. 218; *New York Times*, 5/4/33; *New York Times*, 5/6/33; Telegram from Felix Frankfurter to Raymond Moley, April 28, 1933, Moley Papers, Box 68; Letter from Senator Joe Robinson to Felix Frankfurter, April 29, 1933, Moley Papers, Box 68; Telegram from Felix Frankfurter to Raymond Moley, May 16, 1933, Moley Papers, Box 68; Seligman, *Transformation of Wall Street*, 69–70; Lasser, *Benjamin V. Cohen*, p. 80; *New York Times*, 4/9/33; Lash, *Dealers and Dreamers*, p. 135.

46. Seligman, *Transformation of Wall Street*, pp. 70–71; *New York Times*, 5/28/33; *Time*, 4/10/33; *Time*, 6/12/33; William O. Douglas, "How Effective Is Securities Regulation," in Zinn, *New Deal Thought*, p. 117; *Fortune*, August, 1933.

47. Wallace, *Democracy Reborn*, p. 40; Schlesinger, *Coming of the New Deal*, p. 46; Culver and Hyde, *American Dreamer*, pp. 119, 127; Peek and Crowther, *Why Quit Our Own*, pp. 104–5; Wallace, *New Frontiers*, pp. 161, 168–70, 190.

48. Schapsmeier and Schapsmeier, *Henry A. Wallace*, p. 176; Peek and Crowther, *Why Quit Your Own*, pp. 100–101; Saloutos, *American Farmer and the New Deal*, pp. 54–55; Culver and Hyde, *American Dreamer*, p. 122; Lord, *Wallaces of Iowa*, pp. 332, 340; Schlesinger, *Coming of the New Deal*, p. 46; *New York Times*, 5/15/33.

49. Reminiscences of Jerome Frank, 1960, CUOHRO, pp. 12–15, 139; Peek and Crowther, *Why Quit Your Own*, pp. 13–14, 20, 22; Reminiscences of Henry A. Wallace, 1951, CUOHRO, pp. 236, 240; Lord, *Wallaces of Iowa*, pp. 332, 342; Schlesinger, *Coming of the New Deal*, p. 51; Peek and Crowther, *Why Quit Our Own*, pp. 109–10, 116–19; Saloutos, *American Farmer and the New Deal*, pp. 55–56, 59.

50. Wallace, *New Frontiers*, pp. 169, 171–72; Culver and Hyde, *American Dreamer*, p. 123.

51. Wallace, *New Frontiers*, p. 188; Culver and Hyde, *American Dreamer*, p. 123; Saloutos, *American Farmer and the New Deal*, pp. 66–69.

52. Wallace, *New Frontiers*, pp. 173–75, 188; Peek and Crowther, *Why Quit Our Own*, pp. 124–28; Saloutos, *American Farmer and the New Deal*, pp. 66–69; Carter, *New Dealers*, pp. 75, 81; Lord, *Wallaces of Iowa*, pp. 362–63, Culver and Hyde, *American Dreamer*, p. 123; Schlesinger, *Coming of the New Deal*, pp. 60–63; Wallace, *Democracy Reborn*, pp. 52–56.

Chapter 6: "'Social Justice'... Has Been the Maxim of Her Life"

1. Reminiscences of Frances Perkins, 1961, CUOHRO, Pt. 4, pp. 6, 96–100.

2. Carter, *New Dealers*, pp. 174–75; Reminiscences of Frances Perkins, 1961, CUOHRO, Pt. 4, pp. 96–100, 102; Works Progress Administration, *Washington*, p. 959.

3. Reminiscences of Frances Perkins, 1961, CUOHRO, Pt. 4, pp. 104–5, 108, 112; Martin, *Madam Secretary*, p. 24; Jonathan Grossman, *The Department of Labor* (New York: Praeger Publishers, 1973), p. 29; *New York Times*, 7/1/28; *New York Times*, 1/8/33; *Time*, 12/8/30; *Time*, 8/10/31.

4. Reminiscences of Frances Perkins, 1961, CUOHRO, Pt. 4, pp. 123, 127, 140–42.

5. Mohr, *That Woman*, pp. 129, 153; Letter from K. C. Adams to Franklin D. Roosevelt, January 30, 1933, in Ruth Backes Papers, Box 5, Folder 11; Carter, *New Dealers*, p. 174; Reminiscences of Frances Perkins, 1961, CUOHRO, Pt. 4, pp. 116–23; Martin, *Madam Secretary*, pp. 20–21, 25.

6. Reminiscences of Frances Perkins, 1961, CUOHRO, Pt. 4, pp. 117–23; Martin, *Madam Secretary*, pp. 20–21, 25, 27; *New York Times*, 3/22/33.

7. Martin, *Madam Secretary*, pp. 27–29; 245–46; *New York Times*, 3/22/33; Reminiscences of Frances Perkins, 1961, CUOHRO, Pt. 4, p. 212.

8. Reminiscences of Frances Perkins, 1961, CUOHRO, Pt. 4, pp. 206, 249.

9. Reminiscences of Frances Perkins, 1961, CUOHRO, Pt. 4, pp. 230–33.

10. Reminiscences of Charles E. Wyzanski, Jr., 1959, CUOHRO, pp. 183–84; Reminiscences of Frances Perkins, 1961, CUOHRO, Pt. 4, pp. 383–91.

11. Perkins, *The Roosevelt I Knew*, p. 152; *Washington Post*, 3/5/33; *Chicago Daily Tribune*, 1/30/33; *Time*, 8/14/33.

12. *New York Times*, 3/2/33; *New Yorker*, 9/9/33; Reminiscences of Frances Perkins, 1961, CUOHRO, Pt. 4, p. 253.

13. Severn, *Member of the Cabinet*, p. 10; *New Yorker*, 9/2/33; Matthew and Hannah Josephson, *Al Smith: Hero of the Cities* (Boston: Houghton, Mifflin Company, 1969), p. 104.

14. Martin, *Madam Secretary*, pp. 41–42; Severn, *Member of the Cabinet*, p. 10; Dewson, "An Aid to the End," p. 88; Josephson and Josephson, *Al Smith*, p. 104; Wolfskill and Hudson, *All but the People*, p. 50; Interview with Carol Lubin by Ruth Backes, Ruth Backes Papers, Box 12, Folder.

15. Martin, *Madam Secretary*, pp. 42–43; N.Y.S., "Outstanding Service to Mankind: Frances Perkins Labor Secretary," Department of Labor, Industrial Bulletin, February 1964; Ruth Backes, Interview with Allen Bloom, Ruth Backes Papers, Box 12, Folder 5; Perkins, *The Roosevelt I Knew*, p. 57.

16. Reminiscences of Frances Perkins, 1961, CUOHRO, Pt. 1, pp. 2–3; Reminiscences of Frances Perkins, 1961, CUOHRO, Pt. 3, pp. 652–53; Martin, *Madam Secretary*, pp. 5, 44.

17. Michael A. McGerr, *Fierce Discontent: The Rise and Fall of the Progressive Movement in America, 1870–1920* (New York: Free Press, 2003), p. 8; Harlow G. Unger, "Lyon, Mary," *Teachers and Educators* (New York: Facts on File, Inc., 1994); Reminiscences of Frances Perkins, 1961, CUOHRO, Pt. 1, p. 2; John D. Rockefeller, *Random Reminiscences of Men and Events* (Garden City, N.Y.: Doubleday, 1933), pp. 152–54; Martin, *Madam Secretary*, p. 50; Mohr, *That Woman*, p. 13; Manuscript Register, Annah May Soule Papers, Mount Holyoke College Archives and Special Collections; Manuscript Register, Frances Perkins Papers, Mount Holyoke College Archives and Special Collections; Reminiscences of Frances Perkins, 1961, CUOHRO, Pt. 1, p. 3; "Madam Secretary," *New Yorker*, 9/2/33, 9/9/33; Josephson and Josephson, *Al Smith*, pp. 106–7.

18. Martin, *Madam Secretary*, pp. 46–48, 52; Beatrice Siegel, *Lillian Wald of Henry Street* (New York: MacMillan Publishing Co., 1983), p. 51; Josephson and Josephson, *Al Smith*, pp. 106–7.

19. Martin, *Madam Secretary*, pp. 54, 57; Severn, *Member of the Cabinet*, pp. 18–20; Reminiscences of Frances Perkins, 1961, CUOHRO, Pt. 1, pp. 6, 22–23; Josephson and Josephson, *Al Smith*, pp. 104, 108–9; *New Yorker*, 9/2/33; *New York Times*, 5/15/65.

20. *New York Times*, 5/15/65; Josephson and Josephson, *Al Smith*, p. 104 and n.; *Saturday Evening Post*, 7/27/40; Jane Addams, *Eighty Years at Hull-House* (Chicago: Quadrangle Books, 1969), pp. 5, 15, 19; Jane Addams, *Twenty Years at Hull House*, (New York: Macmillan, 1910), p. 127; Margaret Tims, *Jane Addams of Hull House, 1860–1935* (New York: The MacMillan Co., 1961), p. 44; Allen F. Davis, *Spearheads for Reform: The Social Settlements and the Progressive Movement, 1890–1914* (New Brunswick, N.J.: Rutgers University Press, 1967), pp. x–xi, 17, 27, 29; Reminiscences of Frances Perkins, 1961, CUOHRO, Pt. 1, p. 7; Martin, *Madam Secretary*, p. 60; Josephson and Josephson, *Al Smith*, p. 108; *New York Times*, 2/24/33.

21. Addams, *Eighty Years*, pp. 68, 127, 136; Davis, *Spearheads for Reform*, p. 31.

22. Addams, *Twenty Years*, pp. 22–23, 40, 45, 48, 69; Davis, *Spearheads for Reform*, pp. 123–24; Alan Wolfe, "Becoming Jane Addams," *The New York Times Book Review*, 1/15/2006.

23. Reminiscences of Frances Perkins, 1961, CUOHRO, Pt. 1, pp. 9–14, 18–19.

24. Reminiscences of Frances Perkins, 1961, CUOHRO, Pt. 1, pp. 8–10, 12–14.

25. Reminiscences of Frances Perkins, 1961, CUOHRO, Pt. 1, pp. 19–21; Josephson and Josephson, *Al Smith*, p. 110; Letter of Frances Perkins to Susan Perkins, April 21, 1908, Perkins Papers, Frances Box 118.

26. Reminiscences of Frances Perkins, 1961, CUOHRO, Pt. 1, pp. 23–24, 26–28, 31–34; Ruth Backes, Interview with Allan Bloom, Ruth Backes Papers, Box 12, Folder 5; Namorato, *Tugwell*, p. 25; Mohr, *That Woman*, pp. 28–30.

27. Martin, *Madam Secretary*, pp. 72–74, 493–94; Mohr, *That Woman*, pp. 29–31, 33; Eliot Rosen, *Roosevelt, the Great Depression, and the Economics of Recovery* (Charlottesville: University of Virginia Press, 2005), p. 159; Tugwell, *Brains Trust*, p. 407; Alan Brinkley, *The End of Reform: New Deal Liberalism in Recession and War* (New York: Vintage, 1995), pp. 67–68; Namorato, *Tugwell*, p. 25; Davis, *FDR: The New York Years*, p. 168.

28. Ross Wetzsteon, *Republic of Dreams, Greenwich Village: The American Bohemia, 1910–1960* (New York: Simon & Schuster, 2002), pp. 3, 15, 48–50; Josephson and Josephson, *Al Smith*, pp. 113–14; Reminiscences of Frances Perkins, 1961, CUOHRO, Pt. 1, pp. 26, 37, 41; Martin, *Madam Secretary*, pp. 82–83.

29. Reminiscences of Frances Perkins, 1961, CUOHRO, Pt. 1, pp. 42–44; Martin, *Madam Secretary*, pp. 74, 77; *Muller v. Oregon*, 208 U.S. 412 (1908); Mohr, *That Woman*, p. 38; *New York Times*, 5/15/65; Seth D. Harris, "Convocation Inaugurating the Samuel M. Kaynard Distinguished Visiting Professorship in Labor and Employment Law: Conceptions of Fairness and the Fair Labor Standards Act," 18 *Hofstra Lab. Emp. L.J.* 19, (Fall 2000), pp. 46–48.

30. Philip S. Foner, *Women and the American Labor Movement: From Colonial Times to the Eve of World War I* (New York: Free Press, 1979), pp. 324–25; Reminiscences of Frances Perkins, 1961, CUOHRO, Pt. 1, pp. 43–44, 47–50.

31. Reminiscences of Frances Perkins, 1961, CUOHRO, Pt. 1, pp. 57–60; Ruth Backes, Interview with Alice Cook, Ruth Backes Papers, Box 12, Folder 9; Harris, "Convocation," pp. 51–53.

32. Reminiscences of Frances Perkins, 1961, CUOHRO, Pt. 1, pp. 76, 84, 92–93; Robert A. Slayton, *Empire Statesman: The Rise and Redemption of Al Smith* (New York: The Free Press, 2001), p. 86.

33. Slayton, *Empire Statesman*, p. 86.

34. Reminiscences of Frances Perkins, 1961, CUOHRO, Pt. 1, p. 126; *New York Times*, 3/26/11; *New Yorker*, 9/2/33; *World's Work*, April 1930, in Perkins Papers, Box 151.

35. Leon Stein, *Out of the Sweatshop: The Struggle for Industrial Democracy* (New York: Quadrangle / New Times Book Company, 1977), pp. 196–97; Reminiscences of Frances Perkins, 1961, CUOHRO, Pt. 1, pp. 130–32; Josephson and Josephson, *Al Smith*, p. 122–23.

36. Frances Perkins, *People at Work* (New York: The John Day Company, 1934), p. 50; Severn, *Frances Perkins*, p. 39.

37. Reminiscences of Frances Perkins, 1961, CUOHRO, Pt. 1, p. 132; Josephson and Josephson, *Al Smith*, pp. 124–29; Martin, *Madam Secretary*, p. 103; *New York Times*, 11/15/11.

38. Reminiscences of Frances Perkins, 1961, CUOHRO, Pt. 1, pp. 84, 92–114; Martin, *Madam Secretary*, pp. 91–100, 114; Josephson and Josephson, *Al Smith*, pp. 142; *New Yorker*, 9/2/33; Daniel Czitrom, "Underworlds and Underdogs: Big Tim Sullivan and Metropolitan Politics in New York," *The Journal of American History*, September 1991.

39. Tugwell, *Democratic Roosevelt*, pp. 74–80; Reminiscences of Frances Perkins, 1961, CUOHRO, Pt. 1, pp. 205–6; Martin, *Madam Secretary*, pp. 495–96; Perkins, *The Roosevelt I Knew*, pp. 9–14.

40. Josephson and Josephson, *Al Smith*, p. 129; *New York Times*, 12/6/12; *New York Times*, 10/6/12.

41. Reminiscences of Frances Perkins, 1961, CUOHRO, Pt. 1, pp. 137–44; Martin, *Madam Secretary*, pp. 88–90, 103–4; Lectures of Frances Perkins, Collection /3047, September 30, 1964, Cornell University, Kheel Center for Labor-Management Documentation and Archives, Ithaca, New York; Perkins, *The Roosevelt I Knew*, p. 22.

42. Josephson and Josephson, *Al Smith*, p. 138; David Von Drehle, *Triangle: The Fire That Changed America* (New York: Grove Press, 2003), p. 214–15; Martin, *Madam Secretary*, p. 108; *New York Times*, 7/18/12; *New York Times*, 3/5/13; *New York Times*, 3/24/11.

43. Letter of Frances Perkins to Paul Wilson, July 31, 1912, in Perkins Papers, Box 118.

44. Reminiscences of Frances Perkins, 1961, CUOHRO, Pt. 1, pp. 19–21, 370–73; *New York Times*, 2/25/48; Martin, *Madam Secretary*, p. 74; Mark Schorer, *Sinclair Lewis* (New York: McGraw Hill, 1961), pp. 192–93.

45. Letter of Paul Wilson to Frances Perkins, May 16, 1913, in Perkins Papers, Box 118; Letter of Paul Wilson to Frances Perkins, March 26, 1914, in Perkins Papers, Box 118; Martin, *Madam Secretary*, p. 125; Josephson and Josephson, *Al Smith*, p. 181; Reminiscences of Frances Perkins, 1961, CUOHRO, pt. 1, pp. 245–46.

46. Martin, *Madam Secretary*, pp. 122–26; Mohr, *That Woman*, pp. 56–57; Letter from Paul Wilson to Mrs. Wilson, September 20, 1913, in Perkins Papers, Box 118.

47. Josephson and Josephson, *Al Smith*, p. 152; *The Encyclopedia of New York City*, ed. Kenneth Jackson (New Haven: Yale University Press, 1995), pp. 764–65; *New York Times*, 12/14/14; *New York Times*, 10/23/15; *New York Times*, 10/18/15; *New York Times*, 10/17/15.

48. Martin, *Madam Secretary*, pp. 128–29, 134–35; *New York Times*, 9/17/17; Dewson, "An Aid to the End," p. 89; Tomlin Coggeshall Interview; Trattner, *From Poor Law to Welfare State*, p. 218.

49. Martin, *Madam Secretary*, pp. 132–33; *New York Times*, 7/7/18; Jackson, *Encyclopedia*, pp. 764–65; Robert Sherwood, *Roosevelt and Hopkins: An Intimate History* (New York: Harper & Brothers, 1948), p. 25.

50. Tomlin Coggeshall Interview; Reminiscences of Frances Perkins, 1961, CUOHRO, Pt. 3, pp. 488, 640–43; Martin, *Madam Secretary*, pp. 135–36.

51. Reminiscences of Frances Perkins, 1961, CUOHRO, Pt. 1, pp. 439–44; Josephson and Josephson, *Al Smith*, pp. 102, 194; Mohr, *That Woman*, p. 63.

52. Reminiscences of Frances Perkins, 1961, CUOHRO, Pt. 2, pp. 23–25; *New York Times*, 11/7/15; *New York Times*, 2/19/19.

53. Perkins, Work, April 1930, Perkins Papers, Box 151; Reminiscences of Frances Perkins, 1961, CUOHRO, Pt. 2, pp. 27–33; Reminiscences of Frances Perkins, 1961, CUOHRO, Pt. 4, p. 114–16; Martin, *Madam Secretary*, pp. 151–62; Slayton, *Empire Statesman*, p. 182; *New York Times*, 7/17/19.

54. Perkins, *The Roosevelt I Knew*, pp. 9–12; Reminiscences of Frances Perkins, 1961, CUOHRO, Pt. 2, pp. 62–63, 67–69.

55. Martin, *Madam Secretary*, pp. 169–72; *New York Times*, 11/13/21; *New York Times*, 2/12/22; Reminiscences of Frances Perkins, 1961, CUOHRO, Pt. 2, 92–93.

56. Reminiscences of Frances Perkins, 1961, CUOHRO, Pt. 2, pp. 67–69, 385–86, 441–42; Josephson and Josephson, *Al Smith*, pp. 296–97; Mohr, *That Woman*, p. 76; Perkins, *The Roosevelt I Knew*, pp. 9–12.

57. Martin, *Madam Secretary*, pp. 184–85; Slayton, *Empire Statesman*, pp. 208–9, 214–15; 219–20; Perkins, *The Roosevelt I Knew*, p. 37; Josephson and Josephson, *Al Smith*, pp. 308, 317; Smith, *FDR*, pp. 209–12.

58. McGerr, *Fierce Discontent*, p. 316; Martin, *Madam Secretary*, pp. 186–90, 194; Laurence Tribe, *American Constitutional Law* (New York: The Foundation Press), pp. 311–12 and nn.; *Bailey v. Drexel Furniture Co.*, 259 U.S. 20 (1922); Jean Bethke Elshtain, *The Jane Addams Reader* (New York: Basic Books, 2001) p. 298.

59. Josephson and Josephson, *Al Smith*, pp. 325, 329–32, 342–43; Freidel, *Triumph*, p. 11; Frances Perkins, "Do Women in Industry Need Special Protection?" *The Survey*, February 15, 1926; *New York Times*, 1/8/25.

60. Perkins, *The Roosevelt I Knew*, pp. 41–43; Smith, *FDR*, 224–25; Reminiscences of Frances Perkins, 1961, CUOHRO, Pt. 3, p. 293.

61. Perkins, *The Roosevelt I Knew*, pp. 46–47; Martin, *Madam Secretary*, p. 204; Josephson and Josephson, *Al Smith*, pp. 380–81, 388–89; Christopher Breiseth, "The Frances Perkins I Knew," unpublished manuscript, Ruth Backes Papers, Box 4, Folder 2; Reminiscences of Frances Perkins, 1961, CUOHRO, Pt. 2, pp. 592, 673.

62. Perkins, *The Roosevelt I Knew*, pp. 44–45.

63. Ibid., p. 55; Mohr, *That Woman*, p. 79; Reminiscences of Frances Perkins, 1961, CUOHRO, Pt. 2, p. 723.

64. Perkins, *The Roosevelt I Knew*, pp. 57–59; Martin, *Madam Secretary*, pp. 206–7; *New York Times*, 12/25/28.

65. Frances Perkins, "My Job," *The Survey*, March 15, 1929; Frances Perkins, "Address to 66th Annual Convention of New York State Federation of Labor," Perkins Papers, Box 4; Mohr, *That Woman*, p. 83; *New York Times*, 2/1/29.

66. *FDR Papers*, Vol. 1, pp. 80–86, 221; Perkins, *The Roosevelt I Knew*, p. 91; Reminiscences of Frances Perkins, 1961, CUOHRO, Pt. 3, pp. 214–26; Reminiscences of Frances Perkins, 1961, CUOHRO, Pt. 3, pp. 168, 221, 572; *FDR Papers*, Vol. I, p. 83; *New York Times*, 1/2/24.

67. Reminiscences of Frances Perkins, 1961, CUOHRO, Pt. 3, pp. 214–26; Perkins, *The Roosevelt I Knew*, p. 91; Breiseth, "The Frances Perkins I Knew."

68. Reminiscences of Frances Perkins, 1961, CUOHRO, Pt. 3, pp. 453–55; Perkins, *The Roosevelt I Knew*, pp. 95–96; Davis, *FDR: The New York Years*, p. 151; Bellush, *Roosevelt as Governor of New York*, p. 128; *New York Times*, 1/22/30.

69. "Statement of Frances Perkins, Industrial Commissioner, State of New York, in Regard to the Release of the U.S. Public Employment Service that Employment in July had Shown a Definite Expansion,"

August 26, 1932, p. 1, Perkins Papers, Box 4; *The Roosevelt I Knew*, pp. 95–96; Martin, *Madam Secretary*, p. 213; *New York Times*, 1/23/30; *New York Times*, 2/6/31, Davis, *FDR: The New York Years*, pp. 155, 157; Reminiscences of Frances Perkins, 1961, CUOHRO, Pt. 3, pp. 453–57.

70. Perkins, *The Roosevelt I Knew*, pp. 100–101; *New York Times*, 3/31/30; Martin, *Madam Secretary*, pp. 214–16; Davis, *FDR: The New York Years*, p. 157; Bellush, *Roosevelt as Governor of New York*, p. 129.

71. Davis, *FDR: The New York Years*, p. 157; Perkins, *The Roosevelt I Knew*, pp. 100–101; *New York Times*, 3/25/30; *New York Times*, 4/21/30; *New York Times*, 5/11/30; *New York Times*, 11/16/30; Martin, *Madam Secretary*, pp. 214–16; Frances Perkins, Address to the League of Women Voters, "Constructive Measures to Avoid Unemployment Crisis" (draft), Perkins Papers, Box 4; "Excerpts from Address at Session on Stabilization, Relief and Economic Problems, at Second Annual Conference on Management Problems of Smaller Industries," p. 1, Perkins Papers, Box 4; Frances Perkins, "The Experience of New York Industries in Meeting the Industrial Depression," December 5, 1931, p. 1, Perkins Papers, Box 77; *New York Times*, 10/9/30; Freidel, *Triumph*, p. 135; Reminiscences of Frances Perkins, 1961, CUOHRO, Pt. 3, pp. 140–43.

72. Martin, *Madam Secretary*, pp. 214–16; *New York Times*, 11/14/30; *New York Times*, 11/16/30; Frances Perkins, "Unemployment Insurance: An American Plan to Protect Workers and Avoid the Dole," *Survey Graphic*, November 1931.

73. Reminiscences of Frances Perkins, 1961, CUOHRO, Pt. 3, pp. 171–75, 594; Perkins, *The Roosevelt I Knew*, pp. 100–110.

74. Frances Perkins, "Unemployment Insurance"; Martin, *Madam Secretary*, pp. 224–25; Severn, *Member of the Cabinet*, p. 103; Perkins, *The Roosevelt I Knew*, pp. 100–101, 107; *New York Times*, 3/23/31; *New York Times*, 3/25/31; *New York Times*, 3/26/31; "Conference of Governors on Unemployment," Albany, January 23–24, 1931, Perkins Papers, Box 4; Bellush, *Roosevelt as Governor of New York*, pp. 182–83; "Concerning Governor Roosevelt's Labor Record," p. 1, Perkins Papers, Box 4; Reminiscences of Frances Perkins, 1961, CUOHRO, Pt. 3, pp. 297–98; *New York Times*, 7/1/30; Freidel, *Triumph*, pp. 138–39; *Colliers*, 8/5/44; Davis, *FDR: The New York Years*, pp. 165–66.

75. Reminiscences of Frances Perkins, 1961, CUOHRO, pp. 277–85; Bellush, *Roosevelt as Governor of New York*, p. 168; Freidel, *Triumph*, pp. 80–81, 118–31, 165, 167; *FDR Papers*, Vol. I, p. 222; *New York Times*, 10/14/30.

76. *FDR Papers*, Vol. I, pp. 100–110; *FDR Papers*, Vol. II, pp. 225–26; Martin, *Madam Secretary*, pp. 225–26; Freidel, *Triumph*, pp. 184, 195–97; Perkins, *The Roosevelt I Knew*, pp. 104–8; Reminiscences of Frances Perkins, 1961, CUOHRO, Pt. 3, pp. 182–87; *New York Times*, 1/8/31; *New York Times*, 1/24/31; *New York Times*, 4/22/31; *New York Times*, 4/26/30; "Conference of Governors on Unemployment," Perkins Papers, Box 71.

77. *New York Times*, 8/29/31; *New York Times*, 9/27/31; Bellush, *Roosevelt as Governor of New York*, p. 140; Freidel, *Triumph*, pp. 219–21; Rosenman, *Working with Roosevelt*, pp. 50, 52; Reminiscences of Samuel Rosenman, 1960, CUOHRO, pp. 59–60; *FDR Papers*, Vol. I, pp. 457–68.

78. Brock, *Welfare, Democracy, and the New Deal*, pp. 94–102; George McJimsey, *Harry Hopkins: Ally of the Poor and Defender of Democracy* (Cambridge, Mass.: Harvard University Press, 1987), p. 45; Rosenman, *Presidential Style*, p. 301; Jeff Singleton, *The American Dole: Unemployment Relief and the Welfare State in the Great Depression* (Westport, Conn: Greenwood Press, 2000), pp. 76–78; June Hopkins, *Harry Hopkins: Sudden Hero, Brash Reformer* (New York: St. Martin's Press, 1999) pp. 154–56; Freidel, *Triumph*, pp. 221, 223 and n.

79. Frances Perkins, "Radio Address 'On behalf of the campaign of the National Democratic Committee for Roosevelt and Garner,'" St. Louis, October 25, 1932, p. 2; Frances Perkins, "Campaign Speech for Governor Roosevelt: 'Concerning Governor Roosevelt's labor and welfare programs,'" p. 3, Perkins Papers, Box 4; *New York Times*, 1/20/30; *New York Times*, 11/13/32; Reminiscences of Frances Perkins, 1961, CUOHRO, Pt. 3, p. 463; Reminiscences of Frances Perkins, 1961, CUOHRO, Pt. 3, pp. 295–96, 460–64; Josephson and Josephson, *Al Smith*, p. 428.

80. *FDR Papers*, Vol. I, pp. 786–89.

81. *Washington Post*, 11/6/32; Reminiscences of Frances Perkins, 1961, CUOHRO, Pt. 3, pp. 295–96, 503.

82. Dewson, "An Aid to the End," pp. 78–79; Letter of Mary Dewson to FDR, Dewson Box 4, Roosevelt,

Franklin D. 1928–1944, FDR Library; Notes of Agnes Leach interview by Joseph Lash, 12/13/67, Lash Box 44, FDR Library; E. Roosevelt, *This I Remember*, p. 5; Ruth Backes Interview with Allan Bloom, Ruth Backes Papers, Box 12, Folder 5; Freidel, *Launching the New Deal*, pp. 145, 156; *Los Angeles Times*, 3/2/33, 9/14/30; *Chicago Daily Tribune*, 1/29/33; Moley, *First New Deal*, pp. 73–74.

83. Tomlin Coggeshall Interview; Ruth Backes, Interview with Maurice Neufeld, Ruth Backes Papers, Box 12, Folder 12; Notes of Agnes Leach interview by Joseph Lash, 12/13/67, Lash Box 44, FDR Library; *New York Times*, 3/8/33; Reminiscences of Frances Perkins, 1961, CUOHRO, Pt. 3, pp. 560, 639–44, 646–47, 560; *Chicago Daily Tribune*, 1/29/33.

84. Reminiscences of Frances Perkins, 1961, CUOHRO, Pt. 3, pp. 522, 559, 643–44; *New York Times*, 12/11/32; "Letter of Felix Frankfurter to FDR," January 28, 1933, in PPF 140, Frankfurter, Felix, 1932–April 1933, FDR Library; Freidel, *Launching the New Deal*, p. 156; Frances Perkins, "The Cost of a Five-Dollar Dress," *Survey Graphic*, February 1933.

85. Reminiscences of Frances Perkins, 1961, CUOHRO, Pt. 3, pp. 519, 570; *Washington Post*, 2/5/33.

86. Reminiscences of Frances Perkins, 1961, CUOHRO, Pt. 3, pp. 570–75, 587–608; Frances Perkins, "Eight Years as Madam Secretary," *Fortune*, September 1941; *Collier's*, 8/5/44; Martin, *Madam Secretary*, pp. 239–41.

87. Martin, *Madam Secretary*, p. 241.

88. Reminiscences of Frances Perkins, 1961, CUOHRO, Pt. 3, pp. 639–47; Maurice Neufeld Diary, Ruth Backes Papers, Box 6, Folder 4.

89. *Washington Post*, 2/5/33; *Los Angeles Times*, 3/2/33; *Los Angeles Times*, 3/2/33; Reminiscences of Frances Perkins, 1961, CUOHRO, Pt. 4, p. 298; *The New Republic*, 3/8/33; Carter, *New Dealers*, p. 59.

90. *The New Republic*, 3/8/33; *New Yorker*, 9/9/33; Freidel, *Launching the New Deal*, p. 158.

91. Reminiscences of Frances Perkins, 1961, CUOHRO, Pt. 3, pp. 650–54; *Chicago Daily Tribune*, 4/3/33; *Los Angeles Times*, 3/3/33; *Los Angeles Times*, 3/2/33; Freidel, *Launching the New Deal*, p. 158; Mohr, *That Woman*, p. 2; *Saturday Evening Post*, 7/27/40.

92. *New Yorker*, 9/9/33; *Chicago Daily Tribune*, 3/4/33; *Chicago Daily Tribune*, 3/2/33; *Washington Post*, 3/2/33; *New York Times*, 3/2/33.

Chapter 7: "Just So We Get a Public Works Program"

1. Grossman, *Department of Labor* pp. 3, 9; Works Progress Administration, *Washington*, p. 960; Frances Perkins, "The Department of Labor as an Agency of Government," lecture to Cornell School of Industrial and Labor Relations, April 24, 1957, Ruth Backes Papers, Box 5, Folder 1.

2. Grossman, *Department of Labor*, pp. 12, 22–24, 29; Reminiscences of Frances Perkins, 1961, CUOHRO, Pt. 4, pp. 104–5, 108, 112; *New York Times*, 7/1/28; *New York Times*, 1/8/33; *Time*, 12/8/30; *Time*, 8/10/31; Perkins, "The Department of Labor as an Agency of Government."

3. Reminiscences of Frances Perkins, 1961, CUOHRO, Pt. 4, pp. 117–23; Martin, *Madam Secretary*, pp. 20–21, 25; Mohr, *That Woman*, pp. 129, 153; Carter, *New Dealers*, p. 174.

4. Peter H. Irons, *The New Deal Lawyers* (Princeton, N.J.: Princeton University Press, 1982), p. 23; Dewson, "An Aid to the End," p. 83; Mohr, *That Woman*, pp. 154–55; Grossman, *Department of Labor*, pp. 58–59.

5. Reminiscences of Frances Perkins, 1961, CUOHRO, Pt. 4, p. 133; Rexford Tugwell, Interview of Henry A. Wallace; Martin, *Madam Secretary*, pp. 302–3; Carter, *New Dealers*, pp. 169–70, 174.

6. Reminiscences of Frances Perkins, 1961, CUOHRO, Pt. 4, pp. 299–300; Severn, *Member of the Cabinet*, p. 112.

7. Reminiscences of Frances Perkins, 1961, CUOHRO, Pt. 4, pp. 303–4; Martin, *Madam Secretary*, pp. 251–52.

8. Reminiscences of Frances Perkins, 1961, CUOHRO, Pt. 4, pp. 308–11; Martin, *Madam Secretary*, pp. 253–54; *New York Times*, 6/26/21.

9. Reminiscences of Frances Perkins, 1961, CUOHRO, Pt. 4, pp. 67–70, 186–90.

10. Tully, *F.D.R.: My Boss*, p. 195; Mohr, *That Woman*, p. 3; Ickes, *Diary*, p. 407; Tugwell, *Brains Trust*, p. 78; Dewson, "An Aid to the End," pp. 83–84; *New York Times*, 5/7/33; *New York Times*, 5/15/65;

Louis Baldwin, *Women of Strength: Biographies of 106 Who Have Excelled in Traditionally Male Fields, A.D. 61 to the Present* (Jefferson, N.C.: McFarland, 1996), p. 24.

11. Reminiscences of Frances Perkins, 1961, CUOHRO, Pt. 4, pp. 148–51, 301; Mohr, *That Woman*, p. 148.

12. Reminiscences of Frances Perkins, 1961, CUOHRO, Pt. 4, pp. 148–53; *Washington Post*, 3/15/33; Martin, *Madam Secretary*, pp. 278–79; *New York Times*, 12/19/34; Ruth Backes, Interview with Gerard Dennis Reilly, Ruth Backes Papers, Box 12, Folder 13; *Time*, 8/21/33; Mohr, *That Woman*, pp. 36, 148–49; Carter, *New Dealers*, p. 69.

13. Martin, *Madam Secretary*, pp. 279–82; Reminiscences of Frances Perkins, 1961, CUOHRO, Pt. 6., p. 488; "All Saints Episcopal Convent," in Ruth Backes Papers, Box 4, Folder 2.

14. *FDR Papers*, Vol. II, pp. 82–83; Walter Lippmann, "Today and Tomorrow," *New York Herald Tribune*, 2/7/33; Badger, *FDR*, p. 86; Williams, *Federal Aid for Relief*, p. 49; Letter from Allen Burns, Executive Director of the Association of Community Chests and Councils, to Raymond Moley, March 23, 1933, Moley Papers, Box 63.

15. *FDR Papers*, Vol. II, pp. 19–20.

16. Reminiscences of Frances Perkins, 1961, CUOHRO, Pt. 4, pp. 468–70.

17. Reminiscences of Frances Perkins, 1961, CUOHRO, Pt. 4, pp. 501–3; Lewis Douglas draft reminiscences, "Budget Years," p. 4, Douglas Papers, Box 5.

18. Moley, *First New Deal*, p. 274; Freidel, *Launching the New Deal*, p. 430; Reminiscences of Frances Perkins, 1961, CUOHRO, Pt. 4, pp. 468–69.

19. Reminiscences of Frances Perkins, 1961, CUOHRO, Pt. 4, pp. 468–69; Harold Ickes, *Back to Work: The Story of the PWA* (New York: The MacMillan Co., 1935), pp. 5–6, 9; Leighninger, *Long-Range Public Investment*, p. 36; *The New Republic*, 3/15/33; *One Third of a Nation: Lorena Hickok Reports on the Great Depression*, ed. Richard Lowitt and Maurine Beasley (Urbana: University of Illinois Press, 1981), pp. xvii–xviii; Huthmacher, *Senator Robert F. Wagner*, pp. 61, 76–77, 89–90; *New York Times*, 4/15/33.

20. Reminiscences of Frances Perkins, 1961, CUOHRO, Pt. 4, pp. 468–70; Perkins, *The Roosevelt I Knew*, p. 269; Tugwell, *Diary*, p. 327.

21. Letter of Lewis Douglas to W. R. Mathews of December 29, 1932, in Douglas Papers, Box 238; Letter of Lewis Douglas to Franklin Roosevelt of January 19, 1933, in Douglas Papers, Box 238; Tugwell, *Diary*, p. 411; Reminiscences of Frances Perkins, 1961, CUOHRO, Pt. 4, pp. 468–69; James Sargent, Interview with Lewis Douglas, p. 42, Douglas Papers, Box 119, Folder 5; F. Roosevelt, *FDR: His Personal Letters*, p. 342; Browder and Smith, *Independent*, pp. 85, 96; Schlesinger, *Coming of the New Deal*, p. 9; Moley, *First New Deal*, p. 252; *New York Times*, 5/19/33.

22. Sargent, Interview with Lewis Douglas; Tugwell, *Roosevelt's Revolution*, p. 9; Tugwell, *Diary*, p. 411.

23. Reminiscences of Charles E. Wyzanski, Jr., 1959, CUOHRO, p. 175; Reminiscences of Frances Perkins, 1961, CUOHRO, Pt. 4, pp. 468–69, 471–72, 477–78; Ickes, *Back to Work*, pp. 5–6, 9; Hugh S. Johnson, *The Blue Eagle from Egg to Earth* (New York: Doubleday, Doran & Company, Inc., 1935), p. 189; *New York Times*, 4/15/33.

24. Reminiscences of Frances Perkins, 1961, CUOHRO, Pt. 4, pp. 471–72, 477–78; *New York Times*, 4/15/33; J. Hopkins, *Sudden Hero*, p. 161.

25. McJimsey, *Ally of the Poor*, pp. 45, 51–52; Reminiscences of Frances Perkins, 1961, CUOHRO, Pt. 4, pp. 471–77.

26. Perkins, *The Roosevelt I Knew*, pp. 184–85; Reminiscences of Frances Perkins, 1961, CUOHRO, Pt. 4, p. 474–75.

27. Letter from Lewis Douglas to Raymond Moley, May 4, 1964, Douglas Papers, Box 118; Moley, Diary, 3/24/33; Moley, *After Seven Years*, pp. 173–74; Moley, *First New Deal*, pp. 267–68; *FDR Papers*, Vol. I, p. 625; *FDR Papers*, Vol. II, p. 13; *Washington Post*, 3/12/33.

28. John Salmond, *The Civilian Conservation Corps, 1933–1942: A New Deal Case Study* (Durham, N.C.: Duke University Press, 1967), pp. 4–5, 8; Moley, *After Seven Years*, pp. 173–74; William James, *Memories and Studies* (New York Longmans, Green and Co., 1912), pp. 290–91; Letter from James Rolph, Governor of California to FDR, August 5, 1932, Moley Papers, Box 113; Moley, *First New Deal*, p. 268;

Reminiscences of Henry A. Wallace, 1951, CUOHRO, p. 243; Leslie Alexander Lacy, *The Soil Soldiers: The Civilian Conservation Corps in the Great Depression* (Radnor, Pa.: Chilton Book Company, 1976), p. 19; Tugwell, *Diary*, p. 388.

29. Memorandum from Franklin Delano Roosevelt to Raymond Moley, January 18, 1933 (enclosing report on a Florida program that proposed putting the unemployed to work outdoors), Moley Papers, Box 113; Moley, *After Seven Years*, pp. 173–74; Moley, *First New Deal*, p. 269; Freidel, *Triumph*, pp. 225–26; *FDR Papers*, Vol. II, p. 654; Tugwell, *Diary*, pp. 387–88; Reminiscences of Henry A. Wallace, 1951, CUOHRO, p. 243; Salmond, *Civilian Conservation Corps*, pp. 3–5, 8; Tully, *F.D.R.: My Boss*, p. 17; Blum, *Morgenthau Diaries*, p. 26.

30. Salmond, *Civilian Conservation Corps*, pp. 3–4; Moley, *First New Deal*, p. 269; F. Roosevelt, *On Our Way*, p. 40.

31. Moley, *First New Deal*, p. 269.

32. Frances Perkins, "Memorandum for the Cabinet Meeting, March 31, 1933, Perkins Papers, Box 64; Moley, *First New Deal*, p. 268; Moley, Diary, 3/14/33; Reminiscences of Frances Perkins, 1961, CUOHRO, Pt. 4, p. 480; Freidel, *Launching the New Deal*, p. 258; Breiseth, "The Frances Perkins I Knew"; Sargent, *Roosevelt and the Hundred Days*, p. 110; Perkins, *The Roosevelt I Knew*, p. 177.

33. Memorandum for the Secretary of War, the Secretary of the Interior, the Secretary of Agriculture, and the Secretary of Labor, March 14, 1933, OF 15, Department of Labor, Box 1, FDR Library; Moley, *After Seven Years*, pp. 173–74; Reminiscences of Frances Perkins, 1961, CUOHRO, Pt. 4, pp. 481–83, 504; Salmond, *Civilian Conservation Corps*, p. 11; Moley, *First New Deal*, p. 268–69.

34. Moley, Diary, 3/24/33; Letter from Lewis Douglas to Raymond Moley, May 4, 1964, Douglas Papers, Box 118; Presidential Press Conference, March 15, 1933, *Complete Presidential Press Conferences*; Freidel, *Launching the New Deal*, p. 259.

35. Moley, *After Seven Days*, pp. 174–75; Moley, *First New Deal*, p. 269; Presidential Press Conference, March 17, 1933, *Complete Presidential Press Conferences*.

36. *Washington Post*, 3/22/33; *Chicago Tribune*, 4/3/33.

37. Reminiscences of Frances Perkins, 1961, CUOHRO, Pt. 4, pp. 347–48, 367–68; Dewson, "An Aid to the End," p. 87; *New York Times*, 3/8/1933.

38. Reminiscences of Frances Perkins, 1961, CUOHRO, Pt. 4, pp. 239, 343–56, 368; Smith, *FDR*, pp. 309–10; Dewson, "An Aid to the End," p. 87.

39. Ruth Backes, Interview of Allan Bloom; Dewson, "An Aid to the End," p. 87; Reminiscences of Frances Perkins, 1961, CUOHRO, Pt. 4, pp. 239, 342–45, 368; *Collier's*, 8/5/44; Grossman, *Department of Labor*, p. 58.

40. Freidel, *Launching the New Deal*, pp. 259–60 and n.; *FDR Papers*, Vol. II, pp. 80–81; Moley, *First New Deal*, pp. 270–71.

41. *FDR Papers*, Vol. II, pp. 80–81.

42. Ibid.

43. Jordan A. Schwarz, *The Interregnum of Despair: Hoover, Congress, and the Depression* (Urbana: University of Illinois Press, 1970), pp. 168–69.

44. *New York Times*, 3/22/33; *Time*, 4/3/33; Salmond, *Civilian Conservation Corps*, p. 14.

45. Salmond, *Civilian Conservation Corps*, pp. 14–15.

46. Ibid., pp. 7, 16; *New York Times*, 3/24/33; *Washington Post*, 3/24/33; *New York Times*, 3/30/33.

47. *Time*, 4/3/33; Reminiscences of Frances Perkins, 1961, CUOHRO, Pt. 4, pp. 491–92.

48. Salmond, *Civilian Conservation Corps*, pp. 16–18; *New York Times*, 3/25/33.

49. Moley, Diary, 3/24/33; Sargent, *Roosevelt and the Hundred Days*, p. 75.

50. Presidential Press Conferences, March 24, 1933, Complete Presidential Press Conferences; Lewis Douglas, Memorandum of December 30, 1933, in President's Personal File, File 1914 (Lewis Douglas), FDR Library; Freidel, *Launching the New Deal*, pp. 260–61; Sargent, *Roosevelt and the Hundred Days*, pp. 167–69; Letter of Lewis Douglas to James Sargent, March 19, 1973, Douglas Papers, Box 119.

51. *FDR Papers*, Vol. II, pp. 95–96; Salmond, *Civilian Conservation Corps*, pp. 20, 23, 88; *New York Times*, 3/30/33; *Washington Post*, 3/26/33.

52. Salmond, *Civilian Conservation Corps*, pp. 26–29; Martin, *Madam Secretary*, p. 251; Reminiscences of Frances Perkins, 1961, CUOHRO, Pt. 4, p. 493; *FDR Papers*, Vol. II, pp. 107–9.

53. *FDR Papers*, Vol. II, pp. 107–9; Salmond, *Civilian Conservation Corps*, pp. 27–28, 30–31; Lacy, *Soil Soldiers*, p. 20; Dickson and Allen, *Bonus Army*, p. 208.

54. Reminiscences of Frances Perkins, 1961, CUOHRO, Pt. 4, pp. 311–12; "Agenda for the Labor Conference," Perkins Papers, Box 71; Press Release, "For Release to Morning Papers, March 23, 1933," Perkins Papers, Box 71.

55. Reminiscences of Frances Perkins, 1961, CUOHRO, Pt. 4, pp. 312–16; *New York Times*, 4/1/33; *New York Times*, 3/31/33.

56. Reminiscences of Frances Perkins, 1961, CUOHRO, Pt. 4, pp. 312–18; *New York Times*, 4/1/33.

57. Deborah C. Malamud, "Engineering the Middle Classes: Class Line-Drawing in New Deal Hours Legislation," *Michigan Law Review* 96 (August 1998), pp. 2212, 2234; Newman, *Hugo Black*, p. 157; Freidel, *Triumph*, p. 418; Lindley, *Roosevelt Revolution*, p. 113; *New York Times*, 4/9/33; *New York Times*, 4/8/33; *New York Times*, 4/7/33; *Time*, 4/17/33.

58. Reminiscences of Frances Perkins, 1961, CUOHRO, Pt. 4, pp. 439–48, 450–52; *New York Times*, 4/9/33; Newman, *Hugo Black*, pp. 144–45; Martin, *Madam Secretary*, pp. 260–61; Perkins, *The Roosevelt I Knew*, pp. 192–94; *New York Times*, 4/8/33; *New York Times*, 4/7/33.

59. Reminiscences of Frances Perkins, 1961, CUOHRO, Pt. 4, pp. 440–48, 450–52; Perkins, *The Roosevelt I Knew*, pp. 192–93.

60. Newman, *Hugo Black*, p. 156; Harris, "Convocation," pp. 104–5; *New York Times*, 4/7/33; *New York Times*, 4/8/33; *New York Times*, 4/9/33; *Time*, 4/17/33; David Roediger and Philip Foner, *Our Own Time: A History of American Labor and the Working Day* (New York: Verso, 1997), p. 247.

61. *New York Times*, 4/13/33; *New York Times*, 4/16/33, 4/21/33; *Time*, 4/24/33.

62. Sargent, *Roosevelt and the Hundred Days*, p. 124; *FDR Papers*, Vol. II, p. 141; *New York Times*, 4/13/33; *New York Times*, 4/14/33; *New York Times*, 4/15/33; *New York Times*, 4/21/33.

63. Ickes, *Back to Work*, p. 13; Lindley, *Roosevelt Revolution*, p. 155; Martin, *Madam Secretary*, pp. 261–62; *New York Times*, 4/18/33; *New York Times*, 4/19/33; *New York Times*, 4/20/33; *New York Times*, 5/2/33; *Time*, 4/17/33.

64. Lindley, *Roosevelt Revolution*, p. 155; Martin, *Madam Secretary*, pp. 262–63; *New York Times*, 4/26/33; *New York Times*, 4/27/33; *New York Times*, 5/11/33.

65. "Radio Address by Secretary of Agriculture Henry A. Wallace," April 1, 1933, Wallace Papers, Box S1; Report of the Honorable Harry L. Hopkins, Federal Emergency Relief Administrator, July 18, 1933, Hopkins Papers, Box 43, FDR Library; Frances Perkins, "Radio Speech: 'Emergency Conservation Work,'" July 17, 1933, Perkins Papers, Box 46; Lacy, *Soil Soldiers*, pp. 24–25; Lindley, *Roosevelt Revolution*, pp. 103–4, 275; Perry H. Merrill, *Roosevelt's Forest Army: A History of the Civilian Conservation Corps* (Montpelier, Vt.: Perry H. Merrill, 1981), pp. 9, 11–15, 55; Freidel, *Launching the New Deal*, p. 264; Salmond, *Civilian Conservation Corps*, pp. 31–32; Sargent, *Roosevelt and the Hundred Days*, p. 261; *Time*, 4/17/33.

66. Merrill, *Roosevelt's Forest Army*, pp. 58, 60, 92–93, 95, 97–98; Tugwell, *Democratic Roosevelt*, pp. 278–79.

67. Joint Statement by Mrs. Roosevelt and the Secretary of Labor, June 1, 1933, OF 15, Dept. of Labor, Box 1, FDR Library; Monthly Report of the Federal Emergency Relief Administration, OF 444 FERA, FDR Library; *New York Times*, 5/1/33; Freidel, *Launching the New Deal*, p. 265; *New York Times*, 8/27/33; Salmond, *Civilian Conservation Corps*, pp. 33–34; Leighninger, *Long-Range Public Investment*, pp. 15–18; Lacy, *Soil Soldiers*, pp. 74–77.

68. Dickson and Allen, *Bonus Army*, pp. 207–23; Rollins, *Roosevelt and Howe*, p. 386; Schlesinger, *Coming of the New Deal*, p. 15.

69. Rollins, *Roosevelt and Howe*, pp. 386–88; Dickson and Allen, *Bonus Army*, pp. 215–16; Schlesinger, *Coming of the New Deal*, p. 15; Cook, *Eleanor Roosevelt*, Vol. II, pp. 45–46; Smith, *FDR*, pp. 282, 329–30; E. Roosevelt, *This I Remember*, pp. 112–13; Salmond, *Civilian Conservation Corps*, p. 36; Frank Friedel, Interview of Eleanor Roosevelt, Small Collections Oral History, FDR Library.

70. Stott, "FDR, Lewis Douglas, and the Raw Deal"; Dickson and Allen, *Bonus Army*, pp. 216, 220; Smith, *FDR*, pp. 329–30; *New York Times*, 5/12/33; *New York Times*, 5/13/33.

71. Moley, *After Seven Years*, pp. 184–85; Sternsher, *Rexford Tugwell and the New Deal*, pp. 154–57; Freidel, *Launching the New Deal*, p. 409; Schlesinger, *Coming of the New Deal*, p. 93; Moley, *After Seven Years*, p. 370.

72. Rexford G. Tugwell, "Planning Must Replace Laissez Faire," in Zinn, *New Deal Thought*, p. 88; Moley, *After Seven Years*, pp. 184–85; Sternsher, *Rexford Tugwell and the New Deal*, pp. 9, 154–57, 351; Freidel, *Launching the New Deal*, p. 409; Schlesinger, *Coming of the New Deal*, pp. 93; Josephson, *Infidel*, p. 60.

73. Moley, *After Seven Years*, pp. 184–85, 370; Sternsher, *Rexford Tugwell and the New Deal*, p. 156; Lindley, *Roosevelt Revolution*, pp. 156–57; *FDR Papers*, Vol. I, p. 752; Letter of Henry Harriman to Franklin Roosevelt, May 11, 1933, Of 466, Box 1 (NRA Jan.–May 1933), FDR Library.

74. Reminiscences of Frances Perkins, 1961, CUOHRO, Pt. 3, pp. 593–94; Pt. 5, pp. 10–11, 28–29; Tugwell, *Roosevelt's Revolution*, p. 210; Tugwell, *In Search of Roosevelt*, p. 301; *Hammer v. Dagenhart*, 247 U.S. 251 (1918); *Lochner v. New York*, 198 U.S. 45 (1905).

75. *FDR Papers*, Vol. I, pp. 752, 784; Tugwell, *Democratic Roosevelt*, pp. 91, 142–43; Sternsher, *Rexford Tugwell and the New Deal*, pp. 156–57; *New York Times*, 7/19/22.

76. Memorandum to Raymond Moley from Adolf Berle, November 10, 1932, Moley Papers, Box 63; Tugwell, *Diary*, pp. 293–94; Rosen, *Brain Trust*, p. 118; *New York Times*, 4/14/33; Freidel, *Launching the New Deal*, pp. 422–23; Moley, *First New Deal*, pp. 286–91; Badger, *FDR*, p. 89; Moley, *After Seven Years*, pp. 185–88; Schlesinger, *Coming of the New Deal*, pp. 88–89, 97; Freidel, *Triumph*, pp. 409–10, 416–17; Letter of Henry Harriman to Franklin Roosevelt, May 11, 1933.

77. Sternsher, *Rexford Tugwell and the New Deal*, p. 157; Johnson, *The Blue Eagle*, pp. 193, 196; Freidel, *Launching the New Deal*, pp. 423–24; *New York Times*, 5/11/33; Moley, *After Seven Years*, p. 188; Freidel, *Triumph*, pp. 417, 423; "Notes of Raymond Moley and Hugh Johnson Expressing Ideas that Led to NRA," March 9, 1933, Moley Papers, Box 282; Badger, *FDR*, p. 93; Carter, *New Dealers*, pp. 31–32.

78. Johnson, *The Blue Eagle*, pp. 172–73, 193, 196; Sternsher, *Rexford Tugwell and the New Deal*, p. 157; Freidel, *Launching the New Deal*, pp. 423–24; Moley, *After Seven Years*, p. 188; Lindley, *Roosevelt Revolution*, p. 160; *New York Times*, 5/11/33.

79. Reminiscences of Frances Perkins, 1961, CUOHRO, Pt. 5, pp. 19–20; Johnson, *The Blue Eagle*, p. 193; Sternsher, *Rexford Tugwell and the New Deal*, p. 157; Huthmacher, *Senator Robert F. Wagner*, pp. 145–47; Freidel, *Launching the New Deal*, pp. 423–24; Sargent, *Roosevelt and the Hundred Days*, p. 200; Tugwell, *Diary*, p. 351.

80. James Sargent, Interview with Lewis Douglas, p. 58, Douglas Papers, Box 119, Folder 5; Perkins, *The Roosevelt I Knew*, pp. 198–99, 269–70; Reminiscences of Frances Perkins, 1961, CUOHRO, Pt. 4, pp. 499–500, 506–7, 535–36; Pt. 5, pp. 28–30, 34–35.

81. Reminiscences of Frances Perkins, 1961, CUOHRO, Pt. 5, pp. 54–69; Perkins, *The Roosevelt I Knew*, pp. 199–200; Leuchtenburg, *Franklin D. Rooosevelt and the New Deal*, pp. 56–57; Schlesinger, *Coming of the New Deal*, pp. 90, 136; Martin, *Madam Secretary*, p. 263; Francis Perkins Lecture of December 16, 1957, Cornell School of Industrial and Labor Relations, Ruth Backes Papers, Box 5, Folder 1; Reminiscences of Frances Perkins, 1961, CUOHRO, Pt. 5, pp. 62–63; Huthmacher, *Senator Robert F. Wagner*, p. 145; Badger, *FDR*, pp. 90–91; Carter, *New Dealers*, p. 58.

82. Perkins, *The Roosevelt I Knew*, pp. 198–99, 269–70; Reminiscences of Frances Perkins, 1961, CUOHRO, Pt. 4, pp. 499–500, 506–7, 535–36; Pt. 5, pp. 28–29, 34–35; James Sargent, Interview with Lewis Douglas, p. 58, Douglas Papers, Box 119, Folder 5.

83. Reminiscences of Frances Perkins, 1961, CUOHRO, Pt. 4, p. 536; Reminiscences of Frances Perkins, 1961, CUOHRO, Pt. 5, pp. 10–11.

84. Ickes, *Diary*, p. 11; Reminiscences of Henry A. Wallace, 1951, CUOHRO, p. 199.

85. Letter from Wallace to Louis Howe, April 28, 1933, Wallace Papers, Reel 18, Frame 846, FDR Library; Letter of Henry Wallace to Dante Pierce, June 19, 1933, Wallace Papers, Reel 18, Frame 895, FDR Library; Tugwell, *Diary*, pp. 324, 359; Letter from Lewis Douglas to James Douglas, April 23, 1933,

Douglas Papers, Box 239, Folder 4; Freidel, *Launching the New Deal*, p. 251; Reminiscences of Henry A. Wallace, 1951, CUOHRO, p. 199.

86. James Sargent, Interview with Lewis Douglas, pp. 45–46, Douglas Papers, Box 119, Folder 5; Letter from Lewis Douglas to James Douglas, April 23, 1933.

87. Lewis Douglas draft reminiscences, "Budget Years," p. 4, Douglas Papers, Box 5; Browder and Smith, *Independent*, pp. 96–97; *New York Times*, 4/24/33.

88. Browder and Smith, *Independent*, p. 97; Farley, *Behind the Ballots*, p. 218.

89. Ickes, *Diary*, p. 28; Moley, *First New Deal*, pp. 273–74; *New York Times*, 5/2/33; Reminiscences of Charles E. Wyzanski, Jr., 1959, CUOHRO, pp. 152–53; Charles Wyzanski, Letter to Parents, April 29, 1933, in Freidel, *Launching the New Deal*, p. 431; *FDR Papers*, Vol. II, p. 141.

90. Ickes, *Back to Work*, p. 14; Sargent, *Roosevelt and the Hundred Days*, p. 205.

91. *FDR Papers*, Vol. II, pp. 160–68; Sargent, *Roosevelt and the Hundred Days*, pp. 203–4; Moley, *First New Deal*, p. 290.

92. *FDR Papers*, Vol. II, pp. 164–68; Sargent, *Roosevelt and the Hundred Days*, pp. 203–4.

93. *New York Times*, 5/7/33.

94. Tugwell, *Diary*, pp. 350–51; Schlesinger, *Coming of the New Deal*, pp. 97–99; Ickes, *Diary*, p. 34; Huthmacher, *Senator Robert F. Wagner*, pp. 147–48; Sargent, *Roosevelt and the Hundred Days*, p. 205.

95. Tugwell, *Diary*, p. 351; Huthmacher, *Senator Robert F. Wagner*, p. 147; Sargent, *Roosevelt and the Hundred Days*, p. 206; Johnson, *The Blue Eagle*, p. 204; Reminiscences of Frances Perkins, 1961, CUOHRO, Pt. 5, p. 52–53; *New York Times*, 5/11/33.

96. Reminiscences of Charles E. Wyzanski, Jr., 1959, CUOHRO, p. 175.

97. Reminiscences of Frances Perkins, 1961, CUOHRO, Pt. 4, pp. 460–61.

98. Ibid.

99. Ibid., p. 461–63.

100. Reminiscences of Frances Perkins, 1961, CUOHRO, Pt. 5, pp. 54–69; Perkins, *The Roosevelt I Knew*, pp. 199–200; Huthmacher, *Senator Robert F. Wagner*, p. 147; Freidel, *Launching the New Deal*, p. 422; Leuchtenburg, *Franklin D. Roosevelt and the New Deal*, pp. 56–57; Francis Perkins Lecture of December 16, 1957, Cornell School of Industrial and Labor Relations, Ruth Backes Papers, Box 5, Folder 1; Badger, *FDR* pp. 90–91.

101. Reminiscences of Frances Perkins, 1961, CUOHRO, Pt. 5, pp. 75–85; Browder and Smith, *Independent*, p. 96; Moley, *After Seven Years*, p. 175.

102. Reminiscences of Frances Perkins, 1961, CUOHRO, Pt. 5, pp. 80–82.

103. Ibid., pp. 80–83.

104. Reminiscences of Frances Perkins, 1961, CUOHRO, Pt. 3, p. 593; *Hammer v. Dagenhart*, 247 U.S. 251 (1918); Freidel, *Launching the New Deal*, pp. 432–33; Schlesinger, *Coming of the New Deal*, pp. 98–99; Black, *Roosevelt*, p. 286; *New York Times*, 5/18/33, 5/19/33; *Time*, 5/29/33.

105. *FDR Papers*, Vol. II, pp. 202–4; Sargent, *Roosevelt and the Hundred Days*, pp. 206–7; *New York Times*, 5/18/33.

106. *New York Times*, 5/18/33, 5/19/33, 5/20/33, 5/24/33.

107. Schlesinger, *Coming of the New Deal*, p. 99; Freidel, *Launching the New Deal*, p. 447; *New York Times*, 4/23/33; *New York Times*, 5/23/33; *New York Times*, 5/27/33; *Chicago Daily Tribune*, 5/27/33.

108. *New York Times*, 6/7/33; *Time*, 6/13/33.

109. Schlesinger, *Coming of the New Deal*, pp. 99–100; Freidel, *Launching the New Deal*, pp. 444–50; *New York Times*, 6/4/33; Melvyn Dubofsky, *The State and Labor* (Chapel Hill: The University of North Carolina Press, 1994), p. 112.

110. Schlesinger, *Coming of the New Deal*, pp. 99–102; *Time*, 6/13/33, 6/19/33; *New York Times*, 5/23/33, 6/7/33, 6/8/33, 6/9/33, 6/14/33.

111. Perkins, *The Roosevelt I Knew*, pp. 200–201; Martin, *Madam Secretary*, pp. 269–270; Reminiscences of Frances Perkins, 1961, CUOHRO, Pt. 5, pp. 18–22; James Sargent, Interview with Lewis Douglas.

112. Martin, *Madam Secretary*, pp. 270–72, 274–75; Johnson, *The Blue Eagle*, p. 208; Sargent, *Roosevelt and the Hundred Days*, p. 7; Perkins, *The Roosevelt I Knew*, p. 201; Reminiscences of Frances Perkins, 1961, CUOHRO, Pt. 5, pp. 99, 147–151.

113. Tugwell, *Roosevelt's Revolution*, p. 80; Moley, *First New Deal*, p. 291; Moley, *After Seven Days*, p. 189; Schlesinger, *Coming of the New Deal*, p. 98; *New York Times*, 5/8/33; *New York Times*, 5/4/33.

CHAPTER 8: "HE MUST BE PART OF THIS HISTORIC SHOW"

1. James T. Patterson, *America's Struggle Against Poverty, 1900–1985* (Cambridge, Mass.: Harvard University Press, 1981), pp. 20–21, 58; Williams, *Federal Aid for Relief*, p. 9.

2. Trattner, *From Poor Law to Welfare State*, p. 273; Brock, *Welfare, Democracy, and the New Deal*, p. 133, Williams, *Federal Aid for Relief*, p. 15.

3. Hopkins, *Spending to Save*, pp. 44, 59; Sherwood, *Roosevelt and Hopkins*, p. 46; Myers and Newton, *Hoover Administration*, p. 63; Theodore Whiting, *Final Statistical Report of the Federal Emergency Relief Administration* (Washington, D.C.: United States Government Printing Office, 1942), p. 2; Schwarz, *Interregnum*, p. 31–32, 150; Williams, *Federal Aid for Relief*, p. 22; Trattner, *From Poor Law to Welfare State*, p. 277.

4. Hearings Before a Subcommittee of the Committee on Manufactures, United States Senate, 72nd Congress, Second Session, on S. 5125, Pt. 1, Jan. 3 to 17, 1933, p. 107, in Hopkins Papers, Box 42; *FDR Papers*, Vol. II, pp. 82–83; Brock, *Welfare, Democracy, and the New Deal*, pp. 136–39; Schwartz, *The Civilian Works Administration*, p. 21; *Washington Post*, 3/5/33.

5. Brock, *Welfare, Democracy, and the New Deal*, pp. 169–171; Arthur E. Burns and Edward A. Williams, *Federal Work, Security, and Relief Programs* (Washington, D.C.: U.S. Government Printing Office, 1941); pp. 19, 22; Huthmacher, *Senator Robert F. Wagner*, pp. 140–41; J. Hopkins, *Sudden Hero*, p. 161; Williams, *Federal Aid for Relief*, pp. 62–63.

6. *FDR Papers*, Vol. I, pp. 463, 777; Moley, *First New Deal*, p. 267.

7. Huthmacher, *Senator Robert F. Wagner*, pp. 140–141; Schlesinger, *Coming of the New Deal*, pp. 264–65; Schwarz, *Interregnum*, p. 56.

8. Reminiscences of Frances Perkins, 1961, CUOHRO, Pt. 4, pp. 476–79; Telegram from Franklin D. Roosevelt to Herbert H. Lehman of May 19, 1933, OF 444, FERA, FDR Library; McJimsey, *Ally of the Poor*, p. 52.

9. J. Hopkins, *Sudden Hero*, pp. 10–13; McJimsey, *Ally of the Poor*, p. 3; *New Yorker*, 8/14/43; Sherwood, *Roosevelt and Hopkins*, pp. 14–15.

10. J. Hopkins, *Sudden Hero*, pp. 13–16, 21; McJimsey, *Ally of the Poor*, pp. 4, 39; *Fortune*, July 1935; Sherwood, *Roosevelt and Hopkins*, p. 15; *New Yorker*, 8/14/43, p. 27.

11. McJimsey, *Ally of the Poor*, p. 7; J. Hopkins, *Sudden Hero*, pp. 13–16, 21; *Fortune*, July 1935; *The Nation*, 12/4/48.

12. Sherwood, *Roosevelt and Hopkins*, pp. 14–15, 49; *The Nation*, 12/4/48.

13. J. Hopkins, *Sudden Hero*, pp. 18–19, 21, 25; McJimsey, *Ally of the Poor*, pp. 5, 8–10, 21–25; Works Progress Adminstration, *Iowa: A Guide to the Hawkeye State*, Compiled and Written by the Federal Writers' Project of the Works Progress Administration for the State of Iowa (New York: The Viking Press, 1938), p. 52; Jackson, *Encyclopedia of New York*, p. 1060.

14. Sherwood, *Roosevelt and Hopkins*, pp. 16–17, 21–22; *New Yorker*, 8/14/43; *Fortune*, July 1935, p. 60–61; Reminiscences of Frances Perkins, 1961, CUOHRO, Pt. 3, pp. 13–33; Hopkins, *Spending to Save*, p. 4; McJimsey, *Ally of the Poor*, pp. 9, 12, 17; J. Hopkins, *Sudden Hero*, pp. 29, 31–32.

15. Christodora House, Christodora House Papers, Box 3, Folder 1, Columbia University; Northover Camp, Information for Staff Members, Christodora House Papers, Box 4, Folder 11, *New Yorker*, 8/14/43; Sherwood, *Roosevelt and Hopkins*, p. 22; J. Hopkins, *Sudden Hero*, pp. 31–33. *New York Times*, 8/25/22; *New York Times*, 12/23/28.

16. "History of Christodora House," as Told by C. I. MacColl to a Group of Residents, November 19, 1933, in Christodora House Papers, Box 3, Folder 1; J. Hopkins, *Sudden Hero*, pp. 35–37; Jackson, *Encylopedia of New York City*, p. 220; Allison Giffen and June Hopkins, *Jewish First Wife, Divorced: The Correspondence of Ethel Gross and Harry Hopkins* (Lanham, Md.: Lexington Books, 2002), p. 4.

17. Edward Steiner, "Christodora, 1897–1940," unpubl. manuscript, n.d., Christodora House Papers, Box

3, Folder 3; untitled article, Christodora House Papers; Box 4, Folder 10; *Christodora Yearbook 1915*, p. 11, Christodora House Papers, Box 1, Folder 12.

18. Irving Howe, *World of Our Fathers: The Journey of the Eastern European Jews to America and the Life They Found and Made* (New York: Simon and Schuster, 1976), pp. 148, 545; Jackson, *Encyclopedia of New York City*, pp. 432, 696, 770.

19. *Christodora Yearbook 1915*, p. 25–27; *New Yorker*, 8/14/43; Sherwood, *Roosevelt and Hopkins*, p. 23.

20. Hutchins Hapgood, *The Spirit of the Ghetto: Studies of the Jewish Quarter of New York* (New York: Schocken Books, 1976), pp. 76–85; J. Hopkins, *Sudden Hero*, pp. 44–47, *Fortune*, July 1935; Sherwood, *Roosevelt and Hopkins*, p. 23; McJimsey, *Ally of the Poor*, p. 18.

21. *Fortune*, July 1935; McJimsey, *Ally of the Poor*, p. 18; Giffen and Hopkins, *Jewish First Wife*, pp. 3–4, 9, 22, 27 n., 34.

22. J. Hopkins, *Sudden Hero*, pp. 50–51; Giffen and Hopkins, *Jewish First Wife*, pp. 2, 10, 34.

23. Sherwood, *Roosevelt and Hopkins*, pp. 23–27; *Fortune*, July 1935; *New Yorker*, 8/14/43; McJimsey, *Ally of the Poor*, pp. 22, 36–37; *New York Times*, 2/1/14, *New York Times*, 11/18/13, 1/30/14; J. Hopkins, *Sudden Hero*, pp. 50, 57, 110.

24. Sherwood, *Roosevelt and Hopkins*, pp. 24–25; J. Hopkins, *Sudden Hero*, pp. 61–64; McJimsey, *Ally of the Poor*, pp. 20–21; *New York Times*, 3/1/14.

25. McJimsey, *Ally of the Poor*, pp. 22–23; J. Hopkins, *Sudden Hero*, pp. 65, 67–68, 110–15, 126; *Fortune*, July 1935.

26. Sherwood, *Roosevelt and Hopkins*, pp. 26–27; McJimsey, *Ally of the Poor*, pp. 23–24, 24–29; Giffen and Hopkins, *Jewish First Wife*, pp. 10–15, 141, 153; *Fortune*, July 1935; J. Hopkins, *Sudden Hero*, pp. 127–28, 144.

27. Letter from Linsly Williams to Harry Hopkins, June 7, 1933, Harry Hopkins Papers, Container 7, Pre-Works Progress Papers, FDR Library; *New York Times*, 2/28/24; Sherwood, *Roosevelt and Hopkins*, pp. 27–29; Jackson, *Encyclopedia of New York City*, p. 1202; Frances Perkins, "The People Mattered," *Survey Midmonthly*, February 1946.

28. Sherwood, *Roosevelt and Hopkins*, pp. 29–30.

29. *New Yorker*, 8/14/43; Sherwood, *Roosevelt and Hopkins*, pp. 35–37; McJimsey, *Ally of the Poor*, pp. 40–43; Giffen and Hopkins, *Jewish First Wife*, pp. 187–88; J. Hopkins, *Sudden Hero*, pp. 145–46.

30. *New Yorker*, 8/14/43; *New York Times*, 9/29/31, 8/30/31, 10/8/31, 3/22/32; Freidel, *Triumph*, pp. 222–23.

31. Folsom, *America Before Welfare*, p. 269; Brock, *Welfare, Democracy, and the New Deal*, pp. 94–95; McJimsey, *Ally of the Poor*, pp. 46–49; Freidel, *Triumph*, p. 223; Wecter, *Age of the Great Depression*, p. 27; *New York Times*, 10/24/31; *New York Times*, 1/21/32; *New York Times*, 12/29/31; *New York Times*, 6/8/32.

32. Sherwood, *Roosevelt and Hopkins*, p. 33, 82–83; *New York Times*, 6/21/32, 10/29/32, 11/10/32, 11/12/32.

33. Hearings Before a Subcommittee of the Committee on Manufactures, United States Senate, 72nd Congress, Second Session, on S. 5125, Pt. 1, Jan. 3 to 17, 1933, pp. 79–81, in Hopkins Papers, Box 42; Blum, *Morgenthau Diaries*, p. 234; Brock, *Welfare, Democracy, and the New Deal*, pp. 95, 100–1, 129–31, 167–68; J. Hopkins, *Sudden Hero*, p. 72; McJimsey, *Ally of the Poor*, p. 51; Singleton, *The American Dole*, p. 109.

34. McJimsey, *Ally of the Poor*, p. 49; Sherwood, *Roosevelt and Hopkins*, p. 34; Freidel, *Triumph*, p. 222; *Fortune*, July 1935.

CHAPTER 9: "PEOPLE DON'T EAT IN THE LONG RUN—THEY EAT EVERY DAY"

1. Tully, *F.D.R.: My Boss*, p. 143; *New York Times*, 5/20/33; Lindley, *Roosevelt Revolution*, pp. 294–95; *Washington Post*, 5/23/33; McJimsey, *Ally of the Poor*, p. 52; J. Hopkins, *Sudden Hero*, p. 162.

2. Monthly Report of the Federal Emergency Relief Administration, OF 444 FERA, FDR Library; McJimsey, *Ally of the Poor*, p. 52; Wecter, *Age of the Great Depression*, p. 39; Bird, *Invisible Scar*, pp. 30, 33; Lowitt

and Beasley, *One Third of a Nation*, p. xviii; Josephson, *Infidel*, pp. 74–75; Charles, *Minister of Relief*, p. 5; Hopkins, *Spending to Save*, pp. 67, 71, 93; Sargent, *Roosevelt and the Hundred Days*, pp. 99–100; J. Hopkins, *Sudden Hero*, p. 160; *New York Times*, 4/23/33; *New York Times*, 5/3/33; *New York Times*, 5/26/33.

3. Hopkins, *Spending to Save*, pp. 102–3; *Time*, 10/16/33; *New York Times*, 6/4/33; *New York Times*, 6/17/33; *New York Times*, 1/30/46; Norman K. Risjord, *Giants in Their Time: Representative Americans from the Jazz Age to the Cold War* (Lanham, Md.: Rowman & Littlefield, 2005), p. 100; Gertrude Springer, "The New Deal and the Old Dole," *Survey Graphic*, July 1933; J. Hopkins, *Sudden Hero*, p. 162; Raymond Clapper, "Harry Hopkins and His Four Million Jobs," *Review of Reviews and World's Work*, January 1934; *Washington Post*, 5/23/33; *New York Times*, 5/23/33; Charles, *Minister of Relief*, p. 5; *Fortune*, July 1935; Moley, *First New Deal*, p. 271; McJimsey, *Ally of the Poor*, p. 52; Telegram from Harry Hopkins to Governors Who Had Received Finance Corporation Funds, May 23, 1933, Hopkins Papers, Box 22; Telegram of Harry Hopkins to Hon. Miriam A. Ferguson, May 23, 1933, Hopkins Papers, Box 22.

4. Harry Hopkins, "The Cities and Relief," Address to the Annual Meeting of the United States Conference of Mayors, September 23, 1933, Speeches and Articles, 1933–36, Hopkins Papers; *New York Times*, 8/19/31; Sherwood, *Roosevelt and Hopkins*, p. 46; Lindley, *Roosevelt Revolution*, pp. 294–95; *Fortune*, July 1935.

5. McJimsey, *Ally of the Poor*, p. 55; Hopkins, *Spending to Save*, p. 99; Charles, *Minister of Relief*, p. 24; *Time*, 4/2/34; Wolfskill and Hudson, *All but the People*, p. 104; Raymond Clapper, "Who Is Hopkins?" *Forum and Century*, December 1937; *New York Times*, 5/2/65; *New York Times*, 6/15/33; *New York Times*, 8/19/31; Sherwood, *Roosevelt and Hopkins*, p. 46; *Fortune*, July 1935; Arthur Schlesinger, *The Politics of Upheaval*, (New York: Houghton Mifflin, 2003), p. 355; *Time*, 2/1/82.

6. Harry Hopkins, "The Federal Relief Job," *The Survey*, July 1933; *New York Times*, 5/2/65; *Fortune*, July 1935; *Collier's*, 11/9/35; Charles, *Minister of Relief*, p. 25; Works Progress Administration, *Washington, City and Capital*, pp. 916–23; Schwartz, *Civil Works Administration*, pp. 27–28; *Time*, 2/19/34.

7. J. Hopkins, *Sudden Hero*, p. 168; Sherwood, *Roosevelt and Hopkins*, pp. 46–49; Harry Hopkins, "The Federal Relief Job," *The Survey*, July 1933; *Fortune*, July 1935; Charles, *Minister of Relief*, p. 29; Schwartz, *Civil Works Administration*, pp. 27–28; *Time*, 2/19/34; *Time*, 7/8/35.

8. *FDR Papers*, Vol. II, p. 183–84; Brock, *Welfare, Democracy, and the New Deal*, p. 172.

9. Harry Hopkins, "How Can the States Help?" article prepared for the American Legislators' Association, in Hopkins Papers, Box 54, Folder 1; McJimsey, *Ally of the Poor*, p. 54; *New York Times*, 6/15/33; *New York Times*, 6/17/33, 6/18/33; J. Hopkins, *Sudden Hero*, pp. 165–66; Carter, *New Dealers*, p. 183; Report of the Honorable Harry L. Hopkins, Federal Emergency Relief Administrator, July 18, 1933, Hopkins Papers, Box 43; Charles, *Minister of Relief*, pp. 37–38.

10. Brock, *Welfare, Democracy, and the New Deal*, pp. 174–75; J. Hopkins, *Sudden Hero*, pp. 166–67; Press Release, June 14, 1933, Hopkins Papers, Box 9.

11. Whiting, *Final Statistical Report*, p. iii; Doris Carothers, *Chronology of the Federal Emergency Relief Administration: May 12, 1933, to December 31, 1935* (Washington, D.C.: United States Government Printing Office, 1937) p. 7; Singleton, *The American Dole*, pp. 112–13, 116; Hearings Before a Subcommittee of the Committee on Manufactures, United States Senate, 72nd Congress, Second Session, on S. 5125, Pt. 1, January 3 to 17, 1933, p. 89, in Hopkins Papers, Box 42; Brock, *Welfare, Democracy, and the New Deal*, pp. 98, 175, 191–92; Williams, *Federal Aid for Relief*, p. 96; Folsom, *America Before Welfare*, p. 334.

12. "Conference of Governors and State Relief Executives at the Mayflower Hotel," Speeches and Articles, 1933–36, Hopkins Papers; "Federal Emergency Relief Administration," Press Release, June 7, 1933, OF 444 FERA, FDR Library; Monthly Report of the Federal Emergency Relief Administration, OF 444 FERA, FDR Library; *FDR Papers*, Vol. II, pp. 237–41; *New York Times*, 6/14/33; *New York Times*, 6/15/33.

13. Whiting, *Final Statistical Report*, pp. 19–21, 59–73; Carothers, *Chronology*, pp. 13–15, 19–20; Memorandum to Governors and State Relief Administrators, August 19, 1933, Hopkins Papers, Box 22; Works Progress Administration, *Washington*, p. 1039; Schwartz, *Civil Works Administration*, p. 129; Hopkins, *Spending to Save*, pp. 126–27.

14. Whiting, *Final Statistical Report*, pp. 19–20, 59–73; Carothers, *Chronology*, pp. 13–15; Brock, *Welfare,*

Democracy, and the New Deal, p. 178; Schwartz, *Civil Works Administration*, p. 129; Hopkins, *Spending to Save*, pp. 126–27; Folsom, *America Before Welfare*, p. 239.

15. Carothers, *Chronology*, pp. 3–4; Whiting, *Final Statistical Report*, pp. 8–9; "Address by Harry L. Hopkins, Federal Emergency Relief Administrator, Before the National Conference of Social Work at Detroit, Michigan," June 17, 1933, Speeches, 1933–36, Hopkins Papers, Box 9; Frances Perkins, "The People Mattered," *Survey Midmonthly*, February 1946; Schwartz, *Civil Works Administration*, p. 43; Bernstein, *A Caring Society*, p. 32.

16. Schwartz, *Civil Works Administration*, pp. 129, 132–33; 135–39; *Time*, 2/19/34.

17. Lowitt and Beasley, *One Third of a Nation*, pp. 19, 28–29, 62, 150; John F. Bauman and Thomas H. Coode, *In the Eye of the Great Depression: New Deal Reporters and the Agony of the American People* (De Kalb: Northern Illinois University Press, 1988) pp. 17–16.

18. Sherwood, *Roosevelt and Hopkins*, pp. 53–54.

19. Perkins, *The Roosevelt I Knew*, p. 187.

20. Hopkins, *Spending to Save*, p. 107.; McJimsey, *Ally of the Poor,* p. 55.

21. Tugwell, *Diary*, p. 411; J. Hopkins, *Sudden Hero*, p. 163.

22. Tugwell, *Diary*, p. 411; McJimsey, *Ally of the Poor*, p. 55; *Collier's*, 11/9/35; Whiting, *Final Statistical Report*, p. iii; Carter, *New Dealers*, pp. 181–84; Lindley, *Roosevelt Revolution*, p. 140.

23. Walter Lippmann, "Today and Tomorrow," *New York Herald Tribune*, 3/7/33; Kennedy, *Banking Crisis*, pp. 103–28, 209, 213; Ron Chernow, *The House of Morgan* (New York: Grove Press, 1990), p. 356; *New York Times*, 3/1/33.

24. Sargent, *Roosevelt and the Hundred Days*, p. 240; Moley, *First New Deal*, pp. 316, 319; Smith, *FDR*, pp. 331–32; Freidel, *Launching the New Deal*, pp. 441–43; Kennedy, *Banking Crisis*, pp. 203–5, 208–9, 212–13; *New York Times*, 6/14/33; Lindley, *Roosevelt Revolution*, pp. 137, 139–40.

25. Kennedy, *Banking Crisis*, pp. 214–17; Leuchtenburg, *Franklin D. Roosevelt and the New Deal*, pp. 60–61; *New York Times*, 6/25/33.

26. Moley, *First New Deal*, p. 319; Freidel, *Launching the New Deal*, pp. 441–43, Sargent, *Roosevelt and the Hundred Days*, pp. 240–42; Press Conference, April 12, 1933, *Complete Presidential Press Conferences*; *Time*, 6/5/33; Kennedy, *Banking Crisis*, p. 219; *New York Times*, 6/7/33; *New York Times*, 6/14/33, 6/25/1933.

27. Moley, *First New Deal*, pp. 170, 316–17, 320; Friedman and Schwartz, *Monetary History of the United States*, p. 434; Freidel, *Launching the New Deal*, pp. 443–44; Sternsher, *Rexford Tugwell and the New Deal*, p. 444; Ickes, *Diary*, p. 50; *New York Times*, 6/25/33; *Time*, 6/5/33.

28. Freidel, *Launching the New Deal*, pp. 413–16; Schlesinger, *Coming of the New Deal*, pp. 20–21, 45; Sargent, *Roosevelt and the Hundred Days*, pp. 222–29.

29. Freidel, *Launching the New Deal*, pp. 448–52; Browder and Smith, *Independent*, p. 98; *New York Times*, 6/1/33; *New York Times*, 6/13/33.

30. Browder and Smith, *Independent*, p. 98; Freidel, *Launching the New Deal*, pp. 448–52; Moley, *First New Deal*, p. 206; Sargent, *Roosevelt and the Hundred Days*, pp. 250–55; *New York Times*, 6/11/33; *New York Times*, 6/13/33; *Time*, 6/26/33; Lindley, *Roosevelt Revolution*, pp. 164–65.

31. *FDR Papers*, Vol. II, p. 154; Sargent, *Roosevelt and the Hundred Days*, pp. 5–6, 240; Browder and Smith, *Independent*, p. 98; Freidel, *Launching the New Deal*, pp. 452–53; *New York Times*, 6/16/33; *New York Times*, 6/13/33 *Time*, 6/26/33.

32. *FDR Papers*, Vol. II, pp. 251–56.

33. Smith, *FDR*, pp. 344–45; Perkins, *The Roosevelt I Knew*, pp. 252; Leuchtenburg *Franklin D. Roosevelt and the New Deal*, pp. 65–69; *Schechter Poultry Corp. v. United States*, 295, U.S. 495 (1935); Martin, *Madam Secretary*, p. 331.

34. Perkins, *The Roosevelt I Knew*, p. 208; *FDR Papers*, Vol. II, pp. 275–77.

35. Leuchtenburg, *Franklin D. Roosevelt and the New Deal*, p. 133; Nick Taylor, *American-Made: The Enduring Legacy of the WPA: When FDR Put the Nation to Work* (New York: Bantam Books, 2008), pp. 523–24.

36. *FDR Papers*, Vol. II, p. 256.

Notes

Epilogue: "A Lot Happened Out of That Determination of a Few People, Didn't It?"

1. Schlesinger, *Coming of the New Deal*, p. 23; *Time*, 6/26/33.
2. Moley, *First New Deal*, p. 336; Arthur Schlesinger, "Sources of the New Deal: Reflections on the Temper of a Time," in *Interpretations of American History*, ed. Gerald N. Grob and George Athan Billias (New York: The Free Press, 1978), pp. 316–28; *The New Republic*, 6/28/33; Lindley, *Roosevelt Revolution*, p. 42.
3. Sternsher, *Rexford Tugwell and the New Deal*, p. 123; Badger, *FDR*, pp. 121–22.
4. Moley, *After Seven Years*, pp. 194, 369–70; Smith, *FDR*, pp. 332 and n., 358; *Time*, 6/26/33; *New York Times*, 6/17/33.
5. Wolfskill and Hudson, *All but the People*, pp. 1–152, 183, 192; F. Roosevelt, 192; *On Our Way*, pp. ix–x; Dudley, *The Great Depression*, p. 127; *Time*, 4/27/36; *Time*, 9/24/34; *New York Times*, 11/1/36.
6. Wolfskill and Hudson, *All but the People*, pp. 119, 125; Dudley, *The Great Depression*, pp. 18–19; *Time*, 12/27/68, p. 277; Smith, *FDR*, pp. 370–74.
7. Smith, *FDR*, p. 370; *Time*, 4/27/36; Rosen, *Roosevelt, the Great Depression*, pp. 156–57; Dudley, *The Great Depression*, p. 21; Walter Lippmann, *Interpretations, 1933–1935* (New York: MacMillan, 1936), p. 249, quoted in McGovern, *And a Time for Hope*, p. 41; Kennedy, *Freedom from Fear*, pp. 217, 289; "FDR & the Depression: The Big Debate," *The New York Review of Books*, 11/8/2007; *New York Times*, 11/7/34.
8. Rosenman, *Presidential Style*, pp. 340–41; Dudley, *The Great Depression*, pp. 18–19; Wecter, *Age of the Great Depression*, p. 73; Smith, *FDR*, p. 349; Alter, *Defining Moment*, p. 317.
9. Brinkley, *The End of Reform*, pp. 23–30, 86–105, 268–71; Alan Brinkley, "New Deal Liberalism and the New Deal State," in *The New Deal*, ed. David E. Hamilton (Boston: Houghton Mifflin Company, 1999), pp. 53–81; Leighninger, *Long-Range Public Investment*, pp. 23–24; Smith, *FDR*, p. 453; Reminiscences of Frances Perkins, 1961, CUOHRO, Pt. 7, p. 15; Anderson, *The President's Men*, p. 23; Sternsher, *Rexford Tugwell and the New Deal*, p. 134; Tugwell, *The Democratic Roosevelt*, p. 449; Kennedy, *Freedom from Fear*, p. 455.
10. Schlesinger, *Coming of the New Deal*, p. 203; Smith, *FDR*, p. 340.
11. Schlesinger, *Coming of the New Deal*, pp. 216–17, 221–23; *New York Times*, 7/9/33; Freidel, *Launching the New Deal*, p. 474; Feis, *1933: Characters in Crisis*, p. 101; Sargent, *Roosevelt and the Hundred Days*, p. 230; *Time*, 4/17/33; *Time*, 5/8/33.
12. Schlesinger, *Coming of the New Deal*, pp. 222–23, 230–31; Moley, *After Seven Years*, pp. 259–61; Freidel, *Launching the New Deal*, p. 486; Lindley, *Roosevelt Revolution*, pp. 210–11, 215.
13. Tully, *F.D.R.: My Boss*, p. 156; Moley, *After Seven Years*, pp. 274–76; Moley, *First New Deal*, pp. 502–3; Schlesinger, *Coming of the New Deal*, pp. 231–32; Tugwell, *Democratic Roosevelt*, pp. 237–38, 323; Carter, *New Dealers*, p. 326; *Time*, 9/4/33; *New York Times*, 8/28/33.
14. Moley, Diary, 5/11/33, 5/12/33; Sargent, *Roosevelt and the Hundred Days*, p. 209; Schlesinger, *Coming of the New Deal*, p. 494; McJimsey, *Ally of the Poor*, p. 75; *New York Times*, 2/23/33; *New York Times*, 3/8/34; *New York Times*, 11/8/34; Moley, *First New Deal*, pp. 508–9.
15. Anderson, *The President's Men*, p. 30; *Time*, 9/11/33; *New York Times*, 2/13/37; *New York Times*, 8/28/33; *New York Times*, 11/2/37; *New York Times*, 3/4/38; *New York Times*, 10/26/38.
16. Moley, *After Seven Years*, pp. 9, 11, 172, 397; Tugwell, *Democratic Roosevelt*, p. 238; *Time*, 10/2/39; Raymond Moley, *How to Keep Our Liberty* (New York: Alfred A. Knopf, 1952); *New York Times*, 9/20/39; *New York Times*, 10/24/40; *New York Times*, 6/18/65; Robert H. Jackson, *That Man: An Insider's Portrait of Franklin D. Roosevelt* (Oxford: Oxford University Press, 2003), p. 225.
17. William Leuchtenberg, "Falling Out with F.D.R.," *Book Week*, January 22, 1967; *Time*, 12/30/66; *New York Times*, 2/19/75.
18. Tugwell, *Democratic Roosevelt*, p. 238; Martin, *Madam Secretary*, p. 388; Moley, *After Seven Years*, pp. 262–63.
19. Ben S. Bernanke, *Essays on the Great Depression* (Princeton, N.J.: Princeton University Press, 2000), pp. 70, 78.

20. Meeting Before the Special Board for Public Works, July 1, 1933, in Douglas Papers, Box 244; Browder and Smith, *Independent*, pp. 85, 101; Schlesinger, *Coming of the New Deal*, pp. 284–85; Tugwell, *Roosevelt's Revolution*, p. 8.

21. *FDR Public Papers*, Vol. I, pp. 810–11; Schlesinger, *Coming of the New Deal*, pp. 289–91; Julian Zelizer, "The Forgotten Legacy of the New Deal: Fiscal Conservatism and the Roosevelt Administration, 1933–1938," *Presidential Studies Quarterly*, June 2000, pp. 338–39; Browder and Smith, *Independent*, pp. 103, 108–9.

22. Lewis Douglas, Memorandum for the President, December 30, 1933; Schlesinger, *Coming of the New Deal*, pp. 289–91; Zelizer, "Forgotten Legacy," pp. 338–39; Browder and Smith, *Independent*, pp. 103, 108–9.

23. Letter of Lewis Douglas to James S. Douglas, March 2, 1934, Douglas Papers; Browder and Smith, *Independent*, pp. 110–11; Carter, *New Dealers*, p. 126–27; Blum, *Morgenthau Diaries*, p. 230; Moley, *First New Deal*, pp. 206–7; James F. Byrnes, *All in One Lifetime* (New York: Harper, 1958), pp. 75–76; *Time*, 3/26/34, 9/10/34, 8/26/35; *New York Times*, 3/29/34.

24. Letter of Lewis Douglas to John N. Garner of September 13, 1934, Douglas Papers, Box 238; Letter of Lewis Douglas to James Sargent, March 19, 1973, Douglas Papers, Box 119; Blum, *Morgenthau Diaries*, pp. 230–31; *New York Times*, 9/2/34.

25. Reminiscences of Frances Perkins, 1961, CUOHRO, Pt. 5, pp. 25, 85–87; Letter of Lewis Douglas to James Sargent, March 19, 1973; Letter of Louis Douglas to Arthur Curlee, May 9, 1934, Douglas Papers, Box 238.

26. Lewis W. Douglas, *The Liberal Tradition: A Free People and a Free Economy* (New York: D. Van Nostrand Company, 1935) pp. xvi, ix, 90; Zelizer, "Forgotten Legacy," pp. 338–41; Browder and Smith, *Independent*, pp. 119–20; *New York Times*, 7/28/35.

27. Zelizer, "Forgotten Legacy," p. 341; *New York Times*, 10/15/36; *New York Times*, 5/22/42; Browder and Smith, *Independent*, pp. 127–28, 130, 139, 152, 163–64, 173.

28. Carter, *New Dealers*, p. 128; *New York Times*, 3/2/63; Browder and Smith, *Independent*, pp. 304, 306, 310, 362–63, 374.

29. Carter, *New Dealers*, p. 75; Wallace, *New Frontiers*, pp. 173–75; Lord, *Wallaces of Iowa*, p. 362; Culver and Hyde, *American Dreamer*, p. 123; Schlesinger, *Coming of the New Deal*, pp. 60–63.

30. Wallace, *New Frontiers*, pp. 179–81; Lord, *Wallaces of Iowa*, pp. 364–65; Culver and Hyde, *American Dreamer*, p. 124; Reminiscences of Jerome Frank, 1960, CUOHRO, pp. 38, 116–17.

31. Wallace, *New Frontiers*, pp. 174, Schlesinger, *Coming of the New Deal*, pp. 64–65; Moley, *First New Deal*, pp. 259–60.

32. Peek and Crowther, *Why Quit Our Own* p. 11; Culver and Hyde, *American Dreamer*, pp. 155–56; Lord, *Wallaces of Iowa*, pp. 357, 404–5; Reminiscences of Jerome Frank, 1960, CUOHRO, pp. 24–25, 74, 115, 179–80; Sternsher, *Rexford Tugwell and the New Deal*, p. 191; Saloutos, *American Farmer and the New Deal*, p. 52; Schlesinger, *Coming of the New Deal*, pp. 57–58, Drew Pearson, "Unequal Benefits in the AAA Met Strong Objections," *Daily Mirror*, 2/11/35, in Moley Papers, Box 94.

33. Schlesinger, *Coming of the New Deal*, pp. 70–71; Lord, *Wallaces of Iowa*, pp. 370–73; *FDR Papers*, Vol. II, p. 182; Moley, *First New Deal*, p. 260; Saloutos, *American Farmer and the New Deal*, p. 76.

34. Letter of Henry Wallace to Raymond Moley, May 27, 1965, Moley Papers, Box 245, Folder 10; Lord, *Wallaces of Iowa*, pp. 456–57, 460–63; Nourse et al. *Three Years*, pp. 18–19; Saloutos, *American Farmer and the New Deal*, p. 264; Schapsmeier and Schapsmeier, *Henry A. Wallace*, p. 243; Culver and Hyde, *American Dreamer*, pp. 157–61, 169–70, 178; *Atlantic Monthly*, August 1948; "Harvesting Poverty" editorial series, *New York Times*, 8/5/2003, 8/15/2003, 11/29/2003, 12/30/2003.

35. Saloutos, *American Farmer and the New Deal*, pp. 255–56; Nourse et al., *Three Years*, pp. 420–48; *Life*, 9/2/40; McGovern, *And a Time for Hope*, p. 47.

36. "Six Reasons to Kill Farm Subsidies and Trade Barriers," *Reason Magazine*, February 2006; "The Unkept Promise," *New York Times*, 12/30/2003; "The Enduring Political Illusion of Farm Subsidies," *San Francisco Chronicle*, 8/18/2004.

37. Smith, *FDR*, pp. 442, 461–63; Lord, *Wallaces of Iowa*, pp. 474–81; Culver and Hyde, *American Dreamer*, pp. 226–27, 229. *Los Angeles Times*, 3/12/2000

38. Smith, *FDR*, p. 447–49; Lord, *Wallaces of Iowa*, pp. 474–81, 528–29, 535–36; Culver and Hyde, *American Dreamer*, pp. 255, 275, 323, 325, *Los Angels Times*, 3/12/2000.

39. Frances Perkins, "Address at the Summer School of Social Progress, Wellesley College, on the Objectives of the National Industrial Recovery Act," July 8, 1933, Box 46, Perkins Papers, Box 46; David McCullough, *Truman* (New York: Simon & Schuster, 1992), pp. 516–17; Lord, *Wallaces of Iowa*, pp. 555, 579–82; Culver and Hyde, *American Dreamer*, p. 426; Tugwell, *Roosevelt's Revolution*, p. 208; *New York Times*, 10/6/33.

40. *Time*, 11/15/48; Culver and Hyde, *American Dreamer*, pp. 467–68, 481–82, 493; McCullough, *Truman*, pp. 645–46.

41. Culver and Hyde, *American Dreamer*, pp. 512–14; *New York Times*, 5/22/60; *New York Times*, 11/19/65.

42. Leighninger, *Long-Range Public Investment*, pp. 38–39, 86; 1934 Annual Report of the Department of Labor, Ruth Backes Papers, Box 4, Folder 3; Martin, *Madam Secretary*, p. 306; McGovern, *And a Time for Hope*, p. 49.

43. Annual Report of the Department of Labor, 1934, Ruth Backes Papers, Box 4; Perkins, *The Roosevelt I Knew*, p. 210; Annual Report of the Secretary of Labor, June 30, 1934, Perkins Papers, Box 85; Barton J. Bernstein, "The Conservative Achievements of New Deal Reform," in *The New Deal: Critical Issues*, ed. Otis Graham (Boston: Little, Brown, 1971), p. 24; Congressional Research Service, "Union Membership Trends in the United States," August 31, 2004; Martin, *Madam Secretary*, p. 306.

44. Perkins, *The Roosevelt I Knew*, pp. 278–81; Schlesinger, *Coming of the New Deal*, p. 307; Martin, *Madam Secretary*, pp. 341–43; Kennedy, *Freedom from Fear*, pp. 224–25; Eliot, *Recollections*, p. 92.

45. Perkins, *The Roosevelt I Knew*, pp. 286–97; Schlesinger, *Coming of the New Deal*, p. 304; Martin, *Madam Secretary*, pp. 247–48; "The Social Security Bill: 25 Years After," *Atlantic Monthly*, August 1960; Eliot, *Recollections*, p. 111.

46. Perkins, *The Roosevelt I Knew*, pp. 300–301; Martin, *Madam Secretary*, pp. 355–56.

47. Ibid., pp. 382–86; Huthmacher, *Senator Robert F. Wagner*, pp. 190–98; Kennedy, *Freedom from Fear*, pp. 290–91; McGovern, *And a Time for Hope*, p. 204.

48. Leuchtenburg, *Franklin D. Roosevelt and the New Deal*, pp. 162 n., 262–63; Martin, *Madam Secretary*, pp. 378–80, 387–95; Kennedy, *Freedom from Fear*, pp. 297 n., 344–45; Mohr, *That Woman*, pp. 248–49, *New York Times*, 6/19/33.

49. Perkins, *The Roosevelt I Knew*, pp. 316–19; Martin, *Madam Secretary*, pp. 407–17, 437; Reminiscences of Frances Perkins, 1961, CUOHRO, Pt. 6, pp. 371–542; Tugwell, *Democratic Roosevelt*, p. 450; Smith, *FDR*, p. 472; Reminiscences of Charles E. Wyzanski, Jr., 1959, CUOHRO, p. 189; Ellsworth Barnard, *Wendell Willkie* (Amherst: University of Massachusetts Press, 1971), p. 249.

50. Perkins, *The Roosevelt I Knew*, p. 375; Martin, *Madam Secretary*, pp. 448–51.

51. *Life*, 7/9/45; Perkins, *The Roosevelt I Knew*, p. 393; Martin, *Madam Secretary*, pp. 459–63.

52. Jerry Kluttz and Herbert Asbury, "The Woman Nobody Knows," *Collier's*, 8/5/44.

53. Ruth Backes, Interview with Gerard Dennis Reilly, Ruth Backes Papers, Box 12, Folder 13; Neufeld Diary and Interview with Maurice Neufeld; Ruth Backes, Interviews with Susanna Coggeshall, Ruth Backes Papers, Box 12, Folder 7; Tomlin Coggeshall Interview; Letter of Frances Perkins to Susanna Coggeshall, August 1, 1951, Perkins Papers, Box 118B; Ruth Backes, Interview with Allan Bloom.

54. Ruth Backes, Interview with Gerard Dennis Reilly, Ruth Backes Papers, Box 12, Folder 13; Neufeld, Diary; Martin, *Madam Secretary*, pp. 476–80; Ruth Backes, Interview with Allan Bloom.

55. Breiseth, "The Frances Perkins I Knew"; *New York Times*, 5/22/60; *New York Times*, 5/15/65; Martin, *Madam Secretary*, p. 475.

56. Breiseth, "The Frances Perkins I Knew"; Neufeld Diary.

57. Breiseth, "The Frances Perkins I Knew."

58. Ibid.

59. Ibid.; Neufeld Diary.

60. J. Hopkins, *Sudden Hero*, p. 165.

61. Jonathan Mitchell, "Alms-Giver: Harry L. Hopkins," *The New Republic*, 4/10/35; Harry Hopkins,

"The War on Distress," *Today*, 12/16/33; McJimsey, *Ally of the Poor*, pp. 58–59; J. Hopkins, *Sudden Hero*, pp. 169–70; Tugwell, *Diary*, p. 411; *New York Times*, 5/2/65, p. 68; Hopkins, *Spending to Save*, p. 117; Reminiscences of Jerome Frank, 1960, CUOHRO, pp. 36–37. Badger, *The New Deal*, pp. 203–4.

62. *The New Republic*, 4/10/35; McJimsey, *Ally of the Poor*, pp. 76–79; J. Hopkins, *Sudden Hero*, pp. 186–88; McGovern, *And a Time for Hope*, p. 49.

63. Taylor, *American-Made: The Enduring Legacy of the WPA*, pp. 2, 524; McJimsey, *Ally of the Poor*, p. 111; Charles, *Minister of Relief*, p. 235; *New York Times*, 1/30/46; *New York Times*, 5/2/65.

64. *Forum and Century*, December 1937; Leighninger, *Long-Range Public Investment*, pp. 49, 64; McJimsey, *Ally of the Poor*, pp. 89–90; *New York Times*, 1/30/46.

65. Frances Perkins, "The People Mattered," *Survey Midmonthly*, February 1946; Diana and James Halsted, Interview with Franklin D. Roosevelt, Jr., January 11, 1979, Small Collections Oral History Interviews, Hopkins Papers; Sherwood, *Roosevelt and Hopkins*, p. 448.

66. McJimsey, *Ally of the Poor*, pp. 120, 124–29; Smith, *FDR*, pp. 377–89, 409–15; Anderson, *The President's Men*, pp. 71–72; *New York Times*, 1/30/46; Reminiscences of Jerome Frank, 1960, CUOHRO, pp. 45–50; *New York Times*, 10/8/37; *Time*, 8/5/40; *The Nation*, 5/22/35.

67. McJimsey, *Ally of the Poor*, pp. 136–38, 145–46, 340–41, 363–69, 397; Sherwood, *Roosevelt and Hopkins*, pp. 202–5, 805; Anderson, *The President's Men*, pp. 66, 71, 75, 80; *Atlantic Monthly*, November 1948; *New York Times*, 1/30/46; *Time*, 11/12/34.

68. Letter of Frances Perkins to Harry Hopkins, August 26, 1940, Hopkins Papers, Box 94.

69. Richard N. Goodwin, *Remembering America: A Voice from the Sixties* (Boston: Little, Brown and Co., 1988) pp. 259, 272.

70. *Boston Globe*, 11/4/2007; Robert Kuttner, "Friendly Takeover," *The American Prospect*, 3/18/2007.

71. *New York Times*, 3/2/2007.

INDEX

Abbott, Edith, 269
Addams, Jane, 9, 13, 164, 165, 178
Aebisher, Joseph, 225
After Seven Years (Moley), 292, 293
Agricultural Prices (Wallace), 119
agriculture, 3–4, 6, 7, 9, 10, 16–17, 30, 39, 40, 60, 61,
    63, 108, 109–32, 133–46, 154–56, 279
    Agricultural Adjustment Act, 3–4, 133–46,
        154–56, 221, 231, 246, 251, 279, 286, 298–301
    Agricultural Adjustment Administration, 140,
        154–55, 219, 245, 284
    domestic allotment plan, 9, 25, 113, 123–24,
        126–30, 133–36, 139, 140, 145, 155
    Douglas and, 94, 234
    Farm Belt depression, 116, 120, 123–25
    Farm Credit Act, 279
    Farm Credit Administration, 4, 140
    farmers' debts and foreclosures, 48, 54, 110, 115,
        124, 125, 140, 141, 144, 145, 237
    Farm Tenancy Act, 300
    and FDR's affinity for farmers, 112, 127
    Hoover and, 3, 27, 115, 116, 122–24, 126, 128, 129
    McNary-Haugenism and, 113, 116, 117, 122, 123,
        128, 133–37, 140, 154, 155, 299
    overproduction in, 121–22, 130, 133, 139
    Smoot-Hawley Tariff Act and, 123
    in Tennessee Valley, 147
    Tugwell as assistant secretary of, 6, 111–13
    Wallace as secretary of, 9, 25–26, 109–13, 118,
        128–32, 133–41, 145–46, 154–56, 298–301
Allen, Robert, 28
Altmeyer, Arthur, 305
American Federation of Labor (AFL), 90, 168, 191,
    198, 215, 220, 222, 223, 232
American Friends Service Committee, 2

American Individualism (Hoover), 27
American Legion, 86, 101–2
Arizona, 88–91, 96, 205
Arizona Daily Star, 97
army, 217, 235
Ashurst, Henry Fountain, 105
Association for Improving the Condition of the
    Poor (AICP), 258, 259, 261, 270, 275
Astor, Vincent, 55, 131, 291
Atlantic Monthly, 15
automobile industry, 14, 50
Awalt, F. G., 68–70

Baker, Newton, 61
Ballantine, Arthur, 68–70, 80
Baltimore Sun, 78
Bane, Frank, 268
Bankhead, John, 129
banks and banking, 3, 5, 6, 11, 17, 40, 47–56, 63,
    66–84, 86, 103, 111, 131, 137, 203, 276–79, 318
    Banking Act of 1933 (Glass-Steagall Act), 3, 72,
        79, 277–79, 281, 317
    deposit insurance and, 277–79
    Emergency Banking Act, 3, 8, 77–80, 83, 99–101,
        106, 111, 134
    holidays for, 3, 17, 50–53, 68–71, 73, 75, 76, 80,
        81, 143
    Hoover administration and, 3, 49, 50–53, 67–70,
        72, 76, 82, 94, 277
    Moley and, 8, 52, 66–71, 76–80, 82, 83
    separation of deposit and investment banking,
        277, 317
    Woodin and, 52, 54, 68–73, 76–80
Barnum, Gertrude, 165–66
Baruch, Bernard, 85, 122, 140, 142, 230, 231, 245, 246

Beard, Charles A., 51, 58
Beard, Mary, 51
Beck, James, 243
beer, 43, 105–6
Benchley, Robert, 73
Bendiner, Robert, 48
Benjamin, Herbert, 216–17
Berle, Adolf A., Jr., 6, 60–62, 64, 239–40
Berry, George, 220
Beyer, Clara, 196
Bisbee, Ariz., 88–91
Bisbee, Dewitt, 89
Black, Hugo, 221–24, 245, 250
Black, Ruby, 216
Black Bill, 221–24, 227
Bloom, Allan, 309
Bloor, Ella Reeve, 16
Bluestein, Abe, 287
Board of Child Welfare, 259
Borah, William, 37, 80, 143, 245
Bradley, Charles, 144–45
Brain Trust, 7, 56, 59–63, 111, 189, 228, 265, 286
    Moley has head of, 6–7, 8, 59–63, 66, 67
Brand, Charles J., 155
Brandeis, Louis, 152, 153, 167–68, 228, 229, 304
Bridges, Harry, 307, 309
Brinkley, Alan, 289
Brisbane, Arthur, 48
Brown, Edgar, 277
Brown, John Young, 104
Browning, Gordon, 102
Bruere, Henry, 175, 184
Bryan, William Jennings, 57, 114–15, 124, 142
Bullitt, William Marshall, 85
Bush, George W., 317
BusinessWeek, 55
Byrnes, James F., 97, 143, 295

Cabinet, 43–45, 71–72, 87, 129, 130, 142,
    151, 302
    bedside, 8, 87, 101
    Perkins as first female member of, 190, 191,
        199–200, 212, 216
capitalism, 6, 28, 30, 83, 205, 286
Cardozo, Benjamin, 44, 45
Carson, Sara Libby, 255
Carter, John Franklin, 7, 82, 156, 276, 298
Carver, George Washington, 117–18
Cermak, Anton, 36
charities, 4, 28, 202, 248, 249, 258, 261, 270
Chicago Daily News, 267
Chicago Tribune, 42, 161, 190, 193, 212
Christodora House, 254–58
Churchill, Winston, 173
Civilian Conservation Corps (CCC), 4, 208–11,
    214–20, 224–27, 237, 271, 284, 285, 288, 289,
    295, 311
Civil Service Commission, 309–10

Civil Works Administration (CWA), 273, 283, 312,
    288, 308, 312–13, 316
Clapper, Raymond, 235
Clark, Bennett, 244
Cleveland, Grover, 115
Clinton, Bill, 317
Coggeshall, Tomlin, 190
Cohen, Bejamin, 151–53
Collier's, 46–47, 57, 268, 276, 285, 308–9
Committee for the Stabilization of Industry,
    184–85, 187, 204
Committee on Economic Security, 304–5
communism, 16–17, 30, 159, 228, 251, 302, 307
Comstock, William, 51
Conant, H. N., 99
Conant, James, 297
Concentraton and Control (Van Hise), 228
Congress, 7, 10, 38, 66, 82, 94, 130, 146, 279, 285, 301
    agriculture and, 113, 138–39, 154
    banking crisis and, 70, 73, 77, 79–80
    Civilian Conservation Corps and, 215–16
    Douglas in, 8, 93–99
    Economy Act and, 100–106, 295
    federal budget and, 86
    Federal Emergency Relief Act and, 251, 263
    Glass-Steagall bill and, 79, 278
    McNary-Haugen bill and, 117, 122
    Securities Act and, 153
    Tennessee Valley Authority and, 148–49
    Thomas Amendment and, 144
    Wheeler Amendment and, 143
Connally, Thomas, 106, 280
Connery, William P., Jr., 103, 215, 216, 218
Constitution, U.S., 106
    Prohibition and, 105
Consumers' League, 167–69, 171–72
Coolidge, Calvin, 21, 23, 27, 47, 50, 84, 121, 177, 178
    agriculture and, 116–17, 122
Corcoran, Thomas, 151–52
Costigan, Edward, 204, 207, 208, 211, 214, 215, 250,
    250
Coughlin, Father Charles, 131, 288
Cox, Archibald, 196
Cox, James M., 21, 177
Crash of 1929, 1–2, 14, 28, 48, 93, 122–23, 149, 182,
    196, 261, 276, 288
Creel, George, 14
Cullen, Thomas H., 105
Cummings, Homer, 71, 150–52, 205, 305
Curlee, Arthur, 98
Cutting, Bronson, 83, 202

Davies, Joseph E., 253–54
Davis, Chester, 299–300
Davis, James J., 182–83
Davis, John W., 23, 178
Dawes, Charles, 50
deflation, 4

Degler, Carl, 31
Democratic Roosevelt, The (Tugwell), 293
depression, Farm Belt, 116, 120, 123–25
Depression, Great, 1–2, 5–6, 14–17, 63
  and attitudes toward poverty, 248–49
  Crash of 1929, 1–2, 14, 28, 48, 93, 122–23, 149, 182, 196, 261, 276, 288
  Hoover's handling of, 2, 15, 23, 26–32, 34
  New Deal and, 288
DePriest, Oscar, 218, 226
Dern, George, 44, 205, 210–11, 214, 215, 235–36
Des Moines Register, 131
Dewey, John, 167
Dewey, Thomas E., 293, 302–3
Dewson, Molly, 43, 47, 190, 191, 200
Dickinson, John, 231–32, 239
Dickinson, L. J., 218
Dies, Martin, 307
Doak, William, 157–60, 196
Dodge, Mabel, 167
Dos Passos, John, 16
Douglas, James, 89–90
Douglas, James S. "Rawhide Jimmy," 89–92, 94–95, 99, 104
Douglas, Josephine Williams, 89
Douglas, Lewis, 8, 56, 66, 87–99, 137, 143, 226, 283, 293–98, 317
  as ambassador, 297–98
  in Arizona state legislature, 92–93
  background of, 8, 88–92
  as budget director, 8–9, 86–88, 98–108, 233–35, 293–96
  budget views of, 94–99
  in Congress, 8, 93–99
  conservative views of, 10
  inflation and, 142
  on Johnson, 245
  lectures given by, 297
  Perkins and, 205–6, 296, 303
  relief programs and, 203, 205–6, 211, 217–18, 233, 235–36, 239, 242, 269
  resignation of, 296–97
  Roosevelt and, 87, 96–98, 106
  Thomas Amendment and, 144
  veterans' benefits and, 92, 95–96, 99, 100, 107, 279–81, 295
  in World War I, 91
Douglas, Margaret "Peggy," 92, 93
Douglas, Paul, 187
Douglas, Walter, 90, 91
Douglas, William O., 152
Dulles, John Foster, 153

Early, Stephen, 18–19, 65, 78
economics, 6, 11, 61, 63, 85, 167, 182, 204, 318
  see also federal budget
Economy Act, 9, 10, 84, 87, 99–108, 111, 134, 208, 217, 222, 233, 235, 289, 295, 297

Eisenhower, Dwight D., 298, 309, 317
electric power, 146–49, 186, 242
Eliot, Thomas, 46, 196, 305
Elks, 110
Emergency Banking Act, 3, 8, 77–80, 83, 99–101, 106, 111, 134
Emergency Farm Mortgage Act, 145
Emergency Railroad Coordination Act, 279
Emergency Relief and Construction Act, 250
employment, *see* labor; unemployment
Ezekiel, Mordecai, 135, 154

Fair Labor Standards Act, 282, 286, 289, 307, 309
Farley, James, 24, 58, 59, 62, 197, 200, 205, 235
Farm Credit Act, 279
Farm Credit Administration, 4, 140
Farmers' Holiday Association, 125, 136, 139, 299
farms, *see* agriculture
Farm Tenancy Act, 300
Fechner, Robert, 219, 226
federal budget, 8–9, 11–12, 30, 40, 63, 84–88, 97–108, 111, 217, 279
  deficit spending, 11–12, 84, 289, 295
  Douglas as director of, 8–9, 86–88, 98–108, 233–35, 293–96
  Douglas's views on, 94–99
  dual, 217–18
  Economy Act, 9, 10, 84, 87, 99–108, 111, 134, 208, 217, 222, 233, 235, 289, 295, 297
  Hoover administration and, 6, 84, 85
  Roosevelt recession and, 289
  veterans' benefits and, 85–87
  Wallace and, 131
Federal Deposit Insurance Corporation, 278
federal employees, 102, 106
federal relief programs, 4, 9, 10, 11, 40, 63, 84, 202–4, 206–7, 211, 220, 248–52, 279
  Emergency Relief and Construction Act, 250
  Federal Emergency Relief Act, 206–8, 237, 250–52, 263–64, 285, 311–32
  Federal Emergency Relief Administration (FERA), 4, 251, 252, 265–76, 284, 288, 305, 308, 311–12, 315
  Hoover and, 28–32, 202, 204, 210, 249–51, 267, 270
  Hopkins-Hodson plan, 206–7, 211, 248, 250, 252, 264
  industrial, 4, 7, 11, 221, 223, 227–32, 233, 236–47, 271, 279, 281–83, 285
  Perkins and, 161, 192, 202–4, 206–8, 211, 264, 308, 310
  Temporary Emergency Relief Administration, 188, 202, 206–7, 261–63, 274
  see also public works programs
Feis, Herbert, 290
Felbinger, Joseph, 266
Ferguson, Miriam A. "Ma," 267
Fess, Simeon D., 251

First New Deal, The (Moley), 293
Flynn, Edward J., 62
Flynn, John T., 151
Ford, Henry, 50–51
Fortas, Abe, 155
Fortune, 1, 154, 268
Frank, Jerome, 136, 155, 299–300, 312
Frankfurter, Felix, 58, 91, 151–54, 155, 193, 196
Friedman, Milton, 278

Garner, John Nance, 23, 36, 93, 200, 203, 205, 249, 278, 296, 301
Garsson, Henry, 159, 196, 203
Garsson, Murray, 159, 160, 196, 203
Gaus, John, 107
Gerard, James W., 21
Gifford, Walter S., 30, 250
Gingrich, Newt, 317
Glass, Carter, 54, 55, 68, 80, 105, 142, 144
Glass-Steagall Act (Banking Act of 1933), 3, 72, 79, 277–79, 281, 317
gold, 51, 52, 68, 69, 72–74, 80, 131, 142, 143
   standard, 4, 30, 52, 54, 57, 68, 73, 114–15, 124, 142–44, 237, 279, 289, 293–94
Goldberg, Jacob, 260, 261
Goldmark, Pauline, 174
Goldsmith, Samuel, 270
Goldwater, Barry, 317
Gompers, Samuel, 90–91, 168
Goodwin, Richard, 316
Gore, Thomas, 244
Green, William, 191, 193, 197–98, 215, 216, 221, 232, 243
   Black Bill and, 222–24
Greenway, Isabella, 97
Gregory, Clifford, 134
Grinnell, Josiah Bushnell, 253
Gruening, Ernest, 71
Gunther, John, 86

Hapgood, Hutchins, 257
Harding, Warren G., 21, 27, 115–16, 177
Harper's Bazaar, 73
Harriman, Averell, 291, 297
Harriman, Henry, 243
Harrison, Pat, 160, 244
Hart, Henry, 196
Hartson, Louis, 254–55
Haseltine, Edna, 273
Haugen, Gilbert, 116
Hearst, William Randolph, 5, 286
Hibbard, Benjamin, 118
Hickok, Lorena, 76, 274
Hillman, Sidney, 198, 219, 220
Hine, Lewis, 169
Hiss, Alger, 155
Hodson, William, 206–7, 211, 248, 250, 252, 264, 261–62, 316

Hoffman, Clare, 162
Hofstadter, Richard, 20
Holden, Charles, 266
Holden, Perry G., 118
Holmes, Oliver Wendell, 44
homeless and transients, 272
Home Owners' Loan Act, 141
Hoover, Herbert, 5, 23, 24, 26–35, 39, 43, 47, 62, 78, 94, 102, 107, 130, 146, 180, 181, 186, 247, 293
   agriculture and, 3, 27, 115, 116, 122–24, 126, 128, 129
   banking crisis and, 3, 49, 50–53, 67–70, 72, 82, 94, 277
   Depression and, 2, 15, 23, 26–32, 34
   elected president, 27
   in election of 1932, 2, 23, 26, 32, 33, 52
   European war debts and, 64
   farmers and, 3, 27
   FDR and, 26, 34–36, 41–42, 51–53, 68
   government as viewed by, 11, 12, 28
   government spending and, 6, 84, 85
   individualism as philosophy of, 2, 11, 27, 28, 32, 249, 318
   New Deal and, 31–32, 41–42
   poor and, 4
   relief programs and, 28–32, 202, 204, 210, 249–51, 267, 270
   as secretary of commerce, 27
   unemployment and, 182–83, 188, 197
   as U.S. food administrator, 27, 49, 115
   veterans' bonus and, 31, 50, 226, 227
Hoover, Lou Henry, 53
Hoovervilles, 2, 15, 17, 60, 262, 272
Hopkins, Adah, 252, 254
Hopkins, Anna, 252–53, 258
Hopkins, Barbara Duncan, 261, 314
Hopkins, David, 258–61
Hopkins, David Aldona "Al," 252–53, 258
Hopkins, Ethel Gross, 258–61, 315
Hopkins, Harry, 8, 9–10, 188, 252–64, 283, 287, 305, 311–16, 318
   FDR's relationship with, 314
   as FERA head, 252, 265–76, 311–12, 315
   as foreign policy aide, 315
   Perkins's letter to, 316
   relief work of, 206–7, 211, 248, 250, 252, 258–59, 261, 264
   as secretary of commerce, 315
   as TERA head, 261–63, 274
Hopkins, June, 253
Hopkins, Louise Macy, 315
Hopkins, Lewis, 252, 263
Hopkins, Robert, 260, 261
Hopkins, Stephen, 261, 315
Horner, Henry, 69
House, Edward M., 106, 142–43
Howe, Julia Ward, 13

Howe, Louis, 21, 22, 55, 56, 59, 64–65, 71, 131, 225
  Bonus Army and, 226–27
  death of, 314
  FDR's inaugural address and, 38–39
How the Other Half Lives (Riis), 164
*How to Keep Our Liberty: A Program for Political
  Action* (Moley), 293
Huddleston, George, 16
Hughes, Charles Evans, 36–37
Hull, Cordell, 23, 44, 45, 77, 203, 279
  Moley and, 290–91
  at World Economic Conference, 289–90
Hull, Mrs. Cordell, 199
Hull House, 9, 13, 164–65, 168
Hundred Days, 2–4, 5, 7, 8, 10–12, 246, 284–86,
  316, 318
  national philosophy and, 284–85
  New Deal and, 11
  spending and, 6, 63
Hunt, George W. P., 92, 93
Hunter, Robert, 164
Hyde, Arthur, 109

Ickes, Harold, 15, 25, 44, 213, 231, 234, 246, 279, 308
  on Perkins, 200
  public works and, 205, 210–11, 214, 215, 235–36,
    246, 282–83, 312, 313
immigrants, 13, 42, 49, 58, 158–60, 164, 177, 195–96,
  256, 260
individualism, 2, 11, 27, 28, 32, 249, 285, 318
industry, 14, 39, 63, 249
  relief for, 4, 7, 11, 221, 223, 227–32, 233, 236–47,
    271, 279, 281–83, 285
inflation, 115, 124, 141–44, 237, 295
insurance, 192, 304–5, 309, 310, 317–18
  bank deposit, 277–79
  unemployment, 185–87, 192, 194, 197, 213, 220,
    285, 304, 305, 309
International Workers of the World (Wobblies), 90
investment trusts, 48
Irwin, Will, 173

Jackson, Andrew, 36
Jacobstein, Meyer, 231–32
James, William, 208
Johnson, Hiram, 281
Johnson, Hugh S., 122, 136–37, 230–32, 33, 238–39,
  244, 294
  as NRA head, 245–46, 282
Johnson, Lyndon, 316
Jones, Jesse, 68
Jones, Marvin, 129–30
Josephson, Matthew, 16, 262
Jurkowitz, Frances, 157, 158

Kahn, Dorothy, 15
Katz, Milton, 47
Kelley, Florence, 163, 167, 171–72, 176

Kent, Fred, 231–32
Keynes, John Maynard, 84, 204, 294
Kieran, James M., 59
Kingsbury, John A., 258, 260, 261, 275
Krall, Charles, 225
Krock, Arthur, 35, 44, 95–96, 230, 243

labor, 11, 33, 40, 157–94, 195–247
  Arizona mines and, 90–91
  Black Bill and, 221–24, 227
  Bureau of Labor Statistics, 197
  child, 4, 9, 11, 165, 169, 173, 181, 184, 192, 220, 229,
    237, 242, 254, 282, 285, 304, 306–9
  Department of, 195–96
  Douglas and, 93
  Fair Labor Standards Act, 282, 286, 289, 307, 309
  immigration and, 158–60, 177, 195–96
  National Labor Relations Act, 282, 286, 288, 306
  National Labor Relations Board, 286, 306
  Perkins as secretary of, 5, 13, 157–61, 189–94,
    195–246, 282
  Perkins's background and experience in, 161–89
  Shirtwaist Strike, 168
  unemployment, *see* unemployment
  unions, *see* unions
  wages and hour regulations, 4, 9, 11, 161, 165,
    168, 169, 171–72, 181, 192, 194, 196, 210, 220,
    221–24, 229, 232, 237, 242, 282, 285, 304, 306–9
Ladies' Home Journal, 48
La Follette, Robert, Jr., 94, 106, 121, 197, 202
  public works and, 204, 207, 208, 211, 214, 215
  relief legislation and, 250, 263
Laffoon, Ruby, 269–70
La Guardia, Fiorello, 138
Lamont, Thomas, 51
Landis, James, 151–53
Landon, Alfred, 288, 292, 297
Leach, Agnes, 190
Lee, Frederic, 136, 155
LeHand, Missy, 75
Lehman, Herbert, 69, 206, 252, 263
Lemke, William, 138
Lewis, John L., 193, 198, 213, 220, 249
Lewis, Sinclair, 174
Liberty, 83
Life, 110
Lincoln, Abraham, 11, 13, 36, 43, 316, 318
Lindley, Ernest K., 4, 11, 53, 73, 111, 267, 285
Lippmann, Walter, 33–34, 37, 45, 143, 144, 276,
  287–88
Litchfield, Paul W., 229
Literary Digest, 88, 114
Lloyd, Henry Demarest, 164
Long, Huey, 79–80, 104–5, 244–45, 278, 288
Lord, Russell, 133, 154
Los Angeles Times, 193
Lubin, Isador, 197
Luce, Robert, 251

Lund, Robert L., 244
Lyon, Mary, 163

McAdoo, William Gibbs, 51, 104, 178
MacArthur, Douglas, 217, 235
Macaulay, Thomas Babington, 83
MacColl, Christina, 255
McCormick, Anne O'Hare, 104
Macdonald, Dwight, 114
MacDonald, Ishbel, 224
MacDonald, Ramsay, 290
McDuffie, Irwin, 74–75
McDuffie, John, 95, 102–3
McIntyre, Marvin, 65, 75
McKinley, William, 115
McNary, Charles, 116
McNary-Haugenism, 113, 116, 117, 122, 123, 128, 133–37, 140, 154, 155, 299
Madison, James, 19, 43
Malthus, Thomas, 167
Masses, 167
Matthews, William, 97, 205, 261
Means, Gardiner C., 60–61
Mellon, Andrew, 49
Mencken, H. L., 286
Mercer, Lucy, 21
Meyer, Eugene, 51, 53
Miller, Maurice, 227
Mills, Darius Ogden, 67
Mills, Frederick C., 61
Mills, Ogden Livingston, Jr., 53, 67–71
mining industry, 8, 88–92, 93, 213, 249
Mitchell, John Purroy, 174, 259
Mitchell, William D., 51
Moley, Eva Dall, 58
Moley, Raymond, 5, 6, 8, 21, 41, 53, 54–66, 75, 82, 106, 112, 127, 130, 217, 282, 285, 289–93, 306
  agriculture and, 128, 129, 136–37
  as assistant secretary of state, 65–66, 82
  background of, 8, 10, 57–59
  banking crisis and, 8, 52, 66–71, 76–80, 82, 83, 277, 279
  Brain Trust headed by, 6–7, 8, 59–63, 66, 67
  Cohen and Corcoran and, 152
  Economy Act and, 99–100, 102
  FDR's first meeting of, 59
  FDR's relationship with, 63, 291, 293
  FDR's speeches and, 37–39, 63–64, 236–37, 242, 246–47
  federal budget and, 84
  ideology of, 8, 10, 67, 291–93
  industrial planning and, 228–29, 230–31
  inflation and, 143–44
  memoirs of, 292, 293
  Muscle Shoals power project and, 148
  public works and, 208, 210–12, 217
  resignation of, 291
  role of, 8, 56–57, 64, 82–83, 290, 291, 293

stock sale regulation and, 149–51, 153
war debts and, 64
at World Economic Conference, 290
Morgenthau, Henry, 45, 126–29, 140, 209, 294, 305
mortgages and foreclosures:
  farm, 4, 48, 54, 110, 115, 124, 125, 140, 141, 144, 145, 237
  home, 4, 141, 237
Moulton, Harold, 231–32
Murphy, Charles F., 169
Murphy, J. Prentice, 266
Muscle Shoals power facility, 146–49
Mussolini, Benito, 208, 244

Nation, 18, 37, 90, 128, 249, 269, 277, 314
National Economy League, 85, 107
National Farmers' Union, 2, 133–35, 139
National Industrial Recovery Act (NIRA), 4, 11, 242–47, 271, 279, 281–83, 285–87, 294, 303–4, 306, 312
National Labor Relations Act, 282, 286, 288, 306
National Labor Relations Board, 286, 306
National Recovery Administration (NRA), 4, 245, 281–82, 284, 306
Nesbitt, Henrietta, 39
New Deal, 10, 284, 287–89, 317–18
  Agricultural Adjustment Act and, 145
  Berle and, 61, 62
  Consumers' League and, 168
  critics of, 12, 268, 275, 286–87, 289, 314
  deficit spending and, 11–12
  Douglas and, 8–9
  duplicate assignments in, 150
  Emergency Banking Act and, 83
  FDR's pledge of, 33, 34
  FDR's role in, 7
  federal budget cut and, 84
  Great Society and, 316–17
  Hoover and, 31–32, 41–42
  Hopkins and, 276
  Hundred Days and, 11
  introduction of phrase, 63
  Moley and, 82
  Perkins and, 5, 289, 309, 310
  Second, 288, 293
  start of, 73
  TERA and, 188
  as unified plan, 5
New Republic, 16, 28, 37, 83, 145, 151, 193, 205, 285, 302, 313
Newsweek, 63, 291
New York *Daily News,* 42
New York Herald, 259
New York Herald Tribune, 23, 37, 99
New York Times, 3, 35, 39, 42, 44, 59, 70, 73, 74, 81, 88, 95–96, 106, 138, 161, 168, 182, 183, 212, 217, 230, 237–38, 243, 265, 280, 292, 297, 303, 313

New York Tuberculosis Association, 188, 260, 261, 270
New York World, 90
New York World-Telegram, 15
Niebuhr, Reinhold, 16
Norris, George, 30, 146, 148, 149, 244
Norton, Mary Teresa, 104

O'Connor, Basil "Doc," 61
O'Neal, Edward, 110
"Ordeal of Herbert Hoover, The" (Degler), 31
Other People's Money (Brandeis), 152
Oits, James, 162

Pan-American Union, 18–19
Panic of 1907, 77
Patman, Wright, 102
Patten, Simon Nelson, 167, 193, 238
Patterson, Eleanor "Cissy," 41
Peabody, Endicott, 23, 24
Pearson, Drew, 28
Pecora, Ferdinand, 276, 277
Peek, George, 46, 122, 128, 134–36, 140–41, 154–55, 219, 230, 245, 299
Pegler, Westbrook, 82–83
Perkins, Cynthia Otis, 162–63, 166
Perkins, Frances, 6, 8–10, 13–14, 17–19, 24–26, 33, 41–45, 65, 260, 283, 293, 303–11, 318
 background and experience of, 9, 13–14, 17–18, 161–89
 Black Bill and, 221–24
 at Cornell, 310–11
 Douglas and, 205–6, 296, 303
 on FDR's character and views, 22, 23–24, 180–82, 185–86
 FDR's meeting of, 172
 as first female Cabinet member, 190, 191, 199–200, 212, 216
 Hopkins's letter from, 316
 housing of, 200–201
 on Industrial Commission and Industrial Board, 176–80
 as industrial commissioner for FDR, 180–83, 308
 industrial planning and, 229, 231, 233, 238–39, 240
 marriage of, 174, 190–91, 212–13, 216, 305–6
 memoir of, 172, 275, 309
 New Deal and, 5, 289, 309, 310
 NIRA and, 303–4, 306
 press and, 212–14, 237–38, 308–9
 public works and, 161, 192, 193, 204, 206, 208, 210–12, 214–16, 219–21, 223, 229, 232, 233, 235–36, 238, 241–42, 246, 303, 308
 relief programs and, 161, 192, 202–4, 206–8, 211, 264, 308, 310
 religious faith of, 23–24, 201–2
 resignation of, 308
 as secretary of labor, 5, 13, 157–61, 189–94, 195–246, 282
 Triangle Shirtwaist Fire and, 9, 170, 171, 198
 unions and, 165, 168–69, 192–93, 197–98, 232, 240, 306
Perkins, Frederick, 162–64
Perkins, Susanna, 18, 19, 24, 26, 41, 43, 175, 192, 193, 212, 309
Persons, W. Frank, 218
Pierce, Dante, 139, 141
Plato, ix
Poole, Margaret, 193
Pound, Roscoe, 58
Poverty (Hunter), 164
power, public, 146–49, 186, 242
Prairie Farmer, 134
President's Emergency Committee for Employment, 29–30
President's Organization on Unemployment Relief (POUR), 30
Progressive Era, 10, 18, 89–90, 166
Progressive Party (Bull Moose Party), 21, 173, 177, 255, 302, 305
Prohibition, 43, 105–6, 129
public works programs, 4, 9, 10, 11, 30, 63, 97, 158, 185–88, 204–6, 208–12, 214–21, 233, 235–36, 249, 271
 Civilian Conservation Corps, 4, 208–11, 214–20, 224–27, 237, 271, 284, 286, 288, 289, 295, 311
 Civil Works Administration, 273, 283, 312, 288, 308, 312–13, 316
 Douglas and, 94, 97
 Economy Act and, 101
 Hoover and, 204
 industrial policy and, 230, 236, 239–43
 large-scale, 5–6, 9, 11, 63, 208, 211–12, 214, 215, 217, 220, 233, 235–36
 NIRA and, 242, 243, 246, 271, 281–83
 Perkins and, 161, 192, 193, 204, 206, 208, 210–12, 214–16, 219–21, 223, 229, 232, 233, 235–36, 238, 241–42, 246, 303, 308
 Public Works Administration, 282–83, 285, 312
 Works Progress Administration, 273, 283, 285, 288, 308, 313–16
Pyle, Ernie, 268

Rainey, Henry T., 79, 102, 199
Rankin, John, 102, 103, 149
Raskob, John J., 48
Rayburn, Sam, 7, 151–53
Reagan, Ronald, 317
Reconstruction Finance Corporation (RFC), 31, 49–50, 94, 152, 250, 266, 297
Red Cross, 29, 218, 259–61, 268
Reed, David A., 37, 52, 138
Reisner, Christian, 74
relief programs:
 charities and, 4, 28, 202, 248, 249, 258, 261, 270
 federal, *see* federal relief programs
 state, 6, 33, 187–89, 202–3, 214–15, 251, 252, 261–63, 269–72

Reno, Milo, 125, 126, 136, 145
Republic, The (Plato), ix
revolution, 10–11
Richberg, Donald, 231, 239
Rifkind, Simon, 236
Riis, Jacob, 164
Ritchie, Albert, 96
Rizzo, Fiore, 224
Robinson, Arthur, 105
Robinson, Joseph T., 72, 79, 145
Roerich, Nicholas, 120
Rogers, Edith Nourse, 96
Rogers, Will, 4–5, 30, 47, 81, 187
Roos, Charles, 120
Roosevelt, Eleanor, 24, 42, 43, 47, 53, 224
    Bonus Army and, 226–27
    Civilian Conservation Corps and, 225
    Economy Act and, 102
    and FDR's affair with Mercer, 21
    FDR's polio and, 22
    marriage to FDR, 20
    Perkins and, 190, 213
    press conference held by, 76
    public role of, 76
Roosevelt, Franklin Delano (FDR):
    as assistant secretary of the navy, 21, 177
    background of, 19–20
    Brain Trust of, *see* Brain Trust
    Cabinet of, *see* Cabinet
    conflicting views of, 5–6, 7
    as Cox's running mate, 21
    education of, 20
    elected president, 2, 23, 26, 32–35, 52, 188–89,
      263, 285
    fireside chats of, 3, 5, 11, 80–81, 179, 236–37,
      246–47
    first day as president, 74–75
    as governor of New York, 5, 6, 23, 32–33, 59, 81,
      147, 179–88, 251, 261
    Hundred Days period of, *see* Hundred Days
    inaugural address of, 3, 26, 37–40, 41, 42, 63–64,
      70, 72, 283
    inauguration of, 13, 14, 17–19, 23–26, 35–43
    marriage to Eleanor, 20
    Mercer's affair with, 21
    as New York State senator, 20–21
    nominating speech for Smith given by, 22–23,
      178
    philosophy of government, 11, 187
    polio contracted by, 19–20, 22, 178, 180
    reelection of (1936), 12, 286–88, 297
    religious faith of, 23–24
    second inaugural address of, 12, 288
    thriftiness of, 84, 86
    as tree lover, 209
    U.S. Senate campaign of, 21
Roosevelt, Franklin Delano, Jr., 314
Roosevelt, James (father of Franklin), 20, 23

Roosevelt, James (son of Franklin), 19, 24, 35, 36,
    53, 178
Roosevelt, Sara Delano, 20, 24, 37
    and FDR's affair with Mercer, 21
    FDR's polio and, 22
Roosevelt, Theodore, 20, 21, 115, 179, 255
Roosevelt I Knew, The (Perkins), 172, 275, 309
Roosevelt Revolution, The: First Phase (Lindley), 11
Roosevelt's Revolution (Tugwell), 11
Root, Elihu, 254–55
Roper, Daniel, 150–51, 200, 205
Rosenman, Samuel, 59, 61, 64, 81, 83, 147,
    188, 292
Rumsey, Charles Cary, 201
Rumsey, Mary, 201, 232, 246, 291, 309
Ruutul, Oscar, 270

St. John's Episcopal Church, 19, 24–25, 41
Saturday Evening Post, 18, 125, 135, 173
Schlesinger, Arthur M., Jr., 3, 31–32
Schneider, Louis I., 225
Schneiderman, Rose, 170, 198
school lunches, 272
Schwab, Charles M., 28
Schwartz, Anna, 278
Securities Act of 1933 (Truth in Securities Act), 4,
    149–54, 286, 295
Securities and Exchange Commission, 286, 295
Shaver, Robert, 225
Sheehan, William, 21
Sherley, J. Swagar, 97, 98, 99
Sherwood, Robert E., 26, 263–64, 315
Shoemaker, Francis, 227
Showalter, Mrs. William, 42
silver, 142, 143
Simkhovitch, Mary Kingsbury, 167
Simmons, Robert, 98
Simpson, John, 139
Sinclair, Upton, 118
Smith, Alfred E., 22–23, 27, 32, 44, 55, 59, 67, 81,
    122, 169, 170, 208
    Perkins and, 173, 176–81, 188
Smith, Ellison, 139–40
Smoot-Hawley Tariff Act, 28, 123
Snell, Bertrand H., 79, 102, 104
Social Security, 189, 285, 288, 305, 309, 310, 317
Soil Conservation and Domestic Allotment Act,
    300
Somers, M. J., 270
Soule, Annah May, 163
Special Board for Public Works, 303
Starling, Edmund W., 47
Steagall, Henry, 72
    Glass-Steagall Act (Banking Act of 1933), 3, 72,
      79, 277–79, 281, 317
Steiner, Edward, 254
Stevenson, Adlai, 155
Stewart, Ethelbert, 197

stock market, 4, 11, 47–48, 82, 93, 318
    Crash of 1929, 1–2, 14, 28, 48, 93, 122–23, 149, 182, 196, 261, 276, 288
    Securities Act, 4, 149–54, 286
Straus, Jesse Isador, 45, 261, 262
Supreme Court, U.S., 91, 178, 304
    Agricultural Adjustment Administration and, 300
    Brown v. Board of Education, 298
    child labor and, 229
    FDR's effort to pack, 289, 292, 293
    maximum hours laws and, 167–68, 169, 229
    NIRA and, 282, 306
Survey, 18
Survey Graphic, 191
Swanson, Claude, 23, 203, 205, 296
Swope, Gerard, 224

Taft, William Howard, 115, 195
Talmadge, Eugene, 268
Tammany Hall, 21, 102, 169, 171, 172, 174, 177, 179, 276
Tarbell, Ida, 189
tariffs, 28, 123
taxes, 317
    income, 29
    sales, 94
Temporary Emergency Relief Administration (TERA), 188, 202, 206–7, 261–63, 274
Tennessee Valley, 146, 147
Tennessee Valley Authority (TVA), 4, 148–49, 237
Thomas, Elmer, 143
Thomas, Norman, 42, 287
Thomas Amendment, 143–44
Thompson, Huston, 150–52
Thompson, William, 34
Thoreau, Henry David, 38
Thurmond, Strom, 303
Time, 8, 15, 22, 25, 37, 45, 56, 71, 105, 136, 141, 153, 160–61, 216, 245, 273, 278, 280, 286, 290, 293, 314
Tobin, Daniel J., 192–93, 220, 221
Today, 291
Townsend, Francis, 288, 304
Trading with the Enemy Act, 51, 70, 71, 72, 78
Trammell, Park, 107
transients and homeless, 272
Traylor, Melvin, 71
Triangle Shirtwaist Fire, 9, 170, 171, 198
Truman, Harry, 293, 297, 302–3, 308, 309
Truth in Securities Act (Securities Act of 1933), 4, 149–54, 286, 295
tuberculosis, 100, 113, 256, 257, 260
    New York Tuberculosis Association, 188, 260, 261, 270
Tucson Citizen, 88
Tugwell, Rexford, 6, 9, 11, 12, 17, 35, 60–64, 67, 69, 75, 83, 128, 129, 234, 246, 282, 285, 289, 299, 306
    as assistant secretary of agriculture, 6, 111–13, 133–35, 137–40, 145

Douglas and, 87, 97, 99, 296
    federal budget and, 85, 87
    Hoover and, 182–83
    on Hopkins, 276
    industrial planning and, 228–29, 231, 233, 238, 239
    memoir of, 293
    Moley and, 291–92
    Perkins and, 200
    political views of, 111
    public power projects and, 148
    public works and, 205, 206, 208
    Wallace and, 109–10, 126
Tully, Grace, 53, 209, 265, 291

unemployment, 6, 7, 14–18, 29, 31, 75, 94, 101, 108, 261, 265–66, 285, 288
    Economy Act and, 103, 105
    governors' conference on, 187, 202
    Hoover and, 182–83, 188, 197
    Hopkins and, 258–59
    insurance, 185–87, 192, 194, 197, 213, 220, 285, 304, 305, 309
    layoffs, 86
    in New York City, 258–59, 262, 263
    Woods Committee and, 29–30
    see also federal relief programs; public works programs
unions, 4, 7, 10, 92, 158, 195, 210, 243, 306
    Arizona mines and, 90
    Black Bill and, 221–24
    Civilian Conservation Corps and, 215–16, 218, 219
    in labor conference, 219–21
    organizing protection for, 232, 240, 242, 244, 306
    Perkins and, 165, 168–69, 192–93, 197–98, 232, 240, 306
Untermyer, Samuel, 149–51

Vandenberg, Arthur, 144
Van Hise, Charles, 228
veterans:
    benefits for, 85–87, 92, 95–96, 99, 100–3, 105, 107, 279–81, 295
    bonus for, 31, 50, 226–27

Wagner, Robert F., 31, 94, 105, 169, 170, 173, 197, 306
    federal relief and, 250, 251, 264
    industrial recovery and, 231–32, 233, 236, 238–39, 240, 243–44, 282
    public works and, 204, 207, 241–42
Wagner Act, 306
Walker, Frank, 274
Wallace, Annabelle, 114, 131
Wallace, Henry, 8, 10, 25–26, 41, 44, 86, 113–32, 283, 298–303, 305, 318
    background and experience of, 9, 25, 113–28
    corn company of, 119–20

Wallace, Henry (cont.)
at Cornell, 310–11
Douglas and, 234, 295–96
FDR's meeting of, 126–29
foreign policy and, 301–2
plants as viewed by, 117–18, 133, 310
presidential campaign of, 302–3
public works and, 205, 210, 210–11, 214, 215, 224, 235–36
as secretary of agriculture, 9, 25–26, 109–13, 118, 128–32, 133–41, 145–46, 154–56, 298–301
spirituality of, 120, 201–2
Wallace Henry Caldwell "Harry," 113–18, 120–21
Wallace, Ilo Wilson, 26, 41, 119, 303
Wallace, May Brodhead, 114, 117–18
Wallace, "Uncle Henry," 113–16, 124
Wallaces' Farmer, 9, 25, 109, 114, 115, 117–25, 127–30, 132
Wall Street Journal, 101, 151
Walsh, David, 29
Walsh, Mina Perez Chaumont de Truffin, 36
Walsh, Thomas, 36, 42, 45, 71, 75
Walsh-Healy Act, 306, 309
Warburg, James, 137, 217, 230
Warm Springs, 22, 38, 43, 55, 64, 129, 147, 148, 179
Washington, George, 11, 316, 318
Washington Daily News, 98
Washington Herald, 41
Washington Merry-Go-Round (Pearson and Allen), 28
Washington Post, 148, 189, 191, 212, 291
Washington Star, 87
welfare policies, 185, 248, 317
Wheeler, Burton K., 142
Wheeler Amendment, 142–43
White, Robe Carl, 158, 159

White, William Allen, 34, 125, 189–90
Whitney, A. F., 215
Willard Hotel, 13, 18, 19, 157, 200–201
Williams, Aubrey, 268–69
Williams, John, 89
Williams, Joseph, 42
Willkie, Wendell, 289, 292, 297, 307
Wilson, Edith Galt, 18
Wilson, Edmund, 1, 14
Wilson, M. L., 123, 124, 126–28, 145, 154–55
Wilson, Paul, 174–75, 184, 190–93, 212–13, 305–6, 309
Wilson, "Tama" Jim, 114, 115
Wilson, Woodrow, 19, 21, 51, 54, 61, 90–91, 115, 255
Winchell, Walter, 292
Withrow, Gardner, 103
Wolman, Leo, 198
Women's Democratic News, 102
women's suffrage, 175, 176
Woodin, William, 43, 44, 54–56, 82, 131, 143, 177
banking crisis and, 52, 54, 68–73, 76–80, 278
Woods, Arthur, 29–30
workers' rights, see labor
Works Progress Administration (WPA), 273, 283, 285, 288, 308, 313–16
World Economic Conference, 279, 289–90
World War I, 27, 31, 146, 178, 259
Douglas in, 91
European debts from, 64
farmers and, 116
veterans of, see veterans
World War II, 288, 297, 307, 315
Wyatt, Walter, 56, 68, 72, 82
Wyzanski, Charles E., Jr., 196–97, 206, 239, 307

Zangara, Giuseppe, 36